THE ORIGINS OF GREAT POWER RIVALRIES

Michael F. Joseph's *The Origins of Great Power Rivalries* advances a comprehensive rationalist theory of how great powers assess emerging threats; why enduring great power rivalries unfold through either delayed competition or delayed peace; and how diplomacy functions when rising powers emerge on the scene. In an important departure from traditional realist theory, Joseph argues that countries are motivated by distinct principles – normative values that shape foreign policy beyond simple security concerns. Exploring instances of great power competition, he explains why rational states draw qualitative inferences about rivals' intentions by examining the historical context of their demands, not just military capabilities. Offering an analysis of great power rivalries since 1850, Joseph illuminates British reactions to Stalin at the beginning of the Cold War, among other rivalries. He animates a theoretically sophisticated defense of America's approach to China in the post-Cold War era with hundreds of Washington-insider interviews.

MICHAEL F. JOSEPH is an assistant professor in the Department of Political Science at the University of California, San Diego. He harnesses a decade of foreign policy experience working across five countries and two conflict zones and sophisticated research skills to shed light on modern national security problems. His research has been recognized with the 2021 Formal Theory Section Award from the American Political Science Association, the 2023 Palmer Prize from the Peace Science Society, and a $450,000 National Science Foundation Grant for National Security Preparedness, among other accolades. Policy insights from this research have attracted policy-maker attention in Washington, DC, and appear in the *Washington Post, War on the Rocks*, and other leading outlets.

The Origins of Great Power Rivalries

A Rational Theory of Principled Motivations, and Historical Context

MICHAEL F. JOSEPH

University of California, San Diego

CAMBRIDGE
UNIVERSITY PRESS

Shaftesbury Road, Cambridge CB2 8EA, United Kingdom

One Liberty Plaza, 20th Floor, New York, NY 10006, USA

477 Williamstown Road, Port Melbourne, VIC 3207, Australia

314–321, 3rd Floor, Plot 3, Splendor Forum, Jasola District Centre,
New Delhi – 110025, India

Cambridge University Press is part of Cambridge University Press & Assessment,
a department of the University of Cambridge.

We share the University's mission to contribute to society through the pursuit of
education, learning and research at the highest international levels of excellence.

www.cambridge.org
Information on this title: www.cambridge.org/9781009752824
DOI: 10.1017/9781009752787

First published 2026

A catalogue record for this publication is available from the British Library

A Cataloging-in-Publication data record for this book is available from the Library of Congress

ISBN 978-1-009-75280-0 Hardback
ISBN 978-1-009-75282-4 Paperback

Contents

An online appendix for this publication is available at www.cambridge.org/Joseph.

Figures

Tables

1

Introduction

The 2017 National Security Strategy (White House, 2020, p. 25) warns China is a revisionist power that "seeks to displace the United States in the Indo-Pacific region, expand the reaches of its state-driven economic model, and reorder the region in its favor." A shift in US policy has followed that some characterize as a second Cold War (Daly, 2022; Bekkevold, 2022). It was not always this way. When the Cold War ended, the US was deeply uncertain about China's strategic intentions. In the two decades that followed, the US's China strategy is best described as cautious hedging that left open the possibility of either a rivalry or a stable peace.

Looking back, critics want to know why it took the US so long to recognize that China was an adversary and turn from hedging to competition? They argue that hedging was a mistake and the blame lies with two kinds of national security elites. Some argue that policy-makers ignored a well-established finding that shifting military power inevitably drives great powers into security competition (Allison, 2017). In their view, policy-makers should have turned to competition during the 1990s when they first realized that China's rise was inevitable. They argue that this mistake was especially egregious because policy-makers hastened China's rise by promoting economic integration.

Others argue that hedging was prudent because intelligence reports were uncertain about China's strategic intentions. After all, competition is tragic, and the benefits of economic integration are large. These critics fault the intelligence community for failing to warn, despite clear indicators that China's intentions were vast. As Congress has pointed out, the intelligence community closely watched as China rapidly militarized, built offensive weapons, instigated crises against Taiwan and Tibet, consolidated authoritarian rule, and brutally suppressed democratic movements. However, the intelligence community did not revise its estimates of China's intentions until about 2011 (Schiff, 2020).[1]

If two decades of hedging is a policy or intelligence failure, it is a common failure that dominates the historical record. Since Carr (1945), scholars have justifiably obsessed over a handful of great power cases such as the World Wars, the Anglo-American peace, the Cold War, the Great Game, and the rise of German antagonism. We obsess over these cases because they all inexplicably start out the same way as Sino-American relations: A status quo power (a Defender) tolerates slow revisions of the status quo in the hopes of achieving a lasting peace with the revisionist power (a Challenger). In some cases, the Defender realizes that the Challenger is a rival and lasting peace is impossible. This realization triggers a switch from hedging to competition. In others, great powers achieve a stable peace following limited concessions. Cases only arrive at these endings after the Challenger has had significant time to consolidate its forces and extend its economic and military influence through its region.

Take three examples from the decline of Britain. In 1932 British elites were uncertain if Hitler was a "madman" bent on world domination, or if he sought limited objectives. Some worried as Hitler rapidly militarized, orchestrated the assassination of the Austrian chancellor, and took the Rhineland (Wark, 1985). But competition did not come. Instead, Hitler allayed Britain's fears through diplomacy. He argued that militarization was necessary to take a few valuable concessions but promised that his intentions were limited. Only after Hitler violated the Munich Agreement did British elites infer that Hitler held expansive aims. British elites updated their beliefs because they believed Hitler's demands for the rump of Czechoslovakia were different from his demands in the Rhineland; and therefore a more informative signal of Hitler's aggressive intentions.

Five years later, this pattern repeated. Following a week-long diplomatic meeting at Yalta, Churchill concluded that "poor Neville Chamberlain believed he could trust Hitler. He was wrong. But I don't think I'm wrong about [trusting] Stalin."[2] British and American elites remained optimistic that long-term cooperation was possible as Stalin installed communist governments in Romania and Poland. However, they inferred Stalin's aims were vast following the Iran Crisis (1946). Finally, consider a case that

---

[1] Schiff's criticism echoes more extensive criticisms found in a 2020 House Select Committee on Intelligence report "The China Deep Dive: A Report on the Intelligence Community's Capabilities and Competencies with Respect to the People's Republic of China."

[2] Nicholson and Nicolson (2004), diary entry, February 27, 1945. Discussion about Soviet strategic intentions.

ended in peace. In 1823 President Monroe declared that the United States would remove European powers from the Americas over the next century. This demand for 20 percent of the world's land mass was followed by one of the fastest rates of economic growth in human history and rapid militarization.[3] The US exploited its power to instigate crises in Alaska and then Venezuela. As early as 1830, Britain predicted that the US would rapidly expand its influence and eventually exclude Britain from the Americas. But competition never came. Instead, the British conceded at Venezuela, then Alaska, before forging a special friendship and lasting peace in 1907 (Schake, 2017).

There is a historical pattern here that puzzles researchers. As power transition scholars expect, Britain understood that shifting military power would cause tension (Organski and Kugler, 1980; Powell, 1999). But against their prediction, Britain did not select competition when power shifts were most rapid.[4] As defensive realists expect, British elites closely monitored each Challenger's costly military actions to draw inferences about their intentions (Glaser, 2010; Kydd, 2005). But against defensive realist predictions, British elites remained hopeful as each Challenger invaded territory, undermined status quo norms and institutions, and built large offensive militaries. In fact, Britain was reassured by each Challenger's costless diplomatic promises as the Challenger used costly military actions to revise the status quo. As a result, hedging lasted an inexplicably long time.[5]

This pattern leads us to a broader research question that can shed light on Sino-American relations: *When and why do status quo powers shift their strategy from hedging to competition?*

Like many of those just cited, I believe that the answer lies in the Defender's perceptions of the Challenger's strategic intentions. However, my analytical bet is that we can better answer this question if we enrich how we conceptualize state motives. I do that in two steps. First, I develop a new way to conceptualize state motives that celebrates each state's rich historical and cultural context. Second, I develop a novel framework to analyze strategic interactions between states that hold these richer motives and generate systematic predictions about patterns of competition and peace during the critical cases that have puzzled us.

---

[3] The US started with a modest military, allowing for a rapid increase. US militarization increased again in absolute spending after the Spanish–American War.

[4] Specifically, in the Anglo-American case, or in the years where power shifts were most rapid in the other cases.

[5] Anglo-German policy is often labeled appeasement. As I explain later, appeasement is a variant of hedging at the level of detail that I study.

1.1 Argument in Brief

I theorize that a Challenger's specific foreign policy objectives depend on a combination of their intrinsic foreign policy motives – which I call a principle – and their historical context. For example, states that prioritize ethno-nationalism (one principle) covet different concessions than states that prioritize security, prestige, uniting historical borders, or some other principle. Depending on the principle, the specific territories, institutions, and normative issues that they care about the most depend on their history and culture. For example, states that want to restore their historical borders care about territories they historically controlled. I do not assume that a Challenger can be motivated by a single principle (e.g., security or greed). Rather, I assume that Challengers can be motivated by one of many principles, and each principle implies that the Challenger holds a specific set of core interests. I assume that Defenders are uncertain about the Challenger's true principle. Thus, Defenders do not know which, and how many, core interests the Challenger holds. However, Defenders have a lot of information about the Challenger's history and culture, and can use that information to learn the Challenger's true principle over time.

By appreciating that there are many reasons that states can hold limited aims, I illuminate new information problems and new mechanisms for forming threat perceptions in world politics. I call these mechanisms *qualitative inferences.*[6] They are *qualitative* because Defenders update their beliefs about the Challenger's motives based on how specific demands (a demand for Austria, not Poland) correspond to a principle, and not the scope of these demands or rates of militarization (e.g., a demand for half, not three-quarters of Austria). Like existing signaling theories, when Challengers make costly demands for a specific issue they reveal that they care about that issue (e.g., Kydd, 2005). But unlike other signaling theories, the inference that the Defender draws about the scope of the Challenger's motives depends on the specific issue that the Challenger signaled that it cared about. My theory explains that Defenders can observe the Challenger take costly military actions and infer that the Challenger's strategic intentions are more expansive, or more limited (or no change at all), than the Defender previously thought. What the Defender infers hinges on the historical context that surrounds what the Challenger hopes to achieve from costly actions.

---

[6] To be clear, the model still assumes Bayesian updating. As I explain later in the book, qualitative inferences differentiate my mechanism from past trust building theories, which rely on the scope of demands and militarization choices.

This insight helps us understand puzzling intelligence estimates of China. For example, American policy-makers believe that inferring "Chinese intentions is the single most difficult and important task we face."[7] For decades, the CIA could not assess China's long-term motives with high confidence. However, they could easily assess that Taiwan provided China with enormous historical and nationalistic benefits but fewer security benefits.[8] When China first instigated a crisis over Taiwan, the CIA made inferences about China's long-term motives based on its understanding of what principles could drive China to contest Taiwan.[9] From this inference, the CIA extrapolated to assess other territories and international institutions that China would and would not contest in the future.[10] The CIA's future estimates were moderated through this understanding. Thus, the intelligence community was not alarmed by China's coercive behavior over Tibet, or Taiwan in the 1990s, or China's decision to brutally suppress those who protested the communist party because all of these actions were consistent with a nationalist motivation.

As we shall see, the intelligence community revised their estimates circa 2011 because they could not explain China's actions in the context of China's declared nationalist aims. For many, China's military deployments surrounding the South China Sea raised concerns. On the surface, China's actions in the South China Sea are no more militaristic than China's deployment during the 1995 Taiwan Strait Crisis. But analysts drew different inferences from each once they accounted for China's historical and cultural context.

Of course, the US and China are locked in a strategic dynamic. We know that revisionist powers face strategic incentives to understate the scope of their intentions (Jervis, 1978). We believe that these incentives make costly signaling difficult and render private diplomacy useless. Can qualitative inferences survive in the complex strategic environment of world politics? If they can, what do they mean for patterns of competition in a strategic setting?

In Chapter 2, I develop a framework that captures how the commitment problem (Powell, 1999) is aggravated by a reassurance problem about the scope of the Challenger's motives (Kydd, 2005) at the origins of great

---

[7] Quote from interview with former CIA Director for Analysis Mark Lowenthal.

[8] Special National Intelligence Estimate (100-12-58) *Probable Developments in the Taiwan Strait Crisis*, p. 1.

[9] SNIE (100-4-59) *Chinese Communist Intentions and Probable Courses of Action in the Taiwan Strait Area.*

[10] SNIE (13-3-61) *Chinese Communist Capabilities and Intentions in the Far East.*

power rivalries, creating strong incentives for instant competition.[11] In Chapter 4, I adjust the Challenger's payoff structure to reflect my conceptual theory of principles. Drawing from an informal analysis of the equilibria, I argue that rivalries can unfold in one of two ways: delayed competition or delayed peace. While the top-line result is simple, a detailed look at my qualitative signaling mechanism explains four of the most puzzling aspects of how great powers forge rationalist threat perceptions, and how these threat perceptions influence patterns of competition, hedging, and peace. I explain: (1) why Defenders are reassured by the Challenger's early diplomatic promises that the Challenger's motives are limited; (2) why Defenders are willing to make many repeated concessions even as the Challenger makes violent demands, takes territory, rapidly militarizes, or seeks to undermine the Defender in other ways; (3) punctuated (rather than gradual) changes in Defender's beliefs about the Challenger's strategic motives; and (4) why some cases end in competition following a specific demand while others end in a stable peace.

The mechanism works as follows. Early on, Challengers with expansive and limited aims face different incentives. Challengers with expansive aims value many issues, thus they care less about which concessions they receive first. However, they want to understate the scope of their motives to avoid competition for as long as they can. Challengers with limited aims each value a different (and specific) set of issues. They want to coordinate to receive valuable concessions first. Past coordination theories assume the Challenger's value for each issue is drawn independently (Trager, 2011; Battaglini, 2002), and thus diplomacy signals a list of issues it claims to care about (Taiwan, Tibet, Uganda). In my theory, Challengers can only value specific combinations of issues (those that are implied by a principle) high. Thus, the Challenger's diplomacy reveals a principle (e.g., nationalism) that motivates its demands. Because diplomacy appeals to a principled reason for revision, it sets an expectation about the total set of issues that the Challenger will want as the interaction unfolds. By locking in this expectation, limited-aims Challengers can exploit diplomacy to partially overcome incentives to understate the scope of their motives for many periods.[12]

---

[11] Powell (1996) is the closest model, and Edelstein (2019) provides the closest informal description of the setting I study.

[12] The lock-in is structural and strategic. It does not rely on public statements that generate audience costs from inconsistencies or norm violations (McManus, 2017; Kertzer and Brutger, 2016).

How the Challenger justifies their demands at the beginning has important implications for patterns of competition later on. Each principle implies that the Challenger cares about specific issues and territories. Once those issues and territories are captured, the Challenger either makes another demand and reveals that the initial justification was dishonest or accepts the status quo. Challengers with expansive aims make another demand and the Defender infers that their motives are more extensive than originally claimed. This revelation triggers competition.

Applying the logic to Anglo-German bargaining, Hitler initially used diplomacy to explain he was motivated by nationalism and therefore would only demand Germanic territories (in addition to violating certain human rights norms, etc.). This message was costless, but it altered how the British interpreted Hitler's future behavior. From that moment on, British elites adjusted their threat perceptions based on how Hitler's costly military actions fit nationalist objectives. They could do this because they held considerable knowledge of Germany's history. For example, British elites did not update their beliefs following the Rhineland (1936) crisis because they knew that Germans lived in this territory and realized that these demands were consistent with nationalist motives. However, when they observed Hitler demand the Slavic parts of Czechoslovakia, they assessed that this was outside what an ethno-nationalist Hitler would seek. Since they could not reconcile Hitler's actions with this principle, they ruled out the possibility that Hitler would stop once he captured territories populated by Germans. This realization drove them to competition.

1.2 Summary of Evidence

I support my argument with a multi-method research design. I leverage a survey experiment with national security elites, archival research about Anglo-Soviet relations at the onset of the Cold War, and a cross-case medium-n analysis of critical great power cases.

Chapter 5 reports evidence from a survey experiment with ninety-three real-world national security elites. Subjects include members of the intelligence community, diplomats, and congressional staff who work on foreign policy issues. In the experiment, subjects are given a war game exercise where they are asked to assess the strategic intentions of an emerging threat. I randomly assign whether the Challenger claims to be motivated by either security from foreign threats, or nationalistic aims. I then randomly assign whether the Challenger fights for an issue that is salient for security or nationalist reasons. Consistent with my theory, I show that almost all subjects coordinate their expectations about what the Challenger would want if it held limited aims based on the Challenger's randomly assigned, costless diplomatic statements. I show that subjects who observe the Challenger invade a territory that fits their declared principle do not infer that the Challenger's aims are expansive. This verifies my argument that the logic of costly signaling is conditional on principles and on historical and cultural context.

More broadly, I use the elite sample to understand the general analytical frames and indicators they use to evaluate the intentions of their rivals. I find that they use a diverse range of indicators in different ways. However, they typically interpret information by tying the Challenger's actions and attributes to principles.

Chapter 6 reports an analytic narrative of a critical but understudied case: British assessments of Soviet motives at the onset of the Cold War. The case draws from primary source research from four different archives, as well as several historical accounts about British perceptions of the Soviet Union. Consistent with my modeling assumptions, I show that British elites began deeply uncertain about Stalin's intentions. In 1940, there was wide conjecture that Stalin could be motivated by many different principles. Consistent with my theory, British elites believed that the missing piece of evidence was a statement from Stalin about what motivated Soviet foreign policy. I show that British analysts converged on an assessment framework following Foreign Minister Anthony Eden's visit to Moscow in 1941, in which Stalin explained to Eden that he was motivated by security from foreign threats. British analysts quickly exploited their knowledge of Russia's history, as well as the strategic landscape that surrounds Russia, to develop a list of territories that fit Stalin's declared aims. For the next seven years, British elites interpreted Stalin's actions based on whether they fit Stalin's declared principle. Consistent with my theory, British elites remained optimistic about Stalin's intentions as he orchestrated a coup in Romania and installed a communist government in Poland because they believed these actions fit Stalin's declared aims. However, they realized Stalin's aims were vast following the Iran Crisis because they could not understand how controlling Iran was necessary for Soviet security.

I also use the case to illustrate how my theory complements those who explore how state preferences are the aggregate of domestic preferences. For example, Schub (2023) argues that elite factions vary in their hawkishness. He suggests that there is a best (rational) assessment, and that elites deviate from it depending on their institutional affiliations or lived experiences. These deviations are not irrational. Rather, they are responses to individual-level preferences and training. I do not dispute that individuals and domestic institutions (like the military) may deviate from an optimal baseline. What I will show in my analysis of British elites that assess Stalin's motives is that my theory provides a better rational baseline than realism and the bargaining framework around which these deviations fall. Consistent with Schub (2023), I find that Foreign Office staff are often more optimistic than military staff about Stalin's motives. But I can also explain how both camps start off reasonably optimistic that cooperation is possible and then both revise their assessment that Stalin's aims are vast.

Chapter 7 tests my behavioral predictions about the timing of competition and peace through a medium-n analysis of great power relations since 1850. My central prediction is that competition will come shortly after the Challenger takes an action that cannot be explained by its declared principles. However, if the Challenger does not take an inconsistent action, competition will not come. Consistent with my central prediction, I find that competition comes within three years of the Challenger's first inconsistent action in twelve out of fourteen cases. I use four case vignettes to illustrate how my theory applies in a wide variety of historical and cultural contexts, and clarify how I conceptualize my variables. Finally, I show that my theory contributes to explaining patterns of competition and peace because it explains well the cases that theories of power struggle to explain. I show that a broader framework that incorporates my motives-based theory and Powell's (1999) theory of shifting military power explains patterns of competition and peace in all cases.

1.2.1 Answering the Sino-American Puzzle: The Past and the Future

In Chapter 8, I evaluate US intelligence and policy towards China through the lens of my theory. First, I show that US intelligence estimates of China closely follow the logic of my theory. Following Kissinger's secret visit to China in 1970, the intelligence community wrote up an assessment framework that assumed China would pursue nationalist ambitions if it was motivated by limited aims. Consistent with my theory, the intelligence community provided a detailed analysis of China's history and culture, and extrapolated from that analysis about what China would want if it held limited aims. Also consistent with my theory, they did not revise their estimates in the 1990s and 2000s because China's choices to consolidate autocratic power, instigate crises over Taiwan and Tibet, and invest heavily in offensive weapons fit China's declared nationalist ambitions. I use a novel survey of over 200 China-watchers (i.e., US national security elites that study China) to show that US estimates of China's motives changed suddenly circa 2011. Using additional, long-form interviews with the most senior intelligence officials at the time, I find that these estimates suddenly shifted because analysts could not explain China's costly military actions as serving a limited-aims principle.

Second, I examine US grand strategy towards China in the post-Cold War period. I find that each president chose a strategy that follows what my theory expects. My theory explains why presidents from different parties, and with different world views and experiences, reliably followed the same China policy. It explains why H. W. Bush, Clinton, and W. Bush hedged against China before 2008. It also explains why President Trump was right to rapidly increase US competition in spite of domestic opposition, and why President Biden largely continued President Trump's policy. My theory also allows for a new evaluation of President Obama's Pivot to Asia policy. This policy was fiercely criticized at the time because it sat awkwardly between competition and collaboration. While many of the details remain secret, my theory sheds light on likely tensions in Obama's thinking, which I circumstantially support with new elite interviews, and an analysis of memoirs and public reports to explain his choices.

At the end of the chapter I make predictions about the future of Sino-American relations. The American public wants to know if recent Sino-American competition is a permanent rivalry that will lead to a second Cold War or a temporary rift that we will soon resolve. Existing research suggest two reasons to be hopeful. First, Allison (2017) argues that the source of conflict is shifting military power. But if China's rate of growth declines, then the source of this tension will decline. There is some hope given China's recent lackluster economic performance, and its vulnerabilities to even limited technical sanctions. Second, leadership changes buttressed with interpersonal interactions can mend these fences. As US and Chinese leaders meet, they may be able to reconcile these differences.

On this question, I have grim news: Sino-American competition is here to stay. It will likely intensify in the coming years and persist for decades. In the past, American policy-makers wanted to work through crises because they believed that long-run cooperation was possible. Now they believe that China's long-term motives are vast, and long-term cooperation is not possible. This assessment has filtered to policy-makers, leading to a strategic shift to competition. Since the shift to competition is driven by a new assessment in China's motives, and not a single crisis, the US is unlikely to turn back. While this prediction is grim, it is important because it calls on the US to craft a comprehensive regional strategy to contain

China. This call is largely consistent with efforts of the Trump and Biden administrations but demonstrates that more can be done.

I also consider other questions that extend beyond my theory, but which my theory informs. Notably, the American public wants to know if competition is likely to boil over into World War Three. Indeed, Allison (2017) argues that if pressures to compete intensify, war is as good as inevitable. On this question, a small extension of my theory and some insights from work on crisis bargaining holds good news. The threat of nuclear escalation and the deep connections with third-party states that both China and the US hold mean that war is unlikely.

If war is not inevitable, will Sino-American relations thaw? On this question, my theory suggests bad news. Because US–China tensions are driven by a fundamental shift in US perceptions of China's motives, the new Sino-American Cold War will likely dominate US foreign policy for the foreseeable future. This does not mean it will unfold the same way. But unlike the last Cold War, the US will not start from a position of strength. Differences between the world today and the world in the 1950s, and between China and the Soviet Union are deeply concerning.

1.3 Contributions to Academic Research

The cases that interest me involve complex strategic dynamics that unfold over years. Consistent with scientific practices, existing scholarship isolates different dynamics within each case to better understand their independent effects. This has led to rigorous research into power transitions (Powell, 1999; Organski and Kugler, 1980; Debs and Monteiro, 2016), costly signaling (Kydd, 2005; Glaser, 2010) and audience costs (McManus, 2017), constructivist accounts about the sources of state preferences (Finnemore, 1996a; O'Neill, 1999), and theories about the indicators that states use to form threat perceptions (Yarhi-Milo, 2014; Jervis, 1989b), how states develop reputations from repeated interactions (Schelling, 1957; Dafoe, Renshon, and Huth, 2014), and the coordinating role of diplomacy (Trager, 2010, 2016; Joseph, 2021).

I provide the connective tissue that links these areas of research together. To do it, I develop a theoretical tool (a model) that integrates salient aspects of each of these research agendas into a single theoretical framework. My model includes three notable features that help me fit these different research agendas together to predict overarching patterns of competition and peace. First, I developed my modeling assumptions using interviews with national security elites (see Appendix A online for details). The interviews were designed to mimic problem-driven research (Lake and Powell, 1999). In them, I asked elites what choices they consider when they think about grand strategy against an enduring rival. The choices I allow states to make in the model, and the prior beliefs that I assume states hold, reflect elite answers. Of course, this is not the only way to construct a theory and there may be dynamics that I miss (see Paine and Tyson, 2020, for review), but my hope is that a model that assumes choices that elites think they can make will illuminate strategic dynamics and predictions that generalize across cases.

Second, my framework induces an interaction between the trust problem caused by uncertainty over the scope of the Challenger's motives (Kydd, 2005), and the commitment problem caused by shifting power (Powell, 1999) that makes peace especially hard at the origins of great power rivalries (Edelstein, 2019). Formally, the framework is most similar to Powell (1996). But it has some advantages that make it easier to examine whether and how cheap-talk diplomacy (Trager, 2011), costly signals (Kydd, 2005), and variation in the Challenger's motives can resolve this tension.

Finally, I develop a novel technique to operationalize and systematically study historical and cultural context in a formal model. Consistent with constructivist logic, I show that unique historical and cultural context can explain why cases unfold differently (Hopf, 1994; O'Neill, 1999). But I also argue that there are commonalities across the contexts of different cases that I can utilize for systematic predictions.

Putting it altogether, my theoretical approach yields three payoffs for academic research into international security. First, the model helps distill nuanced, case-specific variation down into relatively simple predictions about patterns of competition and peace. I show that almost all cases start with a long (but predictable) period of hedging, in which the Defender tolerates the Challenger's revisionist demands. I then explain when and why some cases eventually devolve into competition and others end in peace. Explaining this pattern is useful because rationalist scholars have long puzzled over delayed competition (Schweller, 2004; Organski and Kugler, 1980) or peace (Rock, 2000; Kennedy, 1976) in the face of rapidly shifting power or repeated violent actions. My framework supports both as rational behaviors.

Second, I show how important strategic dynamics for one set of scholars explain puzzling variation for another set of scholars. For example, I argue that a combination of historical context and diplomacy explains why some costly military action will engender mistrust and cause competition and other costly military actions have little impact. I also argue that variation in motives explains when rapidly shifting power will lead to competition straightaway, or when it will lead to competition after a while, or when it will lead to peace. I also argue that knowledge of a rival's history determines when intelligence analysts and other elites will voice their threat perceptions as a function of military signals and when they will voice their threat perceptions as a function of personal interactions. I also argue that the strategic incentives that surround competition explain why specific normative values, such as nationalism, heighten tensions in some cases but promote peace in others (Powers, 2022; Jackson and Morelli, 2011; Mylonas, 2013). In each of these examples, my theory not only shows that these different literatures are connected, it explains exactly when and how the features of one moderate the predictions of the other. The model shows that we can only resolve these puzzles if we consider all of these specific dynamics as part of a holistic strategic process.

Third, the model clarifies the extent to which these different literatures provide scope conditions on each other. For example, I show that if power shifts extremely fast, or if the Defender starts out certain that the Challenger's motives are expansive, or if the Challenger's history and culture imply that even their limited aims are enormous, then that factor alone will dominate the others. Different still, I show that if states avoid diplomacy, then peace will fail even if power shifts slowly and the Challenger likely holds limited aims. But I also show that one feature only dominates the others in extreme ranges. In most empirical cases, the conditions are moderate and all of the factors studied by scholars play an important role.

PART I

THEORY

2

The Strategic Problem at the Origins of Great Power Rivalries

I was motivated to write this book by a modern policy problem: Why have Sino-American relations unfold the way that they have, and how will they unfold over the next decade? To address these questions, I need to analyze the strategic setting at the heart of Sino-American relations. But what type of interaction is it? Scholars of international security describe Sino-American relations as one example of two great powers evolving into a rivalry. Many compare it to Anglo-German (1900s, 1930s), Anglo and Franco-Prussian (1850s), Anglo-American (1900), Anglo-Russian (1800s), and American-Soviet (1940s) relations. While these cases share important moments that deserve dedicated analysis such as militarized crises (Fearon, 1995), periods of institutional development (Keohane, 2005), or arms racing (Coe and Vaynman, 2019), I want to treat each case as a single strategic process so that I can explain (1) why some cases end in competition and others end in peace; and (2) in cases that end in competition, what explains the timing of competition in that case?

I argue that these cases share a common structure that I call the origins of great power rivalry. In this chapter, I fully detail this strategic problem in three steps. First, I provide an informal description of my assumptions: Who are the actors, what are their choices, and what is the value that they accrue from these choices. What I describe is closest to Edelstein (2019, ch 1).[13] In summary, I study a strategic interaction between a revisionist Challenger and a status-quo Defender. My theory starts when the Defender

---

[13] Where we depart is in our addition to the standard story. Edelstein (2019) focuses on time horizons which determine incentives for competition but still assume threat perceptions follow the standard logic; I focus on variation in the Challenger's motives, which moderate threat perceptions in response to costly actions and facilitate effective diplomacy.

first realizes that the Challenger will soon have repeated opportunities to revise the status quo over the coming years (or decades). The interaction unfolds over a revisionist phase where the Challenger is given repeated opportunities to demand one more concession, or stop and accept the status quo. The Defender must chose between making that concession, hoping that the Challenger will stop, or turning to strategic competition.

Second, I review the extensive prior research that has studied these cases. I argue that recent scholarship gains leverage on these cases by isolating one of two strategic problems: a commitment problem that is caused by shifting power (Powell, 1999), and a reassurance problem that is caused by uncertainty about the Challenger's motives (Kydd, 2005). I review the mechanisms, predictions, and puzzles that follow from emphasizing each strategic problem. I then argue that, consistent with structural realists (e.g., Glaser, 2010; Edelstein, 2019; Mearsheimer, 2001; Gilpin, 1983), that the origins of great power rivalries are especially conflict-prone because the commitment and trust problems interact. In many of these cases, if the Defender knew the Challenger held limited aims, the Defender would make concessions believing that the Challenger would stop. But the Defender is uncertain about the scope of the Challenger's motives. Limited-aims Challengers are unwilling to accept peace until they have captured the few core interests that they care intensely about. They try to convince the Defender that, despite violent behavior today, they will soon stop. But their promise is not credible because Greedy types engage in salami tactics. Each period, they demand another concession and promise it is their last. Defenders cannot trust the Challenger's claims of limited aims, and succumb to incentives for early competition.

Third, I formalize this interactive strategic problem. This is important because structural realists typically agree that the origins of rivalries present unique challenges. Where they disagree is in whether and how rationalist states can overcome them. Because my model produces the strategic tension they describe, any researcher can introduce new variables into it to address this long-standing puzzle.

Following Lake and Powell (1999), I initially prioritize parsimony. The value of parsimony is established by methodological (King, Keohane, and Verba, 1994), epistemological (Popper, 1959), and applied researchers (Mearsheimer, 2001; Powell, 1999). The downside of parsimony is that I must initially omit many plausible complications that others have studied. As you are reading, you will rightly wonder how might a more nuanced variation in the rate of shifting power, or the offense–defense balance, impact my predictions; can my theory survive if intelligence analysts cannot agree how a particular issue fits a Challenger's history and culture; what sort of variation in motives can my theory support; and what happens if preferences change (possibly as the result of leadership turnover)? After I present the results from the parsimonious model, I introduce each of these (and many other) complications into my strategic model and ask: How bad does this complicating factor need to be to ruin my main theoretical result? Some provide scope conditions on my argument. But ultimately, my core logic survives under empirically plausible conditions. For a summary of substantively motivated extensions see Boxes 4.1 and 4.2.

2.1 The Setting

2.1.1 Who Are the Actors, and Where Does My Theory Begin?

I theorize about a repeated interaction between two states: a Challenger (C, she) and a Defender (D, he).[14] The Defender is a status-quo power. He benefits from the existing international order, the distribution of territories and normative issues, and his sphere of influence. The Challenger had a limited say in how the international order was constructed. As a result, she has at least one issue, and possibly many more, that she wants to revise if given the opportunity.

Most of the issues that the Challenger could contest are controlled by third-party states, or are otherwise outside the Defender's sovereign control (such as the design of international institutions). Nevertheless, the Defender benefits from the existing order, and will lose something with each revision (Sartori, 2005).

Before the interaction starts, the Challenger and Defender enjoy stable relations where they benefit from cultural, commercial, and political exchange (Powell, 1993). However, they recognize that they have different visions about the world that they want to live in. Their differences do not cause tension because the Challenger is unable or unwilling to revise the status quo.

The rivalry begins when the Defender first realizes that the Challenger will have repeated opportunities to revise the status quo in her favor over the coming years (or decades).[15] In many cases, the Defender's fear of

---

[14] Following other structural theories (e.g., Glaser, 2010; Waltz, 1979; Powell, 1999), I analyze unitary states with fixed motives (Powell, 2017, explains why this is a good choice for strategic theories). Section 4.4.3 more fully considers leadership and regime changes.

[15] Thus, a scope condition is that the Challenger must accrue enough power over time to contest many issues. If the Challenger's rise is minimal overall, there is no strategic problem to solve.

revision is driven by shifting economic or military power (Organski and Kugler, 1980). However, the Defender's fear of revision could also be driven by a power vacuum in the Challenger's region that creates an opportunity for a long standing power to dedicate resources to foreign policy expansion (the end of the Cold War), or the Defender's decline (Friedberg, 2010). Since great powers vie for influence over third-party states, the Challenger could exploit increasing soft power brought on by shifts in economic interdependence, expanding diaspora populations, or by regional states adopting the Challenger's cultural practices or political philosophy. Finally, the Challenger's abilities may not change at all. It is possible that a Challenger has chosen not to exploit its power for a long time, but a radical regime change, or major shifts in the preferences of its constituents has caused the Challenger to alter its core foreign policy motivations.

2.1.2 What Are the Actors' Choices?: Hedging/Revision, Competition, and Peace

I assume that the Challenger and Defender independently select their grand strategies. However, the international relations between them depend on the grand strategies that each selects. I focus on three broad categories of international relations that arise from these grand strategic choices: hedging/revisionism, competition, and peace. In what follows, I characterize these different phases of international relations, and the choices states can make to shift them from one to the other.

I assume that the strategic interaction starts in a revisionist phase. This phase is tense because the Challenger is taking territory and overturning norms and institutions at the Defender's expense. Despite that tension, both states employ grand strategies that focus on coordination and exchange.

In the revisionist phase, the Challenger has the option of piecemeal revisions to the status quo. Even though the Challenger is extracting concessions at the Defender's expense, these states are not enemies at this point. Thus, the Challenger tries to reduce the risk of military conflict with the Defender. Substantively, the Challenger reduces this risk in three ways. First, she targets third-party states where the Defender has no explicit commitments. Second, the Challenger promotes institutions that subtly and indirectly undermine the Defender's global position. For example, China during the 2010s promoted the Shanghai Cooperation Organization and One Belt One Road as institutions to promote sovereignty, enhance regional security against nonstate threats, and increase trade in a manner consistent with global principles. These goals sound consistent with US-led institutions. But American analysts believe that they subtly undermine US liberal values. Third, the Challenger seeks to avoid tensions through public and private diplomacy. On the public side, the Challenger may make public statements that promote the Defender's overall view of world order, but make clear that certain aspects of it are unfair.[16] On the private side, the Challenger will often discuss her revisionist plans with the Defender. Of course, this diplomacy is cheap talk. Scholars have shown that cheap talk can rationally influence crisis bargaining (see Trager, 2016), but researchers still do not understand whether or how it influences the reassurance dynamic at the origins of great power rivalries. I will return to this point later. The important point is that the Challenger's pacific diplomacy is a common feature during the period of hedging.

The Defender's strategy during the revisionist phase is characterized by cautious hedging. On the one hand, the Defender's actions promote integration and stability. The Defender engages the Challenger through trade and cultural exchange, and may even promote economic and diplomatic integration. The Defender is even complicit in the Challenger's revision. The Defender may de-commit from an alliance over a third-party that the Challenger wants to influence, acknowledge the Challenger's legal claim over a contested territory, or sign an institutional agreement that supports the Challenger's normative preferences. By removing himself from a contentious position, the Defender gives the Challenger the opportunity to coerce third-party actors or build institutions while avoiding the possibility of direct conflict. As a result of this coordination, and given that the Defender can choose where to deploy forces and keep commitments, the Defender has some say in the order of concessions that the Challenger gains.

On the other hand, the Defender continues to arm to maintain a favorable position should he decide competition is necessary. The Defender maintains active intelligence to better understand the Challenger's intentions and abilities, and a strong military to make coercive threats if competition becomes necessary.

This description well fits US grand strategy towards China between 1990 and 2012. Supportive analysts often describe the US strategy during this period as cautious hedging, or accommodation (Medeiros, 2005). Critical analysts describe it as appeasement or, worse, inaction. While inaction may

---

[16] This fits China's decision to publicly describe its policy as hiding power, biding time, and peaceful rise.

not be a fair characterization, it still fits the spirit of my argument because the US strategy involved leaving the open the possibility of achieving a stable peace with China, and also prepared for a competition contingency. Historians have also characterized British strategy towards the United States (pre-1904), Russia (pre-1907), and Germany (pre-1938) as appeasement (Rock, 1989; Kennedy, 1989), among other notable cases. While each case was more nuanced, Challenger–Defender relations broadly fit hedging/revision as I define it.

The decision to coordinate during the revisionist phase is a choice that both states make. Thus, either can end this phase by unilaterally changing its strategy. My outcome of interest is when states change their grand strategy and thereby bring about an end to the revisionist phase. Since their strategies during the revisionist phase are different, the options they have to end the revisionist period are also different. The Challenger can end the period of revision by deciding that she is willing to live with the status quo, and peacefully integrate into a world order. Substantively, Challengers that stop revision agree to spheres of influence, rejoin global institutions, sign an arms control agreement, or form alliances and stronger trade agreements with the Defender. The Anglo-Russian Agreement (1907) forged at the end of the Great Game, the special relationship forged between Britain and the United States (1906), and Germany's commitment to world order (1990) all represent cases in which Challengers had the opportunity to make additional demands and decided instead to bind themselves to international institutions, demilitarize, or allow for intrusive monitoring in a way that ended their revision.

The prospect of a stable peace is attractive to both states because it allows them to benefit from commercial and cultural exchange, and share the burden of maintaining world order that benefits both of them. It also allows them to avoid the cost of competition with each other. In fact, one reason that the Defender is willing to tolerate the Challenger's initial revision, is that he hopes that the Challenger will eventually accept peace (Waltz, 1979; Glaser, 2010).

The Defender can end the revisionist phase by selecting strategic competition. Theoretically, the main difference between competition and hedging is the Defender's policy objective. When the Defender hedges, his goal is to reach a lasting peace with the Challenger some time in the future but remain prepared in case competition is necessary. The Defender is willing to tolerate short-term revision because his primary interest is in long-term peace. By contrast, when the Defender competes, his goal is to thwart the Challenger from making future revisions, and otherwise undermine the

Challenger's political and foreign policy objectives. The Defender has no intention of reaching a period when the Challenger peacefully integrates into world order as the Defender has built it.

My focus on variation in strategic goals is different from US grand strategy research. These scholars treat the objectives that the US wants to achieve as fixed, then explain how restraint, selective engagement, and so on, contributes to that policy goal (Posen, 2014; Art, 1998; Brooks, Ikenberry, and Wohlforth, 2013). I am interested in explaining when states change their strategic objectives.

Another difference between competition and hedging involves how the Defender reckons with uncertainty. This is analogous to the different types of information problems that arise in the spiral model and deterrence model (Braumoeller, 2008; Jervis, 1978). When the Defender is hedging, he is concerned about spirals of mistrust. Therefore, when a crisis erupts, the Defender is often willing to coordinate with the Challenger so as to avoid a crisis ruining their broader relationship. This follows because the Defender hopes that the Challenger has limited aims and long-term is possible. When the Defender is competing, he believes that the Challenger has expansive interests. The Defender's goal is to stop the Challenger's advances in any crisis. Thus, the Defender wants to convince the Challenger that he is highly resolved to fight in a specific crisis.

This difference helps clarify how the scope of my theory fits with realism and crisis-bargaining theory. Once the Defender decides to compete, the game devolves into a dynamic studied by crisis-bargaining scholars (Schelling, 1960; Sartori, 2005; Fearon, 1995). In it, the threat of escalation to war is imminent, states face incentives to overstate their resolve to fight at every opportunity, and the Defender hopes the Challenger wants less than what she claims. The period of hedging represents the setting studied by realists (Glaser, 2010; Waltz, 1979), wherein the Challenger faces incentives to understate her long-term strategic aims to avoid competition.

Loosely speaking, the observable policies that correspond with competition include comprehensive sanctions designed to cripple the Challenger's economy,[17] efforts to isolate the Challenger from international institutions, the forward deployment of forces to regions the Challenger could contest (Soviet Containment), an increase in strong defense commitments

---

[17] To be clear, states locked in strategic competition can cooperate on some issues. As Robert Zoellick (2005) has argued, it is plausible that the US and China could sign arms control agreements, or agree on the laws of the sea and still be rivals. Related, the US and Soviets cooperated on arms control during the Cold War. The point is that their main strategic intent is to prevent the other from future advances and undermine their international position.

(e.g., alliances) that prevent the Challenger from expanding into nearby states (such as the construction of NATO), supporting insurgents in the Challenger's sphere of influence, convert actions that target regime change, or major war (World Wars), or a combination of these policies.[18]

These indicators are loose because the specific tools that the Defender utilizes will not neatly correspond with his grand strategic objectives. One reason is that Defenders face frictions that cause a lag between the Defender's decision to compete, and the implementation of competitive policies. It can take years to mobilize forces, or reorientate funding that is already obligated to other regions or military assets. Competition often involves building new institutions and alliances, or renegotiating with existing partners. Working with third-party states takes time. In many cases, firms are responsible for trade with, and technology transfers to, the Challenger. The Defender's government cannot always stop its own firms from executing these lucrative deals. Even if they can, firms lobby hard to slow the pace of change so that they can amortize their losses.

Policy choices are also loose indicators because the Defender holds situation-specific concerns that cause variation in crisis behavior (Schelling, 1957). When competition is the Defender's strategic objective, the Defender may still stay out of a crisis if the Challenger is likely to win it and the costs of intervention are large. Instead, the Defender will dedicate his energies where he can more effectively thwart the Challenger. But even when hedging is the Defender's strategic objective, he may intervene against the Challenger in the rare cases that the stakes are very large. This explains, for example, US choices to commit to Taiwan during the 1990s.

One might ask, why focus on variation in grand strategic choices, and not the sexier and easier-to-measure outcome: war and peace? There are three answers. First, wars do not always coincide with grand strategic orientations given how modern scholars code them. Thus, focusing on these more specific events leads to unusual coding decisions in the most important cases. The most important example is the Cold War.[19] This was one of the most expensive and intense periods of competition in world history. The US and the Soviets fought proxy wars in Vietnam, Korea, Angola,

---

[18] This list of indicators is drawn from Edelstein (2019) (pp. 14–18), who conceptualizes competition in a similar way, but defines it more directly in terms of observable behaviors. By contrast, I conceptually tie competition to the Defender's grand strategic intentions. In the empirical section, when I cannot find direct evidence of the logic behind the Defender's grand strategy, I utilize Edelstein's (2019) indicators to code cases.

[19] There are other examples, many scholars code the Fashoda crisis as a war between France and Britain because it involved fatalities. But Anglo-French relations during this period were cooperative.

and Afghanistan. They also harmed each other through covert actions, economic sanctions, and engaged in highly inefficient arming. However, theories that treat war as the outcome code the Cold War as peace.

Second, the US and China are very unlikely to engage in a direct major war because both nations have large nuclear arsenals and enormous armies (Waltz, 1990). If we want our theories to explain why the US shifted from a long period of hedging during the 1990s to the current state of competition, then we want theoretical models that help us to explain the difference between hedging and competition.

Third, my conceptualization of strategic competition allows me to speak to, and clarify, the most closely related academic research. Notably, certain realists, and power transition theorists motivate their studies with cases that end in war. However, they acknowledge that their theories do not explicitly predict the timing of wars. Rather, they argue that their theories explain the conditions under which the risk of major war is heightened (see, for example, Organski and Kugler, 1980; Glaser, 2010; Waltz, 1979). But it is not exactly clear why a heightened risk exists. In my theory, the shift to competition heightens the risk of war in historical cases because the Defender forward-deploys forces to territories that the Challenger may contest, expands his alliance portfolio, engages in increased risk-taking behavior, takes other actions that harm the Challenger, such as covert operations or sanctions, and deliberately diminishes trade and institutional interdependencies. Thus, we can think about strategies of competition as a conscience choice on the Defender's part to select into a high chance of major war.

2.2 What We Know about the Origins of Rivalries

2.2.1 Shifting Power Generates Incentives for Competition

Power transition scholars argue that expectations of repeated concessions create pressures for competition (see Gilpin, 1988; Organski and Kugler, 1980; Powell, 1999; Spaniel, 2019). Under this logic, the Defender reasons as follows. If I compete today I have the greatest chance of victory. However, I will be forced to pay the enormous cost of competition, and must forgo the gains of economic collaboration. If I wait, I can defer the costs of competition. However, I will be forced to fight from a worse position.[20]

---

[20] The tensions caused by shifting power clearly underpin the cases I study and I explicitly include it in my theory. Recall that my theory begins when the Defender first realizes that the Challenger will have the opportunity to make repeated demands.

How do rivals overcome this commitment problem? In recent years, scholars have used the bargaining model with shifting power to explore this tension systematically. They argue that the answer hinges on the rate of shifting power (Debs and Monteiro, 2016; Joseph, 2023; Frendem, Joseph, and Spaniel, 2025). When power shifts slowly, the Challenger can compensate the Defender today with a large concession to offset the Defender's expected future losses (Powell, 1999). Incentives for war arise with rapid, per-period power shifts because the future is so bad that the Challenger is unable to compensate the Defender for it (see Powell, 2006, theorem 1). The Defender is willing to fight today to prevent that future from materializing. This insight yields the following core prediction:[21]

Bargaining Theory with Shifting Power's Prediction: War is more likely when the expected per-period shift in power is rapid (rather than slow) and the cost of competition is low (rather than high).

Scholars have recovered evidence for this prediction in cross-national studies (Bell, 2017; Kim and Morrow, 1992; Lemke, 2003) and in nuclear proliferation cases (Debs and Monteiro, 2016).[22] But the evidence is more mixed for the conventional great power cases that interest me (Copeland, 2015; Weisiger, 2013). They especially struggle to explain the dogs that don't bark: cases that ended in a stable peace despite rapidly shifting power. For example, in the late 1800s, the United States experienced rapid economic and military growth and set out to expel British influence from the Western Hemisphere. At the point at which American power grew most rapidly, Britain responded by withdrawing from key economic interests and ceding influence to the United States – the opposite of preventive war (Schake, 2017). In recent years, Japan (1980s) and Germany (1990s) experienced rapid economic success, and the United States accommodated them, leading to a stable peace. Furthermore, even when shifting power is correlated with war (or strategic competition), the timing of war often does not coincide with the fastest rate of expected shifting power. For example, Wark (1985, appendix 6) shows that British intelligence assessed that the German military would expand at the fastest rate during 1935 and 1936. In

---

[21] Strictly, Powell (2006) argued that rapid power shifts cause war in the first period. But Krainin (2017) showed that delayed war is possible, and others have shown that war follows punctuation in the rate of shifting power. Generally, the prediction I provide is the fairest test. War never occurs at the beginning of the power transition.

[22] However, even here the evidence is weaker than the theory might expect. For example, one important test finds a robust relationship between the expected rate of shifting power and conflict (Bell and Johnson, 2015). But even their measure of anticipated power shifts explains less than 1 percent of the variance in conflict.

fact, British estimates were suddenly and unexpectedly altered by new evidence in early 1935. These are the ideal conditions for conflict according to shifting power scholars. The incentives for war were amplified because Hitler instigated several crises. He occupied the Rhineland (1936) and funded Franco's war efforts (1937). And yet, the British avoided war until 1939, when power shifts were slower.

Putting it alltogether, the puzzle for power transition scholars is this. The evidence shows that status-quo powers monitor and predict future rates of shifting power. But they often do not fight wars when they anticipate rapidly shifting power, or imminent territorial and normative concessions for reasons other than shifting power. In fact, there are many cases where Defenders find a lasting peace at the times when power shifts most rapidly. Why does the fear of future concessions not trigger preventive competition?

Answering this question will help us understand modern Sino-American relations. Since the end of the Cold War, the US has estimated China would experience a long period of rapid economic and military growth. Indeed, beliefs about China's trajectory caused policymakers to focus on China in the 1990s. But their concern did not cause competition for decades. If anything, US policy was accommodating: The US facilitated China's rise through economic rewards and institutional power.

2.2.2 Costly Signals and the Reassurance Problem Caused by Variation in Motives

A second group of scholars emphasize a trust problem that arises given uncertainty over variation in the scope of the Challenger's motives. At one extreme, scholars conceptualize a status-quo Challenger, who holds no intrinsic value for revision, but who may instrumentally seek revision to assure its security (Waltz, 1979). At the other, a greedy Challenger, who intrinsically values all issues, and will expand opportunistically. In between are limited-aims Challengers who intensely value some core interests, but fewer than global domination (Glaser, 2010, footnote 1).

Uncertainty about strategic intentions creates a trust problem (Jervis, 1978). In recent years scholars have formalized this problem as a repeated, simultaneous-move 'box game' where states either hold prisoner dilemma, or stag hunt preferences (see Ramsay (2017) for review, Jervis (1978) for foundation, and Kydd (2005) for prominent example). These scholars argue that security-seekers credibly reveal their intentions – and achieve peace – by avoiding costly military actions that the greedy Challenger wants to take. Consider the basic logic in the context of territorial revision (Powell, 1996). Taking territory involves direct costs such mobilization and casualties. But it also derives benefits. The amount of benefit that it derives depends on how much the Challenger cares about taking territory. The greedy Challenger intrinsically values taking territory a lot. Therefore, the cost-benefit calculation from taking territory clearly favors revision. The security-seeker does not intrinsically value taking territory. Therefore, the cost-benefit calculation from taking territory is more mixed. The security-seeker may want more territory to assure her security. However, her value from revision is clearly less than the greedy type. If the greedy Challenger desires revision enough and the costs of revision are high, then the greedy Challenger will seek revision and the security-seeker will not.

The strategic dynamic is complicated by two-sided mistrust and the greedy Challenger's incentives to lull the Defender into a false sense of trust (Jervis, 1978; Haynes and Yoder, 2020). However, scholars repeatedly show that conditions arise where security-seekers can partially signal their security intentions by avoiding costly military actions (Kydd, 2005). In fact, scholars have applied this same basic logic to many kinds of costly actions including the Challenger's decision to militarize (or not) (Gurantz and Hirsch, 2017), build offensive (rather than defensive) weapons (Glaser and Kaufmann, 1998), accede to a treaty that either requires intrusive monitoring of military systems or credibly limits arms production (Coe and Vaynman, 2015, 2019), or impose domestic policies that correlate with a trustworthy world view (Goldfien, Joseph, and McManus, 2026). Putting all of this research together, we arrive at the following prediction:

Defensive Realist's Prediction: Costly actions → mistrust → competition The Challenger engenders mistrust and competition if she rapidly militarizes, builds offensive weapons, takes territory, or otherwise takes costly actions to undermine the status quo. The Challenger engenders trust and avoids competition if she forgoes opportunities to militarize, builds few weapons or only unambiguously defensive weapons, avoids making territorial demands or, accedes to arms limitation treaties with intrusive monitoring provisions.

A key feature of this result is that costs are necessary to generate trust. The reason is that all Challengers want to avoid competition. They can only do that if they convince the Defender that they are a security-seeker. Therefore, they all face incentives to say that even though they are taking territory, they promise that their overall objectives are security.

Defensive Realist's Costless Trust Prediction: Costless actions such as private diplomacy have no effect on trust. The Challenger cannot offset the mistrust caused by costly military choices through private or public diplomatic messages of reassurance.

There is clear evidence of costly signaling in the cases that I study. For example, when Hitler acceded to the Munich Agreement, British elites raised their confidence that Hitler's motives could be limited. When Hitler violated the Munich Agreement by taking additional Czechoslovakian territory, British elites inferred that Hitler's aims were vast. This realization triggered competition. More broadly, there is comprehensive evidence that British elites closely monitored Hitler's military actions and drew inferences about his motives based on those actions (Wark, 1985).

However, there are many other inferences that British elites drew that reassurance scholars cannot explain. Notably, the British War Secretary did not give "two hoots" about the Germans reoccupying the Rhineland.[23] The British also did not alter their estimates of Hitler's strategic intentions when they learned Hitler secretly funded local Austrians to overthrow the Austrian Government, or that Hitler withdrew from the League of Nations. Further, British elites ignored the erosion of democracy within Germany, and Hitler's choice to undermine liberal values by implementing policies that systematically discriminated against minorities. It is not only that British elites ignored costly signals that Hitler's intentions were greedy, they were reassured by diplomatic encounters with Hitler and other German elites (Yarhi-Milo, 2014, pp. 85–88).

Putting all of this evidence together, the puzzles for defensive realists are as follows. Why do Defenders often refrain from competition after Challengers take costly military actions? Why do Defenders often fail to make inferences about the Challenger's strategic motives when the Challenger's costly military actions (or inactions) provide a clear signal of aggressive intentions? Why are elites occasionally reassured by the Challenger's costless diplomatic reassurances as the Challenger rapidly militarizes, undermines world order, and takes territory?

Answering these question will help us understand modern Sino-American relations. For example, in 1995, China sought to revise the status quo over Taiwan. China initiated an invasion plan, moved 150,000 forces to its coastline, and executed live-fire drills (Scobell, 2003, pp. 176–177). China backed down only after the United States sailed a carrier through the Taiwan Strait. But even then China did not stop. In 1996, China invested in

---

[23] Quoted in Weinberg (1980) p. 259.

offensive battleships and used live-fire exercises to influence Taiwan's election. According to costly signaling theorists, American intelligence elites should have inferred China's intentions were vast because China made territorial demands, then engaged in rapid arming and purchased offensive weapons (Glaser, 2010; Coe and Vaynman, 2019). However, it did not engender mistrust. In fact, several analysts raised their confidence that China's long-term intentions were "limited to peaceful reunification" (Qimao, 1996). The 1996 National Security Strategy (NSS) shifted US policy towards Sino-American cooperation (pp. 40–41). For the first time it stated, "We have adopted a policy of comprehensive engagement designed to integrate China into the international community as a responsible member and to foster bilateral cooperation in areas of common interest."[24] President Clinton reversed a policy that tied China's Most Favored Nation Status to improved human rights, and started to promote China's entry into the World Trade Organization (WTO). Clinton had decided to expand economic cooperation pre-crisis. However, he didn't revert to competition after China's violent demands. Instead he strengthened his belief that cooperation was necessary.

This is not the only example. As the motivation for this book points out, for the last three decades China has invested heavily in new (and offensive) weapons, stood-up shadow institutions to undermine US-led world order, made provocative claims over many territories, brutally suppressed its domestic population and promoted other autocratic values, and used its coercive power to take territory. To complicate matters further, China made explicit that many revisionist actions did not serve security. And yet, the US did not infer that China's aims were vast, and did not turn to competition.

2.2.3 The Origins of Rivalries Are Conflict-Prone because Commitment and Trust Problems Aggravate Each Other

Structural realists argue that the risk of competition is heightened at the origins of great power rivalries because commitment and trust problems aggravate each other. Their description of the specific tension begins with a complete information counterfactual. If the Defender knew that the Challenger intensely valued a few core interests, then the Defender would tolerate initial concessions believing that the limited aims Challenger could

---

[24] In contrast, the 1995 NSS (p. 29) reads, "We are developing a broader engagement with the People's Republic of China."

commit to peace. By contrast, if the Defender knew that the Challenger was greedy, the Defender would compete straight away because the greedy challenger cannot commit to stopping after a few concessions (Gilpin, 1983, pp. 185–190). Therefore, complete information drives relatively efficient outcomes. States compromise if the Challenger holds limited aims, and engage in competition early if the Challenger has greedy intentions (Edelstein, 2019, pp. 16–18).

But the Defender does not know the Challenger's true motives. This gives rise to a particular variant of the trust problem that follows from salami tactics (Schelling, 1966, 66). Challengers with limited core interests promise to stop after they acquire their core interests. Their promise is genuine; but it is not credible because greedy Challengers understate the scope of their motives to avoid competition also (Mearsheimer, 2001, pp. 85–87). Each period, greedy Challengers make another demand and promise it will be their last (Carr, 1945). Since Challengers with greedy or limited aims all promise to hold limited aims, the Defender cannot be certain if this Challenger makes another demand because it intensely values a few issues, or because it wants to avoid competition while it opportunistically expands (Glaser, 2010, pp. 85–90).

Thus, different strands of structural realism do not ask why peace is hard at the origins of great power rivalries. Rather, they presuppose this problem based on observing it in historical cases, and ask whether and how can rationalist states achieve peace given this problem? Defensive realists believe they can, and offensive realists believe they cannot.

It is difficult to address this question using either of the game theoretic frameworks above because each is built to study one tension in isolation from the other. The bargaining framework does not produce the trust problem because rising powers face strong incentives to overstate the scope of their interests to maximize the size of the concessions that they receive. In fact proponents of the bargaining framework argue that introducing incomplete information about preferences produces "strange historical accounts" (Powell, 2006, p. 174) for the cases that interest me. As Powell (2006, pp. 174–175) explains, in the Anglo-German case, asymmetric information about Hitler's motives undoubtedly impacted British reasoning. However, the explanation for war that follows if we introduce uncertainty into the bargaining model is that Hitler claimed he had expansive aims, and would fight without an enormous concession. British elites realized that Hitler was asserting expansive aims, but thought he may be bluffing. War came because British elites were uncertain if Hitler was as aggressive as he claimed, and this caused the British to low-ball Hitler with a smaller offer than what he would tolerate.

Similarly, it is hard to fully integrate the commitment problem into the standard trust models (Kydd, 2005; Ramsay, 2017). Some scholars do introduce shifting power, but they still examine a single shift in a two-period model (e.g., Yoder, 2019). Even models that allow for more periods do not keep track of what specific territories have changed hands, and thus are not equipped to study a case where limited-aims Challengers could stop after a few specific concessions. Another challenge is that simultaneous moves cannot capture the sequencing of salami tactics because demands and concessions occur in tandem.

One important exception is Powell (1996), who identifies many of the same substantive concerns that I do with the existing formal literature, and builds a model to explore many, but not all,[25] of the aspects of the tension described here. One challenge with this framework is technical. Powell's continuous time model becomes intractable if one introduces more complex preference functions or choices. Thus, while it is carefully designed to setup the puzzle that realists want to solve, it is not easy to introduce important elements into the framework so that we can theorize about how to answer that puzzle.

All of this formal research also operationalizes motives differently from how historically orientated scholars conceptualize them. Structural theorists argue that Challengers vary in the scope of their motives, meaning the number of issues that they are willing to risk competition to acquire (see Yarhi-Milo, 2014, pp. 14–15). By contrast, formal accounts operationalize greedy types as holding a higher value for all contested issues. Substantively, formal accounts assume that if China held limited aims, it would intrinsically hold a lower value for all issues. But realist accounts suggest that if China held limited aims it could intensely value Taiwan, Tibet, and a few other issues, but care much less about peripheral interests. This difference is not trivial. In the costly signaling mechanism, limited-aims Challengers are willing to take a trust-building action because they care less about current issues than greedy types. But if limited-aims China intensely values Taiwan, it is not clear that China would avoid the use of force over Taiwan to signal benign future intentions. Indeed, even though Glaser (2010, pp. 103–105) acknowledges that states vary in the scope of their revisionist demands, he argues that it is appropriate to treat them as greedy because even limited revisionist aims cause the severe tensions that drive competition.

---

[25] For example, Powell (1996) cannot capture salami tactics because it assumes simultaneous moves. Therefore, it predicts war as a function of random strategic choices, and not the Defender's response given the Challenger has made a demand and promises to stop.

2.3 Formalizing the Interactive Tension at the Origins of Great Power Rivalries

I now develop a game theoretic model that captures the interactive problem at the origins of great power rivalries described by structural realists. First, I setup a model that captures the choices and preferences described at the beginning of this chapter. Second, I detail four assumptions necessary to induce the complete information counterfactual that structural theorists assert. Third, I demonstrate that these four assumptions give rise to the strategic problem that structural realists describe. Finally, I argue informally that the model provides a systematic framework for any researcher to ask: Can rationalist states overcome the interactive strategic tensions in historical cases; and if so how? Because the model produces the interactive problem structural realists describe, any researcher can adjust it to theorize about how to overcome it. Along the way, I use the model to precisely define core concepts that the existing literature struggles with. If Challengers vary extensively in the scope of their intentions, how can we differentiate between an unacceptably greedy Challenger and an acceptably limited Challenger; what does it mean for a Challenger to be satisfied, and do satisfied Challengers necessarily stop making demands?

2.3.1 Technical Setup

A Challenger (C, she) and a Defender (D, he) bargain over J foreign policy issues over a time horizon T. Define $q_t^D = \{(q_{1t}^D, q_{2t}^D, \ldots, q_{Jt}^D) | q_{jt}^D \in \{0,1\}\}$, and $q_t^C = \{(q_{1t}^C, q_{2t}^C, \ldots, q_{Jt}^C) | q_{jt}^C \in \{0,1\}\}$. q_{jt}^D indicate whether the Defender controls issue $j \in \{1,2,\ldots,J\}$ at the beginning of period t and q_{jt}^C indicate whether the Challenger controls issue j at the beginning of period t. For each issue j and time t, the control is exclusive, with $q_{jt}^D + q_{jt}^C = 1$.

Players derive utility from controlling issues they value. To capture this, each player is assigned a valuation vector. For simplicity, the Defender's valuation vector is $v^D = (v_1^D, v_2^D, \ldots, v_J^D) = \mathbf{1}$, meaning the Defender values every issues 1. The Challenger's valuation vector is

$$v = (v_1, v_2, \ldots, v_J), v_j \in \{h, l\} \tag{2.1}$$

where v_j denotes the Challenger's valuation for issue j, which can be either high (h) or low (h), with $0 \leq l < h$.[26]

---

[26] Substantively, I focus on foreign policy objectives that the Defender seeks to protect.

Throughout the book, we will focus on variation in the Challenger's strategic intentions. Thus, different value vectors v represent different types of challengers. The complete type-space is defined as $V = \{h, l\}^J$, containing 2^J possible types. To capture the common realist assumption, in this chapter I assume C varies in the scope of her strategic intentions. Specifically, I focus on a subset of this space, denoted $V^J \subset V$, defined as:

$$V^J = \left\{ (v_1, v_2, \ldots, v_J) \,\middle|\, v_1 = h,\ v_j \geq v_{j+1} \text{ for all } j \in \{1, \ldots, J-1\} \right\}. \qquad (2.2)$$

This subset imposes an ordering over the J issues from most to least important and categorizes the challenger based on the number of issues she values as high (h). As a result, the size of the type-space is reduced from 2^J to J. Let $H(v)$ denote the number of high-valued issues for type v, $H(v) \in \{1, \ldots, J\}$. For notation simplicity, label type $v \in V^J$ as $v_{H(v)}$. For example, in the case of $J = 3$ issues, the restricted type-space $V^3 = \{v_1 = (h, l, l), v_2 = (h, h, l), v_3 = (h, h, h)\}$, $H(v_2) = 2$.[27]

Finally, define a costless message from the Challenger at time t as a vector $m_t = (m_{1t}, \ldots, m_{Jt})$ of length J, $m_{jt} \in \{h, l\}$. The message represents C's claim about C's true value vector v. Substantively, the message allows C complete flexibility to identify whether or not she values a specific issue high or low. A message is honest in period t if $m_t = v$.

The game begins with D (the status quo power) controls all of the issues in dispute, that is, $q_{j1}^D = 1, q_{j1}^C = 0, \forall j \in \{1, \ldots, J\}$. D is deeply uncertain about C's motives. That is, Nature draws C's motives v from a discrete uniform distribution over the type-space V^J and shows it privately to C. Then the game unfolds over a revisionist phase of (at most) J revision opportunities. The sequence of moves in a period t of the revisionist phase is as follows:

1. C sends a costless message, m_t, and then either decides to accept the status quo, or demand another concession.
    (a) If C accepts the status quo, the game stops and payoffs are realized.
    (b) If C demands another concession, the game continues.
2. D decides to stop the game in competition or not.
    (a) If D stops the game, the game ends and competition payoffs are realized.
    (b) If D does not stop, D selects one issue (w_t) to transfer to C, and the next period begins.

---

[27] In later sections, when I introduce principal-based types, I will discuss how the analysis based on the reduced type-space V^J can be extended to the full type-space V.

Payoffs accrue once a player stops the game, or D has conceded all J issues. Payoffs are a function of (1) whether a player control issues that they care about when the game stops; and (2) whether the revisionist period stops in peace (C's choice) or competition (D's choice). If C accepts the status quo at period t, she stops the game, leading to stable peace payoffs:

$$U^D(peace,t) = q_t^D 1 \tag{2.3}$$

$$U^C(peace,t) = q_t^C v \tag{2.4}$$

This payoff function makes clear that the specific concessions that C receives and C's true motives both matter. Continuing with the three-issue example, suppose the status quo in period $t=3$ (following two concessions) is $q_3^C = (1,1,0)$ because D has chosen to concede issues sequentially. If the Challenger's true motive is $v_2 = (h,h,l)$, then C's utility from accepting peace is $2h$. However, v_1 type accrues $h+l$.

D stopping the game represents strategic competition. Both players enter a costly lottery (with common cost K) over the issues that D has not yet conceded to C. For each issue that D still controls, C wins the lottery with probability p, and D wins with probability $1-p$. The winner of each lottery captures the issue in dispute.[28] To capture the fact that D begins the game as a powerful status-quo power, we begin with the assumption that $p < 1/2$, which will assure that if D stops the game at the outset, D's expected value from competition is greater than C's. When D stops the game at t, expected utilities are:

$$EU^D(comp,t) = (1-p)q_t^D 1 - K \tag{2.5}$$

$$EU^C(comp,t) = q_t^C v + p q_t^D v - K \tag{2.6}$$

These competition payoffs are close to Powell (1996). I chose this as a point of comparison for two reasons. First, it is the model that explicitly analyzes a long-term reassurance problem. Second, the payoff functions guarantee that as time moves on, D's value for competition and peace are both decreasing, but C's value for competition and peace are increasing. While this does not exactly model shifting power and war in the context of bargaining, it is similar in that the range of acceptable bargains and war payoffs shift in the Challenger's favor over time.

---

[28] A strong assumption is that the Defender cannot win back issues in competition once he has conceded them. I relax it in Section 4.5.2.

Given D's belief of C's type $\hat{v}$, D's strategy, $s^D(\hat{v})$, consists of a concession strategy $w(\hat{v})$ and a stopping strategy $r^D(\hat{v})$. The concession strategy determines the sequence of issues that D gives away in each period if the game does not stop. $w(\hat{v}) = \{(w_t(\hat{v})_{t=1}^n | w_t(\hat{v}) \in \{1, 2, ..., J\}\}$, and for $t \neq t'$, $w_t \neq w_{t'}$. $r^D(\hat{v})$ is a vector of stopping choices $r^D(\hat{v}) = \{(r_t^D(\hat{v})_{t=1}^n | r_t^D(\hat{v}) \in \{0, 1\}\}$, where $r_t^D(\hat{v}) = 1$ if D's choice is to end the game in period t and competition payoffs are realized. $r_t(\hat{v}) = 0$ means D's choice is not to stop, and D gives away issue $w_t(\hat{v})$, and the game continues to the next period.

A strategy for C, $s^C(\hat{v})$, includes a series of costless message $m(\hat{v}) = \{(m_t(\hat{v}))_{t=1}^J\}$ and a stopping vector $r^C(\hat{v}) = \{(r_t^C(\hat{v})_{t=1}^n | r_t^C(\hat{v}) \in \{0, 1\}\}$, where $r_t^C(\hat{v}) = 1$ if C's choice is to stop and accept the status quo at period t, and $r_t^C(\hat{v}) = 0$ if C's choice is to make a demand in period t.

I solve for the Perfect Bayesian Equilibria (PBE), and all proofs appear in Appendix B online. Note that I focus on the stopping strategies r^D and r^C because D's concession strategy $w(\hat{v})$ and C's messaging strategy $m(v)$ are trivial in the baseline model. Since the Challenger's motives vary in scope, all C-types rank issue 1 as the most important and issue J as the least important. Therefore, D always make concessions in the order of 1 to J to minimize the cost of reaching peace. I will show later that no cheap-talk messages can affect outcomes in the baseline model because all Challengers share incentives to both delay competition and to receive concessions in an identical order.

2.3.2 Scope Conditions to Induce the Strategic Problem of Interest

The model induces the dynamics that structural theorists describe when four conditions are met. The first two assumptions assure that the Challenger is willing to fight for core interest and not fight for peripheral interests.

Assumption 1: Challengers prefer to demand a core interest and face competition than live in a world where they will never accrue their core interests.[29]

$$\mathcal{A}_1 = h > \frac{K}{p}$$

[29] If this condition is violated, we increase the conditions under which we can support peaceful equilibria.

Assumption 2: Once the Challenger has captured all of her core interests, she prefers to accept the status quo than face certain competition.

$$\mathcal{A}_2 = l < \frac{K}{Jp}$$

To be clear, I can achieve my results under slightly more general conditions. But these stricter assumptions vastly simplify the analysis and allow me to arrive at a simple definition that is useful for informal discussion.

Definition: A **satisfied Challenger** controls all her high-valued issues in period t. An **unsatisfied Challenger** does not control all her high-valued issues in period t.

The second two assumptions assure that the Defender responds as expected under the complete information counterfactual. Specifically, these assumptions assure that if the Defender knew that the Challenger had sufficiently limited aims, that the Defender would be willing to make limited concession knowing that the Challenger will eventually stop.

While structural theorists often assume that limited-aims Challengers will stop (Glaser, 2010), my model illuminates an underappreciated strategic problem: even satisfied Challengers must have a reason to stop. In a fully strategic account, it is not enough for the Challenger to be satisfied. The Challenger must also be deterred from making another demand. If C believed that D would keep making concessions, then even if C was fully satisfied, C would keep making demands. This insight gives rise to a critical period that represents the last period where D can credibly threaten competition. More specifically, define a period x_1 as the integer that satisfies,

$$J + 1 - \frac{K}{1-p} > x_1 > J - \frac{K}{1-p} \tag{2.7}$$

should one exist. Loosely, $x_1 + 1$ represents the first period that D can no longer credibly threaten competition. More precisely,

Lemma 2.1: *If we can solve for x_1, then the game must stop in either peace or competition at $t \leq x_1$ in every PBE*

The right side of inequality 2.7 assures that in period $x_1 + 1$, D strictly prefers to make the remaining $J - x_1$ concessions rather than compete at

$x_1 + 1$. Thus, if the game had not stopped before players arrived here, C knows D will make all the remaining concessions. Therefore even fully satisfied Challengers make demands. The left side assures that in the prior period, $t = x_1$, D still prefers competition to all remaining concessions. D is also aware that if he makes even one more concession, that his credible threat will unravel. This knowledge makes D's threat at x_1 credible.

This does not assure that hedging will endure until $x_1 - 1$. To get there, D must initially desire to tolerate concession, given D's understanding of when D's threat of competition can induce C to stop. Putting it altogether,

Assumption 3 and 4: We can calibrate D's incentive such that there is a last moment that D can credibly threaten competition (period x_1). In the first period, D prefers making $x_1 - 1$ concessions to first-period competition.

There exists an integer $x_1 \in \{1, 2, \ldots J - 1\}$ that jointly satisfies

$$\mathcal{A}_3 \quad J + 1 - \frac{K}{1-p} > x_1 > J - \frac{K}{1-p}$$

$$\mathcal{A}_4 \quad Jp + K + 1 > x_1$$

To be clear, it is not always possible to satisfy these assumptions. This places an important scope condition on when states may face the basic complete information incentives that structural realists describe. Examining $\mathcal{A}_3$, when K is too high, then D can never credibly threaten competition because D strictly prefers to make all J concessions rather than compete straight away. Thus, if K is too high, we cannot produce the tension we want because competition is too costly. By contrast, examining $\mathcal{A}_4$, if K is too low, then D prefers to compete rather than make even a single concession. In this case, even if D knows C only holds a single core interest, D is not willing to compromise. In this case the game ends in certain competition.

A closer look at what it takes to jointly satisfy $\mathcal{A}_3, \mathcal{A}_4$ provides two other substantive insights about the necessary conditions for the Defender's incentives to jointly hold. First, given that D begins the game more powerful than C, I can only jointly satisfy these conditions if $x_1 < J/2 + 1$. If $x_1 \geq J/2$, then D is either sufficiently resolved to credibly threaten competition at $t = x_1 - 1$, or sufficiently irresolute to tolerate the initial $x_1 - 1$ concession rather than compete straight away. But D cannot be both. This bounds limited-aims Challengers to those who value fewer than half of the available issues. Second, because this is a strict inequality, it instantly follows that we can only satisfy these conditions when $J > 2$. This implies that the problem of the origins of rivalries characterized by structural theorists only applies when states contest at least three distinct issues.

2.3.3 Complete Information Counterfactual and Defining Limited and Greedy Challengers

As stated, structural realists often describe a complete information counterfactual that specifies how the Defender would behave if he knew the Challenger's motives. My model rationalizes this result.

Proposition 2.2: *When $\mathcal{A}_1 - \mathcal{A}_4$ jointly hold, then we can rationalize the complete information counterfactual described by structural theorists. With complete information:*

- *If C is so greedy that $H(v) \geq x_1$, D stops the game in first-period competition.*
- *If C's motives are sufficiently limited ($H(v) < x_1$), then a delayed peace equilibrium always exists, where C acquires all her core interests and stops.*

When the Challenger holds vast strategic intentions, the complete information result is dominated by a well-known commitment problem. The Challenger initially wants to commit to stopping after a few concessions. But because she holds vast aims, she cannot credibly promise to stop before D can no longer threaten to deter her. Realizing that delayed cooperation is unsustainable, D selects competition as early as possible. When the Challenger's aims are more limited, she still refuses to stop until she has acquired all her core interests. However, because D knows she holds limited aims, the Challenger can credibly promise to stop after she receives her core interests. To be clear, delayed peace only includes cases where the Defender makes some but not all concessions. Thus, when states eventually achieve delayed peace they enjoy a stable compromise over the foreign policy issues they contest.

Scholars often struggle to characterize Challengers with varying degrees of limited aims as either cooperative or greedy types (Edelstein, 2019; Glaser, 2010). But the complete information model allows me to endogenously define Challengers as unacceptably greedy or acceptably limited.

Definition: A Challenger is **unacceptably greedy** if her interests are so great that the Defender would turn to competition straight away if the Defender knew the Challenger's motives ($H(v) \geq x_1$).

Definition: A Challenger is **acceptably limited** if her interests are sufficiently limited such that if the Defender knows her preferences, the Defender is willing to tolerate initial concessions and arrive at delayed peace ($H(v) < x_1$).

As shown, x_1 is calibrated based on the Defender's costs of competition, and the scope of the Challenger's intentions. Therefore, these definitions are endogenous to these modeling parameters.

Generally speaking, Challengers with fewer core interests (lower $H(v)$) are acceptably limited. Further, the Defender is willing to tolerate more initial concessions if either the Challenger is more likely to prevail in competition (p is higher) and the cost of turning to competition K is moderate to low.

2.3.4 Incomplete Information: Trust Problems Aggravate Commitment Problems

The conventional wisdom among structural realists is that peace is not assured even if C holds acceptably limited aims because D is uncertain about the scope of C's motives. In the context of power transitions, limited aims Challengers face a reassurance problem. They must convince D that even though they are making initial demands, they will soon stop and accept the status quo. While structural realists agree that the reassurance problem is fundamental, they debate how severe this problem is, and whether it can be overcome via costly signals. We now provide structure to this debate by modeling the two most commonly held assumptions made by both offensive and defensive realists: that C's motives vary in scope, and that D is *initially* deeply uncertain about C's motives.

Under these conditions, we generally find that while cooperation can be resolved, the offensive realist position is closer to what is rationalizable. Both for tractability, and to stack the deck in favor of cooperation, we will assume $J = 3$. This makes cooperation as easy as possible because it assures that D need only wait one period before the players arrive at x_1 and D must learn whether C has acceptably limited aims or not.

Proposition 2.3: *Assume $\mathcal{A}_1 - \mathcal{A}_4, J = 3$. Delayed peace is only rationalizable if $H(v_1) = 1$ and:*

$$2(1-p) > k > 3 - 5p \qquad (2.8)$$

Otherwise, all equilibria end in first-period competition, regardless of C's true motives. In all equilibria, diplomacy is uninformative.

In all equilibria, the strategic problem closely follows the problem intuited by structural theorists. There is a limited-aims Challenger that will stop after 1 concession. However, there is also a greedy Challenger that deploys salami tactics. If allowed to make concessions, the greedy Challenger would promise that she will stop after just one more concession. But in the next period, she would repeat that promise. Because D is deeply uncertain about C's true motives, once C makes the initial demand, D is deeply uncertain if C is the type that will stop next. Diplomacy cannot be effective because all Challengers desire concessions. If it could work, all types would use it.

How D manages these costs and risks depends on the underlying parameters. But we emphasize that cooperation is unlikely given empirically plausible conditions:

Remark Cooperation is unlikely: Delayed peace is impossible if either:

- D initially holds a $\frac{2}{3}$ or greater expectation of victory in competition.
- The cost of competition either exceeds $\frac{1}{3}$ of D's value for control of all contested issues, or is less than $\frac{1}{2}$ of D's value for a single issue.

Remark Costly signals do not help: Limited-aims Challengers never forgo first-period costly demands to communicate their true limited aims.

As in the complete information model, D faces a goldilocks problem (see discussion of x_1 above). The cost of competition must be sufficiently low for D to be able to credibly threaten it if C makes an initial demand but then does not stop. But the cost of competition must be sufficiently high for D to be willing to tolerate the initial concession. Deep uncertainty about C's motives severely exacerbates this problem because it assures that D has no idea if C will actually stop, and this constrains D's incentives to offer initial concessions.

Defensive realists might imagine that limited-aims Challengers overcome this problem with costly signals. But recall that even limited-aims Challengers care intensely about their core interests. Costly signaling is not viable because it would force them to forgo the few issues they highly prize.

To be clear, and to foreshadow what will come, the results are sensitive to D's beliefs about C's type. If we restructure D's prior beliefs so that C is very likely to hold one core interest, moderately likely to hold three core interests, and is very unlikely to hold two core interests, then we can sustain cooperation. Thus, to achieve delayed peace, we must find ways to convince D to take on these beliefs. However, under the substantively appealing assumption that the Defender is deeply uncertain about the Challenger's motives, it is hard to escape competition if the Challenger's motives vary in scope.

2.4 The Baseline Model as a Puzzle

The model produces the puzzle that structural realists who study the origins of rivalry often start with. It shows that under four empirically plausible conditions Challengers and Defenders face both commitment and trust problems at the origins of great power rivalries. If the Challenger's motives vary in scope, and the Defender is deeply uncertain about them, these problems interact to thwart peace under most conditions.

The framework also provides two reasons to be skeptical that costly signals alone can overcome this particular trust problem. First, D is only willing to tolerate initial concessions if D trusts C. In theory, a Challenger could use early costly signals to establish initial trust. But in the setting that interests us, limited aims Challengers initially covet high-valued core interests. Thus, they do not hold the initial incentives to build trust through avoiding costly actions. If they did, they would be forced to forgo core interests that they intensely value.

Second, to achieve peace, the Defender must initially trust C enough to make several initial concessions. But there must be a point where the Defender can credibly threaten competition if the Challenger makes one more demand. Thus, to sustain delayed peace, C's initial revisionist demand must not degrade trust much, but D's later costly actions must substantially degrade trust. Standard costly signaling theory tells us the first action is likely the most informative.

Overall, I view this framework as characterizing a puzzle. It formalizes the intuition that peace is hard in these cases. The puzzle arises because real life states avoid competition in spite of this strategic problem. In almost every great power case, even though the Defender is deeply uncertain about the Challenger's motives, the Defender makes early concessions that give rise to either delayed peace or delayed competition. Why is that so? In the next two chapters, I provide my answer.

3

My Innovation: Enriching How We Understand State-Motives

I argue that we can better explain patterns of competition and peace if we make more detailed assumptions about what motivates Challengers to pursue revisionist foreign policies. Like structural realists, I assume that each Challenger has a set of core foreign policy objectives that they value intensely, and a set of peripheral objectives that they care less about. However, I argue that a Challenger's core interests depend on (1) the *principle* that motivates its foreign policy and (2) its historical, cultural, and geostrategic *context*.

Each of these points requires detailed elaboration. First, I define principles. Second, I explain how the Challenger's historical and cultural context means different principles drive different, but specific, forms of foreign policy ambition. Third, I explain how to systematically study motives as principles. Finally, I show that this conceptualization allows the Defender to draw contextualized inferences from the Challenger's actions, but that we can study these inferences in a generalizable way.

3.1 Principles

A principle is a fundamental truth or proposition that serves as the foundation for a system of belief or behavior. As in other rational theories that allow a Challenger's intrinsic motivations to vary, I assume that principles are primitives that are analytically prior to the action's states take and the beliefs states form, and are held fixed across the analysis (Glaser, 2010, pp. 38–39).[30] Scholars have found evidence that states pursue different

---

[30] Constructivists often endogenize intrinsic motives. In Section 4.4.3, I find my main theoretical results are robust even if motives can change. While this does not fully capture all the ways that certain constructivists model preference change (e.g., Wendt, 1992), it

44

principles. Some fight to unify their ethnic group (Goemans and Schultz, 2017), restore historical borders (Carter and Goemans, 2011), for revenge (Stein, 2015), security, status (Renshon, 2016), or the global spread of their ideology. This evidence shows that not all states prioritize the same principle. Each state, depending on the interests of their constituents and leaders, the configuration of domestic institutions, and their exposure to international norms, may prioritize some principles but not others (Finnemore, 1996a; Moravcsik, 1997).

To help make this abstract concept more concrete, I list common principles that states either truly held, claimed to have held, or could have held in important historical cases. This list is not exhaustive, nor does every principle that I list apply in every historical case.

Status: In the context of international relations, status is a state's standing or ranking in the hierarchy of states (Renshon, 2016). How states accrue status depends on time-variant international norms. During the 1800s, Kaiser Wilhelm II's desire for Germany to take a place in the sun, broadly understood as a status claim, drove him to construct a navy and seek out colonial possessions (Maurer, 1997). Some argue that India, China, and Pakistan pursued nuclear weapons to be recognized as a great power (Bell, 2015). Whatever the means, status is the Challenger's intrinsic motivation if the Challenger's end goal is recognition by others in the international system.

In extreme cases, status motivations can drive a state to pursue regional or global hegemony (where hegemon is a status rank). However, a desire for status will not always push a state this far. If international and domestic norms mean that seeking global hegemony is frowned upon, it is possible that hegemony won't bring the status benefits that a state desires.

Security: Security as an intrinsic motivation refers to a desire to feel safe from foreign military threats against territorial borders or the lives of citizens (Waltz, 1979). This is different from an instrumental need to protect the flow of future benefits (Fearon, 1995). For example, following repeated land invasions and brutal conflict over centuries, Stalin argued that Russia felt an intense fear of future invasion and this fear crippled the country.[31]

does establish that my main theoretical result is not entirely sensitive to the assumption that motives are fixed.

[31] As Chapter 6 shows, Stalin was not genuinely motivated by security. As discussed later, this was his declared principle.

This fear elevated security from an instrumental to an intrinsic concern. Similarly, following the September 11 terror attacks, members of the US public were afraid that they could personally become a victim of terrorism. The desire to crush this fear partly drove public support for the War on Terror.

Prosperity: Some states pursue revisionist foreign policies to enrich themselves. For example, in 1921 Japan listed out twenty-one demands for resource rich territories across Asia. Certain generals in Tzarist Russia wanted to fight wars to capture warm-water ports in Turkey. Belgium took colonies to reap the benefits from enslaving the locals and extracting precious stones and minerals.

Nationalism: Nationalism refers to the identification with one's own nation and support for its interests. Nationalism can manifest in different ways in different cases (Powers, 2022). For example, Hitler claimed to be motivated by *ethno* nationalism (Schultz and Goemans, 2019). He claimed this principle drove him to unify all territories with a majority Germanic population under one government. In contrast, in 1924, the King of Saudi Arabia explained his decision to invade Hijaz in terms of *religious* nationalism.[32] Nationalism can also manifest as a desire to *restore historically controlled borders* (Carter and Goemans, 2011), or protect people with a shared *linguistic* or *cultural* background.

In some cases, there is not much difference between these variants of nationalism; and it is useful to think about nationalism as a single principle. For example, when Prussia sought unification, it wanted to control certain ethnically Germanic territories.[33] Since the Germanic territories had not previously been federated, Prussia had no prior borders to unify. But in other cases different forms of nationalism hold different implications. For example, scholars have analyzed different nationalist perspectives of Haffayez Assad's Syria (Batatu, 2012, p. 293). If Assad was motivated to restore Syria's historical borders, he would have conquered Lebanon. If instead he was motivated to unite Alawite Muslims under one government he would have contested Turkey for salient territory. If instead, Assad pursued Pan-Arabism, he would have sought out normative and institutional objectives across the Islamic world, beyond territorial

---

[32] Tzar Nicholas also appealed to religious nationalism before invading Crimea.
[33] The variant of Prussia's nationalist claims omitted Austria. See Raymond (1921) for an explanation of how Prussia made this clear to Britain.

revision. In a case like this, it is useful to categorize different variants of nationalism as different principles because they each imply distinct territorial, institutional and normative interests.

Ideological Principles other than Nationalism: Ideology is any system of ideas that a state believes it should live by. Variants of nationalism are ideologies. Communism is also an ideology. Stalin was likely motivated by spreading communism globally. Different still, Britain fought the Crusades to free Jerusalem from Muslim rule (Tyerman, 1996, pp. 8–9).

Other Principles: This is not a complete list. States may be motivated by revenge for past wrongs, the belief that the state's role is to enforce contracts for their firms overseas, the right to shape world affairs, etc.

These examples illustrate two things. First, Challengers are intrinsically motivated by different principles in different historical cases. Second, there is often uncertainty about the Challenger's true principle. This is especially clear because, in some cases, Challengers declare one principle, but secretly pursue another. In other cases, Challengers honestly reveal their true principle from the start. My theory captures this kind of variation. I start with the assumption that Defenders are initially uncertain about the Challenger's true intrinsic motivation. The reason is that there are many different principles that could serve as the Challenger's intrinsic motivation. The Defender knows that the Challenger is motivated by a specific principle. But the Defender does not know what that principle is.

My focus on variation in principles is different from three ways that scholars typically study variation in preferences. First, it is different from variation in resolve, which determines a Challenger's preference for standing firm in a specific crisis given the probability of victory and cost of war (Kertzer, 2016). In my theory, a principle determines the total set of specific issues that a Challenger values high absent the situation-specific factors. This difference holds implications for what information is learned from one crisis to the next. For example, when Hitler first re-militarized the Rhineland he explained that ethnic-nationalism motivated his foreign policy. The British understood that even if Hitler was motivated by ethnic-nationalism, the Rhineland was not the end of his revision. However, the British also believed that there was a natural limit to the concessions "ethnic-nationalist" Hitler would demand. In my theory, the question is whether Hitler was actually motivated by the principle he claimed (ethnic-nationalism) or something else (regional or global hegemony); and is not how resolved is Hitler to fight in all future disputes on average.

Second, it is close to, but different from, how Glaser (2010); Waltz (1979), and other realists conceived of security versus greedy states. Like these theorists I largely focus on intrinsic motives that are "primitive and inherent to states" (Glaser, 2010, p. 38).[34] A state's intrinsic motives determine how much value a state accrues from the world the way that it is. However, most defensive realists focus exclusively on security versus greedy intrinsic motivations (e.g., Glaser (2010, p. 39) and Kydd (2005, p. 34)). Because there are only two potential motivations, there is no practical difference between an intrinsic motivation and a principle in these theories. I allow states to potentially hold a wider range of intrinsic motivations. This makes the distinction useful. The reason is that a principle only becomes an intrinsic motivation if it is what truly motivates a state's foreign policy. Because I allow different states to hold different intrinsic motivations, there will inevitably be some principles that do not serve as intrinsic motivations. In the language of formal theory, there are theoretically many types of Challengers that are not realized. Each type represents a principle that could have motivated the Challenger.

Third, a principle is different from a norm. A norm is a standard of appropriate behavior (Finnemore and Sikkink, 1998). This implies a norm is a principle that actors believe each other is supposed to follow (Finnemore, 1996b). I do not restrict the set of principles that can motivate states to those that are appropriate. In my theory, states can be motivated by a principle, such as global domination, that is not commonly viewed as a standard of appropriate behavior. As we shall later see, I also do not assume that states which pursue principles that are broadly seen as appropriate (inappropriate) are always perceived as holding acceptably limited (or unacceptably greedy) aims.

I am not the first to acknowledge that states hold nuanced intrinsic motivations. In fact, some of the most important innovations in international security research follow because scholars make different assumptions about intrinsic motivations. For example, Gilpin (1983) and Keohane (2005) both start with the assumptions that Waltz (1979) made about the structure of world politics and the choices states can make. But they derive different predictions about competition and peace because they assume states are motivated by status and prosperity respectively. We get different predictions still if we assume that states respond to parochial military

---

[34] Motives could change over the course of a fifty-year interaction between great powers (Rosato, 2015). One extension in Section 4.4.3 demonstrates my theory is robust if the probability that the Challenger's motives will change is not too large.

interests (Snyder, 1993), political survival, or adopt normative preferences but otherwise behave rationally (Fearon and Wendt, 2002; Mitzen, 2006).

This research provides an important clue that variation in intrinsic motivation can help us unlock insights about patterns of great power competition. However, each of these innovations assumes only one intrinsic motivation at a time (which I call a principle). My theoretical move is to acknowledge that all of these important innovations describe a state's true motives in a particular set of cases. But through history, different Challengers have been primarily motivated by different principles, that Defenders are uncertain about which principle motivates the Challenger, and this uncertainty creates opportunities and difficulties for great power cooperation. My goal is to conceptualize a broader framework that acknowledges there is heterogeneity in the goals that great powers could pursue, that this heterogeneity drives uncertainty about what really motivates any great power in any particular case, and then develop a structured way to analyze the implications of this uncertainty for patterns of competition and peace between states.

For ease of exposition, I describe a Challenger that prioritizes a single principle (meaning that they value issues related to that principle above the rest). As we shall see in Chapter 7, Challengers through history have justified their initial revisionist demands by appealing to a single dominant principle (or at most a couple). Thus, this simplifying assumption also fits the historical record. However, the predictions I report at the end of Chapter 4 are not entirely sensitive to this one-principle assumption. I generate the same predictions if I allow the Challenger to prioritize certain combinations of principles.[35]

At this point, you may have noticed that anything could be a principle. But in each case some principles are more plausible than others. For example, to my knowledge, no analysts considered if Hitler was motivated by the responsibility to protect. But some did consider whether Hitler was motivated by nationalism or status. Why are some principles plausible and others are not, and why is the Defender uncertain about the Challenger's principles? While these questions are beyond the scope of my theory,[36] it

---

[35] It requires that enough combinations of principles that are plausible drive the Challenger to hold a sufficiently small number of core interests, or that the probability of valuing two principles is low.

[36] As we shall see, I only assume that the Challenger could be motivated by different principles. I am agnostic about where principles come from.

is useful to loosely answer them for two reasons.[37] First, it helps bridge constructivist and psychological theories of the origins of preferences, and rational accounts of their strategic effects into a single framework. Second, it informs the empirical problem of coding feasible principles in case material.

I conjecture that the set of plausible principles that most likely motivate the Challenger follows from the preferences of domestic and transnational actors, or prevailing norms, that could influence a Challenger's foreign policy. Thus, one factor that makes certain principles less likely than others is the preferences of domestic or international interest groups. In any particular case, there is variation in what different individuals and interest groups think the Challenger should be using their foreign policy tools to achieve. Individual-level preferences could form as the result of lived experiences that include exposure to international norms, family, cultural, and religious values, or elite cues (Saunders, 2011). They can also form around economic and professional incentives (Moravcsik, 1997). These different experiences and incentives inform public opinion (Knecht and Weatherford, 2006), the interests of lobby groups, and the interests of political elites including the nation's leader, military and diplomatic elites, and other important political and market actors (Snyder, 1993; Schub, 2023). On the international side, transnational actors and international organizations often explicitly lobby governments in an effort to delegitimize specific foreign policy goals and promote others (Finnemore and Sikkink, 1998). Another factor arises from prevailing norms at the time. Norms influence the lived experiences of elites, and also the priorities of transnational actors. The idea that true motives are likely constrained by the social context of the time is consistent with Bull (2002, pp. 23–39), who argues that interests groups in European states have differently coalesced around European, Christian, or global values in different moments of history. The nature of dominant values at the time, determined the potential motivations that interest groups or states could hold in each period (see also Finnemore, 2003, ch 5).

Many, but not necessarily all, of these groups voice their preferences. Defenders spend time examining different interest groups that could influence the Challenger's main foreign policy principle. Therefore, Defenders loosely understand the set of principles the Challenger *could* prioritize based on different groups who may be influencing the Challenger's

---

[37] A tight answer would require a second book, and I do not want to constrain important ideational work that could theorize about sources I have not covered.

decision-makers. Thus, we might expect that when Defenders start to theorize about what could motivate a Challenger, that they likely analyze the interest groups that could influence the Challenger's foreign policy priorities to acquire a list of plausible principles the Challenger may pursue.

The Defender is likely uncertainty about the Challenger's true principle because he does not perfectly observe how the specific preferences of different interest groups aggregate, which substate actors decide the state's foreign policy preferences, and which groups the decider is most sensitive to (Powell, 2017). This is true in highly transparent democracies. For example, with decades of hindsight and declassified archives, scholars still cannot agree on how US foreign policy preferences form. Some suggest that the US is highly sensitive to public opinion, but others still suggest that the US public is ignorant about foreign policy and they respond mainly to elite cues (Foyle, 1997; Ardanaz, Murillo, and Pinto, 2013). Recently, Stephen Walt (2018) has argued that the 'blob' – a group of foreign policy experts who have spent their career working on US grand strategy and foreign policy – determine US foreign policy objectives. But even in his telling, the way that the blob influences policy is multifaceted and shadowy even to its members. In autocracies, a smaller group of actors could influence state motives. However, these domestic actors are usually more secretive. For example, when Kim Jong Un took power, the CIA knew that North Korea's goals would either be governed by the new leader, the military, or the power brokers that kept Kim Jong-il in power. What they did not know, was the interests of these actors. For example, they knew that Kim Jong Un had studied in Europe and had been exposed to Western ideas. They also asserted that some military elites saw value in opening up. But they did not know whether these values and preferences dominated other concerns. Thus, uncertainty persisted about what his motivations could be (Goldfien, Joseph, and Krcmaric, 2023). To be clear, this does not mean that Defenders remain ignorant or are unable to learn. As I will discuss next, Challengers can communicate their principles through their actions. Therefore, as the case unfolds the Defender is able to learn about the Challenger's principles.

3.2 Historical and Cultural Context

Holding the Challenger's true principle constant, the tangible, real-world objectives a Challenger wants to achieve depend on its historical, cultural, and geostrategic *context*. A state motivated by the principle of ethnic nationalism, for example, will be most interested in territories that contain its ethnic group, and may seek to overturn international norms that call for the fair treatment of minorities. But if that same state, with the same context, was motivated by revenge from a prior conflict it would seek different objectives. Further, two states that are motivated by the same principle will value different concessions. For example, if China and Poland both wanted to restore their historical borders, their foreign policy objectives would be different because Poland's historical context is different from China's.

Since a Challenger's value for different territories corresponds with an underlying principle, there are some combinations that are unlikely. For example, if China is motivated by a nationalist project that is grounded in the Middle Kingdom narrative, then it is very likely to values territorial control over Taiwan, Tibet, and several islands, and influence in parts of East Asia. But it is less likely that China values a colony in Uganda. Indeed, it is hard to think of a principle that implies China holds an intense value for territorial control over Taiwan, Uganda, and nothing else.

The Defender is uncertain about the principle that the Challenger prioritizes. While the Defender does not know the principle that drives the Challenger, he knows a lot about the Challenger's historical and cultural context. The Defender acquires that information by employing intelligence and foreign policy experts that read about the Challenger, and otherwise communicate with the Challenger's elite (Lowenthal, 2019). As a result, the Defender has a reasonably good understanding about what the Challenger would want if the Challenger was motivated by a specific principle. However, as we will consider later, some ambiguity remains.

The combination of principles and context both drive and limit a state's desire for expansion. There are many territories that have little financial benefit to them and would not be worth fighting for if states were purely motivated by prosperity (Brooks, 1999). For example, the Gaza Strip is a desert, with no natural resources, and is in a woeful strategic position. The reason Palestinians and Israel fight over it is because of a normative attachment. However, that same normative attachment could limit a state's desire to fight. For example, a state motivated by nationalism may be unwilling to send its army to take an oil field because it risks the lives of patriots for the financial gain of a few elites.

It is tempting to say that some principles uniquely drive expansive aims and others uniquely drive states towards limited aims. But variation in historical context means that one principle holds widely different implications about the scope of foreign policy objectives in different historical contexts. Consider the example of restoring historical borders. If Australia was motivated by restoring its historical borders, then it would hold no territorial ambitions, and no revisionist demands over international laws and norms. If instead Indonesia was motivated by restoring its historical borders, it would want territorial control over Timor Leste, and other territories historically controlled by Indonesia. In contrast, if, as Putin recently claimed, Russia was motivated to restore Soviet borders it means that Russia would seek direct control over Eastern Europe, and the Balkan states, informal influence over Finland and Central Asia, and the dismemberment of Germany.

Consider a different kind of principle: globalist ideologies. Many intuit that globalist ideologies generate extreme tension between great powers. For example, the Western allies believed it was intolerable for Russia to pursue the global spread of communism. But some globalist ideologies lead to collaboration. For example, at the end of World War two it became clear that the United States would surpass Britain as the world leader (Friedberg, 2010). At this point in history, the United States pursued a global foreign policy that included a commitment to the Liberal International Order, free markets, and democracy (Ikenberry, 1998; Monteiro, 2014). US ambitions were global. But these global ambitions were largely consistent with Britain's interests.[38] Thus, Britain did not perceive US global ambitions as a threat. In the modern era, if the US perceived that China wanted to be a global power that promoted and protected the existing Liberal International Order, then the US would likely continue to facilitate China's rise.

This nuance can reconcile two puzzling features of existing studies. First, many researchers start with the assumption that benign states intrinsically hold a status-quo motivation, or otherwise conflate intrinsic security motives with a preference for sustaining the status quo (e.g., Goddard, 2018, p. 12). This forces them to twist the definition of the status quo to fit key historical episodes. For example, Glaser (2015) argued the US should not be concerned about China's militaristic posture towards Taiwan because China and the US disagree about what the status quo is. In other words, the only way Glaser could reconcile US perceptions of China's actions against Taiwan as benign is to assert that the status quo was not objective. I can explain how states have benign interests even if they are not status-quo powers, and how states can shift from status-quo to non-status-quo powers over time. States are satisfied under the status quo because they control all the issues and territories that are connected to their principle.

---

[38] There was disagreement over whether Western states should control colonies. But this was minor, relative to the scope of agreement.

Suppose Australia wanted to restore its historical borders. Then Australia is a status-quo power because it controls all the issues and territories that fit that principle. However, if China took Tasmania, Australia would no longer be a status-quo power. Rather, it would hold well-defined limited aims over Tasmania.

Second, existing studies usually assert a single reason that states hold limited aims. This creates an overlooked empirical problem. For example, during the 1990s China never asserted that security was their primary intrinsic motivation. Rather, it argued that it sought the limited aim of restoring its position in Asia (we will define this more precisely later). Realists assume that if states do not hold security intentions, they are greedy (Glaser, 2010). Thus, they cannot explain why the US did not instantly assume China held vast aims.[39] As we shall see, by allowing for many reasons that states hold limited aims, my theory can account for this.

3.3 Structuring These Insights Generates New Mechanisms for Learning

Figure 3.1 provides a semi-realistic, but still stylized, representation of how one could operationalize motives as feasible principles in the Anglo-German (1930s) case. In this representation, I focus on nine issues and territories and six different principles. This is for illustrative purposes only. As discussed in Section 4.4.2, my predictions survive a setting with more (or less) issues and potential principles, and much more variation in how principles determine the Challenger's value for each issue. In this example, each panel represents a different principle that could have motivated Hitler. I then ask: If Hitler was motivated by this principle, what issues and territories would fit Hitler's core interests? I assume that the British were initially uncertain about which principle motivated Hitler (is Hitler motivated by security from a Russian threat, ethnic-nationalism, etc.?), therefore British elites did not know which panel represents Hitler's true interests. However, British elites did know what Hitler would want if he was motivated by a specific principle (if Hitler is motivated by security from a Russian invasion, I know that he values a buffer zone in Poland). Again, this presentation is illustrative. In Section 4.4.2 I demonstrate my theory is robust if either: a principle only determines which issues the Challenger values low with probability because the Challenger may hold idiosyncratic preferences; or

---

[39] See Powers (2022) for a similar problem.

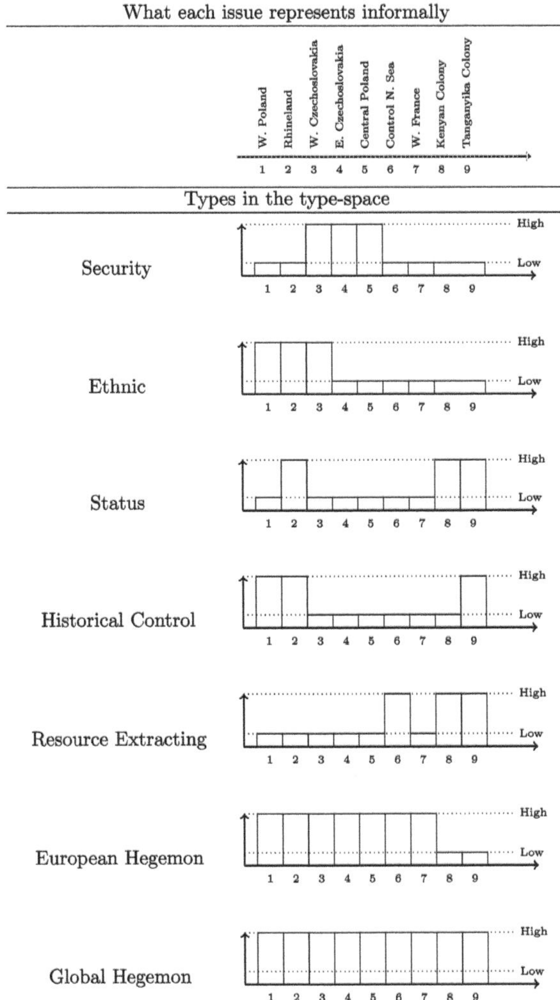

Figure 3.1 Stylistic presentation of Hitler's possible motives.

Note: Each panel represents a different principle that could have motivated Hitler and draws nine real-world territories that Britain and Germany could contest. The bars represent whether a specific principle implies Hitler values a specific territory high or low. The motives and issues visualized are not representative nor exhaustive, and certain codings could be contested. The main purpose of the figure is to illustrate how the updating process could work with empirical referents.

the Defender is uncertain about which issues the Challenger values low because the Defender holds imperfect intelligence about the Challenger's historical context.

This presentation does include three ideal-type features that are substantively appealing because they fit, to a large extent, the informal discussion of state motives. First, the Challenger's motives can plausibly vary in scope: some types want more than others. If Hitler is motivated by ethnic-nationalism, security from a Russian threat, or status, he has fewer than four core interests. But if Hitler wanted to become the European or global hegemon more than seven issues fall within his core interests.

Second, Challengers are more likely to care about specific issues depending on the principle that motivates them. As a result, Challengers vary in their preference ordering over different issues and territories. When we introduce uncertainty about the Challenger's motives, this has important implications. Even if the British agree that Hitler holds limited aims, they may not agree about what Hitler's core interests are. Hitler could have limited aims because he was motivated by security from a Russian invasion, or because he wanted to unite Germans under one government. His specific core interests would be different in each case.

Third, even though there is variation in scope and the nature of core interests, principles influence what combinations of core interests are most likely to arise. While the Challenger's preferences may not perfectly fit a particular principle, it is most likely that if the Challenger holds limited aims, his core interests correspond to a set of issues implied by a specific principle. In practice this means that it is more likely that Hitler cared about Western Poland, Western Czechoslovakia, and the Rhineland – not eastern Poland; than it was that he cared about a Kenyan Colony, Western Poland, and not the Rhineland. The reason is that there is one underlying principle that explains the former, but none that explain the latter.

3.3.1 Qualitative Inferences: How Defenders Learn about a Challenger's Motives

The value of conceptualizing motives as principles is that it drives a mechanism for learning that fits within the Bayesian framework, but takes on a different form. I call this mechanism for learning a qualitative inference. The Defender's inference is qualitative because his beliefs are mediated through an understanding of how specific actions are connected to specific principles. That is, I am most interested in how the Challenger's choice reveals information about the specific issue that a Challenger cares about (Communicating I value Austria high not low), and how that issue connects to a principle (nationalism). I am less interested in how a specific action generates a level of cost (I build three tanks and not four, or take three-quarters of Austria and not half of it), which signals the Challenger's overall interest in all the issues in dispute.

To provide the clearest account of qualitative inferences, I describe the process in a strategy-free environment. That is, I assume that the Defender makes inferences as an outside observer, who cannot react to the Challenger's actions. Since the Defender cannot react, the Challenger's actions are based on the direct costs and benefits of her actions and not an incentive to misrepresent. In Chapter 4, I will demonstrate that qualitative inferences produce novel predictions if we introduce them into a model at the origins of great power rivalries. But it is important to understand the general mechanism because it likely influences how threat perceptions change in other strategic contexts.

Qualitative inferences unfold in three steps. First, the Challenger is faced with a contextualizing choice. By contextualizing, I mean that the choice maps onto a specific set of issues and territories, or gives the Challenger an opportunity to reveal a principle. For example, a local crisis may erupt in Austria that gives the Challenger the opportunity to intervene or not (the choice) in the crisis over Austria (the context).

Second, the Defender exploits his knowledge of the Challenger's history and culture to better understand what principle motivates the Challenger. The Defender can do this because he knows which issues and territories are associated with each principle. When the Challenger fights (does not fight) for specific issue, Defenders think about which principles imply that the Challenger is willing (unwilling) to fight for that specific issue. Using that information, they re-evaluate the principles that likely motivate the Challenger.

Third, the Defender takes his new beliefs about the principles that likely motivate the Challenger, and extrapolates to understand what else the Challenger wants.

Putting it all together, consider the representation of Hitler's motives in Figure 3.1. I'll address the question that British elites wanted to answer the most: Are Hitler's aims vast or limited? Let's start with the assumption that the British are deeply uncertain about Hitler's motives (each principle is equally likely). If true, then British elites start with prior beliefs that Hitler has a 2/7 chance of holding more than seven core interests (call them greedy), and a 5/7 chance that Hitler holds less than four core interests (call them limited aims).

Suppose that Hitler credibly reveals (possibly through an invasion that comes at a high cost) that he values Austria high. Observing this event, British elites infer that Austria is one of Hitler's core interests. Based on their understanding of Germany's history and culture, British elites realize that this action implies that Hitler is not primarily motivated by status concerns, or fear from a Russian invasion. However, they cannot rule out the possibility that Hitler is motivated by ethnic nationalism, restoring Germany's historical position, or European or world domination. Using that information, British elites have a new assessment about Hitler's long-term motives. They now believe that there is a 1/2 chance that Hitler was greedy.

Here, the context – Hitler took *Austria* – is key. Had British elites observed Hitler fight for Western France, they would be certain that he was greedy. The reason is that only the greedy types value Western France. Different still, had they observed Hitler fight for a colony in Tanganyika, they would have inferred a 1/4 chance that Hitler was greedy.

This last example is somewhat shocking. British elites started out thinking that Hitler was greedy with 2/7 probability. They then observed Hitler fight for a colony in Tanganyika. Using that information they became certain that Hitler valued Tanganyika high. And yet, they reduced their confidence that Hitler's long-run aims are greedy from 2/7 to 1/4.

The discussion so far has emphasized a situation where the Defender observe the Challenger take a single action. But qualitative inferences are cumulative. That is, as the Defender observes more of the Challenger's choices, they put the different pieces together to make nuanced inferences about which principles could motivate the Challenger. Each new piece adds a specific insight depending on how it fits with the other pieces.

Returning to Figure 3.1, let's start with the assumption that the British learn that Austria is one of Hitler's core interests. Following that observation, they believe that there is a 1/2 chance that Hitler holds limited aims. Now let's consider two worlds. In the first world, the British learn that a colony in Kenya is also one of Hitler's core interests. In the second world, the British learn that the Rhineland is also one of Hitler's core interests. In each world, the British know only two facts. However, the overall inference that they draw dramatically depends on how these facts are connected through the Challenger's principles. In the first world, learning that Hitler values a colony in Kenya tells the British that Hitler must be greedy. The reason is that only the type that wants world domination values both Austria and a colony in Kenya. In the second world, learning Hitler values the Rhineland high provides the British with no extra information. The reason is that every Challenger that values Austria high, also values the Rhineland high.

In the strategic theory that follows, I will focus on a simple set of actions. In real-world cases, Defenders likely make inferences by piecing together the Challenger's principles from many different actions (Goldfien, Joseph, and McManus, 2022). The Challenger might choose to support (or not) human rights institutions, or institutions that promote sovereignty norms, or nonproliferation norms. The Challenger may also provide foreign aid (or not) to impoverished countries, or only democratic countries, or only allies. The Challenger may also decide to build mission-specific weapons systems that are good for capturing some territories but not others. Also, the Challenger may signal a principle through diplomacy, a public statement, or a Defense White Paper. In each case, the choice provides some information about the principles that may or may not motivate the Challenger.

For example, the Tiananmen Square Massacre made clear that China had little regard for human rights. After the Tiananmen Square Massacre, if China intervened in the Rwandan Genocide under the pretext that their foreign policy was motivated by protecting human rights the United States would not have believed them. The United States would need to reconcile these specific actions with their knowledge about China's history, and the principles that could plausibly motivate China.

In practice, Challengers face complex strategic choices and incentives to misrepresent. As a result, there could be many different logics, such as secretive bureaucratic processes (Joseph and Poznansky, 2024), or diffusion effects (Miller, Joseph, and Ohl, 2016), that could explain the same action. Uncertainty could also arise because the Defender has ambiguous information about the Challenger's history and thus does not fully understand which issues are connected to which principles, or because states can take actions in secret and are unlikely to be exposed (Joseph and Poznansky, 2018). These complications mean the Challenger's actions represent noisy signals. But in a general (i.e., decision model) case, the qualitative mechanism holds up with this uncertainty. But these complexities mean that the Challenger's actions generate noisy signals. The Defender can only draw a partial inference from the Challenger's actions. For example, China's actions at Tiananmen Square may have been complicated by fears of regime stability. If true, intelligence analysts who observed the event may downweight, but not completely rule out, the possibility that China would fight to restore human rights overseas. With this incomplete inference, these analysts could assess that China was very unlikely to intervene during the Rwandan Genocide to restore human rights, but that there was a remote possibility. Even though inferences can be imperfect, it is still the case that partial updating happens. Analysts that observe the Tiananmen Square Massacre will raise their confidence that China does not value human rights, and in turn increase their confidence that China will not intervene in the Rwandan Genocide. Section 4.4.2 will demonstrate that the qualitative signaling is still meaningful given strategic incentives to misrepresent at the origins of great power rivalries.

3.3.2 How Qualitative Inferences Advance Signaling Theories

I advance costly signaling arguments because I provide a systematic way to predict why the same costly actions will engender mistrust in one context but not another. I also explain why the scope of costs is weakly correlated with the changes in the Defender's threat estimate. That is, the Defender may not alter his perceptions following an especially violent crisis, but may suddenly shift after a seemingly benign episode. Different still, I explain punctuated shifts in threat estimates after long periods of constant threat estimates in the face of repeated demands.

As we shall see, these theoretical refinements are empirically salient. Critics of costly signaling often assert that indicator theory is the rationalist baseline (see Yarhi-Milo, 2014, pp. 26–35). In this account, a purely rational Defender should update their threat perceptions following each of the Challenger's costly actions. In many cases, Defenders often fail to update in the face of key indicators. Critics assert that this provides evidence against costly signaling theory, and exposes many puzzling threat perceptions that require nonrationalist explanations (e.g., Rosato, 2015; Goddard, 2018). As we shall see throughout the empirical section, these seemingly puzzling events are easy to account for within the rationalist framework if we accept that Defenders collect historical and cultural information about the Challenger, and therefore should only respond to indicators in particular contexts.

My theory also advances research into diplomatic coordination (Battaglini, 2002). Like my theory, these theories start with the assumption that states can value different combinations of issues (Trager, 2011; Joseph, 2021). They usually focus narrowly on how states use costless diplomacy to clarify motives across multiple crises. However, past coordination theories assume that Challengers are equally likely to care about every combination of issues. As a result, there are real limits to what diplomacy can achieve (Penn, Patty, and Gailmard, 2011). For example, in Trager (2011), if we learn that China values Uganda, we have no extra information to understand how much China values Taiwan, or Kenya, or Australia. The reason is that Trager assumes it is equally likely that China values every combination of issues. I theorize that some combinations of core interests are more likely than others because the Challenger's motives are tied to a specific principle. This creates different opportunities for learning than those we observe in standard theories of coordination. Past coordination scholars allow the United States to ask: "which territories does China value high or low?" By constraining the type-space my theory also allows the United States to ask: "Now that I know that China values Taiwan high, what do I know about how much it values Tibet, and is that different from what I learn about its interest in a colony in Kenya?" The reason is that diplomacy signals information about the Challenger's principle, and not just how much they value a specific territory.

As we shall see in the Chapter 4, once we account for the strategic incentives to reassure at the origins of great power rivalries, this constrained set of possible motives explains how costly military signals interact with costless diplomacy to rationally influence threat perceptions. My strategic theory generates different predictions about threat perceptions in response to all these actions at each moment of the rivalry. However, it is important to note that the aspect of my mechanism that follows from diplomacy is different from social mechanisms for persuasion. First, it does not assume costs from public audiences (cf. Goddard, 2018; McManus, 2017), or costs felt for dishonesty or inconsistency (cf. Schimmelfennig, 2001; Renshon, 2015). This is important because many debate whether audience costs are sufficiently large relative to the stakes involved for great powers who contest world order (Snyder and Borghard, 2011; Rosato, 2015). Second, a persuasive message of limited aims does not need to conform to appropriate norms at a moment in history (cf. Goddard, 2018). Rather, states can reassure by appealing to repugnant but limited aims. Finally, in my theory speech is not required to offset mistrust following every costly action (cf. Goddard, 2018). Rather, it is only necessary during early moments of the case when there is a coordination and clarification problem to resolve. These differences are important because they imply that rationalist speech communicates different pieces of information than what others have examined, operates in both private and public settings irrespective of the costs involved, and differences in the conveyed message will influence perceptions early on, but hold no effect later. I view these differences as complementary with rationalist theories of diplomacy, and certain theories that blend normative and rationalist arguments to study other strategic settings (e.g., Schimmelfennig, 2001; Barnett and Finnemore, 2004). But I also yield different predictions from social theories of persuasion at the origins of rivalries, which I explain in Section 4.3.

4

How Principled Motives and Qualitative Signals Resolve the Strategic Tension at the Origins of Great Power Rivalries

In this chapter, I introduce the assumption that the Challenger's motives are tied to principles into the strategic problem characterized in Chapter 2. In Chapter 2, I showed that if the Challenger's motives varied in scope, that the incentives for instant competition are strong. Here, I show that when motives are tied to principles, a new separating equilibrium emerges – the informative equilibrium – under broad conditions, which forms the basis of my theoretical argument. In summary, I argue that great power rivalries can unfold in one of two ways: delayed competition, or delayed peace. Which way the rivalry unfolds ultimately depends on the scope of the Challenger's motives. If the Challenger holds acceptably limited aims, the rivalry ends in peace. If the Challenger is unacceptably greedy, the rivalry ends in competition. The proximate cause of competition is the Defender's beliefs. If the Defender is sufficiently confident that the Challenger is unacceptably greedy, he selects competition. The mediating variables are the choices (diplomatic messages and territorial demands) that the Challenger makes, and how these choices influence the Defender's beliefs.

To be clear, these variables are similar to past theories of military signaling in great power rivalries. However, my theory generates different predictions about the instances and timing of competition and peace, the role of costless diplomacy, the pattern of observed concessions, and the role of costly signals. I show that the Challenger's violent territorial demands (a costly action) do cause the Defender to learn about the Challenger's motives. But what the Defender learns varies dramatically in ways that defy what we understand from costly signaling theory. My novel predictions follow from my qualitative inferences signaling mechanism. The Defender assesses the Challenger's long-term motives by observing how the Challenger's choices are connected to different principles. When the Challenger fights for a specific issue, the Defender exploits his knowledge of the Challenger's history and culture to infer whether the Challenger's action is associated (or not) with each principle. Over time, the Defender pieces together the Challenger's motives by observing the combination of issues that the Challenger contests, and then asking how that combination of specific actions fits with each principle.

First, I informally describe how I adapt the model constructed in Chapter 2. Second, I informally describe the causal mechanism that my theory produces given one, highly stylized, method for operationalizing motives as principles. Third, I describe the conditions under which the informative equilibrium survives given eight modeling extensions that address two types of substantive concerns. The first type considers different ways that I could model motives as principles. The second type considers alterations to the structure of the international system, such as introducing the offense–defense balance. Finally, I summarize eight empirical predictions that follow from the theory.

4.1 Introducing Motives as Principles into the Model

In the baseline model, I assumed C's motives varied in scope. My conceptual innovation was that the Challenger's motives are attached to principles. To capture this innovation simply, I initially assume that the Challenger's motives are drawn from the type-space presented in Figure 4.1. Section 4.3 considers other ways I could operationalize motives as principles. For interpretability, I attach highly stylistic labels based on the Anglo-German case. In this example, states contest nine issues and territories ($J=9$) that Hitler (the Challenger) could have taken. I assume that if Hitler held limited aims, he was motivated by one of three principles: ethnic-nationalism (ω_1), status (ω_2), and security (ω_3). Each of these types holds three core interests each. But the core interests of each are different. Hitler could have also wanted world domination (ω_4). Obviously this is not an exhaustive set of types and issues from this case.

The setup is otherwise unchanged (see Appendix C.1 online for technical information). However, the flexible offers and messages take on a different character. As in the baseline, the game begins with D, the status-quo power, controlling all the issues. Nature selects C's value vector from a discrete uniform distribution over the type-space (Figure 4.1) and shows it privately to C. Then the game unfolds over a revisionist phase with at most J periods.

Figure 4.2 summarizes the timing of one period in the revisionist phase. I deliberately visualize a case where D does not simply offer issue 1 through

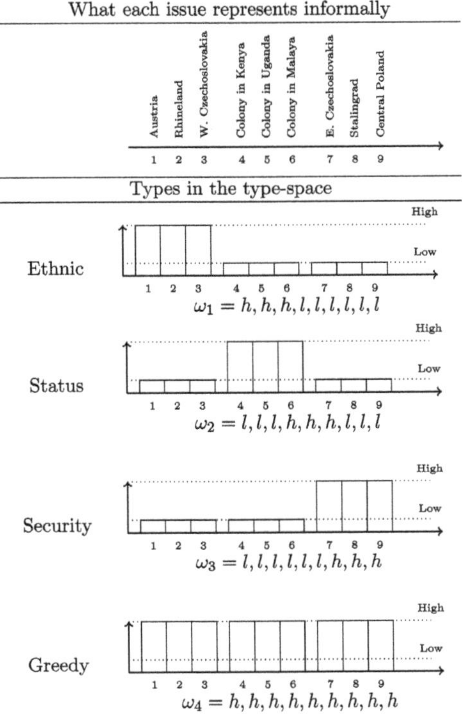

$$\omega_1 = h, h, h, l, l, l, l, l, l$$

$$\omega_2 = l, l, l, h, h, h, l, l, l$$

$$\omega_3 = l, l, l, l, l, l, h, h, h$$

$$\omega_4 = h, h, h, h, h, h, h, h, h$$

Figure 4.1 The set of potential Challenger-motives I assume to illustrate the strategic theory.

Note: For the purpose of clearly articulating my mechanism, I assume states contest nine issues, and C's type (i.e., her true motives) is drawn from this set of four potential motives. To ease the discussion of the strategic model, I label the different issues (columns) and principles (rows) based on an incredibly stylistic mapping onto German interests in the 1930s. I walk through the strategic logic of my theory using this example.

9 sequentially. This was also true in the baseline model. However, because C's motives varied in scope, D's best strategy was to always offer issues sequentially. Now that I attach C's motives to principles, the decision to give D flexibility in the order of offers is meaningful.[40]

---

[40] I assume D decides which issue to concede (which could represent withdrawing support for a local partner). The combination of C's diplomatic statement and D's decision captures the substantive motivation described in Chapter 2 where Defenders, for example, de-commit from alliances or remove forward-deployed forces from territories important to the Challenger as the Challenger declares short-term objectives (Bull, 2002, pp. 163–164). In robustness, I consider what happens if the Challenger plays a more active role in selecting specific concessions.

A revision opportunity (t) begins with a status quo distribution of issues. In this example, we are starting in the third period ($t=3$). Two concessions have been made. C controls issues 1 and 3. D controls issues 2, 4, 5, 6, 7, 8 and 9.

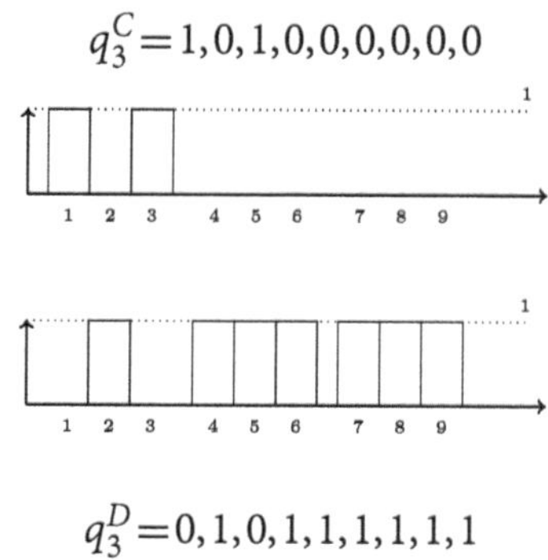

C uses cheap-talk diplomacy to explain her foreign policy interests. In this example, C explains her core interests are issues 1, 3, 7. This statement also specifies that issues 2, 4, 5, 6, 8, 9 are peripheral interests.

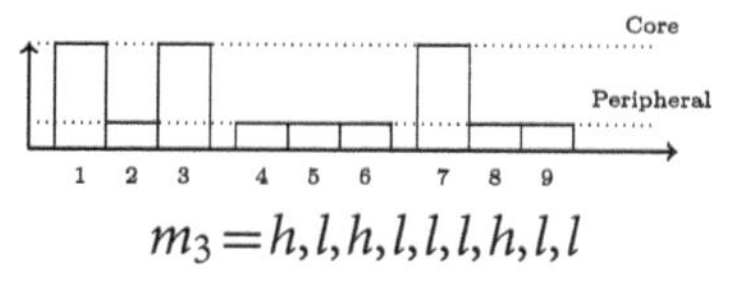

C chooses between accepting peace under the status quo (game stops) or demanding a concession (the period moves to D's choice).

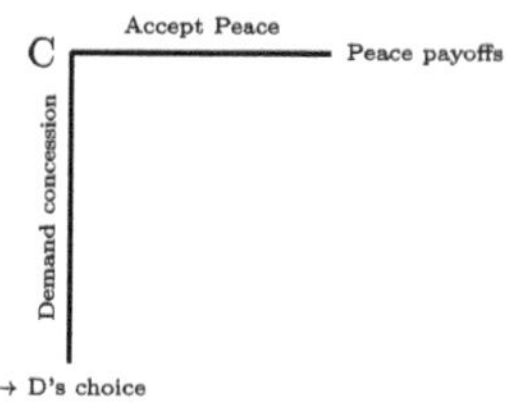

D chooses between competition (game stops), or making a concession.

If D makes a concession, D transfers one issue. This changes the status quo at the beginning of the next period. The example illustrates a case where D concedes issue 7 in the third period. Therefore, C controls issues 1, 3, 7 at the beginning of the 4th period.

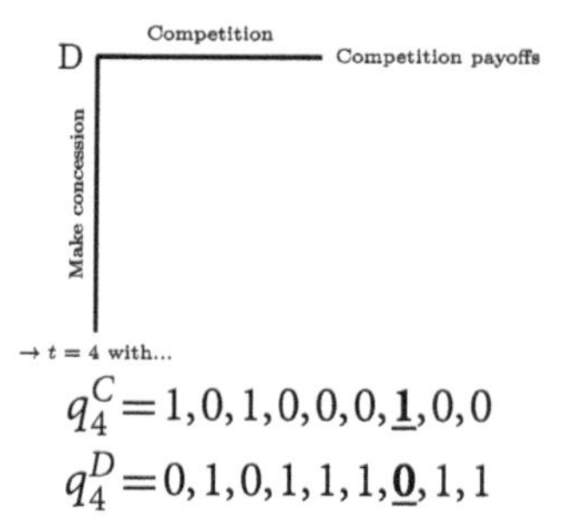

Figure 4.2 One period of the revisionist phase when players select the order of offers ($J=9$).

Finally, it is important to understand more about C's decision to send a costless diplomatic message. I allow C to send a diplomatic message that could, in theory, identify any issues as core interests. However, I interpret the diplomatic message as communicating a principle and not any list of core interests. This is appropriate because, in equilibrium, the Challenger selects her message to communicate information about a specific principle. Further, no matter what message the Challenger sends, the Defender uses it to draw inferences about principles directly. The flexible message has stronger fidelity for the predictions I want to make. To draw the conclusion that diplomacy focuses on principles, it is important that I do not constrain the message space to principles because doing so would force my conclusion. Rather, I will show in the babbling equilibrium that if the Challenger tries to send messages that are disconnected from principles, that she cannot induce either trust nor cooperation. Therefore, the costless message works because it is tied to principles. I'll also use the flexible message to rule out salami tactics: The Challenger cannot change her message by claiming a different principle once she has captured some issues.

4.1.1 The Strategic Problem Is Worse if Motives Are Tied to Principles

As in Chapter 2, assumptions $\mathcal{A}_1 - \mathcal{A}_4$ assure the model produces the interactive trust and commitment problems I hope to solve. We saw in Chapter 2, that when the Challenger's motives varied in scope, and the Defender was deeply uncertain about the Challenger's motives, that greedy Challengers were incentivized to play salami tactics. Each period, they made one more demand, and promised it would be their last. The Defender anticipated this problem, and under almost all empirically plausible conditions responded with first-period competition. This outcome was frustrating when the Challenger's aims were limited, because, in this case, states could have achieved peace if the Defender knew the Challenger's true motives.

There is good reason to believe peace is even harder when motives are tied to principles because a coordination problem emerges that exacerbates the trust problem.[41] Even if the Defender believed the Challenger held limited aims, the Defender does not know which principle motivates the

---

[41] Coordination problems are not specific to coordination games. They arise whenever there are multiple equilibria and one Pareto dominates the other. Chakraborty and Harbaugh (2007) establishes coordination problems in a class of models with heterogeneous preferences and incomplete information because the Defender does not know the optimal order of concessions to make. I fall into this class.

Challenger. Indeed, if we assume that the Challenger's diplomacy is ineffective (i.e., the babbling equilibrium in Appendix C.4.3 online), the Defender always selects first-period competition because he worries he will concede the wrong issues. What is more, since there are many Challengers with limited aims, the Defender worries that the Challenger can change her story as time moves on. She can start out claiming to be one limited-aims Challenger, then once she has gathered those concessions, she can switch to a different claim. For example, at the onset of the Cold War, it is possible that the Western Allies initially believed that security motivated Stalin. Thus, they conceded territories that related to security. But then they might come to believe that Stalin cares about protecting Orthodox Christians. Again, they are willing to make concessions, but now they must make different (but still limited) concessions. Over time, if Stalin can change his story, then the Western Allies will allow Stalin to make more and more concessions. Consistent with the logic of salami-slicing, the Defender is unwilling to make a first concession if he fears that the Challenger can change her story from one limited aims type to another.

4.2 My Causal Mechanism

I argue that Challengers with limited aims can combine costless diplomatic messages and costly military actions to overcome these strategic problems if we assume that their motives are tied to principles. To support this claim, I informally describe an informative equilibrium of the model using the example where C and D contest nine issues, and C's motives are taken on the highly stylized Anglo-German presentation in Figure 4.1. Here we provide an informal summary of the theoretical result. See Appendix C.4.2 online for technical analysis.

4.2.1 What We Observe

I argue that once we include uncertainty about the Challenger's principles, great power rivalries unfold in one of two ways: delayed competition or delayed peace. The way that the informative equilibrium unfolds depends on whether the Challenger has limited or greedy motives. Table 4.1 summarizes the on-path behaviors of these two pathways in column (a) and (b). Figure 4.3 summarizes D's beliefs about C's motives at different stages of the game that correspond with the equilibrium behaviors reported in Table 4.1.

Table 4.1 *On-path actions for the informative equilibrium*

C's type	Limited $\omega_1, \omega_2, \omega_3$	Greedy ω_4
First period:		
C's message	Honest, informative $m_1 = v$	Dishonest, informative $m_1 \in \{\omega_1, \omega_2, \omega_3\}$
C makes demand?	Yes	Yes
D Competes?	No	No
What D offers:	Matches C's message	Matches C's message
Second period:		
C's message	Honest, consistent with first period, uninformative	Dishonest, consistent with first period, uninformative
C makes demand?	Yes	Yes
D Competes?	No	No
What D offers:	Matches C's message	Matches C's message
Third period:		
C's message	Honest, consistent with first period, uninformative	Dishonest, consistent with first period, uninformative
C makes demand?	Yes	Yes
D Competes?	No	No
What D offers:	Matches C's message	Matches C's message
Fourth period:		
C's message	Honest, consistent with first period, uninformative	Dishonest, shifts to another limited aims type, uninformative
C makes demand?	No **(game stops)**	Yes
D Competes?	Would compete, but C stops.	Yes **(game stops)**
How it ends:	fourth-period status quo	fourth-period competition

Note: Assumes C's motives are drawn from the example in Figure 4.1. States contest nine issues. Thus, the interaction could have unfolded over nine periods. Changing the number of issues, and the specific configuration of the type-space will change the period in which D competes if C does not stop, but not the basic logic of the argument. See discussion on pp. 71–72.

As Figure 4.3 shows, the Defender starts out deeply uncertain about the Challenger's motives: he believes that each Challenger-type is equally likely (each type has a probability of 1/4). In the first period, all Challengers make a demand. Limited-aims Challengers use diplomacy to honestly

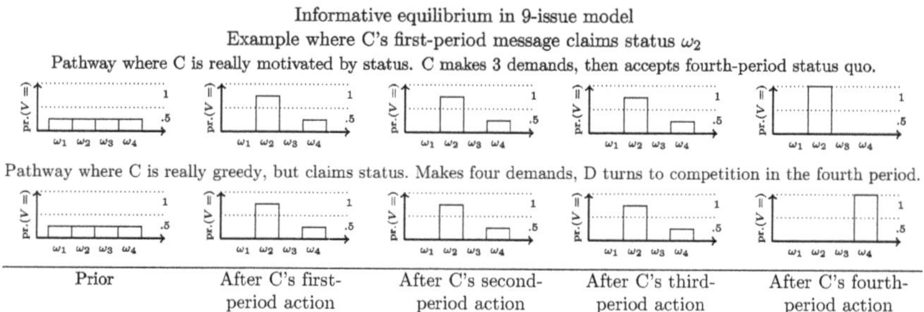

Figure 4.3 D's beliefs in the informative equilibrium with nine issues.

communicate their principle. However, the greedy Challenger understates her true intentions by claiming that she values one of the limited aims principles. She may claim to value status (but could also claim security, or nationalism). As a result, the Defender always observes that the Challenger justify her first-period demand is in service of a single-issue principle.

To be clear, diplomacy is informative even though the Defender knows that the Challenger could be greedy. If the Challenger claims to value status, the Defender infers that there is a 3/4 chance that the Challenger really is the status-seeking type. Since the Defender knows the Challenger could have lied, the Defender still believes that there is a 1/4 chance that the Challenger is greedy.[42] The Defender rules out the possibility that the Challenger values security or nationalism.

Based on these beliefs and expectations about future strategies, the Defender makes a first-period concession. The Defender does not know the Challenger's motives for certain. But the Defender does know (1) what the Challenger said that she wanted; and (2) which territories are tied to which principles. Exploiting that information he targets his first concession at the issue that is consistent with the Challenger's declared principle.

In the second period, all Challengers, no matter their true motives, make a second demand and repeat their first-period diplomatic message. In reply, the Defender makes a second concession targeted at another of the Challenger's declared core interests. The third period follows the second.

Even though the Challenger continues to make demands in the second and third periods, the Defender's beliefs about the Challenger's motives remain constant. For example, suppose the Challenger claimed to value status in the first period. Then at the beginning of the second period, the

---

[42] To be clear, the precise probabilities depend on the type-space that I assume. But the direction of updating is identical in each model.

Defender believes that there is a 3/4 chance that the Challenger truly values status; and a 1/4 chance that the Challenger is greedy. At the end of the third period, the Defender's beliefs are exactly the same.

In the fourth period, the limited-aims Challenger (who sent an honest first period message) accepts the status quo, leading to peace. The greedy Challenger makes another demand. The greedy Challenger tries to claim that she can be satisfied with one more concession. For example, if she claimed to value status in the first period, she now claims that she really values security in an effort to get another concession. The Defender does not believe this second message. The Defender ignores fourth-period diplomacy and instead draws inferences about the Challenger's type based only on the Challenger's costly decision to make a demand (or not). Based on this inference, the Defender selects competition if the Challenger makes a fourth-period demand.

Had the Defender not selected competition in the fourth period, the Challenger would have continued to make demands until there was nothing left to give. Each period, the Challenger would have promised that she could be satisfied with just a few more concessions.

To be clear, you should not infer from this example that competition will come after four concessions in every case. The exact timing of competition in a specific case relies on the different sets of motives the Challenger could hold, the number of issues in dispute, the Challenger's historical context, and the Defender's threshold for acceptably limited Challengers.

What you should infer, and what is common across many cases, is an initial period of hedging followed by a sudden shift to either competition or peace in the middle. In each case the Defender is willing to tolerate a limited number of concessions, the Challenger communicates a principle that implies fewer concessions than the Defender is willing to tolerate, and the Defender makes those concessions. Once the Defender makes those concessions, unacceptably greedy Challengers make one more demand and competition comes. However, acceptably limited Challengers accept the status quo and we enter a period of peace.

Another assumption that influences the exact timing of competition or peace is that the Challenger gets one revision opportunity at a time. This assumption matches important historical cases. For example, Hitler did not take the Rhineland, the Sudetenland, Austria, and Western and Eastern Czechoslovakia all at once. Rather he capitalized on revision opportunities one at a time. However, in other cases Challengers sometimes revise a handful of issues simultaneously. As a result, you should not conceive of periods as a constant unit of time (e.g., two periods is two years). Rather, you should think about each new period as a new revision opportunity over a specific, contested issue. The real time in between these opportunities could vary within and across cases.

4.2.2 Why We Observe It: Explaining Three Surprising Facts

This pattern of behaviors and beliefs leaves us with three lingering questions. First, the existing rationalist literature tells us that diplomacy should be ineffective because the Challenger faces an insurmountable incentive to understate the scope of her motives (see Glaser, 2010; Yarhi-Milo, 2014). Thus, we want to know: Why does diplomacy change D's beliefs in the first period, and how can this change facilitate trust and concessions? Second, there is a phase in the middle where the Challenger makes repeated violent demands and the Defender does not alter his beliefs about the Challenger's motives. Rather, the Defender holds his beliefs constant and continues to make concessions. Why do the Defender's beliefs shift in response to diplomacy in the first period, and in response to violent demands in the fourth period, but remain insensitive to either in the middle?

Finally, things change dramatically in the fourth period. If C makes a fourth-period demand, D dramatically updates his beliefs that C is greedy and turns to competition. Why does a fourth demand cause alarm, but not the three demands that came before; and why does diplomacy reassure in the first period but not the fourth?

Starting with our first question. C's credible first-period message relies on the incentives for different Challenger-types to send *specific* first-period messages. In our working example, each limited aims Challenger cares about three *specific* issues. They prioritize receiving their core interests over delaying competition as long as possible. Their message is informative because D promises to (1) target his concessions against the issue that C claims to value high; and (2) select competition in the fourth period. Thus, limited aims Challengers do not do equally well if they send any acceptable message. Rather, they want to make sure D targets his concession at the specific issues they value high.

The greedy Challenger does not face the same incentives to coordinate because she values all issues high. Her priority is to avoid competition for as long as she can. She knows that if she dishonestly claims to hold limited aims she will receive three concession. If she does anything else, she will face first-period competition. She dishonestly claims (through diplomacy) to be motivated by a limited principle. But since she really values all of the issues, she does not care what lie she tells because any message leads to a high-valued concession. Thus, the greedy Challenger does equally well if she claims to be motivated by security, status, or ethnic-nationalism. In the model, she picks from these lies at random.

The key to the result rests on this insight: Even though the greedy Challenger is willing to lie to receive three concessions, she must pick one lie to tell. The Defender factors in his beliefs about how likely each Challenger is to send each message. Suppose the Defender observes the Challenger say, "I am motivated by status." The Defender knows one of two things is true. It is possible that the Challenger is being honest. If the Challenger truly is the status-seeking type, she would definitely send this honest message. Alternatively, the Challenger could be greedy and understating her aims by passing herself off as the status-seeker. But the greedy type could have sent any limited-aims message. There is only a 1/3 chance she would claim to be the status-seeker.

D's prior belief is that there is a 1/4 chance that C seeks status. But, D re-weights his posterior that C seeks status to account for these two possibilities:

$$\frac{\text{Initial belief C seeks status} \times \text{pr. status-seeker claims to seek status}}{\text{Initial belief C seeks status} \times \text{pr. status-seeker claims to seek status} + \text{Initial belief C is not status-seeker} \times \text{pr. not status-seeker claims to seek status}}$$

Translating these beliefs into numbers given deep initial uncertainty about C's type:

$$\frac{1/4 \times 1}{1/4 \times 1 + 3/4 \times 1/9} = \frac{3}{4} \tag{4.1}$$

Of course, D is not certain that C seeks status. It is still possible that C is the greedy type. However, the result holds together because, given the costs and risks of competition, D would prefer to make three concessions targeted at the status-seeker's interests, and accept a 1/4 chance that C was dishonest (meaning competition in the fourth period), than compete in the first period. As we make the model more complicated, the result still holds together if we can find a first-period message that coordinates enough so that the benefit of delayed competition outweighs the cost.[43]

---

[43] Diplomacy raises trust relative to a counterfactual message where D does not reveal a principle.

Turning to the second question, I claim that D observes C make a second, and then a third violent demand but does not update his beliefs in the second and third period. Rather, D's beliefs are invariant to any of C's actions. C makes two additional demands, and D makes a second and third concession but does not alter his beliefs. Past theories suggest that violent demands are a critical way that Challengers communicate their motives (Yoder, 2019). Each time C does not stop, D should increase his confidence that C is greedy (Powell, 1996). What explains this long period of failure to learn in the face of violent demands?

The answer is partially a function of equilibrium strategies. But these strategies are only possible because of the type-space. I get a different result from past studies because of the way that issues are correlated with different Challenger types. Consider the case where the Challenger initially claimed to be motivated by status. As we have already discussed, this drives the Defender to focus on two possibilities at the end of the first period: C is either greedy, or motivated by status. Notice that these two types share three core interests (issues 4, 5, and 6). Furthermore D expects all Challenger types, no matter the scope of their aims, to do whatever it takes to capture their core interests. Thus, if the status-seeking type has core interests that she has not yet captured, then she can do unspeakable things to capture issues that relate to her core interests. This includes invading foreign countries, extorting them through predatory loans, or orchestrating foreign coups. So long as these actions do not set her apart from the remaining types, the Defender will not update her beliefs.

We see this logic play out in British assessments of Hitler's motives. Early in Hitler's tenure, the British inferred that if his aims were limited, he was motivated by ethnic nationalism. When Hitler remilitarized the Rhineland, the British War Secretary told the German Ambassador, "through the British people were prepared to fight for France in the event of a German incursion into French territory, they would not resort to arms on account of the recent occupation of the Rhineland. The people ...did not care 'two hoots' about the Germans reoccupying their own territory."[44]

This line of reasoning exposes a subtle feature of how British elites made inferences that matches my mechanism. They understood Hitler's actions in the context of their beliefs about what combination of territories Hitler could plausibly want (the types in the type-space) and what they had learned from Hitler's initial words and actions (nationalism). Since they

---

[44] Quoted in Weinberg (1980) p. 259.

knew that nationalist Hitler cared about the Rhineland, they did not update their beliefs when they observed Hitler fight for it.

Returning to the model, D concedes issue 4 in the first period; then issues 5 and 6 in the next two periods.[45] C's second and third demands provide no extra information because every Challenger that values issue 4 also values issue 5 and 6. There is no updating because none of these demands are discriminating. Like the existing military signaling literature, D's decision to select competition is triggered by the inference that C's motives are expansive (Kydd, 2005). Unlike this literature, D's inferences are mediated through a complex appreciation of the principle that could motivate C, and how different objectives are tied to each principle. D's inference follows from observing what C initially asked for, the concessions that C collects, and then C's demands in the context of what specific territories that she has already captured.

Turning to our third question. I claim that D is reassured by diplomacy in the first period but not in the fourth. In the fourth period, if C makes another demand, D grows instantly mistrustful about C's motives. C tries to claim that her aims are limited through reassuring diplomacy, but D does not believe her. Instead, D ignores C's diplomacy and turns to competition. This raises two questions: what is special about the fourth period? and if diplomacy is reassuring in the first period, why can't it work a second time?

Fourth-period diplomacy is ineffective because it does not discriminate between the preferences of limited-aims types. The Defender knows the Challenger's history and culture. Therefore, he knows which issues are associated with status. After the third period, the Defender has conceded all of the status-seeking type's core interests. Once the Defender has conceded those issues, the Challenger faces a choice: stop making demands or keep making demands and expose that you hold core interests that are not associated with status. In this version of the theory, the fourth period matters because the limited-aims Challengers care about three issues each. However, in versions where the Challenger's motives vary more extensively, what matters is whether the Challenger's motives are type-discriminating. What matters is that the Defender can rule out the possibility that the Challenger is motivated by status.

Still, one might wonder why diplomacy fails to reassure in the fourth period. After all, diplomacy overpowered violent demands in the first period. Why can't it overpower demands a second time? The reason that first-period diplomacy is so effective is that each limited-aims Challenger sent a distinctive message because each held different (and specific) core

---

[45] Strictly, D randomizes over the order of these three concessions.

interests. Thus, when the Defender sees the Challenger claim to value status, he rules out the possibility that the Challenger is motivated by nationalism or security. When we arrive at the fourth period, the status-seeker stops and the greedy type keeps making demands. The greedy type would like to claim to be something else. But there is nothing else to claim because all other limited-aims Challengers sent a different first-period message.

4.3 Robustness and Scope Conditions

In Appendix C.5 online I analyze modeling extensions that introduce substantively motivated changes to the main model and ask: Can I still support my theory, and if so, under what (potentially narrower) conditions? While the equilibrium analysis for each extension is different, I say my theory (i.e., the informative equilibrium) survives (often with scope conditions) if I can sustain an equilibrium with the following four properties:

- D makes a specific number of initial concessions before turning to competition if C has not yet accepted peace.
- If C's aims are acceptably limited, C stops in peace after some initial demands. If C is unacceptably greedy, she never accepts peace, and continues to make demands one at a time.
- Each limited-aims Challenger sends a distinctive first-period diplomatic message.
- The Defender finds that initial message partially credible and targets concessions to match the message.

The extensions address two kinds of substantive concerns. First, I walked through the mechanism under the assumption that states contested nine issues, and C's motives were drawn from the type-space constructed in Figure 4.1. You will likely wonder, are my predictions specific to nine-issues, or the baseline type-space? Box 4.1 summarizes extensions that consider these complications, and the scope conditions they place on my theory. Second, the framework I developed in Chapter 2 is sparse. Would the informative equilibrium survive given realistic variation in the structure of the international system, or the choices states can make? Box 4.2 summarizes extensions that consider these complications, and the scope conditions they place on my theory.

In what follows, I summarize each kind of robustness check. If the results are straightforward, I provide a simple overview. If the theoretical result is nuanced, or empirical debates may cause you to wonder if my scope conditions are reasonably met in real life, I detail the extension.

Box 4.1 Complicating the ways in which C's motives are tied to principles

Motivations: My conceptual definition of principles allows for the possibility that states contest any number of issues, some limited aims principles are more likely than others, there are more or less limited aims principles, or that the Challenger is generally more likely to be greedy than limited. It is also possible that different limited aims challengers hold overlapping core interests, or vary in the number of core interests each holds. Does the theory survive such variation?

Adjustment 1a: $J > 2$ issues, $L > 1$ limited aims Challengers who (a) each value x_2 or fewer core interests, (b) cannot be fully nested within another limited aims Challenger. pr. C is greedy is $1 - \zeta$, pr. C is a specific limited aims Challenger is $\zeta \zeta_l$. (App C.5.1)

Scope Condition 1: If there are at least three limited aims Challengers and D is deeply uncertain about C's motives then no restrictions beyond $\mathcal{A}_1 - \mathcal{A}_4$ is needed. If C is likely to be greedy ex-ante and states contest few issues (J is low), then the informative equilibrium requires that we can find enough limited aims Challengers with fewer core interests (x_2 must be lower). However, for any prior expectation that C is greedy and any x_2, the informative equilibrium is possible if states contest enough issues (J is large).

Motivation: You acknowledge conceptually that because history is complex, (a) limited aims Challengers may hold *idiosyncratic preferences* disconnected from principles; (b) Defenders have *imperfect historical knowledge* and thus are uncertain which issues connect to which principles. For example, if China has limited nationalist aims it may or may not care about the Senkaku Islands. Some US analysts may believe the Senkaku Islands genuinely serves China's nationalist ambitions, others may not, and others may be uncertain because China's historical connection is *ambiguous.*

Adjustment 1b: If C is assigned limited aims, Nature switches every low-valued issue to high value with *pr.* ϵ (App C.5.2). This implies:

- Almost all types are realizable. C can values anywhere between two to nine issues high (including multiple greedy types) and can value any combination of issues high or low.
- As ϵ increases, C's motives are increasingly disconnected from principles.

Scope Condition 2: The informative equilibrium fails if the limited aims Challenger's value for *each* issue is sufficiently disconnected from principles.

(**continued**)

Box 4.1 (continued)

Scope Condition 3: The informative equilibrium fails if D is sufficiently unable to use his ex-ante knowledge to identify how each limited aims principle connects to *each* specific core interests.

Motivation: The Challenger's preferences might change because of *leadership or regime transition*. The limited aims Challenger might become greedy because the *appetite comes with the eating*. The greedy Challenger might become limited because of *socialization* or *enmeshment*.

Adjustment 1c: Each period of the hedging phase, the Challenger turns greedy with pr ϵ (App C.5.3).

Scope Condition 4: The informative equilibrium fails if the per-period probability that the Challenger becomes greedy is large. However, socialization (the risk greedy types turn limited) broadens the conditions for the informative equilibrium.

Motivation: Is the mechanism "general" (Paine and Tyson, 2020) in that you can substantiate it in the simplest variant with fewest parts? Appendix C.4.1 online rationalizes the informative equilibrium given $J=3$.

Box 4.2 Complicating the structure of the system

Motivation: Variation in the rate of shifting power.

Adjustment 2a: Vary the number of issues conceded per period.

Scope Condition 5: The informative equilibrium fails if power shifts so fast that D prefers instant competition to concessions. Intuitively, in a model that also included discounted preferences, we would expect the informative equilibrium to fail if power shifted too slow.

Motivation: C pays a cost to send a dishonest message or behave inconsistently because of *normative and psychological costs from deception*, or because the message is conveyed in a public speech that carriers *audience costs* or *multi-vocality costs*.

Adjustment 2b: C pays a cost for sending a dishonest message (Appendix C.6.4).

Scope condition 6: The informative equilibrium fails if the cost of sending a message is so high that greedy types are not willing to under-state their motives.

Box 4.2 (continued)

Motivation: D can win back conceded issues in competition. The probability that D wins them back is increasing in the *offense balance* and decreasing in the *defense balance*. Does the theory survive if you introduce these complications?

Adjustment 2c. In competition D wins unconceded issues with pr. $1-p$ and conceded issues with pr. $1-p_H$. Note the baseline is a special case of extreme defense advantage ($p_H=1$). In the extension, there is a defense advantage if $p_H > p$ (Appendix C.6.2)

Scope condition 7: The informative equilibrium fails if it is easier to win back issues rather than retain them because D wants to concede issues, and thus cannot threaten first period competition.

Motivation: C and D's *preferences conflict* because D also intensely values a particular issue. For example, the US and China both intensely value Taiwan.

Adjustment 2d. Offense/Defense advantage, + adjust D's value vector such that D values $\tau_D > 1$ and C values that same issue $\tau_C > h$. We also consider a weaker variant of $\mathcal{A}_2$ where C will accept peace given all but 1 core interest (Appendix C.6.3).

Scope condition 8: The informative equilibrium fails if both states intensely value the same issue, and either (a) defense advantage is too strong, or (b) C is not willing to settle for all but one core interest issue.

Motivation: During hedging, C may decide to take issues via *fiat accompli*, without coordinating with D.

Adjustment 2e (sketched only Appendix C.6.5) After diplomacy, Nature gives D the opportunity to offer with pr. γ and gives C the opportunity to take with probability $1-\gamma$.

Scope condition 9: Diplomacy is always effective. But it is not always necessary to produce a shift in beliefs if C has complete ($\gamma=0$) control over initiating crises because D draws qualitative inferences from C's selection. However, if limited aims Challengers hold overlapping preferences, diplomacy is necessary for D to infer C's limited principle early. Further, if γ is sufficiently large, we cannot sustain the informative equilibrium absent diplomacy.

Note: Unless otherwise stated, all adjustments begin with the baseline $J=9$, and type-space assumed in Figure 4.1.

4.4 Complicating How I Operationalize Motives as Principles

The message from this book is that I get different predictions about patterns of competition and peace *because* the Challenger's motives are tied to principles. To make this claim as broadly as possible, I need to show that (a) if I operationalize motives in a way that is consistent with my conceptualization, I can rationalize the informative equilibrium; and (b) if I operationalize motives in ways that are inconsistent with principles, I cannot. In Section 3.3 I argued conceptually that, beyond some variation in scope,[46] any operationalization of motives as principles should include two substantively motivated features. In what follows, I detail two extensions that introduce these two features. I also consider that state motives can shift over decades-long interactions (Rosato, 2007; Mearsheimer, 2001), and tie it to debates about leadership and regime change.

4.4.1 Varying the Number of Issues, Prior Beliefs, and the Scope of Overlap between Limited-Aims Challengers

I made the conceptual claim that when motives were attached to principles, that Challengers with acceptably limited aims did not exclusively vary in the scope of their intentions. That is, for at least two Challengers with acceptably limited aims, the core interests of one are not completely nested within another. Substantively, this allows for variation in

- The number of issues states contest (J).
- The scope of the Challenger's interests that the Defender finds acceptably limited ($H(v) < x_1$).
- The relative likelihood of different Challenger preferences (assumed uniform).
- The amount that Challengers with limited aims hold overlapping core interests.
- The number of core interests different limited-aims Challengers hold.

In Appendix C.5.1 Online I consider a model with an arbitrary $J >$ 2[47] and assume the following type-space. There is one greedy type $\omega_G = \{h, h, h....h\}$. There are $L \geq 2$ acceptably limited aims types $\omega_1, \omega_2, ...\omega_L$ with

---

[46]   Trivially, if all Challengers valued the same number of issues then either all are greedy or acceptably limited, and there is no trust problem to solve.

[47]   Chapter 2 shows that if $J = 2$, I cannot sustain delayed competition even under complete information.

value functions that satisfy two properties: (a) Each holds less than x_2 core interests; and (b) no one limited aims type is perfectly nested in another. To be clear, we allow (as an example) for ω_1 to hold more core interests than ω_2, and there to be some overlap in their core interests. Given the theoretical constraint identified in Chapter 2, I assume that $x_2 \leq x_1 < J/2$.

I now assume Nature assigns C as greedy with probability $1 - \zeta$, and limited with probability ζ. This adjustment acknowledges the fact that there is only one greedy type but potentially many limited-aims types. ζ balances the relative probabilities between all limited types and the greedy type. If limited, Nature assigns a specific limited-aims type with probability ζ_l. This allows for the possibility that some limited-aims Challengers are more likely than others.

In this generalization, I find a variant of conditions $\mathcal{A}_3, \mathcal{A}_4$, which we require to both produce D's strategic problem of trust with repeated concessions and sustain the informative equilibrium. First, equivalent to the condition that gave rise to $\mathcal{A}_3$, D's threat of competition at x_2 is credible if:

$$J - x_2 + 1 > \frac{k}{1 - p}$$

Second, equivalent to the condition that gave rise to $\mathcal{A}_3$, D is initially willing to tolerate concessions hoping C will stop at x_2 if:

$$\zeta > \frac{(x_2 - 1)(1 - p)}{(J - x_2 + 1)p + k}$$

A closer look at the mechanism alleviates two other important concerns. First, how can we sustain peace if some limited-aims Challengers value more issues than others? In this case, wouldn't the greedy type pool with those who value the most? We overcome this concern with pure strategies because D is willing to tolerate at least $x_2 - 1$ concessions no matter what C's aims really are.[48] Thus, in equilibrium, D tolerates all limited-aims Challengers making exactly $x_2 - 1$ demands even if they hold fewer core interests. This has an important substantive analog. In certain cases, we may observe the Defenders tolerate a few concessions that clearly extend beyond the Challenger's principles. Such cases would remain consistent with my theory, so long as the Defender facilitated these additional concessions with the understanding that is consistent with the agreed-upon strategy. If however, the Challenger made demands that were surprising to the Defender, I would expect mistrust and competition to follow.

---

[48] We can also overcome it with mixed strategies.

Second, it does not matter that some limited-aims Challengers are more likely than others. The reason is that greedy types can always adjust their diplomatic strategies so that they are more likely to pool with the most likely limited-aims types, and least likely to pool with the least likely limited-aims types. Thus, even if Stalin was unlikely to be motivated by security, Britain should not be suspicious if Stalin asserts security, because greedy types are unlikely to send the least-credible justifications. The same basic logic clarifies how the informative equilibrium holds if there are different greedy types. Because each greedy type values different things, they face stronger incentives to pool with some types and not others. We can still sustain the informative equilibrium by adjusting the frequency each sends a specific diplomatic message.

Summing up, I made the conceptual claim that if motives are attached to principles, Challengers with acceptably limited aims do not exclusively vary in the scope of their intentions. I have just shown that we can sustain the informative equilibrium under many different ways that we can construct this problem. This suggests that so long as we meet the assumptions from Chapter 2, then any operationalization that meets these specifications can induce the informative equilbrium. Recall in chapter 2, I showed that if motives vary in scope then we could never rationalize effective diplomacy. Further, if the Challenger's motives varied in scope, and the Defender was deeply uncertain, then instant competition was assured. Thus, we can also say that this source of variation is important for rationalizing the informative equilibrium.

4.4.2 Because History Is Complex, (a) Limited-Aims Challengers May Hold Idiosyncratic Preferences Disconnected from Principles; (b) Defenders Are Uncertain Which Issues Connect to Which Principles

I made the extreme modeling assumption that principles fully determined the Challenger's motives, and the Defender was certain which issues attached to which principles. Importantly, other scholars argue for, or adopt for simplicity, the opposite extreme assumption: The Challenger does not hold objectives to identify in advance, and the Defender cannot exploit their historical knowledge to estimate which issues fit which principles. An important assumption for Goddard (2018) is that issues do not contain objective value. Rather, the Challenger's value for issues, and the Defender's perceptions of the Challenger's value are socially constructed through the Challenger's rhetorical justifications. Rosato (2015); Mercer

(1996) both rely on the supposition that history is so complicated that any state can justify how their desire to contest a single issue fits their limited aims.

In Chapter 2 I argued conceptually that real life likely lies somewhere in between. Even if a Challenger was mainly motivated by a limited principle, they still could hold idiosyncratic preferences. For example, historians have argued that George H.W. Bush held a particular fondness for China because he developed personal connections with CCP leaders while stationed there as the chief of the US Liaison Office (Engel, 2010). I also argued that while the Defender's expert intelligence analysts hold a strong understanding of the Challenger's history and culture (Lowenthal, 2019), leading for example, the US to believe with high confidence that China has a strong nationalist attachment to Taiwan but not Uganda, that their knowledge is incomplete. There will be cases where the Defender is uncertain if a specific issue fits a specific principle.

The important question is: Does the informative equilibrium survive if we accept C's motives may be partially disconnected from principles, and D is uncertain about which issues are connected to which principles? One reason to be skeptical is pretext creep (Mearsheimer, 2001). For example, suppose the US is uncertain about whether the Senkaku Islands is consistent with China's nationalist aims. Before China embarks on revision, it can slightly extend its claims by digging up a pretext that suggests the Senkaku Islands is consistent. Presumably, China could do this for many issues, given China's complex global history and vast diaspora population. Rosato (2007) argues that the capacity to pretext creep makes peace intractable.

I analyze this problem as follows. I start with a nine-issue model, with one greedy Challenger, and three limited-aims Challengers that each hold two specific core interests each. I then assume that if Nature assigns the Challenger limited aims, then Nature switches every low-valued issue to high value with probability $\epsilon > 0$. The probabilities nature switch each issue are independent and therefore it is possible that the Challenger could hold between two and nine core interests, and also value almost any combination of core interests. Variation in ϵ captures how close C's motives are connected to principles. When $\epsilon \to 0$, the Challenger's motives are (and D believes that they are) deeply connected to principles. As ϵ increases, the Challenger's motives are increasingly disconnected from principles, and the Defender is unable to say what the Challenger values high, even if the Defender knows the principle that motivates the Challenger.

I find that the informative equilibrium survives so long as the Challenger's motives are *sufficiently* connected to principles, but degenerates otherwise. Similarly, it survives when the Defender has at least moderate information about the Challenger's historical context and fails otherwise. This speaks to the importance of my conceptual claim: When motives are *sufficiently* tied to principles, the informative equilibrium is possible, but when they are not, it is not.

Does the level of knowledge in real-life cases meet this threshold? Extrapolating from evidence presented in other contexts it is likely that individual analysts with extensive experience and knowledge of the Challenger's history can more easily connect issues to principles than inexperienced analysts or generalists (Saunders, 2017; Grynaviski, 2018). National-level estimates may be uncertain about specific issues because different analysts disagree about how issues connect to principles based on different personal experiences, backgrounds, training, and access to materials (Schub, 2023; Lowenthal, 2019).

Those who make the opposite assumption might still say that pretexts arise in critical cases. China has asserted that the Senkaku/Diayu Islands is an historically salient core interest. Some US analysts argue that China's claims are genuine, but others argue that they are not. Clearly, China was able to exploit its complex history to assert a pretext in this narrow example. A closer look at the modeling extension explains why the Defender is partially persuaded by (and tolerates) a small number of early pretexts, but refuses to tolerate many pretexts. The reason is that there are so many issues that the Defender understands he has likely mis-estimated the Challenger's interest for some of them. However, the Defender is intolerant of many pretexts because it is unlikely that the Defender has underestimated the Challenger's historical connection to many issues. Thus, if the Challenger asserted a high value for many ambiguous issues, the Defender infers that the best explanation is that the Challenger was greedy from the start. Therefore, evidence of a few pretexts alone is insufficient to say that states cannot rely on estimates from their read of history.

Indeed, taking a broader view of Sino-American relations, pretext cases are rare. US foreign policy elites know that Taiwan, Hong Kong, and Tibet fit China's declared principles, but control over Australia, Africa, Europe, and the Americas – and even territorial control over Japan — does not. Indeed, I interviewed the Director of National Intelligence about estimating China's intentions. After he listed out the territories and normative issues that fell within China's limited interests, he explained, "Determining core interests has a long and honorable place in analysis. It is not that difficult [to do]. You ask any 50 China-analysts and they'd

give you that same list of things that I came up with."[49] He then went on
to explain that analysts spend years acquiring expertise on China's history
and culture to form these judgments.

Still, the broader concern that the connection may be too distant to support the informative equilibrium is reasonable. If there is high ambiguity
over many issues, then the case is out of scope for my theory, and in scope
for alternatives. I do not take the scope of ambiguity in any particular case
for granted. Rather, Expectations 1 and 2 below test it explicitly. In each
case, I verify that Defenders can list out how most issues fit principles.
When they cannot, I say the case is out of scope for my theory.

4.4.3 Shifting Motives, Leadership Change, Regime Change

A Challenger's motives could change over the course of a fifty-year interaction. The most plausible reason is that leaders and regimes change
in ways that alter the motives of the Challenger (Chiozza and Goemans, 2011). But it is also possible that the appetite comes with the
eating (Rosato, 2015): The more the Challenger takes, the more the Challenger gets a taste for revision. Offensive realists assert that the possibility that limited-aims Challengers can become greedy makes reassurance
intractable (Mearsheimer, 2001). To my knowledge, there is no systematic
test of this claim. I study a model where in any period of the revisionist
phase Nature turns the Challenger into the greedy type with probability ϵ
and keeps C's type the same with $1 - \epsilon$. This assumption stacks the deck
against my theory because I assume that C can only become more aggressive over time. It also well reflects cases where Defenders initially worry
that, in the future, a Challenger's leader will come to power with expansive
intentions.

I find that so long as ϵ is small, I can still generate the informative equilibrium.[50] The reason is that the Defender does not care if the Challenger
started out greedy or became greedy over time. What the Defender cares
about is whether the Challenger is greedy when the Challenger is faced with
the costly action that only the greedy type will take. In the baseline model,
the Defender is willing to delay competition in the first period because he
believes that it is unlikely that the Challenger is greedy. In the modeling
with shifting preferences, the Defender is willing to delay competition if

---

[49] Author's interview with Denis Blair.

[50] Under reasonable conditions, I can generate my results if the cumulative probability of
leadership change is less than about 50 percent.

he believes it is sufficiently unlikely that the Challenger starts out, or will become greedy before the discriminating period.

To be clear, this robustness does not depend on whether the Challenger's preferences do in fact change. Rather, it depends on the Defender's initial expectation that a new leader will come to power with a different motivation at some point during the transition period. In equilibrium, if preferences do change, the new (greedier) leader will continue to adopt the strategy of the acceptably limited type until she is forced to reveal her true nature. Thus, so long as the Defender starts out with a reasonably low expectation (e.g., lower than 20 percent) that the Challenger will become greedy over the transition period, the results hold up even if a new leader with aggressive motives does comes to power.

The important substantive question is this: At the beginning of these rivalries, do Defenders hold strong beliefs that the Challenger's intrinsic motivations will become greedy during the transition period? Cross-national evidence shows that Defenders ought to believe that the risk a Challenger's motives will turn greedy is within the bounds of the informative equilibrium. However, the logic is different against democratic and autocratic Challengers. In democracies, leaders and parties change regularly, and can bring new world views and priorities (Saunders, 2011). However, domestic institutions that select leaders bound the variation we observe on questions of core foreign policy principles (Wolford, 2007).[51] Even if a leader or party emerged with truly outlier foreign policy aims, democratic institutional constraints limit what they can achieve. A recent studies on US estimates of how foreign democracies would behave at key foreign policy moments focused more on regime and institutional actors than leaders (Goldfien and Joseph, 2023).

By contrast, when personalist dictators come to power, they may hold very different motivations than those who came before. They also can purge the existing ruling classes, and face fewer institutional constraints over foreign policy. Thus, when autocrats face severe domestic resistance, and leadership changes are likely, my theory would not apply. Fortunately for my theory, autocratic states with high turnover rates are rarely Challengers to global order (Goemans, Gleditsch, and Chiozza, 2009). This is likely because an autocrat's ability to sustain power is correlated with economic and military power. Further, autocrats often prioritize

---

[51] Variation in world views shifts how leaders go about achieving a principle more than what the principle is.

domestic threats over foreign policy expansion (Talmadge, 2015). Thus, at moments they face severe threats to their rule, they are unlikely to challenge international rivals.

4.5 Complicating the Structure of the International System

As Box 4.2 shows, the informative equilibrium is bounded by the rate of shifting power, the offense–defense balance, or because both Challenger and Defender care intensely about the same issue (e.g., the US and China both intensely value Taiwan). However, when these complications are sufficiently extreme to cause the informative equilibrium to fail, it often fails because the core tension described in Chapter 2 degenerates. For example, if power shifts too fast, then D always selects competition even if D is certain about C's motives. Therefore, the trust problem described by structural realists does not arise because the commitment problem described by bargaining theorists dominates. I conjecture that if I introduced discount factors and very slow rates of shifting power then the informative equilibrium would also fail because D could not credibly threaten competition even if D knew that C was completely greedy. Thus, conditional on observing the basic strategic problem that structural realists describe, then I can typically sustain the informative equilibrium if motives are tied to principles. Still, several of these complications warrant more discussion because they illuminate related debates about how structure constrains state choices at the origins of great power rivalries.

4.5.1 Private Diplomacy versus Public Speech – Speech versus Fait Accompli

I assume the Challenger uses costless, private diplomacy. Recent scholarship argues that public speech is credible because it drives inconsistency costs (Fearon, 1994). This raises two questions. First, would introducing the costs associated with rhetoric weaken my predictions? If speech is costly, it is easier to facilitate trust to a point because only greedy types send a dishonest message. However, if the costs of sending a dishonest message are very large, then there is no reassurance problem to speak of. The greedy type simply prefers to reveal aggressive intentions from the outset. This reveals a puzzle for certain normative theories that assert diplomacy works because it is costly enough to bind (Goddard, 2018). If the costs are large enough to influence greedy types, then there is no reassurance problem to solve.

Second, why focus on private diplomacy? The main reason is that private diplomacy presents the toughest and most important theoretical test. As detailed in the introduction, empirical scholars have shown that diplomacy effectively reassures at critical moments of critical enduring rivalry cases. But scholars struggle to explain why it works at all, and why it works at some moments and not others. I resolve this enduring puzzle by providing a rational foundation for effective diplomacy during enduring rivalries.

Thus, while these alternatives predict that only the costliest forms of public speech should influence perceptions, I find that any form of speech can play a coordinating role. Thus, I directly address the empirical puzzle of effective costless diplomacy during great power rivalries. This is especially valuable because some show that the costs of public speech are low in any setting (Snyder and Borghard, 2011), and it is commonly believed that the costs are especially low for great powers which contest world order (Mearsheimer, 2001; Rosato, 2015).

A broader question is whether speech is necessary, or if states can communicate using directed costly military actions. In the formal theory I present, speech is necessary because the Defender must choose the order of concessions. But Challengers choose where to deploy their forces (Tarar, 2016). As stated in the decision model presented in Chapter 3, the Defender could draw qualitative inferences depending on whether the Challenger targeted territory A or B. Over enough targeted demands, the Defender would infer the Challenger's motives. Thus, it is possible to derive some similar predictions about patterns of competition and peace absent any verbal communication in a stylized fait accompli model. However, in a complete theory, these mechanisms compliment each other for three reasons. First, costless speech is more efficient (Kurizaki, 2007). Thus, if it works, we would intuitively expect Challengers to use it because it costs less. Second, the Defender often has alliance commitments and forward-deployed forces in territories that the Challenger wants. Diplomatic coordination is necessary to minimize escalation risk. Third, the Challenger cannot perfectly select the order of revision opportunities. In many cases, local unrest or politics outside the Challenger's control causes a crisis that the Challenger can capitalize on. For example, visits made by the Taiwanese leadership facilitated the 1995 Taiwan Strait Crisis. If we assume that the Challenger holds only partial control over the order of concessions, then diplomacy is still necessary because the Defender must worry about the coordination problem before he can discern the Challenger's preferences from the Challenger's demands.

This illuminates how costly military actions and costless speech work together in real life. Costless speech is less credible than a costly military action in the face of incentives to misrepresent, but allows the sender to articulate a principle directly. For example, the Defender may be wondering what a Challenger wants when the Challenger invests heavily in her navy. The Defender may infer that the Challenger is interested in islands or maritime issues more than contiguous territories. But it is possible that status, or security can drive the Challenger to contest maritime disputes. The Defender cannot know from the decision to construct a large navy alone. In contrast, a diplomatic message can precisely articulate the reason that the Challenger rapidly builds a navy. Thus, the military actions can overcome the credibility problem, but the speech can refine the message by explaining the reason behind the military action when there are several benign types.

4.5.2 Competition, War, and the Offense–Defense Balance

I assume that if the Defender turns to competition, the issues the Defender has conceded to the Challenger up until that point are protected, and that the Defender cannot win them back. In practice, when Defenders launch competition, they have some chance of protecting the issues they still control, and recapturing the issues that they have conceded. Whether the Defender prevails in competition over a specific issue depends on the offense–defense balance (Glaser and Kaufmann, 1998). To capture these dynamics, I alter the competition payoffs of the model to:

$$EU^D(comp,t) = (1-p_H)q_t^C 1 + (1-p)q_t^D 1 - K \qquad (4.2)$$

$$EU^C(comp,t) = p_H q_t^C v + p q_t^D v - K \qquad (4.3)$$

The key change is that Defenders can win back conceded territory with probability $1-p_H$. It is still the case that D wins unconceded territories with probability $1-p$. Substantively, $p_H - p$ represents the offense–defense balance. When $p_H > p$, it means defense has the advantage (i.e., a state is more likely to win issues it controls than issues it does not control). Further, as p_H increases, it means that it is easier to defend rather than attack. Finally, we can think of the baseline model as a special case of extreme defense advantage ($p_H = 1$).

I find that I can support the delayed peace equilibrium under some parameter ranges so long as defense has the advantage ($p_H > p$). My theory degenerates when offense has the advantage ($p_H < p$) but only because the underlying reassurance problem entirely disappears. When it is easier to take territory than to defend it, even if D is certain that C is greedy, D wants to delay competition until the last moment. If it were easier to attack than defend, the best strategy is to concede everything before you initiate competition.

This scope condition fits many of my historical cases: The amount of effort and expense necessary to take a specific issue is usually larger than the expense and effort necessary to defend it (Glaser and Kaufmann, 1998). For example, during the Cold War, when the US decided to contain the Soviet Union, it had little chance of liberating many Central Asian and Eastern European states from the Soviet Bloc in the early decades of the Cold War. Rather, the US accepted these territories were lost for a long period, and focused on areas that lay outside the Iron Curtain, such as Korea, Afghanistan, Cuba, Vietnam, and so on. Even in cases such as World War two, where tanks made offense easier relative to other periods of history, the loss exchange ratios were larger for offensive operations. To be clear, over many different issues, there could be an advantage to offense because the attacker can choose to concentrate forces and the Defender must distribute them (Garfinkel and Dafoe, 2019). But holding the level of force constant at the issue-level, defense often has the advantage.

The results illuminate two debates about the offense–defense balance. First, realists that examine the decision-making logics of elites argue that the offense–defense balance – including expectations of victory over controlled versus noncontrolled territories – weighs on the minds of decision-makers (van Evera, 1998; Levy, 1984). But Fearon (1995) shows that only the first strike advantage can rationally cause war in a bargaining model. My theory illuminates a difference between Fearon's crisis model and the reassurance setting discussed by offense–defense scholars. If we construct a model that is closer to the setting realists describe, we can rationalize new ways that the offense–defense balance can influence patterns of competition and peace.

Second, offense–defense scholars are puzzled because they believe that peace should be more common when defense advantage increases (Glaser, 2010; Jervis, 1978; Gortzak, 2005). But competition arises with indistinguishable regularity during historical periods where defense is relatively stronger or weaker (Levy, 1984; Fearon, 1997). My theory provides a possible answer: Incentives for competition are non-monotonic in the offense–defense balance because offense advantage diminishes the trust problem. Initially, the Defender worries that if he makes concessions and the Challenger is greedy, then the Defender will not get those concessions back once he turns to competition. This concern is most extreme when the Challenger has complete defensive advantage $p_H = 1$. By contrast, if defense advantage is lower, the Defender knows he may win these issues back once competition starts. This makes the risk of being exploited later more palatable.

4.6 Empirical Expectations

My theory holds many empirical implications about the instances and timing of competition, how and when the Defender forms and updates his threat perceptions in response to the Challenger's actions, and the logic of effective diplomacy. But most of the action happens at two critical junctures. I call these critical junctures **the moment of focus** and the **moment of truth**. In between these two junctures is a **period of consistency** that I exploit to emphasize many null predictions that parse me from existing theories. In what follows, I detail general expectations that separate my theory from the major alternatives. In each empirical chapter, I develop even more nuanced predictions that tailor these general expectations to the specific evidence I use.

4.6.1 Initial Assumptions

My theory relies on assumptions that may not arise in every case. I presuppose that Challengers could be motivated by different principles, and each principle implies that the Challenger cares about a specific set of issues and territories. As a result, the Defender starts out uncertain about which and how many issues and territories the Challenger wants in the long run. This creates a dynamic where the Defender's goal is to discern the Challenger's principle, using knowledge about how specific issues connect to specific principles. These assumptions are an important departure from the existing literature. If they are wrong, my theory will unravel. Since these assumptions are novel (they differ from others) and essential (without them I cannot generate my predictions) I search for evidence of them.

Expectation 1: *Defenders are initially uncertain about how many and which issues and territories a Challenger cares about because they are uncertain about the principle that motivates the Challenger.*

Expectation 2: *Defenders evaluate a Challenger's long-term demands by theorizing about different principles that may motivate them and how those principles connect to specific issues and territories. Defenders list issues that connect to specific principles before a crisis begins. They do not theorize about the scope of the Challenger's interests independently of an underlying principle.*

This claim is different from assumptions commonly made in alternative theories. Defenders could start out confident that they are unable to determine the Challenger's motives (Mearsheimer, 2001), or that the Challenger can value any combination of territories without any underlying logic for why issues are connected (Joseph, 2021). Finally, the Defender may be unable or unwilling to list out issues and territories that fit specific principles because the history is too complex (Rosato, 2015) or the Challenger's preferences are socially constructed through the actions and rhetoric of their constituents (Goddard, 2018).

To be clear, my theory only assumes that Challengers *can* tie most issues to principles with at least moderate confidence. Thus, it supports my theory if we initially observe elites complete this task loosely as they theorize about the principles that could motivate the Challenger. However, I do not expect elites to provide a detailed report on exactly how every territory connects to every hypothetical principle at the outset. The reason is that an analyst's time is valuable and any Challenger's history is complex. To provide a comprehensive estimate analysts must conduct a time-intensive historical review and engage many experts. What is more, since they expect the Defender to reveal a single principle through diplomacy, it is not necessary to compile a detailed report for each principle. They are better off waiting until the Defender has revealed a candidate principle before they undertake a detailed review. I do expect, however, that analysts compile a thorough report on how issues tie to the Defender's *declared* principle.

I also assume that there is variation in the principles that could motivate a Challenger. In practice, if all Challengers through history were motivated by security or were otherwise greedy, then Defenders would likely always assume that their rival's motives could be described along a single dimension. Thus, for my theory to hold, we must ensure that Challengers through history have not always appealed to one primary motivation such as international security, or that Challengers uniformly balanced either prosperity (Keohane, 2005), or status (Gilpin, 1983), against security; or followed one of a handful of kinds of nationalist motivations (Powers, 2022).

Expectation 3: *Across historical cases, different Challengers will appeal to different limited-aims principles. Challengers that truly held limited aims will have pursued different principles.*

4.6.2 The Moment of Focus

The moment of focus occurs early in a rivalry when the Challenger first explains what principle motives her foreign policy. Before the moment of focus, the Defender is deeply uncertain about what the Challenger wants. He believes that the Challenger could be motivated by many different principles. Each principle implies that the Challenger holds different long-term demands. After that moment, the Defender raises his confidence that the Challenger is motivated by the Challenger's declared principle, and rules out all other potential limited-aims motivations. The Defender still believes that the Challenger could be greedy. However, he is willing to make a concession because he is sufficiently optimistic that C's initial explanation was honest.

This leads to some predictions that I can test across cases.

Expectation 4: *A Defender will increase his confidence that he understands the Challenger's long-term strategic intentions after the Challenger explains the principle that motivates her foreign policy, through either public or private speech. If instead*

- *the Challenger promises limited aims but does not appeal to a principle, the Defender will not increase his confidence that he knows what the Challenger wants.*
- *the Challenger does not reveal a principle and pursues revisionist policies anyway, the Defender will turn to competition.*

As previously discussed, my core argument holds if the Challenger uses public or private statements to convey a principle. Either is surprising for many structural scholars, who argue that the stakes involved during great power rivalries are high relative to the audience costs the Challenger could accrue from public statements (Snyder and Borghard, 2011; Rosato, 2015). However, expectation 4 is most surprising if it follows from private (costless) diplomacy. Indeed, rationalist scholars argue that private messages cannot convey information in this strategic setting (Glaser, 2010; Kydd, 2005; Edelstein, 2019; Ramsay, 2017), and even prominent constructivists assert that public rhetoric is necessary to alter the Defender's threat perception in this strategic setting (e.g., Goddard, 2018). As we shall see, private diplomacy plays an important role in many cases.

Of course, others argue that diplomacy is influential because of psychological distortions. In these accounts, Defenders learn because of the tone of what is being said, and the mannerisms and facial expressions of the subjects (Holmes, 2013). Further, meeting attendees overestimate their capacity to read their counterparts and rely on these vivid experiences (Yarhi-Milo, 2014). By contrast I argue that diplomacy works at certain moments (but not at other moments)[52] because of the content of what is said (it includes a principle), and the strategic setting. To pit my theory against these alternatives I derive some qualitative expectations about the role of diplomacy that I can use to verify my mechanism in case material.

Expectation 5:   *At the moment of focus:*

- *The Challenger and the Defender will seek out an opportunity (such as a diplomatic meeting) for the Challenger to explain the principle that motivates her foreign policy.*
- *Defenders are partially persuaded by the Challenger's appeals to a principle because they recognize that it creates an opportunity cost: The Challenger denies herself easy demands for some specific territories in exchange for easy demands for others.*
- *Elites who cannot attend a diplomatic meeting are persuaded by a transcript of the meeting, or a description of the meeting where those who attended explain the principle that the Challenger revealed.*

4.6.3 The Moment of Truth

The moment of truth follows the point at which the Challenger has taken the concessions that are consistent with the limited-aims principle that she initially claimed. At this point, she must choose between remaining satisfied with the status quo, or exposing that her long-term intentions are greater than what she originally promised. This period is critical because it presents the first opportunity for the Defender to learn if the Challenger's initial justification was honest. I predict that if the Defender discovers that the Challenger's initial claim was dishonest, he becomes mistrustful of the Challenger's long-term motives. This change in beliefs will trigger D to

---

[52] Psychological accounts do not make arguments about the moments of a case where face-to-face diplomacy is more likely to work. This also contributes to making expectations 6 and 7 surprising.

shift from cooperation to competition. This leads to predictions about the timing of competition that we can test across cases.

Expectation 6: *If a Challenger takes an action that is inconsistent with the principle she declared at the moment of truth, then the Defender will:*

1. *increase his confidence that the Challenger's intentions are greedy.*
2. *turn to widespread strategic competition.*

This logic follows from (1) the Defender's qualitative inferences about the Challenger's motives; and (2) a close connection between the Defender's beliefs about the Challenger's motives and the Defender's decisions to engage in widespread strategic competition. In any specific case, I expect to see my strategic reasoning play out in the case material:

Expectation 7: *If the Challenger is unacceptably greedy, then at the moment of truth, intelligence analysts for the Defender will explain that their new assessment about the Challenger's motives is based on their belief that the Challenger's actions reveal that the Challenger does not value the principle that they initially claimed. By a process of eliminating all feasible limited-aims principles, their new assessment is that the Challenger's aims are vast (although they may not know exactly what motivates the Challenger).*

4.6.4 The Period of Consistency

In between these two critical moments, I predict a period of consistency. During the period of consistency, the Challenger may do unspeakable things. However, so long as those things are consistent with the Challenger's declared foreign policy principle, they will not influence the Defender's beliefs.

Expectation 8: *Suppose the Challenger takes provocative actions that are consistent with the principle she declared at the moment of focus. These actions will not change the Defender's beliefs about the Challenger's strategic motives. The Defender will continue to negotiate with the Challenger, and make concessions, hoping to eventually achieve a lasting peace. These actions will not trigger a turn to competition so long as they are consistent.*

While my theory makes sparse assumptions about the Challenger's actions, we can parse my theory from alternatives by demonstrating that no updating occurs at key moments that others expect to see updating.

Therefore even if my theories coincide with others at other times, we can use my null predictions during the period of consistency to adjudicate different explanations. Alternative theories suggest that a wide variety of actions induce distrustful beliefs and/or competition. The Challenge could:

- Build offensive military capabilities;
- Rapidly militarize;
- Take territory;
- Brutally suppress domestic resistance or other illiberal actions;
- Violate treaties, international laws, and norms;
- Take morally repugnant actions, or fail to justify violent actions through rhetoric;
- Engage in aggressive diplomatic negotiations that engender negative personal impressions; or
- Orchestrate coups in foreign countries.

For example, scholars predict that military spending, or the use of force to take territory reliably causes shifts in threat perceptions (Glaser, 2010; Edelstein, 2019). However, my theory predicts that these actions do not always cause the Defender to update beliefs or select competition even if they are very costly. Whether they matter depends on the Challenger's historical and cultural context, and the issues that the Challenger chooses to act over. Parts of this prediction contrast my theory with institutional expectations that states form trust by making either public or formalized commitments to confine their ambition. Other parts contrast my theory with constructivist accounts that argue Defenders should infer the Challenger is aggressive if the Challenger takes repugnant actions that show the Challenger is not committed to international laws, norms, or institutions (Goddard, 2018; Krebs and Jackson, 2007; Hoffman, 2002). My theory makes no such claims. The Defender can perceive the Challenger's actions as truly repugnant, and in violation of basic laws and norms, and still trust the Challenger's strategic aims are limited.

Contrasting the events that trigger mistrust at the moment of truth with the events that do not during the period of consistency further illustrates how my theory is different. During the period of consistency, the Challenger may take very costly actions (such as invade and take territory), refuse to justify them with public speech or to meet the Defender face-to-face, or violate longstanding norms and treaty commitments, and the Defender will not update. By contrast, relatively minor events that do not fit a principle will drive massive shifts in threat perceptions at the moment of truth.

PART II

EVIDENCE

My theory yields empirical implications about the instances and timing of competition and peace, and how and when threat perceptions shift in response to costly actions and diplomatic reassurances. In this section I furnish three kinds of evidence to test these implications: an elite survey experiment (Chapter 5), archival evidence of British assessments of Soviet motives (Chapter 6), and a medium-n analysis of great power rivalries since 1850 (Chapter 7).

No piece of evidence tests all of my predictions, but, as Table PII.1 summarizes, each piece focuses on a different aspect of my theory. At one extreme, the experiment focuses on the Defender's beliefs about the Challenger's motives. At the other, the medium-n analysis focuses on the Defender's competition choices. The archival material does some of both.

I also accept that each method I use suffers from inferential concerns. But, as Table PII.2 summarizes, the weaknesses of one method are complemented by the advantages of the others. I use the experiment to causally identify the most unique and difficult to observe predictions of my theory: how decision-makers form and update their beliefs about a Challenger's strategic motives. Using an experiment on an elite sample, I can say that elites update their beliefs about a Challenger's motives when a Challenger fights *because* what the Challenger is fighting over is inconsistent with the Challenger's long-declared principle.

Table PII.1 *How I use different evidence to test my predictions*

	Observable Outcome	Evidence I Use
	Initial Assumptions	
E1	Defender is initially uncertain about Challenger's objectives	Case study, Experiment
E2	Defender theorizes about specific principles and connect them to objectives	Case study, Experiment
E3	Challenger varies in declared and actual principles in space and time	Medium-n
	The Moment of Focus	
E4	Defender changes beliefs about Challenger's motives following early diplomacy	Experiment, Case study
E5	Defender seeks out diplomatic meeting, Challenger reveals principles, all elites (even those who only read a transcript) update their beliefs	Case study
	The Moment of Truth	
E6(1)	Defender updates beliefs about Challenger's motives follow inconsistent action	Experiment, Case study
E6(2)	Defender's competition choice follows beliefs in E6(1)	Medium-n, Case study
E7	Defender's beliefs adjust due to qualitative inferences	All
	Period of Consistency	
E8	Defender's beliefs about the Challenger's long-term motives remain constant (Null prediction)	All

I use the medium-n analysis to verify that my theory is well correlated with the instances and timing of competition across all great power rivalries since 1850. I show that my theory outperforms other frameworks and also explains the cases that others have struggled to explain. In short, the medium-n analysis answers the so-what question: Can your motives-based framework explain patterns of competition and peace across the critical cases that fill our history books better than power-based theories that follow from realism and the bargaining model with shifting power?

I use the case study to trace all of the features of my mechanism through the strategic reasoning of elites in a single case. I validate my unique

Table PII.2 *What my evidence does*

Evidence	What it helps validate	Advantages	Disadvantages
Experiment	How elites process information and form beliefs	• Precise measure of beliefs • Measures changing beliefs in response to specific events • Exploits random assignment to causally identify mechanism	• Cannot connect beliefs to competition choices • Unclear if it generalizes to a real rivalry, where Defenders construct their own possible principles, and Challengers make strategic choices • Reports average beliefs, not state beliefs following aggregation
Case Study	Qualitative learning connects to competition choices in a real case	• Process traces my complete logic • Validates my core assumptions • Documents reveal decision-maker logic • Examines beliefs/choices made by individuals in institutional context	• Case is complex. Causal identification difficult • Results are case-specific, may not generalize
Medium-*n*	Predictions about instances and timing of competition across universe of cases	• Covers all cases. • Explores variation in competition choices • Exposes variation in declared principles	• No evidence of mechanism/causal identification

assumptions about how Defenders use principles to assess the long-term motives of Challengers, and show that beliefs about motives are directly connected to competition choices. Finally, I analyze elite debate to track the aggregation process from individual-level to state-level assessments and policies.

In the following Chapters 5, 6, and 7 I test my predictions using each piece of evidence. In each chapter, I also develop a distinct set of alternative explanations. These alternatives represent the dominant explanations in the literature for the aspect of great power interactions that I focus on in the chapter. My experiment examines how diplomacy and military actions impact a Defender's threat estimates about a Challenger's long-term intentions. Thus, I pit my theory against theories of military and diplomatic signaling, perceptions and misperceptions under the security dilemma, and intelligence analysis. My medium-n analysis seeks to explain the instances and timing of competition across all one-way great power rivalries. Thus, I pit my theory against theories about power and war in long-term rivalries; including power transition theory, balance of power theory, bargaining theory with shifting power, and realism. My case analysis of Anglo-Soviet relations covers several steps in my mechanism. At each step, I translate my theory into case-specific predictions. I pit my theory against a wide range of alternative theories including all those described above, and organizational theories, and historical accounts of Anglo-Russian relations.

Pitting my theory against different alternatives in each chapter provides a fair test of alternatives explanations. The reason is that I am careful to only evaluate each alternative theory in the empirical domain it was designed to explain.

It also creates a tough test of my theory. The reason is that my theory is built to explain a long and complex interaction (i.e., the entire rivalry), but many of these alternative explanations are purpose-built to explain only one a few decisions at a few moments. For example, social theories of diplomacy are built to explain why elites form trust following diplomatic interactions when realists claim that diplomacy should not work. Detailed historical work verifies these explanations in the cases that I study. Given the rigor of the case research, we might think that these theories comprehensively explain, for example, why British elites trusted Stalin. I show that my rationalist explanation can help us understand these deliberative processes.

Inside the Analyst's Mind: Experimental War Game Simulation with US National Security Elites

How do national security elites form and update their beliefs about a rival's strategic intentions? The standard rationalist story is that states rely on a series of indicators, such as regime type, and strategic terrain to form prior estimates about the scope of a rival's interests. Then they examine their rival's costly military behavior to update these beliefs over time. When they observe violent behavior, they move towards mistrust. My theory suggests that these insights are incomplete in three ways. First, Defenders examine costly military choices, but they use them to alter their perceptions through the logic of qualitative inferences. Second, costless speech can influence the Defender's perceptions if it appeals to a principle. Third, costly and costless actions interact because they are either consistent with a principle or not. In the end what matters is whether the entire history of the Challenger's actions fit together to serve (or dis-serve) a specific principle.

It is difficult to precisely test these claims with observational data. Great power rivalries last for decades. As they unfold, leaders turn over, third-party threats emerge, and technology changes.[53] Furthermore, the overarching rivalry involves a complex strategic process. What Challengers say during diplomatic meetings, their choice of military targets, and who they choose to meet with are all strategic decisions that I must account for in an empirical analysis. Furthermore, Challengers often take many actions at a time. Thus, it is hard to know the specific choices that drive the Defender's beliefs.

Even if I could control for these factors, it is difficult to systematically measure elite beliefs. Elites rarely write down or state their assessments of a Challenger's motives. In many cases, elites change their beliefs but do

---

[53] This creates unanticipated disjunctures in economic and military fortunes.

not document their reasoning with enough detail to evaluate a social science theory.[54] Even when elites report their assessments with frequency, they rarely use the same scale. Finally, I cannot always trust what they say because elites are subject to desirability bias that can lead them not to report, or over-report certain types of assessment.

To overcome these issues, I test some of my most surprising predictions about how elites form and update their perceptions of a Challenger's motives using an elite survey experiment. This survey departs from most other survey experiments in international relations in three ways. First, subjects were ninety-three real-world foreign policy elites. Focusing on elites is important because I want to know the indicators that elites use to evaluate intentions. If it is true that elites are trained to focus on particular behaviors, or that they succumb to unique biases that cloud their judgment, then I want to reflect those elite-specific beliefs in my experiment.

Second, the vignette was a detailed hypothetical scenario that closely reflected a real-life war game exercise that national security professionals participated in, rather than a stylized game or a short vignette. In it, I presented subjects information about a fictional rising power named Bandaria. Subjects were randomly assigned information about Bandaria's diplomatic explanation for its limited revisionist aims, and the targets of Bandaria's military interventions to take territory. They are then asked to assess Bandaria's long-term intentions as information was revealed.

Third, the actions that subjects observe Bandaria take are identical in each treatment group. In all treatment groups, Bandaria makes a diplomatic claim that its motives are tied to a specific principle (ethnic or security). Then subjects all observe Bandaria use force to take territory that is tied to one of these principles. If costly actions drove Defenders to update, we should observe no differences across these treatment groups. What changes is whether the diplomatic statement and the military action serve the same principle. My theory predicts subjects will pay attention to how the qualitative features of Bandaria's actions are tied to a single principle (or not) and use these features to arrive at different estimates.

In addition to a randomly assigned war game scenario, I ask post-survey questions. These questions include long-form answers where subjects explain the logic of their choices. They also include specific questions to determine if non-rationalist argument could be explaining my results.

---

[54] Although, as we shall see in the next section, there is some evidence that gives a window into the minds of important decision-makers at enough points in history to evaluate my argument in at least one case.

I find strong support for all the predictions that I test, and the post-survey questions further substantiate my mechanism is prominent in elite decision-making relative to alternatives from sociology and psychology.

I proceed in four steps. First, I explain how an elite war game survey experiment helps me make claims about the population that interests me. Second, I review the theories that motivated my experimental design. Third, I detail my vignette structure. Fourth, I detail my measures and results. Finally, I describe the results of post-survey questions.

5.1 A Scenario-Based Elite Survey Experiment

My goal was to answer the following question: when *national security experts* are tasked with evaluating the strategic intentions of an adversary, what indicators do they use? When do those indicators affect their beliefs?

To get leverage on this question I made two important choices. First, subjects were foreign policy elites. Second, the vignette was a detailed hypothetical scenario that closely reflected a real-life war game exercise that national security professionals participated in, rather than a stylized game or a short vignette.[55] Next, I explain the advantages of this approach, and the design choices that help me overcome its shortcomings.

It is important to recruit elites because extensive research in international relations shows that training and personal experiences distinguish foreign policy elites' decision-making processes from the general population's (see Saunders, 2011). In a recent study Kertzer (2020) shows that while elites and the general public respond similarly in many political experiments, the differences are more stark in international relations than any other sub-field. If foreign policy elites rely on specific indicators, or use them in a way that is different from the general public, I cannot draw inferences about their behavior from experiments administered to a general population. This is especially true in the post-survey questions where I seek to understand the comparative power of my analytical framework to others.

In other contexts, it has been shown that professionals with specialized expertise approach their work differently than an average educated adult would the same task. For this reason, behavioral researchers increasingly turn to convenience samples to identify effects for medical doctors (Arber et al., 2006; Feldman et al., 1997), CEOs (Abdel-Khalik, 2014; Cen and Doukas, 2017; Lieb and Schwarz, 2001), or lawyers

---

[55] Additionally, it asks about an assessment and not approval.

and judges (Redding et al., 2001), rather than a representative sample of educated adults. These convenience samples often derive consistent result in repeated experiments on elite samples (Redding et al., 2001). And when the vignettes are sufficiently detailed, this can lead to different results from the general public (Lieb and Schwarz, 2001; Cen and Doukas, 2017).

Given the population of interests – foreign policy analysts who brief policy-makers – I define my sample frame as follows. Subjects were eligible if they had briefed a Deputy Assistant Secretary, Congressperson or similarly ranked official on foreign policy issues. Subjects were asked sample inclusion questions at the end of the survey to ensure they met the elite sample frame.[56] 139 subjects answered at least one question, 131 completed the survey, and ninety-three passed attention checks. I analyze these ninety-three responses below.

My sample is a good proxy for high-level elites for two reasons. First, all participants are successful, political officials focused in foreign affairs. It is precisely this group of people that NSC members are drawn from. Second, subjects were selected because they provide information to senior decision-makers. High-level elites rely on facts and analysis that they receive from people in this sample. Thus, the sample has considerable influence in shaping the information that their superiors see.

It is true that convenience samples can make generalizability difficult. Drawing from the economic research above, I took four steps to increase my confidence that the results are not an artifact of my sampling method. First, I solicited elites using two distinct sampling techniques that I describe in Appendix D.1 online. Each sampling method had its own link to an identical survey. I demonstrate that the treatment effects hold controlling for the different sampling methods in Table D.1. Thus, I can say with confidence that one method of sampling did not determine the results because I get the same results using different sampling techniques on different sub-populations of elites. Second, I collected biographical information on President Trump's first-term NSC and President Obama's final NSC. Figure D.1 reports the summary statistics for my sample (panel a) broken out by sampling procedures and the real NSC staff (panel b) broken out by president. The variation across my sampling frames is consistent with variation in real-world NSC selection. Third, I report metadata on response attributes and attrition rates recommended by Eysenbach (2004) in Appendix D.1.3 online. Fourth, I conducted pilot surveys on M-Turk to test features of the vignette recommended by Steiner et al. (2017). The results are supportive.

---

[56] See Appendix D.1.2 for solicitation information and D.4 for balance tests.

My second design choice was that I use a very detailed scenario that involves a fictional country. My vignette is slightly adapted from three declassified war games that real-world national security elites participated in. This is different from two other choices I could have made. A stylistic vignette with numerical payoffs, or a vignette that involved real countries (i.e., a China scenario).

This design choice draws from recent insights from behavioral economics, medicine, and law. Increasingly, researchers that survey elites use scenario based exercises rather than stylized games with precise numerical payoffs (Collett and Childs, 2011; Arber et al., 2004). The reason is that elites make judgments in complex strategic environments that cannot be captured in stylistic games. In the national security setting, challengers are not simply profit maximizers that respond to well defined purchasing choices (like individuals in markets may). There are several dimensions of preferences and outside options that may effect decision-making.[57] As a result, stylistic choices do not well reflect the complex assessment process that leaders face when they assess their rival's military behavior.

National security experts are better suited to hypothetical scenarios than the average American or even other groups of experts because they participate in hypothetical war game exercises as part of their daily work. Real war plans[58] and National Security Estimates[59] are informed by war games that involve hypothetical countries. The vignette I developed took features from real war games that national security experts had participated in. After I developed the vignette, I received review from five foreign policy experts including a former Deputy Director of an intelligence agency to make sure the amount of detail in the vignette was consistent with the scenarios that foreign policy experts use. The design also reflects the exercises that analysts go through during the analytic training program (CAP) at the Central Intelligence Agency.

One concern with vignettes is that policy-makers choose policies not only based on their beliefs about their rivals, but on complex inter-agency dynamics and select incentives (Allison, 1971). These do not apply in my case for two reasons. First, my dependent variable is beliefs, not policy choices. In the instrument, I am careful to ask subjects about their beliefs in this scenario, rather than actions they would take or policies that they

---

[57] In the crisis bargaining literature defenders can use force in different ways, and this produces different strategic interactions.

[58] That is, the US military's specific plans to invade other countries.

[59] That is, the intelligence community's assessments of foreign threats.

would recommend. Second, the subjects I recruit serve analytical roles and not policy roles.

A second concern is that subjects do not take hypothetical scenarios seriously. In Appendix D.2 online I describe design features, attention checks, and metadata that demonstrate the subjects took the vignette seriously.

Real-world analysts also run war game scenarios with real countries. I chose a hypothetical scenario over a real example (e.g., a China scenario) because I did not want subjects to import outside information about a case into their answers. I deliberately avoided this because any country that poses a threat to the United States has already taken many different actions that analysts would use at the start of their estimate. For example, if subjects thought the scenario was about China, they may have started the experiment with specific beliefs about the principles that motivate China based on what China has done. I describe design features that ensured subjects did not systematically invoke a historical case and responses that demonstrate those measures were effective in Appendix D.3 online. In short, if I used a real country, I could not ask what is the analytical frame analysts use to approach an estimate. I could only ask whether they adopt existing frameworks given long-standing estimates on a current threat.

5.2 How Theory Informs My Design

How should analysts form and update their estimates of a rival's strategic intentions? At the broadest levels scholars argue that elites should focus on two kinds of indicators to draw inferences about a rivals intentions: attributes of regimes and states; and costly military actions (broadly defined). My experiment is designed to support my argument while taking into account the concerns of indicator theories. Beyond specific indicators, scholars seek to understand how heuristics, and qualitative features of communication influence the Defender's perception (usually in a nonrationalist way). My main experiment is designed to make sure these arguments do not confound my study. However, I explore other ways that analysts form impressions relative to my argument using post-survey questions.

5.2.1 Indicator Theories

The first set of indicators are features of the Challenger's domestic politics. Notably, consolidated autocratic regimes are prone to expansionist aims (Weeks, 2008). Further, when Challengers and Defenders are ruled by different types of regimes (Oneal et al., 1996), or diverge in their ethnic and cultural backgrounds (Jackson and Morelli, 2011) they are prone to competition. These features rarely vary within a single case. But even when they do not change, they should impact the Defender's prior beliefs (Kydd, 2005). Some scholars argue that these non-varying indicators amplify the effects of costly signals (Schweller, 1992). In this telling, democratic Defenders will be highly sensitive to a Challenger's choice to use force to take territory if the Challenger is an autocrat (especially if they have consolidated power), or if the Challenger's ruling elites herald from an ethnic or cultural background that is different from the Defender's background.

The second set of indicators are the Challenger's costly military actions. According to defensive realism and other costly signaling theories of trust, Defenders should closely monitor all kinds of costly military actions including military spending (Glaser, 2010), and offensive weapons purchases (Garfinkel and Dafoe, 2019). But perhaps the strongest signal of aggressive intentions is the decision to invade a foreign territory and annex it (Kydd, 2005). This is especially the case if the Defender is the strongest state in its region, its economic power is increasing and its region is separated from others by a large body of water. In a situation like this, it is hard to argue that the choice to take territory through force serves status-quo objectives.

Defensive realists also provide clear predictions about the indicators that Defenders should ignore. Notably, defensive realists argue that costless messages should have little or no effect on estimates of the Challenger's intentions in the context of an enduring rivalry (Glaser, 2010; Powell, 1996). Most notably, private diplomatic reassurances should be unpersuasive if elites rationally account for the Challenger's incentives to misrepresent (Kydd, 2005). This view that private statements should not be rationally influential is shared by certain constructivists (Goddard, 2018). But realists also believe that public reassurances or Defense White Papers should also have little impact on the Defender's perceptions (Waltz, 1979).

Indeed, these core predictions influence perceptions of certain policymakers. As stated in the Introduction, Congress has recently chastised the intelligence community (IC) for failing to infer China's aims were vast. Congress argued that the IC should have relied on these indicators but didn't. This insight motivates my experiment because there is indeed a conventional wisdom that specific indicators matter, but evidence that they do not amongst the real-world elites that we charge with drawing inferences about a Challenger's motives.

I argue that indicators only matter in the context of qualitative inferences. Unlike defensive realists I argue that costless speech can play a coordinating role. This coordinating role has direct effects on the Defender's perceptions (i.e., even absent costly signals) and also moderates the implications of the Challenger's military actions. To be clear, I do not predict that diplomacy always plays a coordinating role. Rather, diplomacy only coordinates if it explicitly appeals to a principle that explains why the Challenger's motives are limited.

This leads to my first hypothesis based solely on the Challenger's diplomatic actions.

Hypothesis 1. Cheap-talk diplomacy coordinates if it is tied to a principle: Subjects who observe the Challenger justify her demands in terms of a specific principle during a private diplomatic meeting will increase their confidence that they know what the Challenger wants if the Challenger holds limited aims. Subjects who observe the Challenger promise that her motives are limited but without a reference to a specific principle will not.

My theory is also different because I argue that costly military actions only cause concern when they rule out a limiting principle. Defensive realists predict that using force to take territory should always engender some mistrust. My theory suggests that this result only holds when the Challenger uses force to take territory that does not fit with a declared principle, or otherwise with the set of actions that the Challenger has previously taken. However, I also argue that the Challenger can do unspeakable things, even take territory, and not engender mistrust so long as the Challenger's actions fit the declared principle.

This leads to two closely related hypotheses.

Hypothesis 2a: Subjects that observe the Challenger take territory that matches a previously declared limited aims principle will trust the Challenger more than subjects who observe the Challenger take territory that does not match a previously declared limited principle.

The second hypothesis explores variation in individual-level responses over time.

Hypothesis 2b: Subjects who observe a Challenger use force to take territory that matches a declared principle will not change their estimate that the Challenger's intentions are vast.

H2b is a tough test given what we think in indicator theory. It means that a group of subjects will not change their estimates if they observe violent military actions.

For my mechanism to work, it must be the case that Challengers cannot continuously stake their reputation on new limiting principles as their power increases. According to offensive realists, the main reason that trust-building is hard is that the Challenger can continually revise their territorial claims by saying "I want just one more concession." I showed formally that when different limited-aims Challengers want different things, the problem of salami-slicing claims is surmountable because limited-aims Challengers faced a strong incentive to receive valuable concessions before competition. This leads to a final set of hypotheses:

Hypothesis 3a: Subjects are less likely to trust the Challenger's future statements in diplomatic meetings once they have verified that the Challenger's initial limiting principle was not valid.

The second hypothesis explores variation in individual-level responses over time.

Hypothesis 3b. Diplomacy can coordinate only once: Subjects who observe the Challenger use force to take territory are no less likely to trust the Challenger in future diplomatic meetings.

The vignette that follows is designed to test my theory on its own terms, and given the insights of these alternative theories.

5.2.2 Beyond Indicator Theory

There are many other ways that elites could form impressions. Elites could rely on heuristics (Snyder et al., 1987), or analogise to a recent experiences (Khong, 1992). Elites could also avoid doing the work on their own by seeking out expert advice and adopting the perceptions of those experts (Grynaviski, 2018).

None of these concerns impact the causal identification of my experiment. However, if they are highly salient, then they will overshadow the effects of my theory in real cases. In the post-survey question, I ask elites about the extent to which they rely on these other indicators and mechanisms rather than the indicators suggested in my theory. My intuition is that analysts rely on a wide range of analytical frames. And my hope is that the logic of qualitative inferences is prominent relative to these alternatives.

Others argue that private diplomacy matters but for an entirely different reason. Their basic logic is that diplomats judge whether their counterparts are honest during in-person interactions. Diplomats then use these in-person inferences to update their beliefs about the Challenger's intentions. Some argue that diplomats can learn from face-to-face encounters because of neurological processes (Holmes, 2013), and others argue that diplomats develop skills of reading the mannerisms of their counterparts (Bull, 2002). Some argue that diplomats correctly draw these inferences, but others suggest that diplomats overestimate their ability to read people (Yarhi-Milo, 2014). Either way, the broad consensus is that that salient feature of diplomacy is that it occurs face-to-face.

None of these concerns impact the causal identification of my experiment because subjects only observe the transcript of a diplomatic meeting. The vignette is carefully designed so that I do not describe personal impressions, or features of the elites during diplomatic meetings. Thus, these psychological accounts would predict no effect precisely because the subjects never attend a real meeting, and therefore cannot develop personal impressions.

However, it is possible in real meetings these personal impressions overshadow the coordinating mechanisms that I propose. I ask the questions proposed by Holmes (2013), in addition to some other questions, to determine if this is the case. Again, my intuition is that analysts exploit diplomacy in many different ways. My hope is that the logic of qualitative inferences is prominent relative to these alternatives.

Finally, some argue that public statements post-crisis offset the mistrust caused by costly military actions. In my theory, rhetoric does not matter per se. What matters is whether actions fit a principle. To stack the deck against my theory, I include a post-crisis statement of reassurance which, if Goddard (2018) is right, should wash out differential effects between the consistent and inconsistent treatment groups.

5.3 Experimental Vignette

The survey instrument has three phases. In each phase, subjects are presented with new information about Bandaria then asked standardized questions about Bandaria's intentions and resolve. Subjects also write text responses. See Appendix D.7 online for full text.

Phase 1 provides all subjects with the same prompt and baseline information. Subjects are told that Bandaria is an emerging world power, and the American president will soon meet the Bandarian prime minister. Subjects are asked to provide the president an assessment of Bandaria's long-run intentions and resolve in preparation for that meeting.

Phase 1 provides three pages of detail about Bandaria. In general, I included many details to address confounding concerns raised by Dafoe et al. (2016). Further, interviews with senior intelligence officials and my review of war games operated in the IC suggest that the level of detail was necessary to make the scenario consistent with war game scenarios that are common at the CIA's analytic training program (CAP) as well as war games operated by the Department of Defense.

But I chose specific details to match my theory and create a tough test for my hypothesis. To match the reassurance setting that my theory describes, phase 1 tells subjects that Bandaria is experiencing economic growth that outpaces others in the region. Further, Bandaria has embarked on a period of increased military spending.

To account for the domestic political indicators described in Section 5.2.1, subjects are told that Bandaria is a consolidated autocracy with a majority ethnic composition that departs from the United States. As stated, some existing scholars argue that these features will amplify concerns that Bandaria holds aggressive intentions. Furthermore, and against the conditional logic of H2 and H3, these details should attune all subjects to infer that Bandaria's intentions are vast if Bandaria takes any military action.[60]

Most critical for my theory, phase 1 also provides a map of Bandaria and its surrounding countries. The map is presented in Figure 5.1. The map and accompanying discussion illuminates two plausible dispute areas based on different kinds of principles that Bandaria could hold. First, Bandaria's international security is vulnerable to port closures in the Lebang Bay. These ports are controlled by New Kasper. Second, poorly treated ethnic Bandarians live in a neighboring country (Arcadia). Crucially, there is no information about which of these issues Bandaria cares about the most.

In *phase 2*, subjects are randomly assigned into a *diplomatic message treatment* where Bandaria explains it is motivated by either: (1) security or (2) ethnic-nationalism. I also include (3) a counterfactual condition, that reflects the case where Bandaria promises it is peaceful, but does not appeal to a principle. In the counterfactual condition, the Bandarian prime minister talks about confidence building measures and Bandaria's general interest in peace.

---

[60] Phase 1 provides a lot of other information. For example, it details Bandaria's trade networks and intergovernmental organization (IGO) affiliations.

Table 5.1 *Treatment groups at the end of phase 2 (diplomatic message)*

Diplomacy declares (randomized):	Associated Territory
Ethnic core interest	Arcadia/Greywall
Security core interest	New Kasper/Lebang Bay
Appeal to peace	Undefined

Figure 5.1 Bandaria and its neighbors.

Table 5.1 shows variation in observed information at the end of phase 2. I include two core interest treatments to make sure the revelation of core interests generally and not the particular issue (security- or ethnic-based grievances), is doing the causal work. As an example, the ethnic treatment is:

In a private meeting, the American president asked the prime minister of Bandaria to explain Bandaria's military spending. The Prime Minister replied: "Grave injustices have been done to ethnic Bandarians. We have a long history of supporting our Bandarian brothers in Arcadia. Ethnic-national concerns motivate our military policy." He then said, "Of course we want to resolve this issue peacefully. But Arcadia does not realize just how concerned we are about our ethnic kin. We will use any means necessary to ensure our ethnic kin are well governed." He continued, "Once our ethno-nationalist goals are assured, we have no reason to expand our military. All of our other foreign policy and regional concerns are less important and can be managed through UN participation, diplomacy and negotiation."

Experts note that ethnic nationalism concerns have been central to Bandarian foreign policy over the past 10 years. Bandarian elites referred to ethnic-nationalism in private diplomatic conversations and public speeches consistently over the past 10 years.

The language was modeled on declassified minutes, letters, and cables that described conversations between British elites, German Kaiser Wilhelm (1866), US President McKinley (1898), German Chancellor Hitler (1934), and Soviet premier Stalin (1932). Although the language may strike the reader as direct, it is common through history. In what follows, I exploit variation across all three groups to test H1.

In *phase 3*, subjects are randomly assigned into a *military intervention* treatment where Bandaria annexes: (1) territory that surrounds the Lebang Bay in New Kasper, or (2) Greywall. One corresponds with ethnic interests, the other with security interests.

This treatment takes the form of breaking news. For example, the ethnic treatment is:

Breaking News: The Bandarian military occupied Greywall in Arcadia. Greywall is populated by ethnic Bandarians. The move comes after months of political unrest in Arcadia. The Bandarian prime minister announced plans to annex Greywall but promised fair treatment and reparations for aggrieved Arcadian citizens and businesses. The Bandarian Prime Minister insists that these events are entirely consistent with Bandaria's interests long known to the rest of the world and Bandaria remains committed to peace and stability generally.

The treatment groups that follow are depicted in Table 5.2. The rows represent the different diplomatic messages that subjects can observe in phase 2. The columns represent the different military interventions that subjects can observe in phase 3. By the end of the experiment there are six distinct treatment groups. But for H2 and H3, I am mainly interested in the differences between the consistent and inconsistent groups (i.e., I don't care about those who observed the undefined diplomatic message for my main tests).

There are three notable features of this design. First, all subjects observe violent military actions in the third period. Second, subjects in both consistent and inconsistent groups observe violent action over an ethnic territory

Table 5.2 *Treatment groups at the end of phase 3*

	Ethnic Military Dispute	Security Military Dispute
Ethnic Core Interest	Consistent with principle	Inconsistent with principle
Security Core Interest	Inconsistent with principle	Consistent with principle
Core Interest undefined	Pre-conflict Counterfactual	

or a security issue. Third, subjects in both consistent and inconsistent groups observe diplomatic messages that appeal to both principles.

These features allow me to examine how the combination of qualitative details work together to affect subject inferences, but do not force me to rely on any specific combination of declared principles or military actions. To best leverage this feature (and consistent with my preregistered design), I pool consistent and inconsistent groups in the main analysis. However, in Table D.7 I disaggregate the groups to demonstrate that the effects hold when I consider the ethnic-nationalist message and security message separately and then analyze the difference between consistent and inconsistent groups. My results are consistent if I aggregate or treat the qualitatively different justifications separately.

5.4 Results and Measurement

At the end of each phase, I ask subjects: "What is the percentage probability that the following statements are true?" I then present the same list of questions. By repeating the questions, I can verify how perceptions change in response to different stimuli. Responses were recorded using a slide rule from 0 percent to 100 percent that moved in 5 percent increments. I chose this response method rather than a seven-point index for reasons that are peculiar to the subject pool. Each Agency uses a different lexicon to describe probabilities. The CIA uses a confidence scale, Hill staffers and diplomats describe probabilities with no official standard. I did not want to favor one group over another. Second, there is much debate about what confidence levels mean. For some, the level of confidence refers to the primary source material. Thus, low confidence that an assertion is true can refer to either the credibility of the source or that the assertion is false.[61]

I preregistered my hypotheses, analytical tests, and standards for inference via e-gap.[62] Since I randomized treatment on a nonrandom sample, I preregistered analytical tests based on the p-value derived from the permutation test of group means suggested by Strasser and Weber (1999). The test identifies how confident a researcher can be that the treatment had a

---

[61] I chose 5 percent increments because some critical numbers move along that scale. But I wanted to avoid trivially small choices that would distract subjects.

[62] The registration ID is 20160609AA. The book reports registered hypotheses 1–3b (worded slightly differently), survey items to measure them, analysis of data plan for them. For space, some pre-registered tests appear in an Appendix, but results are as predicted. Other analyses reported were not pre-registered.

causal effect on the responses of a nonrandom sample conditional on the responses observed and the independence of the in-sample randomization. Among the many advantages of permutation tests is that inferences are robust to small sample sizes.[63] For a review of the pre-registration and the analytical tests see Appendix D.5 online.

Based on the preregistered analytical tests that rely on p-values from permutation tests, I infer strong support for the expectations that I test. To maximize the transparency of my results, I report the distribution of responses broken out by treatment group.

5.4.1 Predictions about Effective Diplomacy

To test H1, I asked two questions. First, I asked:

A: Although there are many military objectives that Bandaria might pursue, a single target stands out as the most likely.

If my theory is correct, then subjects assigned to either the ethnic or security justification treatment will score high on this question, but subjects who are assigned to the preconflict counterfactual will not. According to the existing literature, there are three reasons that I may not find an effect. First, subjects may not use diplomacy as a good indicator. Second, subjects may only use information derived from in-person aspects of diplomatic encounters to form their impressions. If true, then subjects may not respond to the content of information in the text. Finally, subjects may read that Bandaria is an autocracy with a recent trend in military expansionism, and simply infer that Bandaria does not hold limited aims.

To further investigate the coordinating logic of diplomacy outlined in H1, I also asked:

B: In the last question you were asked to think about a most likely target. Click on the map where that most likely target is.

Subjects are then presented with a map of Bandaria that they can click on. If my theory is correct, I should observe two things. Before subjects observe a diplomatic message (at the end of phase 1) their clicks should be dispersed across the map. If true, this will help validate an important assumption about my theory. I argued that the Defender started out uncertain about the specific principle that motivated the Challenger. I

---

[63] For an explanation of why they are superior to t-tests see Ludbrook and Dudley (1998). The p-values are interpreted like those from t-tests. Using a t-test instead of the permutation test improves the result reported in the paper.

argued that it was plausible that there were many limited principles. This assumption may not be reasonable because it is possible that subjects naturally assume that the Challenger is motivated by a specific principle (e.g., security) if the Challenger holds limited aims. It is also possible that analysts rely on indicators from the Challenger's domestic politics to draw strong inferences about the Challenger's principles. If true, they may all agree on Bandaria's likely principle based on the domestic political information I provided.

If my theory is correct, I should observe a different pattern in clicks after Bandaria justified her demands. After phase 2, subject clicks should vary depending on qualitative differences in the diplomatic message that they observe. Subjects in the ethnic-nationalism or security treatments should coordinate their clicks on the territories associated with those respective claims. However, those who observe the control message will not coordinate.

Figure 5.2 presents results for H1. The top of Figure 5.2 plots click-map responses. Panel (a) plots pre-treatment responses after phase 1. Panel (b) plots responses after the diplomatic treatment in phase 2. Circles received ethnic treatments, crosses received security treatments, and boxes received controls. Prior to treatment, subjects from every (future) treatment groups are well dispersed across the map. Panel (b) shows that the responses of those who observed a diplomatic treatment with a qualitative justification for Bandaria's motives reflect the content of that treatment. Those who see the ethnic (security) message click on the ethnic (security) issue. However, subjects who observed the diplomatic treatment with no principle remain well dispersed after treatment.

The bottom panels in Figure 5.2 plot responses to question **A**. The lighter mass received a diplomatic treatment that contained a principle (group mean is the solid line). The darker mass received the control (group mean is the dashed line). Panel (a) plots responses before subjects received their diplomatic treatment, panel (b) plots results after the diplomatic treatment. Before treatment the group means are the same.[64] After treatment the group means are different. Those that observed Bandaria's diplomacy appeal to a principle became more confident that they understood what Bandaria wanted relative to those who did not. A permutation test confirms that the means of treated and controlled subjects are different post-treatment with 98.5 percent confidence.

---

[64] Although the distributions are shaped differently, the means are the same.

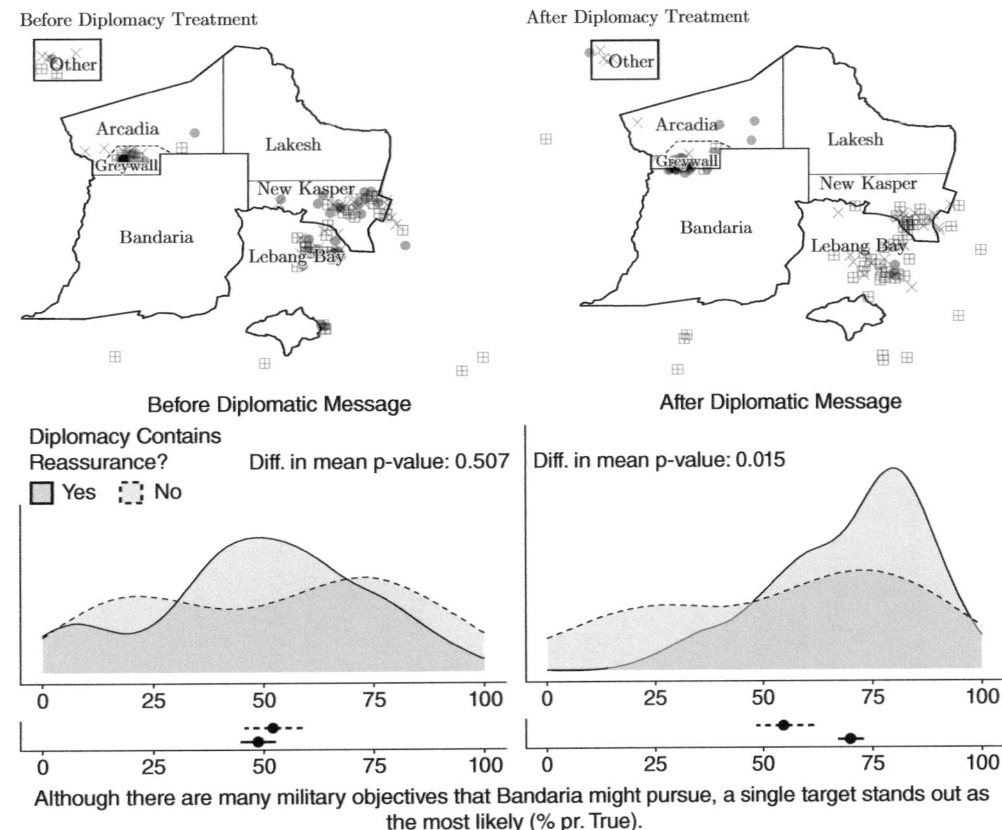

Figure 5.2 Does cheap diplomacy influence beliefs about limited aims?

5.4.2 Predictions about Trust in the Face of Violent Demands

H2a and b ask about subject perceptions of Bandaria's strategic intentions. To test them, I ask

C: Bandaria will use military force to expand its borders whenever the opportunity presents itself.

To test H3a and b I ask:

D: We can trust what the Bandarian Prime Minister says about Bandaria's long-term intentions.

All the subjects observed Bandaria use military force to take territories. Even though they observe identical violent actions, H2a predicts that those who observe inconsistent actions will be more mistrusting than those who observe consistent actions. If true, then subjects in the inconsistent group will score higher on this question than subjects who observed a consistent action.

Similarly, H3a predicts that subjects who observe actions that conform to a single principle will be more willing to listen to future diplomacy (i.e., score higher on question **D**) than subjects who observe actions that, collectively, cannot be supported by a limiting principle.

Figure 5.3 plots the distribution of responses to question **C**. Within each panel, responses are broken out by consistent and inconsistent treatment groups. The darker mass observed a consistent diplomatic message and military intervention (group mean is dashed line). The lighter mass observed inconsistent treatments (group mean is solid line). Panel (a) presents pre-treatment results and panel (b) presents post-treatment results. Before subjects observed military interventions, the mean of both

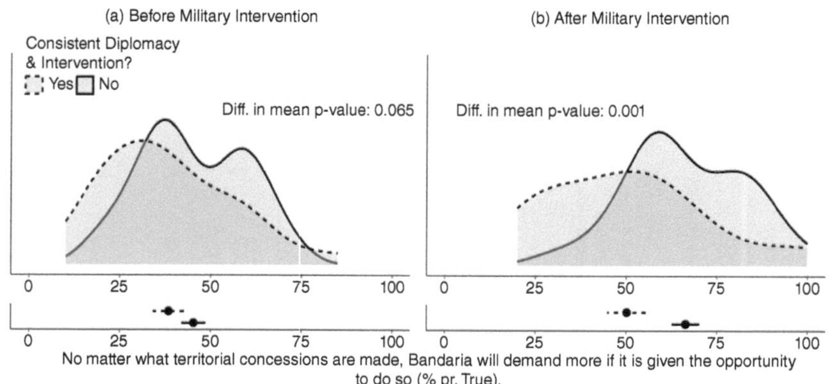

Figure 5.3 Does inconsistent behavior alarm subjects?

groups is not statistically different. The average respondent was more optimistic than not about Bandaria's long-term intentions, but the responses are close to complete uncertainty (50 percent). After the military intervention treatment, subjects that observed inconsistent behavior were concerned about Bandaria's long-term intentions. Subjects that observed consistent behavior remained uncertain. A permutation test confirms there is no difference in treatment group means pre-treatment but a significant difference post-treatment with 99 percent confidence. I infer that subjects who received inconsistent treatments grew worried about Bandaria's long-term intentions compared to those that observed Bandaria fight for what it said that it wanted.

Figure 5.4 addresses H3a. It plots the density of responses to question **D** in the same format as Figure 5.3. Before the military intervention treatment, the group means are nearly identical. Afterwards, subjects that observed inconsistent behavior are deeply mistrustful. Those that observed consistent words and deeds did not, on average, update their assessment. A permutation test confirms the means of these groups are different with 99 percent confidence post-treatment. I infer that subjects who received inconsistent treatments grew mistrustful of Bandaria compared to those that received consistent treatments.

H2b makes claims about how individual subjects change their trust in Bandaria. I focus on the consistent case because it distinguishes me from the standard costly signaling arguments. Where past scholars predict that analysts who observe a state take territory through military force will grow mistrustful, I argue that these subjects will not alter their beliefs if the violent action can be explained by a known principle. To test this, I compute the difference in subject responses to question **C** in phase 3 and phase 2.

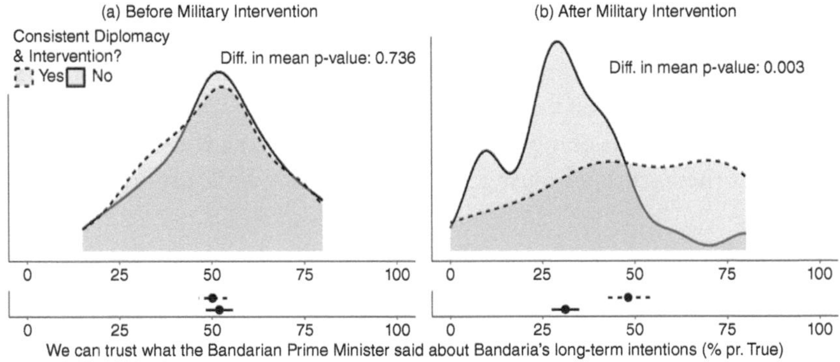

Figure 5.4 Does inconsistent behavior lead to less trust?

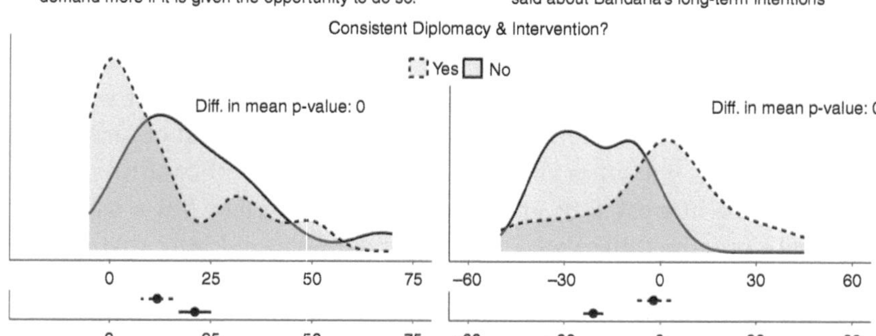

Figure 5.5 Does inconsistent behavior lead subjects to change beliefs across time?

If I am right, and different from signaling theories, the difference in the
consistent group will be indistinguishable from 0. If I am wrong, then subjects who observe Bandaria use force to take territory will increase their
mistrust. To test H3b, I complete the same analysis for question **D**.

The results of these analyses are in Figure 5.5. Panel (a) plots results
to questions **C** (H2b). Panel (b) plots the results from question **D** (H3b).
The x-axis plots the change in respondents' answer to the same question between phase 2 and 3. Responses can range from -100 to 100. The
darker mass received consistent treatments and the lighter mass received
inconsistent treatments.

As I expect, the consistent group is amassed around 0 in both cases. A
permutation test cannot rule out that the consistent group mean is statistically different from 0 in either test. This means that the average subject
in these groups observed Bandaria use force to take territory but did not
update their beliefs that Bandaria's intentions were vast, and were equally
willing to engage Bandaria in good faith diplomacy in the future.

The distributions show that a large portion of subjects updated in the
opposite direction from the conventional wisdom. Notably, 18 percent of
subjects decreased their belief on question **C**, and 45 percent of subjects
increased their beliefs on question **D**. This means that a considerable number raised their levels of trust after observing Bandaria use force to take
territory.

Existing theories simply cannot explain this kind of updating. It is consistent with my broader account of qualitative inferences because these
actions were clearly consistent with Bandaria's declared aims but potentially inconsistent with broader intentions. As a result, it is possible that
subjects ruled out the possibility that Bandaria was motivated by some

aggressive motive, and this caused them to increase their confidence that Bandaria's motives were limited.

To make clear that the results are not a feature of the design, I also plotted the inconsistent group in solid lines. As you can see, this group is dispersed broadly across positive ranges with a mean above 40 in panel (a), and negative ranges for panel (b) with a mean below -25. A permutation test confirms that the way the consistent group updated was different from the inconsistent group in both cases. I infer from these results that subjects did not alter their beliefs when they observed consistent violent behavior. However, subjects that observed inconsistent behavior became more concerned about Bandaria's long-term intentions and were less likely to trust what the Bandarian prime minister said in future diplomatic meetings.

5.5 Qualitative Inferences in Text Responses

To further support my mechanism, I directly asked 1/3 of the subjects the following long-form question:

If other countries have aggressive intentions, they have strong incentives to hide them. So why should we believe anything that their leaders say? In your work, do you consider what foreign leaders say when you evaluate their interests? If so why?

This question is a tough test of my theory for two reasons. First, the question wording was explicitly designed to prompt respondents to say diplomacy does not work. Second, the question does not mention the fact that Challengers can hold different principles, that the logic of diplomacy related to qualitative inferences, or otherwise hint at the idea that Challengers can hold different limited aims. Nevertheless, all but one subject argued that diplomacy was useful (most argued it was very useful). 90 percent of respondents went on to describe a logic that supported the qualitative signaling mechanism.

In one example, a subject explicitly describes the value of interpreting diplomacy within historical context.

I think we need to listen to what we are being told with a critical mind. That does not mean we automatically assume someone is lying to us, nor does it mean we take them wholly at their word... What state leaders say is useful to a country assessment, but must be balanced with other information sources and historical context.

Another explains how diplomacy provides information only combined with a variety of other indicators.

There is seemingly always a gap between a given nation's declaratory policy and their actual pursued policy, but that is not to suggest their is no value in the declaratory. Other sources of information need to be brought to bear (intelligence, domestic politics, past behavior, strategic culture, etc.) in order to often tease out basic strategic truths contained in declaratory policy.

Another explicitly refers to the logic of consistency with principles that is clearly different from a simple Sartori (2005) type logic of consistency between words and deeds.

Obviously actions are generally more indicative of underlying intentions (and in the application of international law are generally considered to be a stronger indication of a nation's position than its statements). However, words can also be quite indicative; other than in full blown war scenarios, international disputes are fought out in multiple spheres, including diplomatic and even public relations ones. Therefore, it could be assumed that nations will attempt to claim a moral position and avoid lying or backflipping. It is for this reason that broad phrases such as acting for its "core security interests" are used. This enables a moral stake to be taken (its reasonable for all countries to be concerned for and, to an extent, act to ensure security for its citizens and interests) and such a broad remit allows it to undertake a wide range of actions under that guise while seeking to argue that its objectives remain consistent. As such, statements that contain or allude to broad, subjective goals or principles can be taken to indicate that those making the statements may want to stake a moral claim yet preserve their ability to take a wide range of paths without diverting from the apparent broad moral principle.

Others also describe the logic of my theory in detail.

Yes, because I still think (as I did here) that it is possible to see undertones of defensive or offensive interests. Furthermore, I think it is important to see how their intentions when said line up or fail to line up with their clear international actions, as indicators of their sincerity.

Yes it was. It gave a benchmark which then factored into a much larger tapestry of facts, informed judgment, history, geopolitical imperatives, and strategic national interest, which – when synthesized – helps determine foreign policy.

Another simply stated, "It is absolutely vital to believe what they say – unless and until facts on the ground contravene what was uttered; as well, one must invariably Trust, but Verify...."

5.5.1 Robustness Checks

In Appendix D.5 online, I present OLS regressions where the dependent variables are responses to questions **C** and **D**. The right-hand side variables include the treatment (consistency) and one of the following controls:

sampling method, diplomatic message that was received, duration of the experiment, subject's work function, employment sector, military service record, nationality, and seniority (measured by the most senior person they have briefed). In every model, the treatment is significant and consistent with the above results. However, the controls are not significant and do not confound the treatment effect. An analysis of the covariance suggests that the treatment does not co-vary with the controls.

Finally, a broader concern is that subjects would change their perceptions in response to the treatments I provide because nothing else has changed. I account for these concerns in my design. Recall my main predictions are that subjects respond to the same information differently. Consider the third phase where all subjects observe Bandaria use force to take territory. If subjects were simply responding to the information, they would have observed Bandaria use force to take territory and increased their confidence that Bandaria's intentions were vast. If this demand effect influenced their perceptions, it would be incredibly difficult for me to validate H2b and H3b because these hypotheses require that one group of subjects observe Bandaria use force to take territory and do not alter their beliefs about Bandaria's motives. Also, the vignette intentionally provides a wide arrange of information in phase 1 and phase 2 to conceal these kinds of effects. As stated, subjects are provided information about Bandaria's regime, domestic politics, military spending, economic development, regional history. After subjects are provided this information they are also asked to respond.

I ease residual concerns in two ways. First, there is no difference in the text responses reported above from those who observed the control diplomatic message relative to those who observed the treatment. Those in the control group still detailed the logic of principles even though they were not primed with a diplomatic message that appealed to a principle. Second, I analyze the causal effect of the treatments on response times. Research shows that subjects who observe information that causes them to develop anxiety have longer response times. If subjects are simply reacting to what they observe without processing the information in detail, then their response times will not vary. However, if subjects are putting the information together to infer that Bandaria is genuinely aggressive, then they should take longer to respond. Consistent with this logic, subjects in the inconsistent treatment arms take 20 percent longer to respond than subjects in the consistent treatment arms following phase 3, but in no earlier period.

5.6 Analytical Frameworks beyond Indicator Theory

The experiment provides strong support for my theory relative to standard indicator theories. Indeed, there is something about the content of what is being said that moderates how intelligence analysts interpret costly signals.

However, and as raised in Section 5.2.2, it is possible that elites rely on entirely different analytical frameworks to evaluate a rival's strategic intentions. One might wonder: In a real case, would analysts gravitate to your analytical framework over other methods for evaluating the intentions of a Challenger? To address this question, I embedded post-survey questionnaires into the design and some additional questions in the main experiment to test alternative theories. Although the results are drawn from a small convenience sample, they shed light on the reasons that real-world decision-makers rely on parts of speech to form their impressions.

The first question is whether analysts rely on observations of the case before them, or whether they rely on a broad range of other heuristics? Prominent international relations theories grounded in psychology and sociology suggest that policy-makers rely on historical analogies, and personal impressions to form their assessments. Organizational theories (both rational and sociological) suggest that policy-makers rely on subject matter experts to form their opinions. Some in decision sciences expect policy-makers to rely on key indicators (although this has not been directly extended to intelligence agencies). To see how analysts approach analytic challenges I included the following a post-survey questionnaire:

Analysts can approach problems in a range of ways. If you were asked to analyze the intentions of a target country that you did not know much about, a good way to approach the problem is to:

- Compare the target to historical cases that were similar and extrapolate from those cases.
- Read what the target's leaders have said about their intentions and determine if their behavior is consistent with what they say.
- Use a standard list of key indicators that suggest a state is aggressive. Then see if the target matched those key indicators.
- Seek meetings with counterparts in the target's government and form impressions of them.
- Ask country experts with extensive historical knowledge of the target and use their analysis.
- Ask country experts with extensive networks in the target country and use their analysis.

Forty-one subjects from the main survey were randomly assigned to this questionnaire, thirty-four responded. Subjects were asked to select from a five-point scale. Figure 5.6 summarizes the responses grouped by Agree (Strongly Agree, Agree) and Disagree/Indifferent (Strongly Disagree, Disagree, Neither Agree nor Disagree). The results clearly show two types of methods are preferred by subjects: consistency between words and deeds, and a reliance on experts. Historical analogies are also more useful than not. Personal impressions formed during diplomatic engagements and key indicators were not thought to be useful by about half of the respondents.

The results also show that analysts positively report on multiple methods. Typically, organizational and state-level explanations are pitted at odds with each other. It is common that scholars will suggest that their method is the dominant way that analysts will process information. These results suggest that individual policy-makers may use a variety of approaches to deal with problems. One reasonable interpretation of this data is that policy-makers gather expert opinions and then use them to evaluate consistency between words and deeds.

A second question is whether secret diplomacy is necessary, or can any form of speech matter. Strictly, my argument departs from others because I find that both private or public speech acts could coordinate. This is different from others that explicitly find verbal communication should not matter in general, but secret diplomacy especially should not matter for reassurance. However, audience cost theory predicts that public statements are more important than private diplomacy. Theories of cognitive biases predict that diplomacy is important because it leaves specific

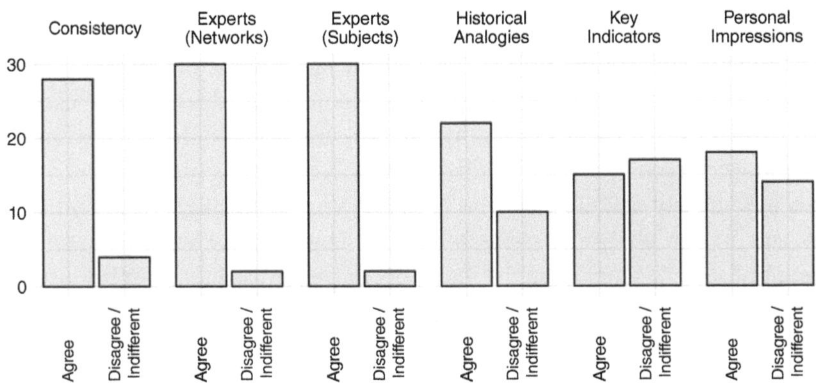

Figure 5.6 How policy-makers approach problems.

personal impressions with policy-makers. This leaves an important question: Do both of these forms of communication convey information? If they do, do they convey the same information (i.e., are substitutes for each other)?

I answer these questions with a second post-survey questionnaire that was randomly assigned to forty participants.

Q1: Think of times when you evaluated the intentions of a foreign counterpart. In these cases, would you find a private meeting with government officials from the target state to be useful for your assessment?

Q2: When you are unable to meet with foreign counterparts, are any of the following sources useful to you to supplement the missing information you would have gathered during these meetings:

- A written transcript from a private meeting between the target's leader and a senior US diplomat where they discuss the target's long-term intentions in detail.
- A brief from a US diplomat that meets extensively with the leader of the target state.
- Speeches the target leader makes to their domestic public about their foreign policy goals.

Q3: Compared to other people in your profession, are you a good judge of character?

Subjects responded to the first two questions with a seven-point Likert scale from Extremely Useless to Extremely Useful. Responses to **Q3** were recorded on a seven-point scale from one of the very best, to one of the very worst.

Audience cost scholars argue that public statements are more credible than private statements because domestic and international audiences punish leaders who walk-back from public statements (Fearon, 1994). I argue that private diplomacy is a vital part of the assessment process. **Q1**, plotted in Figure 5.7, tests these competing conjectures directly. For ease of interpretation I combine the four useless categories together (Extremely useless, Moderately useless, Slightly useless, Neither useful nor useless), the two moderately useful categories (Moderately useful/Slightly useful), and present Extremely useful separately. Very few subjects believed meetings were not useful. More thought they were extremely useful than not useful. Clearly, these policy-makers found private diplomatic meetings are useful to policy-makers.

The question, then, is why? My theory provides a rational explanation. However, some theories argue that elites rely on personal interactions to

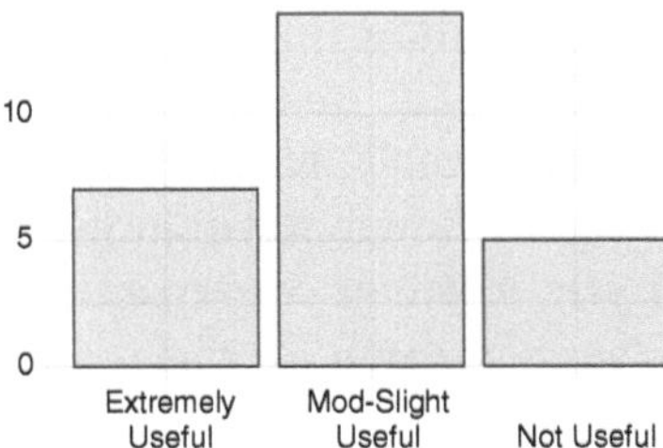

Figure 5.7 Are meetings useful?

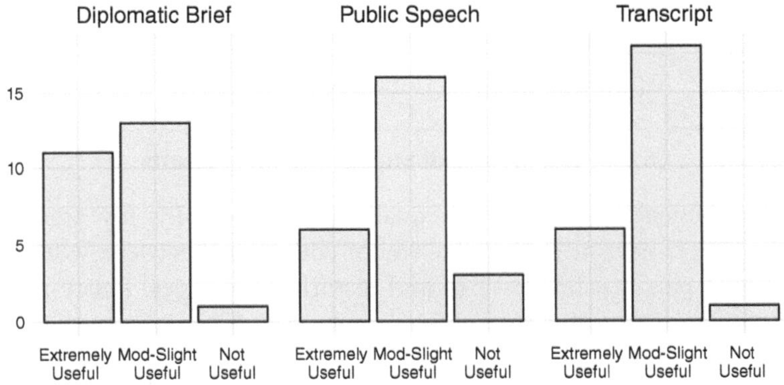

Figure 5.8 What substitutes for personal interactions in meetings?

form their beliefs about the intentions of their rivals. At the most basic level, these theories expect that being present in meetings is a critical feature.

In real life, elites likely draw inferences from the tone and content of meetings. However, it would be good to know which kind of inference is most salient. **Q2**, plotted in Figure 5.8, tests this basic proposition explicitly. If the most salient feature of diplomacy was the in-person interaction, then the transcript would not be useful. However, if the content of meetings was important, then it would be.

Against the predictions of face-to-face diplomacy, all but one policy-maker in the sample believed that a written transcript was a useful substitute for an in-person meeting. One third thought a transcript was extremely useful. Subjects preferred a brief from a senior diplomat who regularly attended such meetings. Both of these results are surprising if the *personal* interaction during meetings generated information. The most reasonable interpretation is that policy-makers infer information from the content of what is said during diplomatic meetings. At minimum it means that the inferences they draw from personalist interactions do not overshadow the content.

Figure 5.8 also confirms that public speeches are the worst substitute for private diplomatic meetings (although still quite good). One interpretation of this result is that private meetings convey different information from public speeches. One plausible reason for this is a paradoxical account of audience costs. Leaders may face domestic political incentives to exaggerate their claims, or make sweeping generalizations in public because the public knows little about foreign policy and would not appreciate the nuance of precise diplomatic speech. Defenders may rely more on diplomatic speech precisely because leaders can explain a nuanced position that better reflects their beliefs.[65]

5.6.1 Discussion of Supplementary Results

The supplementary test provide qualitative support for my argument. Policy-makers have a clear preference for consistency between words and deeds over personal impressions and historical analogies. Policy-makers are conscience that diplomacy helps them make decisions. Even when posed with the problem of cheap talk directly, they still say that diplomacy matters and explain that it is best used to verify events that unfold. Furthermore, policy-makers do not believe that in-person meetings are necessary. Rather, they can get as much information from expert briefs with people who attended meetings or even a transcript of the meeting itself. In short, the content and tone matters much less than the content of what is being said.

There are many inferential challenges with these supplementary results. Yet it is surprising that over a variety of different questions designed specifically to promote the salience of other analytical frameworks, the responses are supportive of my expectations.

5.7 Summary

My experiment sheds light on how real-world national security professional process information and form beliefs in response to different stimuli. Consistent with my initial assumptions (E1, E2), I find that subjects start out deeply uncertain about the Challenger's long-term intentions, but

---

[65] The results of this analysis do not change if I break it out by consistent or inconsistent treatment.

they can reliably assign specific issues to underlying principles (cf. Goddard, 2018; Rosato, 2015). Across subjects, I found wide variation in what subjects instinctively believe Bandaria's core interests were. Individual subject reported low confidence in their initial assessment about Bandaria's long-term motives.

Consistent with the logic of costly signaling and regime theory, I find that subjects monitor these indicators and do update their beliefs in response to them. However, unlike the dominant rationalist theories, the elite subjects did not update in response to military actions out of context. Rather, subjects interpret the actions that they observe the Challenger take, given the context I provide about the Challenger's history and geostrategic position. Notably, subjects who observe an identical set of diplomatic and military actions, update their perceptions in different directions depending on the historical context that surrounds those actions. Based on this evidence, I infer support for E6. Since a violent demand for either the ethnic or security issue could be consistent (or inconsistent), I show that it is the qualitative features of how different actions fit with specific principles that matters holding constant the size of the costly military action.

My experiment also validated that diplomacy plays a clarifying and coordinating role at the moment of focus. I found diplomacy only influenced subject perceptions if it revealed the principle that motivated the Challenger's foreign policy. When subjects were assigned to the security (ethnic) diplomatic treatment, they inferred that if the Challenger held limited aims he was motivated by security (ethnic nationalism). Subjects were not persuaded if diplomacy did not appeal to a principle. In this way, national security elites rely on the content of what is said during a diplomatic meeting to form beliefs. Clearly, this cannot be explained by face-to-face accounts. In fact, many elites thought that a transcript was just as valuable as attending the meeting in person. What is more, I find that subjects are never persuaded by post-crisis public statements. Based on these results I infer support for E4.

Not only do all the results work in concert to support my causal mechanism, but the magnitude of the main effects are substantively meaningful. Let's consider the most important question for US grand strategy – does Bandaria hold aggressive strategic intentions? Suppose we interpreted the mean respondent as the consensus of the IC, which could form the basis of the intelligence estimate that reached the president. Further, suppose that we use the analytical standards recommended by the Director of National Intelligence (2015) to convert the quantitative scores into likelihood judgments. If Bandaria's military action targeted a consistent territory, the IC would continue to estimate that it was unlikely that Bandaria held aggressive strategic intentions. By contrast, if Bandaria's military action targeted an inconsistent territory, they would revise their estimate from unlikely to likely. We could imagine that such a difference could greatly impact US policy.

6

Anglo-Russian Relations and the Origins of the Cold War

In this chapter I trace the logic of my argument through British assessment of the Soviet Union (1941–1946). I selected Anglo-Soviet relations at the onset of the Cold War for four reasons. First, it is both critical and under-studied in political science. Past political scientists focus on tense episodes during the Cold War such as Détente, the SALT negotiations, and the Cold War's end.[66] This is surprising because grand theories assume the Defender is uncertain about the Challenger's long-term aims, and have not yet chosen between competition and peace. As we shall see, the Western allies formed strong opinions about Stalin's long-term strategic intentions by 1947; and these strong opinions led to the origins of the Cold War. Thus, a proper test should examine the pre-Cold War period when the future of Western–Soviet relations was uncertain. Related, the application of my theory to this case illuminates that certain events – such as Eden's visit to Moscow – may be understudied in the historiography.

Second, Britain served as the status-quo power in many great power rivalries between 1700 and 1945. Although it is difficult to use any one case to make general claims, my focus on a common status-quo power increases my confidence that my theory of motives travels to other important cases.

Third, even though many scholars of trust problems assume that Challengers value security or are otherwise greedy, Stalin is one of the few revisionist powers to argue that his demands were in service of security from a foreign threat.[67] Focusing on a declared security-seeker case allows me to explore how my theory advances existing rationalist accounts. It also allows me to fairly contrast my predictions with psychological

---

[66] There are exceptions Holmes (2018, ch 7), Kydd (2005, ch 4), Trachtenberg (2019). While Larson (2000) discusses the early Cold War, she begins post-1947.

[67] See Chapter 7.

theories about how threat perceptions form and change, and social theories about rhetorical persuasion. These theories usually start with the premise that a variant of realism is rational (Yarhi-Milo, 2014; Goddard, 2018; Holmes, 2018), then identify deviations in threat perceptions from the realist baseline to evidence their theory (i.e., when Defenders update following diplomacy, or fail to update following the decision to fight in a crisis). But if the core assumptions of realism do not fit the case, then it is not clear what deviations from rational theory are. For example, Hitler never claimed to be purely motivated by international security. British elites never thought that if Hitler held limited aims he was purely motivated by security. Thus, the deviations from realist theory occur prior to the costly events that these nonrationalist accounts focus on. By isolating a case where the Defender claims security intentions, I can treat these accounts on their own terms.

Finally, the case presents interesting opportunities to validate my predictions and rule out alternatives. The pressures of World War Two led to a unique foreign policy environment. The War Cabinet met (on average) weekly to discuss foreign policy issues. Several intelligence, foreign policy and defense sub-committees analyzed the strategic intentions of the Soviet Union in detail. These now-declassified documents provide a good basis to search for evidence of the reasoning behind British thinking. Furthermore, there was a constant stream of diplomatic, political, and military events that could have affected the British assessment of Soviet intentions. Notably, there were four heads of state, and eight foreign minister meetings, three treaties signed, several political spats, and ominous military interventions. Towards the end of the war, the Soviets and the Western allies explicitly bargained over the fate of Europe. During that time, the Soviet Union made clear its interests in annexing territory. The diversity and frequency of events provide fertile ground to test competing theories that expect a relationship between these events and assessments of intentions.

6.1 Analysis Plan

My analysis is broken into three sections that correspond with my theory's critical periods. I code Anthony Eden's visit to Moscow in November 1941 as the *Moment of Focus*. In the first section, I review Anglo-Soviet relations up until this moment to validate my core assumptions about Defender beliefs at the onset of rivalries, and evaluate my predictions at the moment of focus. I code the *Period of Consistency* between November 1941 and January 1945. I use consistent British estimates of Soviet intentions during this period to trace the aggregation of knowledge from individual assessments, through organizations and bureaucratic processes. I code the *Moment of Truth* between February 1945 and March 1946. During this period, British elites grew mistrustful of Stalin's long-term intentions. I use this period to validate my predictions at the moment of truth, and draw a connection between British beliefs and competition choices.

One challenge for evaluating a social science theory about decision-making logics through archival material is that scholars have amassed many competing theories that make similar predictions at particular moments of the case. As psychological, normative, and rationalist arguments have advanced, the core difference between leading theories are the mechanisms through which individuals or decision-making units process information, form beliefs, and then make choices. We cannot directly observe the private thoughts of elites, and the murky estimates and reasoning of decision-making collectives. The important, indirect evidence from oral and written justifications we can gather is subject to demand bias, and is rarely complete, representative of all important decision-makers, or written with sufficient specificity to validate social science theories. How can I be sure that my theory holds explanatory power given so many alternatives? I use the analytical narrative method (Bates et al., 1998), and refinements to it (Goemans and Spaniel, 2016; Joseph et al., 2022) to provide positive support for my theory. In particular, I will develop and validate case-specific predictions from many important steps in my causal mechanism. If I can find evidence against an important step in my mechanism, then it is hard to say my theory plausibly explains other parts of the case because decisions at one moment are related to the next. The key insight is that this is true of *every* rigorous theory. Thus, even if an alternative theory arrives at the same prediction as my theory at a certain moment of the case, I can increase my confidence that my theory holds important explanatory power by demonstrating that the full mechanism from other theories is not well-supported across the case as a whole. In what follows, I detail my case specific predictions that I must verify to have any confidence in my theory. I then detail the predictions of several leading contenders, paying special attention to where we differ.

6.1.1 Evaluating My Theory on Its Own Terms

Box 6.1 summarizes my case-specific predictions for each stage of my causal mechanism. Box 6.1(a) summarizes what expect to observe if my assumptions are valid. British elites should: start out deeply uncertain about Soviet intentions; theorize about different principles (and start to list of associated issues and territories) that could motivate Stalin's foreign policy; propose many different theories about what principle motivated Soviet foreign policy; and render each proposal with low confidence. If British elites explicitly state that they are very uncertain about Stalin's motives because Stalin has not yet explained his strategic intentions, it would provide especially strong evidence for my theory.

The case deviates from my basic assumptions if any of the following are true. First, British elites do not debate Soviet intentions. Second, British elites reach a consensus about the Soviet Union's long-term intentions based on the Soviet's regime type, Stalin's pre-tenure biography (such as his military history). Third, British elites focus on Stalin's instrumental objectives (such as security for the status quo) and do not seek to understand his intrinsic motivations. Finally, British elites identify principles, but find that the history is too complex for them to understand what issues and territories are tied to what principles.

Box 6.1(b) summarizes my case-specific predictions at the moment of focus. I expect British elites to: seek out a meeting with Stalin to hear what Stalin has to say about his long-term motives; and change their assessments following the first diplomatic encounter between one senior British policy-makers and Stalin in which Stalin justifies his foreign policy in terms of a principle. If my theory is right, then this period would mark a shift in how British elites evaluated Soviet intentions. Subsequent reports would no longer raise different hypotheses about why Stalin held limited aims. Rather, their deliberations will focus on ruling out the principle that Stalin asserts. Strong evidence for my theory would include an analysis of Stalin's meeting with Anthony Eden as the reason for the shift in focus, and documents in which analysts argued that Stalin's claims were credible because they limited what Stalin could plausibly ask for in the future.

Three types of evidence would dis-confirm my theory. First, if British elites do not seek out a meeting with Stalin to learn about his intentions. Second, British assessments of Soviet intentions may not change following Eden's visit to Moscow. Third, Anthony Eden may adjust his assessment following his face-to-face meeting with Stalin, but other elites that did not travel to Moscow may not rely on Eden's report of the meeting.

Box 6.1(c) summarizes my predictions during the period of consistency. I expect that British elites do not alter their assessments of Stalin's intentions during this period. I also expect British elites will refrain from competition even as Stalin rapidly militarizes and takes territory, engenders negative impressions, violates international agreements, displays a disregard for international norms, and rapidly expands Soviet military power.

Box 6.1 How British Elites (BE) have thought about Soviet intentions according to social science

I Theorize	I Am Wrong if
	(a) My Unique Assumptions
BE evaluate Stalin's long-term demands by theorizing about different principles that could motivate Stalin's foreign policy.	BE do not evaluate Stalin's motives because: • It is too difficult • Stalin's motives could change • Stalin's resolve in a crisis is more salient • Power will shift so rapidly questions of motives do not matter
BE identify a handful (more than two) different principles that could motivate Stalin. Each implies variation in the specific territories, and the number of territories, that Stalin will prioritize. Some of these principles imply a few demands, but at least one implies vast aims.	BE evaluate Stalin's motives but do not refer to principles/connect territories to specific principles because they: • Assume that Stalin wants security or is greedy. • Assume Stalin's motives vary in scope. • Assume Stalin can value any configuration of issues. • Cannot tie a principle to specific territorial objectives at all; or • Until Stalin's public rhetoric socially constitutes them.
BE start out uncertain about Stalin's motives (i.e., all assessments made with low confidence).	BE start out confident that they know Stalin's principle; possibly because they use Stalin's biography, or Soviet regime type to infer motives; or because all Challengers want security or are greedy.

(continued)

Box 6.1 (continued)

(b) Moment of Focus

Before the first diplomatic meeting with Stalin, BE are uncertain about Stalin's principle because Stalin had not revealed what motivates his long-term foreign policy. BE seek out a diplomatic meeting with Stalin to learn about Stalin's motives. After Stalin reveals his motives in a diplomatic meeting, BE (1) raise their confidence that Stalin wants what he said he wants; (2) start to evaluate if Stalin's actions match his declared principle.

BE are convinced by diplomacy because it connects to a principle.

BE do not seek-out or rely on diplomacy to infer Stalin's motives. BE dismiss Stalin's diplomacy as cheap-talk. Instead, BE focus on the scope of costly military actions, or violent demands absent diplomat context.

Diplomats who meet Stalin are persuaded by their face-to-face interaction, and their inferences are different from elites who did not travel to Moscow. BE believe Stalin because of personal judgments of his sincerity and not what he says.

Once Stalin communicates that he is motivated by security concerns, BE evaluate his future actions against that claim. They write reports that detail what Stalin will (and won't) demand if he truly values security. To the extent BE debate whether Stalin's aims are limited, the debate centers on whether his actions are consistent with his stated aims.

Beliefs about Stalin's long-term motives remain constant so long as Stalin's actions are consistent with his claim. BE continue to evaluate if Stalin's initial claim was honest.

BE do not turn to competition for any other reason.

BE cannot assess what issues fit with Stalin's declared motives. BE evaluate Stalin's motives based on Stalin's actions outside of whether those actions are consistent with Stalin's initial claim.

BE assessments widely fluctuate despite Stalin's consistent actions because:

- Stalin takes territory, or rapidly militarizes
- Stalin engenders a negative personal impression
- Stalin violates international laws and norms
- Stalin does not justify violent action with rhetoric
- Different BE rise to leadership
- BE time horizons change

BE turn to competition, possibly because:

- Power shifts rapidly
- They confront an indivisible issue
- Their time horizons change
- The balance of power falls out of kilter
- Miscalculation in crisis

(continued)

Box 6.1 (continued)

(d) Moment of Truth

BE observe Stalin do something inconsistent. Update their beliefs about Stalin's long-term motives.	BE observe Stalin do something inconsistent. Do not update their beliefs about. BE logic for updating has nothing to do with how Stalin's actions connect to the principle that motivates him.
BE updated beliefs trigger a policy shift. BE seek to thwart Stalin's expansion, stop offering concessions, turn to widespread containment.	New beliefs do not trigger policy change. Rather, competition choice hinges on another reason: • Fluctuations to rate of shifting power • Power parity • Changing discount factors

Box 6.1(d) summarizes my predictions at the moment of truth. I expect British policy-makers will increase their mistrust after they observe Soviet behaviors that are inconsistent with Stalin's stated security intentions. As a result of their shifting beliefs, the British government shifted its policy towards competition.

I would infer incredibly strong support for my theory if Stalin engaged in a single inconsistent action, all British elites agreed it was inconsistent, and then all called for competition. I can still infer support for my theory if I find individual-level variation in the point at which analysts update their beliefs. The key piece of evidence will be debates between those who did update their opinions and those who did not. For my theory to explain important variation in the case, it must be that analysts disagreed about whether the events they observed were in fact inconsistent with Stalin's reassurance.

Two types of evidence would dis-confirm my theory. First, British elites may not update following blatantly inconsistent Soviet behavior. Second, they may update their beliefs, but may not turn to competition.

6.1.2 My Theory and Defensive Realism

Because Stalin appeals to security, the differences between my theory and defensive realism are subtle in this case. We agree that Challengers vary in their strategic intentions, that Defenders are uncertain about the Challengers' motives, and that Defenders draw inferences by monitoring Challengers' costly actions. Given that we agree on so many points, how can I be sure that my theory holds an independent effect? In this section I clarify five case-specific differences between my theory and defensive realism.

First, realists *assume* that Challengers are motivated by security or are otherwise expansive (greedy). A core question, then, is whether real-life Defenders theorize about different underlying principles the Challenger could hold? This case supplies evidence to address this question at the moment of focus. If British elites start out assuming that Stalin wants security or is otherwise greedy, then the bed rock assumption of realism is plausible. If, instead, British elites theorize about the different principles that Stalin could hold and then extrapolate to predict the kinds of issues and territories that he could desire, then it would support my argument that elites try to draw inferences about principles, and do not simplify down to instrumental motivations.

Second, realists argue that costless diplomacy will not influence British perceptions. In contrast, I argue that costless diplomacy plays a coordinating role. It would be surprising for defensive realists if British elites sought a meeting with Stalin because they wanted to hear Stalin's explanation for his future revisionist actions.

Third, defensive realists typically expect that each time Stalin engages in costly military action it should engender some mistrust (Edelstein, 2019; Glaser, 2010). The amount of mistrust depends on how costly the action is (Jervis, 1989b). It would be surprising for these scholars if Stalin engaged in frequently high-cost military signals and British trust remained intact. By contrast, I do not expect British estimates to change, even following very costly and militaristic actions that fit a declared principle.

Fourth, some interpret this case as a spiral of mistrust that emerges because of two-sided uncertainty (Larson, 2000). My theory simplified away two-sided uncertainty. But I accept that it arises in real life. Indeed, my conceptualization of hedging expects Defenders to forgo their interests to avoid inadvertent escalation over a Challenger's core interest. I do find evidence that British elites made initial concessions because they were concerned about Stalin's mistrust in them. From this, I infer that my theory would be enriched by including two-sided uncertainty. However, for spirals of mistrust to explain the origins of the Cold War, we must assume that Stalin actually held cooperative intentions, and the Cold War was a product of misunderstanding. This point is, at best, contested.[68]

Finally, a different defensive realists logic is that greedy types initially forge trust, then lay in waiting until a costly opportunity arises to cheat their counterpart. Once they cheat their counterpart, mistrust and competition follow. Consistent with this prediction many defensive realists emphasize British reactions to the Iran Crisis.[69] But under defensive realist logic, greedy Challengers who have initially engaged in cooperation to forge trust should only cheat when they can exploit a rival's trust for profit. It would be puzzling if Stalin took a costly action that exposed his intentions at a moment he could not exploit for short-term gain, and even more surprising if he announced his decision to cheat Britain in advance.

6.1.3 My Theory and Individualistic Theories of Irrational Trust

Some scholars debate whether wishful thinking or buying time explains why elites defer competition (Ripsman and Levy, 2008). There are two ways that I can parse my theory from these explanations. First, I am careful to

---

[68] Haslam (2003), Leffler (1999), Gaddis (2006, pp. 10–13).
[69] Trachtenberg (2019, p. 35), Kydd (2005, p. 101).

search for evidence of the reason elites update their estimates. If my theory is correct, then those who update their estimate will say something akin to, "we have changed our estimate because Stalin's behavior in this case cannot be explained by his declared motivations." Second, I will consider if British beliefs change at an opportune strategic time. If they are thinking wishfully, then it is hard to explain why they suddenly change estimates exactly when my theory predicts they would. If they are buying time, then they will wait until the Soviets are vulnerable to enact competition. But we must question the logic of this mechanism if British perceptions change in response to Stalin's costly actions, and this shift in estimates triggers competition.

Another group argues that diplomacy can persuade Defenders because of social and inter-personal properties of face-to-face encounters (Holmes, 2018; Parks et al., 1996). Building on these insights, others claim that these trusting impressions persist even as Challengers take costly military actions because elites succumb to selective attention (Yarhi-Milo, 2014). The selective attention hypotheses holds that senior leaders are especially susceptible to both of these biases. Outside of theories about diplomacy, scholars believe that leaders remain trustful because of motivated reasoning (Barnett, 1986), or voice opinions that they do not hold because of bureaucratic incentives (Schweller, 1992).

There are two ways I can parse my theory from social theories of effective diplomacy and select attention on particular indicators. First, I argue that diplomacy is valuable absent face-to-face encounters and the vivid images that they create. I expect that diplomacy matters not only for the British elites who meet Stalin in person, but those who read reports about the meeting. Thus, it supports my mechanism if British elites who stay home are persuaded by written cables that describe diplomatic encounters with Stalin. Second, these scholars emphasize impressions derived from a diplomat's tone, temperament, and physiological cues. In contrast, I argue that diplomats rely on the content of what is said in meetings. Thus, diplomatic persuasion is not enough to support my theory. It would not support my theory if elite reports only read "I met with Stalin and I just don't trust him because I got a bad impression." If my theory is correct, I would need to see reports that read "I met with Stalin and I just don't trust him because his actions and words cannot be reconciled with a principle that implies he holds limited aims" or alternatively, "I met with Stalin and I trust him because there is lots he could have said to explain his behavior, but he chose to declare a specific, limited principle to explain his motives."

6.1.4 The Aggregation Problem: Individual Evidence and State-Level Decision-Making

The preceding discussion highlights an important disconnect between any structural theory (including my own) and evidence in diplomatic history. Ultimately, my theory is about how states process information, form beliefs, and behave. But diplomatic archives describe individual perceptions.

If all individuals processed information as I predict, then state-level decisions should follow. However, if not all individuals think in this way, or if organizational processes mediate the expert assessments that decision-makers observe, then the most important decision-makers may reach systematically biased assessments. Indeed, there is overwhelming evidence that aggregation is complicated, and biases can creep in.

Even if I find evidence of individual accounts that supports my theory, how do I know that I am focusing on the opinions that matter given how states make choices? I use the Anglo-Soviet case to illuminate how organizational and psychological processes influenced national-level assessments and policies. As we shall see, organizational processes and individual level beliefs (not biases) played an important role in how the British assessed the Soviet Union's intentions. However, the evidence suggests that my theory forms a rational baseline around which these assessments fell. The military was usually more pessimistic than the Foreign Office. But both organizations updated their beliefs about what the Soviets wanted based on an assessment of whether Soviet words and deeds were consistent with a principle. Elite assessments were distributed around what I believe was the rational baseline. As we shall see, some analysts became concerned about Soviet intentions before others. However, all use the same assessment framework: Are Stalin's actions consistent with his declared security motivations. Disagreements follow based on different interpretations of Soviet security needs. I further show that institutional features reduced cognitive biases in the decision-making process leading to rational decision-making in the aggregate.

To capture the complete assessment process in Britain, I examine reports, minutes or other assessments of Soviet intentions that reached the War Cabinet. Thus, I analyze the assessment process of members of the Post-Hostilities Planning Committee (a military organization), the Chiefs of Staff, the Joint Intelligence Committee, the War Cabinet, and the Foreign Office.

I analyze the assessments from several foreign policy experts in Britain, not just the prime minister's assessments, to properly capture state-level decision-making. The broader approach is necessary because foreign policy institutions in Britain ensured that many actors were involved in the assessment and decision-making process. It was common, for example, for the prime minister to submit his foreign correspondence to the War Cabinet for approval. On several occasions, the War Cabinet overruled the prime minister's position leading the prime minister to change his statements. On rare occasions, when time was critical, Churchill made unilateral decisions (e.g., the text of his speech following Hitler's invasion of the Soviet Union was not approved by the War Cabinet). But he apologized for breaking with the norm of deliberation within the War Cabinet. Before high-level meetings with Stalin, Churchill sought approval for talking points and the limits of what concessions he could make. When Stalin's demands exceeded what was authorized by the War Cabinet, Churchill often refrained from striking deals.

There were two ways that analysts below the most senior ministers influenced state-level assessments. Sometimes senior decision-makers tasked specialist sub-committees to analyze critical questions. The War Cabinet asked multiple sub-committees across intelligence, defense, and foreign policy (and mixed committees) to analyze Soviet intentions. These sub-committees conducted independent research, then submitted their reports to the War Cabinet. The War Cabinet debated the different assessments and approved a conjoined summary for the prime minister. Specialists from these sub-committees accompanied the prime minister and foreign minister on international visits. Other times senior decision-makers believed they had sufficient knowledge to make an assessment on their own. Before they acted on their assessment, they circulated memorandum for sub-committees to comment on. As we shall see, lower-level analysts were fiercely critical when they believed their superiors were wrong. In what follows I analyze one case where the foreign minister reversed his opinion based on a single memorandum from an assistant deputy undersecretary (four ranks below him).

Not all analysts had access to all information and each brought in their own specialized training and experience to their assessment. The prime minister and foreign minister understood these limitations. Nevertheless, institutional features ensured that the British assessment process reflected a weighted consensus model. The prime minister and foreign minister were influenced by their subordinates and often formed their opinions based on reporting they received.

Throughout the analysis, I ask and answer three questions that take the aggregation process seriously:

1. When and why do individuals update their beliefs across time?
2. At any point in time do different individuals or organizations have different assessments?
3. How do assessments at the advisor level affect assessments at the head of state level?

6.1.5 Sources

I read over 5,000 declassified cables, minutes, memoranda, and other primary source documents. These documents were available through the online British National Archives, published British cables and intelligence reports, and three private archives accessed by subscription. I also read on Anglo-American correspondence made public in the Foreign Relations of the United States and National Security Archives at the Library of Congress.

I located 121 distinct assessments of Soviet intentions written by a variety of military, intelligence, and foreign policy analysts (and the prime ministers).[70] In many cases, I observed concurrent memoranda that showed precisely who agreed with which assessment. These memos were extremely helpful because they were the forum through which analysts critiqued each others' positions and explained their reasoning processes.[71]

I also read secondary sources including nine diaries and fifteen memoirs from analysts who either partook in the assessment process or observed the prime minister and foreign minister during critical periods. These personal notes allow me to corroborate the primary source records with each analyst's private feelings. I also read several newspaper reports, speeches, and conference proceedings that provide context to events.

Finally, I read approximately thirty history books on Anglo-Soviet relations to make sure that my inferences matched the conventional wisdom in history. Corroborating my account with history books ensures that I did not unfairly weigh one set of analysts over another in my

---

[70] Many additional documents made implicit assessments of Soviet intentions.

[71] Primary sources are cited throughout the text. Where I found sources in digitized national collections, I used the reference system to refer to the series that the document was from. Where a coding reference includes multiple documents I also include a date to help a reader locate the document. For primary sources reprinted in books and periodicals, I cite the book that I located the source from. A complete list of abbreviations is located in Appendix E online.

assessment. I consulted history books that described state-level and organizational-level assessments. I also consulted books that focus on the impact of specific events, such as the Yalta Conference, or the Iran Crisis, on British assessments of Soviet intentions.

6.2 The Onset to the Moment of Clarity

British suspicions of the Soviet Union date back to the latter's founding. Haslam (2021, chs 1 and 2) chronicles how, in the years after the 1917 October Revolution, Lenin and Trotsky openly called for global revolution, and even funded communist agitators across Europe and Asia. However, even Haslam acknowledges that Britain did not seriously consider Russia a major threat because Russia was embattled with domestic conflict, and lacked the military and economic capacity to project power. Further, the identity and direction of Soviet foreign policy was not yet set.[72] By the mid-1920s, Trotsky was ousted by the Comintern, and Stalin, who was known to be far less interested in global revolution, was thrust to power.[73] The Foreign Office inferred from this domestic jockeying that the Comintern may not have held as strong an interest in global revolution as the leaders of the October Revolution did.

As World War Two approached, Stalin moved closer to Hitler, signed the Molotov–Ribbentrop Pact and invaded Poland. During this period there was concern among certain British elites that Stalin would align with Germany. However, British elites did not know if Stalin's maneuvers served an intrinsic motivation to expand territory, or an instrumental need to offset the German threat.[74] Britain was also eased by Soviet domestic dynamics. As Neilson (1993, abstract) argues "the purges in the Red Army in 1937 made the British feel that Soviet military strength had declined, making the appeasement of Germany the best course of action."

As a result of these complications, and given the pressing need to examine German intentions, Britain did not seriously analyze Soviet long-term intentions as a threat to their global interests during the 1930s, or even during the early years of World War Two.[75]

June 22 1941 marked a critical point in World War Two for Anglo-Soviet relations. In the early hours of the morning, German forces launched

---

[72] Gorodetsky (1994); Pons (2012, pp. xii, 54–70)

[73] James (1937, pp. 178–182).

[74] Carley (1999), Churchill (1948, p. 449).

[75] Starting my analysis following the Molotov–Ribbentrop Pact in 1938, or Neilson (1993, p. 207) turning point in 1934 would lengthen the chapter, but not change my findings.

Operation Barbarossa: a full-scale invasion against the Soviet Union. In a speech to cheering crowds on the same day, Hitler declared war against Russia and promised to capture Moscow.[76]

Berlin was not the only place where people were cheering. In London, Prime Minister Churchill was so excited that he sent his foreign minister, Anthony Eden, cigars.[77] For Churchill, Hitler's actions had forged a common Anglo-Soviet cause that would change the war. Churchill was now confident that the Soviets would join the British side.[78]

Within hours Churchill's intuition was confirmed. The Soviet Ambassador in London, M. Maisky, informed British Foreign Minister Anthony Eden that a state of war existed between the USSR and Germany.[79] Under instruction from Stalin, Maisky requested military and economic support.[80] Stalin proposed both an Anglo-Soviet military alliance against German aggression and a political alliance that would maintain their friendly relations after the war.[81]

In Churchill's view, British interests were served by aiding any country that fought against Germany. The Soviet Union was no exception. The question was not *whether* Britain would help, but how much? Would Britain provide simply military aid to sustain the Red Army against the Germans, or would their ties cover political issues as well? To answer the political question the War Cabinet would need to evaluate what Stalin wanted in the postwar settlement.[82]

Given my scope conditions, Operation Barbarossa (1941) is an important moment because it marks the first time that British policy-makers actively debated Soviet *strategic* intentions as a global power anticipating their likely strength in the postwar period. Although the outcome of the war was far from certain, British policy-makers realized that continental Europe would most likely be left with just one powerful state at war's end. France had already fallen and the war between the Soviets and the Germans was all-consuming. If the Soviets defeated the German military, there would be no power in Europe to match them. The British realized that if the Soviets emerged from the fighting victorious, they would

---

[76] Translation published in Hitler (1941).

[77] Kitchen (1986, p. 56).

[78] Berthon and Potts (2007, pp. 82–84).

[79] N3056/3014/38; N3108/3/38; WM(41)62; WM/41/67.

[80] N3138/3014/38; N3260/78/38.

[81] N3108/3/38; WM(41)62; WM/41/67.

[82] In the meantime, Churchill commits to send Stalin supplies through the exchange of personal notes. See: N3955/3955/38.

be battle-hardened, unopposed, and highly industrialized. Although war would ravage them, it would not be long before they would regain enough strength to dominate Europe if they wanted to.

6.2.1 Theoretical Expectations for British Assessments at the Onset

Scholars have proposed that decision-makers use several specific indicators to infer a Challenger's motives at the onset of a great power rivalry. According to most of these theories, the information that the British had about the Soviet Union in June 1941 should have led them to deeply mistrust Stalin's postwar intentions. Realists and rationalist scholars argue that when one state expands its military and uses force to take territory it signals aggressive intentions.[83] If policy-makers thought the way that realists expect, then the British should have been concerned about Stalin. In 1939, Stalin and Hitler formed an alliance and jointly invaded Poland. Russia then annexed Lithuania, Latvia, and Estonia in early 1940. Russia coerced oil-rich Bessarabia and Northern Bukovina from Romania in June 1940. In 1941, Stalin further demanded territorial concessions from Finland. When the Finns refused, Stalin invaded. As war raged in Finland, Stalin turned to the Baltic States. If military spending and territorial ambition are a sign of greedy intentions, then these actions should have deeply alarmed the British.

Other scholars suggest that regime type or opposing political ideologies are a source of concern.[84] Similarly, Challengers with limited electoral competition,[85] autocratic governments,[86] and small selectorates[87] are at greater risk of militarized conflict. The Soviet Union was an authoritarian, communist state. Communist writings during Lenin's time explicitly call for the overthrow of Western capitalist countries. The communist party in Britain was openly subversive of the British government and the War Cabinet worried about links between the Kremlin and British communists.[88] Thus, if regime type or ideology played an important role in reaching an assessment, then the War Cabinet would have mistrusted Stalin.

Arguments based in psychological processes suggest that policy-makers rely on vivid images and recent historical experiences to make judgments.[89]

---

[83] Jervis (1978), Waltz (1979), Edelstein (2002).
[84] Haas (2005).
[85] Schultz (1999).
[86] Doyle (2005).
[87] de Mesquita et al. (1999).
[88] CAB/66/19/17 Oct 19, 1941. Note by the Secretary of the War Cabinet E. E. Bridges.
[89] Jervis (1989a).

Alternatively, decision-makers may turn to historical analogies to form assessments.[90] In both cases, the obvious comparison is between Nazi Germany and Soviet Russia. The image of Hitler was fresh in British minds. If British policy-makers were biased by vivid images, recent experiences and historical analogies then the rise of Stalin should have conjured images of Hitler. These images should also have led the British to a pessimistic assessment of Soviet postwar intentions.

Similarly, the most senior foreign policy elites in Britain rose to power because they opposed cooperation with Hitler. Those in favor of Neville Chamberlain's appeasement were purged from the War Cabinet in 1939. Churchill was notoriously outspoken about his mistrust for Hitler from 1937. Part of the reason Churchill appointed Eden as foreign minister was because he had resigned from the same position in protest of Chamberlain's policies. One might argue that these powerful elites were therefore predisposed to cynicism. If true, then they should have erred on the side of mistrust.[91]

For all of these reasons, the major arguments across political science would suggest that the British War Cabinet should have been deeply mistrustful of Soviet postwar intentions at the outset. If the British leaders thought the way that either realists or those that emphasize vivid images, regime type, or organizational processes expect them to, then we should observe the most senior policy-makers quickly conclude that the Soviet Union had malign long-term intentions.

6.2.2 Assessments of Soviet Intentions June–November 1941

Despite these factors, senior British policy-makers were decidedly uncertain about Soviet intentions in 1941. In a BBC broadcast during October 1939, Churchill noted with frustration that "I cannot forecast to you the action of Russia. It is a riddle wrapped in a mystery inside an enigma." Through 1941, Churchill believed that a "fog of confusion and uncertainty"[92] surrounded British assessments of the Soviet Union.

Below the prime minister, there was wider variance in the assessments of Soviet intentions. At one extreme, some analysts thought Stalin could

---

[90] Khong (1992).

[91] Churchill and Vansittart are excellent examples of this. Both were given considerably more influence after appeasement failed and both were staunch opponents of it. Vansittart wrote "I am convinced that we have got to aim at the destruction of both Nazism and Communism in this war ... the Soviets have been a bloody fraud from the start." Memo from Robert Vansittart. FO 371, 2484529 Mar 1940.

[92] Gilbert (1983, p. 50).

not be trusted. In June, the Chief of General Staff for the British Expeditionary Force, Lieutenant-General Henry Pownall wrote in his diary: "I avoid the expression Allies; for the Russians are a dirty lot of murdering thieves themselves, and double crossers of the deepest dye."[93]

At the other extreme, some thought that Russia was fundamentally peaceful. The Ambassador to Moscow, Stafford Cripps attributed Russia's secretive behavior and military aggression to British deeds. He wrote to Eden,

Russian suspicions are much longer dated than you would seem to imply. They have increased, during the last twenty years by the atmosphere of political antagonism which, started with the intervention by us on behalf of the White Russians... we are treating the Soviet Government without trust and as inferiors rather than as trusted allies. This attitude is similar to that which we have adopted ever since the revolution, and has been the cause of great resentment by the Soviets, and is, I believe, liable to discourage them in their efforts to hold on.[94]

Cripps believed that the Russians would peacefully integrate in the post-war world order and it was Britain's task to convince Stalin of her benign intentions.

The balance of opinions lay in the middle. In a comprehensive report on Soviet intentions, A. R. Dew[95] wrote that Russian foreign policy was driven by "the preservation of Russian interests in the Baltic and Black Seas. We may thus expect demands for Russian access to the Persian Gulf, for a revision of the Montreux Convention, possibly for the establishment of Russian bases in Norway and in Finland and the Baltic States to ensure the security of Leningrad and Kronstadt." Several, including Eden, concurred with Dew's findings. A separate report from the Foreign Office that gained support in the War Cabinet concluded that "they want us to approve the annexation of the Baltic States and Eastern Poland, and to help them secure special rights with regard to Finland, the Dardanelles and access to the Persian Gulf, and an ice-free port in northern Norway."[96]

Others believed that Stalin was interested in securing warm-water ports and was therefore interested in concessions in Turkey. Others still believed Stalin's interests would converge with Tzarist Russia's historical ambitions of power politics in Asia.[97] As a result, Stalin would seek territory in Iran,

---

[93] Quoted in Beaumont (1980, p. 26).

[94] CAB66/19/45. No. 37.

[95] Dew was stationed at Moscow at the time. He died en route to the Yalta Conference.

[96] FO 371/29472.

[97] FO 371/248/4529 Mar 1940. Vansittart was deeply mistrustful of Soviet intentions and thought appeasement would fail.

the Caucasus, the Baltic States, Central Asia and, possibly, India.[98] Finally, a group believed that the spread of global communism motivated Russian foreign policy. Within this group, some thought Stalin wanted to expand the Soviet empire as far as he could, others thought world communism implied Stalin would subvert democracy in Asia and Europe wherever possible.

Although the conclusions of British assessments varied wildly, they shared four features. First, each assessment was based on a theory about the principle that motivated Stalin. Different British elites proposed that Stalin could be motivated by spreading communism, security from foreign threat, access to ports and waterways, or Tzarist ambitions.

Second, each time an analyst described a principle, that analyst explained several specific issues and territories that Stalin would want if Stalin was motivated by that principle. They could do this because each analyst had a working understanding of Russian history and culture, and used their understanding to connect each motivation with tangible objectives. As a result of this process, each analyst suggested that Stalin would seek out specific issues and territories.

Looking across the different assessments, there was variation in which and how many issues and territories Stalin would seek. This validates a critical assumption of my theory: the War Cabinet was exposed to a handful of specific assessments about Stalin's motives; and each assessment implied a different set of territories. As a result, the War Cabinet did not know which, or how many, issues Stalin would pursue.

Third, each assessment was made with low confidence. All came with important caveats that there was not enough information to truly know what Stalin wanted. Many held the view that both extreme accounts were possible. The prime minister's view was that it was possible that Stalin had benign long-term intentions that were largely complementary with British interests (despite some disagreements). As a result, he held out hope that long-term Anglo-Soviet cooperation was possible.

Fourth, many explicitly stated that they could not make a more confident assessment because Stalin had not revealed what his long-term intentions were. For example, when Dew asked rhetorically "What are Russian ideas on war aims and the post-war settlement and what kind of an agreement to be concluded at this stake will satisfy them?" His answer began with the caveat, "the Russians have been extremely reticent in defining their

[98] COS39/66. 6 Oct. 1939.

post-war ideas on war aims and the post war settlement."[99] He therefore had little confidence in his assessment.

Cripps similarly complained that it was "impossible to have any contacts with any Russians and thus to obtain any reliable information as to what is going on in the country."[100] Indeed, the British took the lack of Soviet communication so seriously that they were willing to tie military assistance to it. As the Secretary of the War Cabinet, Bridges instructed military commanders: "Although Russians are still being sticky about telling us their intentions and dispositions, and have not reacted to our offer of Staff Conversations, we must be in a position to give them a firm offer of assistance the moment they show signs of being more forthcoming."[101]

Correspondence between Churchill and Stalin in November 1941 demonstrates the toll this uncertainty was taking on Anglo-Soviet relations. Through September, Stalin had complained to Churchill that the limited British supplies caused grave concern in the Soviet Union about British long-term interests in Soviet success. Churchill offered, "In order to clear things up and to plan for the future I am ready to send General Wavell, the Commander-in-Chief in India, Persia and Iraq, to meet you."[102]

Churchill's offer focused on improving military understanding. Stalin's reply exposed a much deeper lack of knowledge:

I agree with you that we need clarity, which at the moment is lacking in relations between the U.S.S.R. and Great Britain. The unclarity is due to two circumstances: first, there is no definite understanding between our two countries concerning war aims and plans for the post-war organisation of peace; secondly, there is no treaty between the U.S.S.R. and Great Britain on mutual military aid in Europe against Hitler... Until understanding is reached on these two main points, not only will there be no clarity in Anglo-Soviet relations, but, if we are to speak frankly, there will be no mutual trust.[103]

The lack of progress in Anglo-Soviet diplomacy, coupled with a series of spats over military supplies, had led Anglo-Soviet relations to deteriorate. To salvage the relationship, foreign minister Anthony Eden was sent to Moscow to improve relations. Eden realized that "we ought to be examining the question of our post-war relations with the Soviet Government

---

[99] FO371/29472, N5679/3014/38.

[100] N4070/3014/38; N6901/78/38.

[101] CAB99/19/47.

[102] From Churchill to Stalin, Nov. 7, 1941. Published as document 19 in Ministry of Foreign Affairs (1957a).

[103] From Stalin to Churchill, Nov. 8, 1941. Published as document 20 in Ministry of Foreign Affairs (1957b).

as far as it is possible to do so at the present stage of the war. We certainly are prepared… to continue collaboration with the Soviet Government after the war is over for the purpose of working out the terms of the new settlement of Europe."[104] To that end, he had given the subject of Soviet intentions considerable study before embarking on his journey. Yet his extensive research was fruitless. On the eve of his visit to Moscow he still could not reach an assessment of Soviet intentions because he had "not received and explanation from Stalin as to what he himself has in mind when he proposes a post-war alliance."[105] Consistent with my theory, and the assessments of War Cabinet colleagues, Eden believed that conversations with Stalin could help clarify Soviet intentions. The key piece of information was a statement from Stalin himself that explained what Soviet intentions were.

In what follows, I argue that Eden's visit was important for Anglo-Soviet relations. However, historians have not given it much attention. The likely reason is that a week before Eden left for Moscow, Anglo-Soviet relations were overshadowed by Japan's attack on Pearl Harbor. The gravamen of research on British diplomacy focuses on the US's entry into the war, and Churchill's impromptu visit to Washington.[106] Another reason to overlook it is that no tangible product – such as a pact, communiqué – came from Eden's visit. Eden's Moscow visit is mainly discussed by Eden's biographers who are mainly concerned with Eden's performance, and the limits on what he was allowed to offer Stalin.[107] My interest is in an overlooked effect of Eden's visit on British thinking: how it shifted perceptions of Soviet intentions. Indeed, this context presents a tough test of my theory. If select attention had strong influence over estimates (Yarhi-Milo, 2014), then the cables Eden wrote regarding his visit should not represent vivid images for the War Cabinet, who were intensely focused on Pearl Harbor and Churchill's travels. Thus, we might expect no shift in British estimates of Soviet strategic intentions.

6.2.3 Stalin Explains Soviet Intentions

On the first day of Eden's visit to Moscow, in the very first meeting with Stalin and Molotov, Stalin blurted out his postwar interests. By Eden's recollection, "At my first conversation with M. Stalin and M. Molotov on the

[104] Prem 3/395/6, Nov. 10, 1941.
[105] Ibid.
[106] Dutton (1997, p. 189).
[107] Rothwell (1992, p. 62).

16th of December... M. Stalin set out in some detail what he considered should be the post-war territorial frontiers in Europe, and in particular his ideas regarding the treatment of Germany."[108] Eden then recounted Stalin's detailed interests in Europe which included the dismemberment of Germany, Soviet control of Polish territory up to the Curzon line, and control over Baltic States, Finland, and Bessarabia.

It is worth noting the gravity of what Stalin was asking for. Stalin made clear he wanted to permanently take territory of six sovereign states, expand military bases through Europe and Asia, and permanently dismember Germany – the only counterbalance on the continent. His statements left no doubt: The Soviet Union had revisionist intentions. Of special concern for the British was Stalin's Polish demands. Under an Anglo-Polish treaty, Britain entered the war in defense of Polish borders and the Polish Government in exile operated out of London. To make certain that Stalin really wanted territorial concessions from Poland, the next day Cripps asked Stalin (with Eden present), "Could we know whether the phrase 'having full regard to the interests of the U.S.S.R. in the restoration of frontiers,' means the recognition by us of the U.S.S.R. frontiers of 1941?"[109] Stalin replied, "Yes, it does mean the recognition of the right of the U.S.S.R to their 1941 borders."[110]

Stalin did not just make demands, he justified them: "We must have these [frontiers] for our security and safety... if you decline to do this it looks as if you were creating the possibility for a dismemberment of the Soviet Union." The following day Eden made clear that he did "fully realize that you [Stalin] want security on your north-western frontier."[111]

In the end, Eden was not authorized to make postwar concessions.[112] The issues Stalin raised had not been studied and it would take considerable time to do so. Furthermore, Stalin's demands directly contradicted Britain's commitment to the United States. Under the Atlantic Charter, Britain had committed not to settle postwar borders until Germany had surrendered. In the end, the Atlantic Charter provided Eden cover against Stalin's repeated demands for settling postwar frontiers. Eden was able to argue that he could not commit to any postwar settlement without extensive discussion with the United States. No agreement was signed during Eden's visit and both parties agreed that M. Molotov would visit London in May 1942 to conclude the negotiation.

---

[108] Prem 3/394/3 Dec. 18, 1941.
[109] Ibid.
[110] Ibid.
[111] WP(42)8; N109/5/38(1842).
[112] Rothwell (1992, p. 62).

6.2.4 Assessment of Soviet Intentions Following Eden's Visit

Following Eden's visit, there was a clear change in how British analysts evaluated Soviet intentions. Most notably, security entered the debate as the primary motivation for Stalin's postwar aims. Many policy-makers who before Eden's visit were reserved, now mentioned security explicitly as Stalin's most likely motivation. Even many of those who began mistrustful of Soviet postwar aims now described Soviet behavior as in service of "(a) their own victory in the war; and (b) their own security after the war."[113]

Eden himself increased his confidence that security motivated Stalin. In a cable to Viscount Halifax, then the Ambassador to the United States, Eden outlined what he believed should be Britain's response to Stalin's demands:

We might say that, while we cannot agree now to restoration of 1941 frontiers, we and the United States could immediately give assurances that on grounds of Soviet security we would support, when the time comes, a demand by the Soviet Government to establish. Soviet bases in territories contiguous to Russia and especially on the Baltic and Black Seas from which her security might be threatened... [These] offers are based, as any offers clearly must be, on requirements of Russian *security* for which Soviet Union have been striving ever since 1917 Revolution in order that Soviet Government may be enabled to complete unfinished social and economic experiments within Russia without danger of foreign intervention or war.[114]

Eden justified his new assessment.

It must be remembered that Stalin might have asked for much more, e.g. control of the Dardanelles, spheres of influence in the Balkans, one-sided imposition on Poland of Russo-Polish frontier, access to Persian Gulf, access to Atlantic involving accession of Norwegian territory. Stalin's present demand it is true, may not be final, but he may later be in a position to enforce a claim to some or all of these, and we and United States Government would be in stronger position to assert our views if we have established precedent of tripartite agreements in regard to post-war arrangements, and if Soviet Government have not decided to go ahead without regard to our views owing to our giving an entirely negative reply to present demands. Moreover, from strategic point of view, it may well be sound that Russia should be established once again in the Baltic so as to be able better to dispute with Germany the naval command of that sea than was the case since 1918.

Eden's reasoning was presented to and affirmed by the War Cabinet, including Churchill.[115]

---

[113] FO 371/32/876 Feb. 12, 1942.

[114] CAB/66/21/49 (Draft 2) Telegram to Viscount Halifax (emphasis is Eden's).

[115] In his response, Halifax noted that much of Stalin's fears were most likely exaggerated and the threat to Soviet security did not warrant such extensive demands. Yet he acknowledged that Stalin probably held those fears genuinely and accepted security as Stalin's motivation. See WP(42)69; WM(42)18; N798/5/38; N1024/5/38;

There are four important points to Eden's reasoning that follow directly from my theory. First, Eden referred explicitly to Stalin's diplomacy as the reason he focused on security. Second, he recognized that Stalin's talk was cheap: Stalin could easily have lied and there was a concern he would ask for more as he grew stronger. Third, Eden's reasoning for trusting Stalin was based on what Stalin could have asked for but did not. Eden noted that Stalin's omissions made it difficult to adjust claims in the future. Finally, there is no mention of Eden's impressions of Stalin or Stalin's character based on Eden's personal assessment. I have found no evidence in this document or any other that suggests Eden's revised assessment had anything to do with the tone of Stalin's request. Rather, Eden based his assessment on the content of what Stalin said, or didn't say.

The focus on security is further confirmed in how the British reasoned through their counteroffers to Stalin's demands. Halifax, who had not met Stalin at this point, "recognizes the justice of Stalin's claim for security," but noted that it was "difficult at this moment to take a final decision..."[116] on postwar frontiers. As a result, he asked the War Cabinet to devise counterproposals that could guarantee Soviet postwar security without ceding territory from Poland and elsewhere. One suggestion was to divide Germany into zones of occupation such that the Soviet Union would have no one to protect their western border from, and therefore no need for a security buffer.[117]

Following the same line of reasoning, Eden offered Molotov a twenty-year security pact between Britain and the Soviet Union as part of the Anglo-Soviet treaty. In pushing the plan, Eden told Molotov, "Though the treaty did not deal with vexed questions such as frontiers, it was obvious that, if we were to offer a twenty-year pact, it must be our desire that Russia, as our ally, be strong and secure."[118]

6.2.5 Alternative Explanations

Eden's visit marked a clear change in British assessment of Soviet postwar intentions. Up until Eden's visit, British elites were, on average, deeply uncertain about Stalin's postwar intentions. During Eden's visit, Stalin

N1279/5/38; N1526/5/38; T352/2/402 (Churchill Papers); N1300/5/38; T395/2/402 (Churchill Papers); N1395/5/38; N1653/5/38; WM(42)37, C.A. for extensive discussion about Stalin's intentions relating to security between the War Cabinet, Halifax, and Roosevelt.

[116] CAB66/22/26.

[117] N2646/5/48; WP(42)198 Revise; WP(42)218.

[118] N2901/5/38. See also N2902/5/28; N2903/5/28; WM(42)66 C.A; N2904/5/38; N2946/5/38; WP(42)21.

explicitly stated his foreign policy was motivated by the security of the Soviet Union. He claimed that the concessions he demanded were all in service of this goal. Indeed, his demands were large. His requests violated the sovereignty of at least five nation-states, seemed to contradict the Atlantic Charter and called for the complete dismemberment of Germany. Yet the British found them to be somewhat credible. After Eden's visit, British officials focused their analysis on whether or not Stalin wanted security.

The initial uncertainty is difficult to explain for realists. They expect that British decision-makers to immediately viewed Stalin's prewar behavior through the lens of potential security motives. The fact that decision-makers debated a variety of alternative limited aims is inconsistent with realist thinking. This is especially unusual in this case because security was a plausible claim Stalin could have made. Even more remarkably, there was a clear shift following a diplomatic encounter. Realists cannot explain why years of costly military behavior did not affect British thinking whereas as single high-level diplomatic event did. Thus for realists, the case should have ended here. To be clear, some of the evidence does support aspects of realist logic as it relates to the spiral model. As I describe in a moment, British elites worried that Stalin did not trust them, appreciated the logic of two-sided trust and engaged in confidence building measures. Consistent with both realism and my account, these measures helped with instrumental cooperation during World War Two. However, they were not enough to convince British elites that Stalin was a security-seeker. Rather, they only lay the ground-work for the qualitative inferences dynamic that I describe.

Even if British assessments of Soviet intentions changed after Eden visited Moscow, it does not necessarily follow that the reason is rational. Here I consider two alternative explanations for why Eden's meeting could have altered British assessment of Soviet intentions. First, it is possible that World War Two generated organizational incentives for the British to trust the Russians. The British faced a formidable German adversary and were committed to helping the Russians erode Hitler's strength. By July, British public opinion strongly favored the Russians. In a poll conducted in August 1941, the British public were asked "Do you feel that Britain has taken full advantage offered by the German attack on Russia?" The replies, read by War Cabinet, were: Has taken 29 percent; Has not taken 49 percent; and the rest did not know. Indeed, it may be that the British were looking for ways to justify an alliance with Russia and Stalin's diplomacy gave them one.[119]

---

[119] Woodward (1970b, pp. 23–24).

Although plausible, this argument ignores several diplomatic and military confidence building measures between November 1939 and November 1941. If the British wanted an excuse to trust Stalin, any of these earlier events should have altered their assessment.

Britain and the Soviet Union engaged in several joint military and intelligence exercises. Most notably the foreign-imposed regime change in Iran required Anglo-Russian political, military, and intelligence coordination. The status of force agreement (SOF) discussed Soviet and British areas of operations and occupation rights. However, it was impossible for either side to hold the other accountable to this agreement and there was a real risk that the Soviets would exploit opportunities to advance further than agreed upon. The Soviets honored their commitment.[120] Both Eden and Churchill thought the incident was a huge success that improved Anglo-Soviet relations. Eden wrote, "Personally I consider the Persian affair to have been a neat piece of joint military and diplomatic action. In its way it is a minor classic."[121]

Similarly, diplomatic relations between Russian and British military and intelligence services improved as a result of joint operations. In 1941, the Special Operations Executive (SOE) sent Colonel Hill as part of the military mission to Moscow. Hill established a joint operations agreement between the SOE and People's Commissariat for Internal Affairs (NKVD) in September 1941 that governed joint Anglo-Soviet clandestine operations until the war's end.[122] British special operations also dropped Soviet spies behind German lines and commanded a joint Anglo-Soviet special operations force to destroy German-operated oil fields.

Furthermore, the British and the Soviets held high-level diplomatic visits that culminated in several formal agreements. The Minister of Supply, Lord Beaverbrook, visited Moscow in October 1941 accompanied by the American Special Envoy W. Averell Harriman. During this visit the British and Americans committed to sustained supplies for the Soviet Union's war effort. Further, Beaverbrook reported a very positive opinion of Stalin. A notable feature of these meetings was that these British officials never discussed Stalin's postwar intentions. Instead, they constrained their conversation to military and logistical matters.[123]

---

[120] Ibid., pp. 23–27.
[121] Prem 3, 237-2, Eden to PM Sep 9 1941. Quoted in Kitchen (1986, p. 94).
[122] FO 800/301.
[123] Harriman and Abel (1975).

Finally, they institutionalized Anglo-Soviet communication. Immediately following Operation Barbarossa, Churchill and Stalin began direct correspondence. In the year prior to Operation Barbarossa, Churchill addressed just two notes directly to Stalin, and Stalin sent nothing in return. In July 1941 alone, they exchanged nine notes.[124]

Yet as we saw in the previous section, British assessments during this period were consistently uncertain. None of these events proved decisive to structure the debate about Soviet intentions or increase (decrease) optimism about cooperation. If Britain wanted to trust Stalin because it was convenient, then any one of these events would have provided sufficient cover to do so. The timing of the shift in British assessments strongly suggests that something about Eden's meeting with Stalin shifted the balance that differed from other confidence building measures.

A second possible explanation comes from social theories of diplomacy (Holmes, 2018; Yarhi-Milo, 2014). It is possible that Eden overestimated his ability to read Stalin's mannerism during in-person meetings. If true, Eden would have erroneously relied on his conversation with Stalin to form impressions about Soviet intentions. How states form beliefs is likely multicausal. But there are three reasons to believe that my theory provides a significant explanation over social theories. First, Eden's visit had a large and immediate impact on all high-level British beliefs. Face-to-face theories or select attention cannot explain why Halifax, Churchill, Permanent Under-Secretary of State for Foreign Affairs Cadogan, and others adjusted their assessment following a meeting that they did not attend.

Second, this was not the first meeting between Soviet and British elites. As discussed, Lord Beaverbrook visited Moscow in October 1941 accompanied by W. Averell Harriman. The British thought these high-level meetings were essential to a frank exchange of views and they helped develop rapport between these most senior elites. Indeed, Beaverbrook developed a strong positive impression of Stalin. He recalled one discussion where he and Stalin joked about Rudolf Hess's visit to London among other anecdotes that demonstrated Stalin's good nature. Yet these favorable impressions did not translate into an assessment of Soviet intentions. Remarkably, Eden's visit had more of an impact on Beaverbrook's assessment than Beaverbrook's own meetings did. The missing piece was that Beaverbrook never discussed Soviet intentions with Stalin. As a result, his personal interactions with Stalin provided insufficient information to evaluate Soviet intentions.

---

[124] Ministry of Foreign Affairs (1957b).

Finally, it is worth considering the impression Stalin made on Churchill through the exchange of heated cables. Stalin chastized Churchill on November 7, 1941. The message left Churchill so outraged that he threatened to cut off communication entirely. It took a private visit by Maisky to resolve the dispute.[125] Maisky, speaking in an unofficial capacity, told Churchill that Stalin was under extreme pressure and did not mean his harsh tone.[126] Yet these strong negative impressions had no effect on Churchill's assessments of Soviet intentions. A cable from Eden describing a costless diplomatic encounter did.

6.2.6 Inference

Initial assessments of Stalin's motives confirm the basic assumptions of my theory. The War Cabinet heard five different assessments about what Stalin's motives could have been. Each individual assessment started with a theory about the principle that motivated Stalin's foreign policy, then extrapolated from that principle to make predictions about the specific issues and territories that Stalin would want in the long-term. Taken as a group, these assessments meant that British elites were both uncertain about which and how many issues Stalin wanted. Thus, they faced a reassurance problem and a coordination problem.

Consistent with my theory, British policy-makers made explicit that they were uncertain because Stalin had not explained his intentions. The fact that several assessments included this caveat makes clear how important Stalin's assurances were to understanding his intentions. As a result, they sought out a diplomatic meeting with Stalin because they thought Stalin's explanation would ease their uncertainty.

Eden's visit marked a clear change in the British assessment of Soviet postwar intentions. Before Eden's visit, British elites asked: What are Stalin's postwar intentions? After Eden's visit, the question became: Will Stalin be satisfied if we can guarantee Soviet security, or are his postwar intentions greater? Although there was still considerable uncertainty about whether Stalin was honest, there is no denying that security became the focus of assessments. I infer from the change that Stalin's disclosure of post-war intentions caused British policy-makers to update their beliefs about Soviet intentions.

---

[125] Maisky et al. (2016, pp. 404–408).
[126] N6540/3/38; N6586/3/38; Churchill Papers 395/17.C.

Stalin's statements to Eden had a clear impact on British assessments. Once Stalin explained that security motivated his foreign policy, British elites were more confident that they understood what Stalin wanted. Consistent with my theory, these elites believed that Stalin's most likely motive was what Stalin had disclosed (security). Further, they believed that if Stalin was not motivated by security that he probably had very aggressive intentions. They no longer considered other possible motives for limited intentions.

6.3 The Period of Consistency

By the end of 1943, the war had turned and the Allies were confident that victory, eventually, would come. The most pressing concern for the British was that in "ten years, in man-power, in economic resources, in industrial capacity she [Russia] will be immensely strong and, almost certainly, well organized."[127] The question was what to do about it? The answer again hinged on a detailed study of Soviet intentions. Thus, British officials throughout the war exerted "a continual attempt to interpret Russia policy, assess the real intentions of Stalin and the small governing oligarchy of the USSR and estimate the probabilities of an agreement."[128]

Indeed, the rapidly changing political environment of World War Two, and increased Anglo-Soviet communication, meant that regular assessments were required. Many events could have triggered revised British estimates of Soviet intentions. None of them did. Between Anthony Eden's visit to Moscow in 1941 and the Yalta Conference in February 1945, Britain viewed the Soviet Union largely as a "pragmatic and nationalist power, legitimately concerned with its own security."[129] During this period, the Soviets made territorial demands that violated the sovereignty of other states, undermined both democratic governments in Eastern Europe and the Western allies' attempts to build a world order, and brazenly violated several agreements that they had signed, the British "did not feel that Soviet territorial demands were likely to pose any serious threat to British interests."[130] One key theme in this period is that Stalin did not pursue policies that were inconsistent with security motives. These dogs that didn't

---

[127] FO381/43/335 Apr. 29, 1944.
[128] Woodward (1970b, p. 105).
[129] Kitchen (1986, p. 198).
[130] Ibid., Aldrich et al. (2014, ch. 4).

Table 6.1 *Theories of conditional effects*

Type of Bias	Mechanism at individual and organizational level	Potential consequences for British assessments of Soviet intentions
Systematic deviation	Ind: Risk-averse analysts are more pessimistic	Senior decision-makers take more risks $\implies$ more optimistic
	Org: Organizations that profit from fighting make alarmist predictions	The military will be more pessimistic than the FO
Ignores evidence	Ind: experts rely on what they know	Those with military training will privilege military events. Those with Russian specializations will rely on Russia's history more, etc
	Org: Organizations collect and disseminate certain types information	Same as individual
Failure to update	Ind: Discounts information that disconfirms world view, or searches for confirming evidence	Those that start of with a specific assessment will keep that assessment
	Org: Organizations reward members with similar assessments	Same as individual

bark provide evidence that events alone do not impact British assessments of Soviet intentions. If they did, the Cold War would have started long before the conference at Yalta.

I leverage this period of continuity to shed light on the aggregation process from individual assessments, through organizations, to the working knowledge of states. Scholars argue that individual and organizational biases lead states to make systematically biased assessments in three important ways summarized in Table 6.1. First, select incentives, recruitment processes, or risk aversion leads to assessments that are systematically more optimistic or pessimistic than what is rational given the available information. Second, expert knowledge or the organizational privilege of certain sources leads to evaluations that focus on a specific type of evidence and ignore the rest. Third, group-think or confirmation bias leads decision-makers to ignore any information that confounds their original assessment.

In my view, the first two types are largely consistent with my theory to the extent that they create deviance around an otherwise rational baseline. For example, the British military might always reach more pessimistic assessments than the Foreign Office about Soviet intentions. However, the average may be the rational assessment. It is possible that both deviate from the rational assessment but still update, and only update, when they observe inconsistent behavior. Related, the military may emphasize Soviet military behavior in their reporting, whereas the Foreign Office (FO) may emphasize diplomatic and domestic issues. This may explain why the military and FO update at different times and following different events. However, both still use the logic of consistency between words and deeds. What will be important to observe is how far different organizations and specific individuals vary. If, for example, the military is always pessimistic about Soviet intentions, no matter what information they observe, then I could not conclude my theory explains their assessment process. If, however, there is room for updating, then I would conclude that my theory may just provide a rational baseline for organizational theories.

The third type of bias is inconsistent with my theory, because it implies that decision-makers are unwilling to update or consider certain types of information at all. A key part of my theory is that decision-makers are willing to change their minds when confronted with new events.

Of course, the three types of biases may interact. Decision-makers may start off systematically pessimistic and, expecting the worst, not care about Soviet behavior that follows. Furthermore, it might be that Stalin's military behavior and economic and diplomatic behavior are fundamentally inconsistent. If the FO, or people with a certain type of training, were unwilling to consider military signals, then I would find that my theory did not apply to those people (but it may still apply to others).

It is important to realize that national security organizations are explicitly designed to weed out individual-level errors. Through the process of peer-review, classified debate in the War Cabinet, and redundant assessments, organizations may overcome biases at the individual level. Therefore, I may observe irrational individual behavior from time to time, but still observe rational state-level assessments.

I leverage this period of continuity to shed light on my theory in two new ways. First, I focus on variation in assessments based on organizational affiliation (defense, intelligence, and diplomatic). I find that the FO and the military do reach systematically different assessments of Soviet intentions. However, the difference is mainly in their recommendations for the policy implications from an assessment of Soviet intentions and not over the assessment of intentions itself. I find some evidence that the FO was more optimistic that the military over what the Soviets' long-term intentions were, but the variance is small, centered around what I consider to be the rational baseline to be, and still within the framework that my theory expects. Therefore, my theory is compatible with organizational bias theory as it explains the rational baseline from which different organizations will deviate.

Second, I analyze the only deviation from my theory that I find in the data. In April 1944, Anthony Eden temporarily adjusted his assessment of Soviet long-term intentions. This shift cannot be explained by my theory. Fortunately, Eden's deviant assessment corrected itself within a month and he returned to the rational baseline. I compare Eden's behavior to Churchill's over the same period to demonstrate the real limitations of existing theories of cognitive biases in explaining leadership decision-making.

6.3.1 Variance between the Foreign Office, Military, and Intelligence Services

Churchill recognized that assessments of Soviet intentions and British postwar policy may vary. To capture the diversity of these opinions, "within Whitehall a wealth of different organizations were created from 1943 onwards, designed to look towards the post-war world."[131] Among them, the Post-Hostilities Planning Subcommittee (PHPS) headed by members of the Joint Chiefs and other military advisors represented the military's view; and a working group in the FO represented the views of civilian foreign affairs experts.

Both groups studied Soviet postwar intentions,[132] and fiercely debated their positions to reach a joint assessment. The clear divide lay along organizational lines. "The difficulty underpinning them was the polar positions occupied by the FO and the military: in simple terms the former did not appreciate the idea of making plans against a current ally, whilst the latter though that the wartime rapprochement was a temporary aberration, and once war was over the alliance would crumble."[133]

The military argued for an assertive British foreign policy that included British occupation of all liberated territories and the total occupation of

---

[131] Goodman (2014, p. 121).
[132] Aldrich et al. (2014, p. 1).
[133] Goodman (2014, p. 121).

Germany. In February 1944, the PHPS circulated a paper to the War Cabinet that argued British forces should establish zones of occupation in all liberated Eastern European states. The goal was to guarantee these states could form stable, independent governments. The PHPS warned that

if South-Eastern Europe is left entirely to its own devices after this war, it is likely that the resultant anarchy will, in the long run, entail some action by some Great Power, and that if this means unilateral action by the Soviet Union there might be grave danger of a disruption of the Anglo-American-Soviet front. In any event, the possibility of a physical occupation of the whole area by Russia is not one which, on the whole, the United Kingdom could contemplate with equanimity.[134]

In the PHPS's view, the risk of Russian aggression was too great to ignore. The FO did not agree.[135] They issued a paper on Russian intentions and British postwar policy in response. Their paper suggested that, despite it being difficult to predict, that the Soviet Union's foreign policy will most likely be "in the future, as it has been in the past, the search for security against any Power or combination of Powers which might threaten her while she was organizing and developing her domain. In particular, after her narrow escape and tremendous losses she will fear German recovery."[136] The Foreign Office argued that "The Soviet Government is now clearly ready to give co-operation with the United States and Great Britain a trial." Therefore, it is imperative that Britain and the United States "do not appear to the Soviet authorities to wish to deprive Russia of the means of eliminating the menace from Germany (and Japan), do not appear to be supporting a combination against her and give reasonable consideration to her views."[137]

I concede that there was considerable disagreement along organizational lines. However, that disagreement was not centered around an assessment of Soviet intentions, but the implications of that assessment for British policy. The distinction was made clear in June 1944. After exchanging heated memos, the PHPS and FO agreed that the matter was best debated in person. On June 15, Jebbs, Wilson, and other members of the FO working group sat down with the PHPS to debate Soviet intentions. The Vice-Chiefs

---

[134] CAB81/41 Feb. 10, 1944.

[135] As discussed earlier, all Challengers want at least some revision. The question is how extensive that revision will be. Clearly, all British policy-makers preferred it if Stalin did not expand at all. However, they were also willing to accept limited Soviet expansion in Eastern Europe that reflected inevitable shifts in the balance of power so long as these advances were limited. Thus, the question was not: does Stalin want territorial revision, but how extensive would that territorial revision be?

[136] FO381/43/335 Apr. 29, 1944.

[137] Ibid.

and members of the Joint Intelligence Committee were present. The discussion revealed precisely where the disagreement was. As Wilson noted:

> The military say, quite rightly, that the only power in Europe which can, in the foreseeable future, be a danger to us is the Union of Soviet Socialist Republics. They go on to argue that the only way to meet that potential danger is to organize against it now... The view taken in the Foreign Office has been that, in planning along these lines, the military will make inevitable the very danger they are trying to avoid.... We and the military are on common ground (a) in acknowledging as a fact that Russia is the only power in Europe that can be a danger to our security, (b) in wanting to avoid that danger, and (c) in wanting to secure that, in any future war, we and the Russians are on the same and not opposite sides. The difference between us is therefore one of method and not of principle.[138]

Duff Cooper, a diplomat with extensive military experience, then serving as British Representative to the French Committee of National Liberation, explained the problem in a letter to Eden. He wrote that "Russia has never wanted either colonies or Lebensraum, and the true creed of Communism is peace rather than war," there was no need for Britain to "panic." However, a strong Western alliance system would form the basis of defense in depth against the Soviets should it be necessary. "A sort of insurance policy."[139]

The difference was one of emphasis. Both the FO and the Joint Chiefs acknowledged that the Soviet Union had the capability to threaten Britain's strategic interests after the war. The military thought it best to plan as if they would. The FO thought that doing so would guarantee that the Soviets would become an enemy.[140]

As we shall see, the debate was all for naught. "Concern over Russian troop movements towards the Caucasus in late 1945 and in Persia in late 1946... [with alarming reports of Soviet domestic behavior in mid-1946] convinced many that the FO view had been incorrect."[141] Most analysts from all three communities came around to the military position following Soviet behavior deemed inconsistent with their security-seeker goals.

6.3.2 Discussion

These events demonstrate how organizational theories and my own are two parts of an important decision-making process. In a softer interpretation of the organizational bias account, all analysts use a common analytical

---

[138] FO371/40741A Wilson's Minute Aug. 10, 1944.
[139] CAB21/1641 May 22, 1944. See also Kitchen (1986, p. 216).
[140] O. Sargent describes this in: FO 371/43306.
[141] Quoted in Kitchen (1986, p. 217).

framework to evaluate their rival's intentions. Within this framework, there is some "best" assessment, a rational baseline, of a rival's intentions given all the available evidence. Organizations either limit the type of information that their analysts see the most, or select analysts that prioritize some information over others systematically. However, analysts still take into account all the information they observe. Different organizations will therefore reach different assessments that deviate from that underlying rational baseline. But the emphasis is on the baseline, and not the direction of the bias. If the baseline is quite close to "deeply uncertain" then most organizations should reach assessments close to that. If the baseline shifts to "certainly aggressive" then all opinions should shift as well.

What my theory provides is the common analytical framework and baseline that analysts use to evaluate intentions. The case evidence suggests that the FO and PHPS accepted that it was possible that the Soviet Union wanted security and evaluated evidence as consistent or inconsistent with this hypothesis. They disagreed over how best to manage this uncertainty. All sides judged that the Soviets may want security. It was possible, but too early to tell. As we shall see, the members of both organizations updated their assessments of Soviet intentions based on whether or not Soviet behavior was consistent with its diplomatic claims.

To be clear, my theory is agnostic about how different organizations will prioritize different recommendations that flow from their assessments. Consistent with organizational hypotheses about bureaucratic incentives, the evidence clearly suggests that the military emphasized the risk of military inaction and too much talk, whereas the FO emphasized the risk of military action and limited talk. These are important questions that relate to the implications of the assessment that both sides reach. Indeed, organizational influences impacted the recommendations that flow from assessments about Soviet intentions. What is important for my theory is that the assessment of Soviet intentions relied on the logic of consistency across the military and diplomatic services.

6.3.3 Personal Impressions, Face-to-Face Encounters, Norm Violations

Despite the general unwavering assessment of Soviet intentions from all British elites, there was a period in April 1944 where Eden grew unusually pessimistic about Soviet intentions following a baseless but damaging report in the Soviet Newspaper, *Pravda*. The report alleged that the British Government was negotiating a separate peace with Germany. As we shall see, Eden's shift is inconsistent with my theory and, most likely, an emotional response. However, the effect lasts less than a month. Notably, it had been six months since Eden had last seen a Soviet counterpart (Molotov) and that encounter had left a favorable impression. What is most surprising is that Churchill had recently experienced an unfavorable impression of Stalin during the Tehran Conference, and came to question Stalin's compliance with liberal values, yet Churchill still saw the *Pravda* incident for what it was: insignificant.

This incident provides additional support for my theory in four ways. First, it demonstrates the short and trivial effect of poor cognitive abilities to influence the assessments of senior leaders. Second, it demonstrates how organizational practices and time easily correct for any individual level biases. Third, it calls into question the primary mechanism thought to generate cognitive biases: impressions generated via in-person meetings. Finally, it shows that even though Churchill is outraged by Stalin's illiberal position and norm violations, that he can still estimates that Stalin could hold limited aims.

Churchill stays the course despite troubling personal encounters, and morally repugnant actions   In December 1943, the Heads of Government of the three Great Powers met at Tehran. From a planning standpoint the Tehran Conference was a huge success. The Three Powers resolved underlying disagreements and contested issues, to lay the political and military course for the rest of the war. The British and Americans agreed to a timeline to open a second front in Europe. The British also agreed in principle (and in secret) to accept many Soviet territorial demands, including in Poland. Stalin agreed in principle to enter the war against Japan and take part in the United Nations. Stalin further agreed to liberate the territories occupied by the Soviet Union in preparation for peace. Finally, all agreed to a broad structure for occupying and governing Axis powers that conceded (including Italy).[142]

Although Tehran was a success for the allies, it was less successful for Britain than the rest. Partially as a matter of policy, and partially to curry favor with Stalin, Roosevelt made a concerted effort to take Stalin's side on key issues. Roosevelt and Stalin held several private meetings (at the exclusion of Churchill) and stood together against Churchill on key decisions.

---

[142] For a detailed discussion of Tehran, see Kitchen (1986, ch 7) and Woodward (1970a, chs XXXVII–XL).

In addition, several encounters soured Churchill's opinion of Stalin. November 29 was an especially troubling day. In the morning, Churchill learned that the night before Stalin and Roosevelt had privately discussed the postwar status of India. Roosevelt believed that India should be remade, from the bottom up, in the image of the Bolsheviks. Both men quipped that Churchill would be very sensitive to the issue and it best be kept private till a later date.

In the afternoon, Churchill pushed to focus operations on the Mediterranean. Stalin explained that "The operations in the Mediterranean of which Churchill speaks are merely diversionary." He then made clear he mistrusted Churchill's intentions stating, "I would like to know if the British believe in Operation Overlord or simply speak of it to reassure the Russians."[143] British negotiators took Stalin's words to heart. Alan Brooke wrote of Stalin's exchange, "I am absolutely disgusted with the politicians' method of waging war!!... It is lamentable to listen to them."[144]

Over dinner that night a jovial discussion about what to do with the Germans at war's end turned sour. Stalin joked, "50,000 Germans must be killed. Their General Staff must go." Churchill rose from his seat and paced for a minute in silence then commented, "I will not be part of any butchery in cold blood." Stalin repeated, "50,000 must be shot." Churchill stormed out of the room in anger. Stalin followed him and coaxed him back in.[145]

The dinner ended in good humor, but the day had taken a toll. Churchill had formed the impression that Stalin did not share his values, and there was little he could do about it. Lord Moran went to check on Churchill a little after midnight and found him drinking alone in a somber state. Churchill revealed, "I believe man might destroy man and wipe out civilization. Europe will be desolate and I might be held responsible."[146] Lord Moran's analysis of Churchill's full position was that,

until he came here, the PM could not bring himself to believe that, face-to-face with Stalin, that the democracies would take different courses. Now he sees that he cannot rely on the president's support. What matters more, he realizes that Russians see this too. Stalin will be able to do as he pleases. Will he become a menace to the free world, another Hitler? The PM is appalled by his own impotence.[147]

---

[143] Proceedings of the Tehran Yalta and Potsdam Conferences, British National Archives, pp. 7–53. See also Berthon and Potts (2007, p. 223) for a qualitative description.

[144] Alanbrooke (2003), diary entry on November 29, 1943.

[145] All quoted in Moran (2002, pp. 171–173).

[146] Ibid., p. 171.

[147] Ibid., p. 173.

Following the conference, Churchill flew to Cairo where he contracted pneumonia. For the next month, he lay bedridden in Morocco, ill, disconnected from the War Cabinet, and with Tehran fresh in his mind. If ever negative impressions should disrupt Churchill's rational thinking, this was the time. Yet Churchill still believed he could cut deals with Stalin and still operated under the assumption that Stalin was motivated by security. In January, Churchill cabled Eden privately to raise the idea of granting additional concessions to the Soviet Union beyond what was offered at Tehran. He argued that the British should concede to Soviet demands in the Baltic States and Finland. These would alleviate all Soviet security concerns about British intentions and pave the way for peace.[148]

These events demonstrate that in a case most likely to succumb to emotions and personal impressions, that the general trajectory of Soviet behavior trumped any concerns Churchill gathered from his meetings with Stalin.

Eden wavers at the Pravda incident   In January 1944, the Soviet newspaper *Pravda*, allegedly through their press correspondent in Cairo, published a report that representatives of Britain and Germany had met somewhere on the Iberian Peninsula to discuss a separate peace. The report led to anti-British sentiment in the Soviet Union and among communist supporters in Britain.[149] A Soviet press attaché revealed that orders came from the Kremlin to distribute the report widely. Further, the FO established that *Pravda* had no correspondent in Cairo.[150]

To be clear, these events did not violate any specific agreement between the Russians and the British. Several interpreted the report as an attempt by the Kremlin to show they would not compromise over the Polish question.[151] Thus, the *Pravda* incident was a matter of tactics, not strategy. Per my theory, rational British leaders would not have read too much into them.

Yet the events clearly frustrated British officials. The FO cabled the Russian Foreign Ministry to protest. They claimed that the report had global implications that damaged both Britain and Russia and fueled German propaganda. The British asserted the claim was totally baseless and asked

---

[148] N665/506/59; WM(44)8; N506/506/59.
[149] N442/442/38.
[150] For a qualitative account, see Woodward (1970a, pp. 104–110).
[151] N451/442/38.

the Russians what evidence they had of it.[152] The Russians replied that there was no evidence. However, *Pravda* was an independent newspaper over which they had no control.[153]

Churchill then sent a personal note to Stalin explaining that he had been "much impressed ... by the extra-ordinary bad effects produced here by the *Pravda* story to which so much official publicity was given by the Soviet Government."[154] He told Stalin that the incident soured the good will established by the Tehran Conference.[155] Stalin replied that Churchill should not put too much stock into the writings of an unofficial newspaper over which the Soviet government has no editorial control.[156]

The whole incident outraged many at Whitehall. In an internal memo, Churchill wrote that although he had tried to put his sympathies in with the communist leaders, "he could not feel the slightest confidence in them."[157] He said, "trying to maintain good relations with a Communist is like wooing a crocodile... When it opens its mouth you cannot tell whether it is trying to smile or prepare to eat you up."[158] Churchill was concerned by the incident but ultimately thought it had no real bearing on the long-term trajectory of Anglo-Soviet relations.[159]

Yet the event had a different effect on Anthony Eden. In April 1944, Eden wrote to the War Cabinet, "But I confess to growing apprehension that Russia has vast aims, and that these may include the domination of Eastern Europe and even the Mediterranean and the 'communising' of much that remains."[160]

Although this estimate is damning for my theory, it is short lived. In response to Eden's comments, Wilson circulated a memo to the FO and the War Cabinet that made clear Soviet behavior was still consistent with a desire for security. He reminded the War Cabinet that, "fear of a united Europe rather than a desire to dominate must be a major influence in [Russia's] attitude towards Europe," and the likely explanation for the *Pravda* incident.[161] The memo received concurrence from Jebb, Cadogan,

---

[152] N1021/442/38.

[153] N525/442/38. It was widely believed that the Kremlin had complete control over what *Pravda* published.

[154] T130A/4/396 Churchill Papers.

[155] Ibid.

[156] T1179/4/396.

[157] N2128/36/38.

[158] Quoted in Bryant and Alanbrooke (1974, p. 140).

[159] N2128/36/38.

[160] N1908/36/38.

[161] N3554/36/38.

and Sargent before it was sent to Eden. Eden concurred with Wilson's finding. By the end of June, Eden had reversed his opinion in line with Wilson's. He wrote to Churchill that "we should not regard as inevitable a clash of interests," with the Soviet Union.[162] By the time Churchill visited Moscow in October, the entire incident was long forgotten and his assessment again centered on Soviet security interests.[163]

6.3.4 Inference

The *Pravda* incident illustrates that domestic institutions serve as an important check on elite misperceptions. In this example, the British internal cabling system compelled Eden to publicize his assessment to many analysts. Those analysts felt free to debate the merits of Eden's position. All it took was a well-reasoned argument by a (relatively) junior Foreign Officer, four full ranks below Eden, to influence the foreign minister's assessment. Within less than a month, Eden's opinion returned to my rational baseline. This general practice of consensus and collaboration between all levels of government across several organizations demonstrates the real limitations of psychological bias to influence an assessment over key issues such as Soviet intentions.

6.4 The Moment of Truth

By January 1945, Italy had surrendered, the British had pushed back the Nazis in France and the Soviet Union had pushed through the Polish border.[164] With victory in Europe so close, the Great Powers agreed to meet again in Yalta (February, 1945) to discuss planning the postwar world. The period following the Yalta Conference marked the turning point in British assessments of Soviet intentions. Yalta "was the first time that the three leaders reached fundamental agreements on post-war problems as distinct from mere statements of aims and purposes."[165] Therefore, it was the first time that the British saw details of Soviet postwar planning.

From the point of view of my theory, this period marked a critical juncture for British assessments of Soviet intentions because it was the first time

---

[162] WP(44)304; R9092/349/67.

[163] T1828A/4, Tel. 3217 to Moscow (Prisec Churchill Papers/434); JIC(44)395(O) (Final; PMM D(O)1/4); T1840/4/434 No 789, Churchill Papers; T1848/4/434 No 625, Churchill Papers; T1872/4/434, No 790 Churchill Papers; T1881/4/434, No. 626, Churchill Papers; T1891/4/434, No. 791, Churchill Papers.

[164] CAB/66/61/31.

[165] Stettinius (1949, p. 3).

that Stalin had the opportunity to take concessions beyond what could be plausibly argued as security seeking. The Red Army had occupied Poland, Rumania, Northern Iran, Bulgaria, and other parts of Eurasia by 1945. At the very least, Russia could refuse to withdraw its forces. Once Germany surrendered, Russia was less restricted by its reliance on Western material support. Thus, between these conferences, Stalin was able to choose between making more demands and concealing his aggressive intentions.

As we shall see, Britain thought that, even in the best case, Russia would demand revision. Therefore concessions were necessary to achieve peace. The important question was the extent of Soviet demands. Here I argue that the answer to this question hinged on beliefs about Soviet intentions. The British believed that if Stalin truly valued security, an Anglo-Soviet accommodation could be reached. However, if Stalin wanted more, then the British were best off resisting Stalin's demands.

I will analyze both individual- and group-level estimates. At the group level, I code that the balance of estimates, and the national estimate, turned sharply following the Iran Crisis (and to a lesser degree, the Turkish Crisis), and that this triggered a shift in British strategy towards competition. To be clear, there is debate about the origins of the Cold War. But those who would disagree with my coding use a different definition than my theory. One debate centers on disagreements about who truly held aggressive intentions.[166] I take the less-controversial position that Soviet–Western intentions were incompatible (Gaddis, 2006, pp. 10–13), and seek to understand when they realized that fact. Others argue that the Cold War began with the Polish Crisis, the Marshall Plan, or other notable contestation events.[167] But my definition rests on when elites realize that the Defender is vast, and decide to shift their strategy. Based on this definition, my coding of the Cold War's origins for either the US or the UK at the Iran and Turkish Crises is noncontroversial.[168] My goal is to take this coding as given, and examine an underexplored question: what was different about the Iran Crisis, and the costly signals Stalin took in Romania, Poland, Bulgaria, and elsewhere?

At the individual level, I find that analysts come to mistrust Stalin's intentions at different points in time. However, the assessment framework each analyst uses considers whether Stalin's action can be reasonably explained as serving his declared security motivation. Those that grew alarmed early

---

[166] See Haslam (2003); Leffler (1999) for discussion.
[167] See Walker (1986) for review, see also Pollard (1985); Larson (1985).
[168] See Raine (1994); Hess (1974); Fawcett (2014).

point to Soviet behavior as a clear sign that Stalin does not want security, and therefore argue that Stalin must be motivated by something more menacing. Those that did not update argued that Soviet behavior was not necessarily inconsistent with security-seeking motives. They always offered a plausible justification for how Soviet behavior fit within Stalin's original demands based on their interpretation of Stalin's strategic position. The point is that the cleavage is always: Are these events inconsistent with security motives? Overall, I find that estimates shift when British analysts cannot reconcile Soviet actions with security motivations, based on the analysts' historically driven understanding of what is necessary for Stalin to assure his security. Those that grew alarmed early point to Soviet behavior as a clear sign that Stalin does not want security, and therefore argue that Stalin must be motivated by something more menacing. Those that did not update argued that Soviet behavior was not necessarily inconsistent with security-seeking motives.

6.4.1 Understanding Stalin as a Security-Seeker and the Inevitable Conflict in Interest

During 1944, a number of reports were circulated about what the Soviet Union would plausibly ask for if it truly wanted security. This effort culminated in a December 1944 report by the Joint Intelligence Committee (JIC), the peak wartime intelligence body titled, "Russia's Strategic Interests and Intentions from the Point of View of Her Security." The "hugely detailed"[169] report provided information on Russian economic production and resources, postwar intentions towards the Allies, smaller states in Europe, the Middle East, and the Far East. The thirty-page assessment, accompanied by a more detailed annex, included an analysis of Soviet diplomatic, political, and military trends with three annexes that focused on different aspects of Soviet behavior. The report was approved by the FO and the Chief of Staff Committee (COC) and sent to the War Cabinet and prime minister.[170]

The JIC judged that at minimum,

in order to achieve the greatest possible security Russia will wish to improve her strategic frontiers and to draw the States lying along her borders, and particularly

---

[169] Aldrich et al. (2014, p. 121).

[170] The fact that these reports emerge at all is supportive of my theory. No reports, for example, emerged that looked at what the Soviet Union would want if it was motivated by nationalism. See Goodman (2014, ch 8), Aldrich et al. (2014, pp. 120–122) for more details.

those in Europe, into her strategic system. Provided that the other Great Powers are prepared to accept Russia's predominance in these border States and provided that they follow a policy designed to prevent any revival of German and Japanese military power, Russia will have achieved the greatest possible measure of security and could not hope to increase it by further territorial expansion. Nor is it easy to see what else Russia could under such conditions hope to gain from a policy of aggression.[171]

The report identified that "Russia would regard Finland, Poland, Czechoslovakia, Hungary, Romania, Bulgaria and to a lesser extent Yugoslavia as forming her protective screen. She will, however, probably regard Norway and Greece as being outside her sphere."[172] It claimed that Russia would directly involve itself in the internal affairs of these states.[173] Further, the Soviet Union would demand territorial concessions from Poland up to the Curzon Line. The JIC argued that Russia would participate in a world organization so long as the organization granted Russia enough autonomy in its periphery to guarantee Soviet security. Further the JIC judged that Russia would take measure to protect oilfields in the Caucasus and maritime routes in the North and Black Seas, including bases to monitor Northern Persia and Azerbaijan. However, political control over these areas would be beyond Russia's interests in security.[174]

Although the JIC does not explicitly state how it arrived at these conclusions,[175] the detailed appendices suggest that it considered three types of information. First, members of the JIC used deductive logic to determine where Soviet strategic choke points were based on expert knowledge of military and economic warfare. Second, they read the history of Soviet invasions to identify points where the Soviets had previously experienced security threats. Finally, they considered issues that Stalin and Molotov and lower-level Soviet military leaders had raised about their own security during engagements with allied forces.

6.4.2 Implications for Negotiations between the Western Allies and the Soviet Union

By the JIC assessment, Russian interests would conflict with the Western allies even in the best-case scenario. Three important areas for concern

---

[171] Published in Aldrich et al. (2014, p. 129).
[172] Ibid., (2014, p. 126).
[173] Ibid. It did not say to what extent.
[174] Published in Aldrich et al. (2014, pp. 141–143).
[175] I also could not find it in official history (Goodman, 2014).

were Poland, global governance and the treatment of occupied states in Europe.[176]

British and Soviet preferences were furthest apart over Poland. Britain had entered the war in defense of Poland. The Polish government in exile was stationed in London (referred to as the London Poles). Poland was also a critical issue for the Soviet Union. Stalin invaded Poland in 1939 and captured Polish territory east of the Curzon Line. During the war, Stalin had made clear he considered that territory to be part of the Soviet Union. During the war, a group of Polish Communists (known as the Lublin Poles) fought against the German occupying force. In 1944, Stalin recognized the Lublin Poles as the provisional government of Poland.

The deadlock lay between the London Poles on one side and Stalin and the Lublin Poles on the other. Diplomatic relations were severed repeatedly during the war. Adding fuel to the fire, evidence emerged in 1944 that the Red Army had massacred a whole village of Polish citizens during their occupation of Eastern Poland, leading the London Poles to accuse Russia of war crimes. In response, Stalin and the Lublin Poles called members of the exiled government anti-Russian and Fascist sympathizers.[177]

The British were caught in the middle. The British saw the Lublin Poles as a Soviet puppet and would not recognize them as the leaders of a provisional government.[178] Britain wanted a provisional government headed by the London Poles to administer services before a prompt election. They further wanted British and American observers in Warsaw. Thus, on the issue of provisional governance, the British sided with the London Poles. However, Churchill was willing to make concessions on Polish borders.[179] Russia had a strong historical claim to the region. Further, the Red Army was already in position of Eastern Poland. If Stalin did not want to leave, it would be near impossible to force him.[180]

A second concern was the postwar international order. Roosevelt believed that power politics had caused conflict in Europe. He wanted

---

[176] There were several other disagreements including the treatment of Germany, prisoner-exchange protocols and the war in Asia. I choose these three because they shed light on my question. The British and American account of Yalta is available should a reader want more information. For a more detailed account, see Clemens (1970, pp. 8–58), Harbutt (2010).

[177] CAB/66/61/2, Report: The Polish Provisional Government. See (Churchill, 1956, pp. 128–145) for elite reactions.

[178] CAB/65/51/12, Minute 3.

[179] CAB/65/51/10, Minute 1.

[180] CAB/66/63/12 Record of the Political Proceedings of the "Argonaut" Conference held at Malta and in the Crimea, p. 2.

to avoid a world system where Great Powers operated spheres of influence. Instead, he envisioned an international organization where the Great Powers would jointly settle all international disputes.

At Tehran, Stalin had indicated he would join Roosevelt's world organization, subject to some administrative changes. However, he expressed his desire to influence states along Russia's periphery. Stalin claimed he would accept democratic governments in Eastern Europe. However, at a minimum, Stalin wanted to exclude political parties that spoke out against the Soviet Union. It was unclear how much influence would satisfy him.[181] The Western allies worried that Stalin wanted significantly more control.[182]

Churchill's position was between these two. Churchill wanted independent, democratically elected governments in Europe and was willing to join a world organization that protected these rights for all. However, he wanted Britain to have a larger say than the other Great Powers in the affairs of Greece, the Low Countries, India, Egypt, and elsewhere. He accepted Stalin would want the same in Eastern Europe and the Baltic States.[183]

This general discussion about world order had a direct application in the administration of the liberated states of Eastern Europe. At Tehran, the Great Powers had agreed that the liberated states (and most that surrendered) would democratically elect representative governments once the war was over. In the meantime, the Great Powers would implement Control Commissions to administer services during the war. In theory, each Control Commission would include members from all three Great Powers. But in practice, three-way consensus was difficult to implement. In Eastern Europe, the Soviet representatives, made unilateral decisions without consulting the Western Administrators. When the Allies protested, the Soviets replied that swift, unilateral actions were necessary to wage their campaign against the remaining Axis Forces.

In many cases, Soviet military concerns were legitimate. However, Churchill and Roosevelt worried that Soviet policy overwhelmingly favored far left-leaning political parties, and this would unfairly influence elections after war's end. More broadly, the Western allies were concerned that Stalin would maintain his strangle hold in Eastern Europe. Indeed, the assessment of Stalin's intentions from the point of view of his security suggested that tight Soviet control was plausible. As a result, the Western allies were

---

[181] Buhite (1986, pp. 78–79).
[182] Harbutt (2010, p. 94).
[183] Buhite (1986).

unsure if they could prevent the Soviet Union from creating a sphere of influence and worried about the amount of influence the Soviets would demand.

6.4.3 The Yalta Agreement and the Optimism That Followed

The status of Poland was the most contested issue at Yalta. It was discussed at seven of the eight plenary sessions.[184] To wrest concessions from Stalin, Churchill appealed to British prestige. He argued that he could not tell the British people that he had conceded on the very issues that induced Britain to enter the war. Stalin replied that for Russia, Poland was a

question of security, not only because Poland was on the frontiers of Russia, but because throughout history Poland had been a corridor through which Russia's enemies had passed to attack her. During the last thirty years the Germans had twice passed through this corridor. They passed through because Poland had been weak. Russia wanted to see a strong and powerful Poland so that she would be able, of her own strength, to shut this corridor.[185]

Stalin further argued that Russia had a right to a strong Poland, friendly to Russian interests. He claimed that many of the London Poles had shown a dislike for the Soviet Union. To that end, the Russian delegation proposed a provisional government that was an expansion of the Lublin Poles that included some London Poles friendly to Soviet interests. They expected elections could be organized within a few months and so the effect of the provisional government would be minimal.[186]

Consistent with my theory, Churchill was largely persuaded by Stalin's argument based on security.[187] He noted that Stalin's claims over Poland were based on right and not force. However, several concerns remained. Churchill claimed that the Lublin Poles were not popular in Poland and politically inexperienced. Accepting an expansion of the Lublin Government would be tantamount to recognizing the Lublin Government, which neither he, nor the London Poles, could accept. Churchill suggested a *reorganization* of the Polish government that included the London Poles.[188]

In the end, the English translation of the Yalta Communiqué read

---

[184] Churchill (1966, p. 16).
[185] CAB/66/63/12, p. 30.
[186] Ibid., p. 71.
[187] Churchill (1966, p. 16).
[188] CAB/66/63/12, p. 67.

The Provisional Government which is now functioning in Poland should therefore be reorganized on a broader democratic basis with the inclusion of democratic leaders from Poland itself and from Poland abroad... M. Molotov, Mr. Harriman and Sir A. Clark Kerr are authorized as a commission to consult in the first instance in Moscow with members of the present Provisional Government and with other Polish democratic leaders from within Poland and from abroad.[189]

The discussion on Eastern Europe was much shorter because there was little disagreement. The British reaffirmed their preference for the European Control Commissions to govern liberated states in Europe.[190] But the British and Americans acknowledged that the actual "executive and administrative work of the Control Commission will be a matter to be settled on the spot."[191] The implication being that the Soviets would govern the areas they liberated. However, the British and Americans would have a right to membership of any sub-committee or executive organ.

Stalin agreed. He affirmed that he would support free local elections for independent governments once the war was over. However, he noted that three-party consultation was cumbersome. He argued that victory against Hitler was the primary objective and local politics could not slow the Soviet advances.

Finally, Stalin agreed that Molotov would attend the conference at San Francisco to establish the World Organization. He conceded to American preferences for most of the administrative procedures, who should attend, and the voting protocol for the Security Council.

6.4.4 Assessment of Soviet Intentions at the End of Yalta

The Yalta Conference was hailed as a huge success. The *New York Times* reported that the agreement will "justify and surpass most of the hopes placed on this fateful meeting, and in their aims and purposes they [the Big Three] show the way to an early victory in Europe, to secure peace, and to a brighter world."[192] In a speech to the House of Commons two days after he returned from Yalta, Churchill proclaimed,

The Crimea Conference leaves the Allies more closely united than before, both in the military and in the political sphere... Marshal Stalin and the Soviet leaders wish to live in honorable friendship and equality with the Western democracies.

---

[189] The Yalta Communiqué.
[190] CAB/66/63/12, p. 63.
[191] Ibid., p. 108.
[192] Quoted in Stettinius (1949).

I feel that their word is their bond. I know of no Government which stands to its obligations, even in its own despite, more solidly than the Russian Soviet Government.[193]

6.4.5 Discussion

Going into the Yalta Conference, the British understood that even if the Soviet Union was motivated by security, that they had some conflicting objectives. Stalin would use his increasing military power to press for his ideal policy. The Western allies were broadly uncertain about two things: (1) If Stalin truly wanted security, what was his ideal outcome over the territories he had identified as important and how much was he willing to compromise on these issues; and (2) did Stalin truly want security?

Consistent with my theory, British elites and intelligence sub-committees assessed the specific issues and territories that Stalin would want if Stalin was motivated by security. Based on these assessments, policy-makers identified where British and Soviet interests would conflict and developed diplomatic strategies to achieve as many British interests as possible given what a security seeking Stalin would ask for.

It is notable that Yalta was not the first high-level conference, but the first to elicit such an optimistic assessment of Soviet intentions. Indeed, Churchill had conceded on the Polish question, Britain's most critical interest. Further, Churchill recognized the parallels to Munich stating, "Poor Neville Chamberlain believed he could trust Hitler. He was wrong. But I don't think I'm wrong about Stalin."[194] Why was Churchill so optimistic? Churchill would later reflect on this question in his memoirs. He claimed that his confidence in Stalin's limited intentions was based on what Stalin did not ask for. Stalin did not haggle over Poland, Greece, or world governance during the Yalta Conference.[195] Further, Stalin did not revive demands in Persia.[196] Stalin did not press beyond what was reasonably required for Soviet security, or use these issues as bargaining chips, even though he could have. In the words of the Deputy Prime Minister, "ample elbow-room had been retained."[197] The British analysis of Yalta suggested that Stalin could have demanded much more in the name of security. Ultimately, it was Stalin's restraint that made Churchill optimistic.

---

[193] Churchill, Hansard Record of the House of Commons, February 27, 1945.
[194] Quoted in Nicolson and Nicolson (2004, entry 27 Feb, 1945).
[195] Churchill (1966, pp. 26–27).
[196] CAB/66/63/12, p. 63.
[197] CAB/65/51/18, Minute 5.

This dynamic is precisely what my theory expects. Defenders reserve judgment until a point at which the Challenger has achieved all the concessions implied by her limited demands. At that point, if the Challenger stops making demands and integrates into the world system, the Defender increases his confidence that the Challenger's aims are limited. It was precisely this logic that made the prime minister optimistic. He pointed specifically to what Stalin did not ask for as a sign of Stalin's limited aims.

6.5 Events in Poland and Eastern Europe: February–July 1945

Less than three weeks after the Yalta Communiqué was released, Molotov rescinded Soviet commitments over Poland. Under the British interpretation of Yalta, British Ambassador Clark Kerr, American Ambassador Harriman, and M. Molotov would facilitate a conference between the London and Lublin Poles in Moscow to form a Provisional Government in Poland. This was the first step towards free and fair elections for an independent Polish Government. The first meeting was on February 23, 1945. Per the Yalta Agreement, Clark Kerr submitted a list of eight London Poles to Molotov that Britain wanted at the conference to decide the fate of Poland.[198]

The next day, Molotov told Clark Kerr that he had consulted the Lublin Government about his list, and they would not accept seven of the eight names proposed. "In short, the men of Lublin, now installed in Warsaw by the Russians, must have veto power over invitations to any Poles outside their own circle."[199] Clark Kerr explained that the Yalta Agreement did not give the Lublin Poles the right of consultation. After some debate, Clark Kerr agreed to present the Soviet formulation to the War Cabinet but explained it would certainly be rejected.[200] At the same time, troubling reports reached London that Polish citizens who opposed the Lublin regime had gone missing inside Poland.[201] Churchill and Roosevelt sent a joint letter to Molotov on March 19 that affirmed Clark Kerr's protest.[202] Molotov argued that the Western interpretation was "entirely incorrect." Molotov then presented the Russian translation of the Yalta Agreement that read, "... are authorized as a commission to consult in Moscow

---

[198] Harriman and Abel (1975, p. 246).
[199] Ibid.
[200] CAB/65/51/26, WM(45) Minute 5.
[201] Harriman and Abel (1975, p. 246).
[202] Ministry of Foreign Affairs (1957b, Cable Delivered March 19).

with members of the present Provisional Government *in the first instance* and with other Polish democratic leaders from within Poland and from abroad."[203] He stated that based on the Russian translation that the Lublin Poles should form the "nucleus" of the new government of national unity.

Unsure if Molotov's position reflected Stalin's, Roosevelt and Churchill wrote Stalin directly on March 29. The letter, delivered on April 1st, made clear that they could not accept the Lublin Government at the center of a Polish Administration. Churchill stated that he would be forced to report the situation to the House of Commons if Stalin did not change his position within a fortnight. In a "thinly veiled threat"[204] on April 7, Stalin responded that the "question of Poland is for the security of the Soviet Union what the question of Belgium and Greece is for the security of Great Britain."[205] Despite the tone, Stalin promised to use his influence with the Lublin Poles to alter their objections.[206] Ultimately, the most important members of the London Poles were invited to Moscow. However, the conditions were very different than what Churchill thought he had agreed to at Yalta. It was clear that the Lublin Poles would form the basis of government in Poland.

Events in Eastern Europe raised further alarm. On February 19, the Soviet Union orchestrated a coup against the Allied-appointed provisional government in Romania. The Soviets then pressured Romanian King Michael to fill the vacancy with the communist party's leader.[207] By early March, the communist party in Bulgaria had taken control using militias "to intimidate, arrest and kill opponents of the Communists."[208] Intelligence strongly suggested that the unpopular communist party would rig the forthcoming election to guarantee victory. The Foreign Office and JIC assessed that "the Bulgarian Communists have received great encouragement and at least moral support from the Soviet authorities and from the presence of the Soviet army of occupation."[209] A similar situation arose in Hungary.[210] From the perspective of the Western allies, Soviet actions in Romania clearly violate the norms and values that would underpin the United Nations because Russia was deeply unpopular, owing to "historic antagonisms, dating back over many centuries, [which] were exacerbated

---

[203] Quoted in with added emphasis Harriman and Abel (1975, p. 429).
[204] Kitchen (1986, p. 253).
[205] Woodward (1970a, p. 530).
[206] Ministry of Foreign Affairs (1957b, cable delivered April 7).
[207] Lynn (2013, p. 151).
[208] CAB/66/63/29.
[209] Ibid.
[210] FO371/47897 Jul. 20, 1945.

by ethnic rivalries and territorial disputes."[211] The British government was so outraged they protested over these issues, demanding an explanation from Moscow, but received no response.

It was not all bad news. The Soviets showed considerably more restraint with states further afield. As late as July, anti-Soviet political leaders in Finland "continued to play a part in Finnish politics, there is no evidence that the Finnish Communists' demands ... have been encouraged by the Soviet authorities."[212] Although the Soviet authorities were actively engaged in media censorship in Northern Persia, it was largely consistent with their views on free press. Further, the Soviets had stayed within the guidelines laid out for their Control Zone of Persia.[213]

The final cause for concern came from Soviet participation in the World Organization. Specifically, Molotov withdrew his participation from the conference in San Francisco. The Soviets would send their Ambassador to the United States Gromyko in his place. Ultimately, Roosevelt's untimely death prompted Molotov to attend the conference. However, his intention was to skip it.

6.5.1 British Assessments of the Soviet Union, July 1945

Following these events, new debate arose about Soviet long-term intentions. In general, there were three views. An alarmist group argued that Stalin had exposed his true aggressive intentions. A second group called for calm. They argued that Stalin's behavior was still consistent with security. In the middle was a group who called for calm about Stalin's interests, but believed that Stalin did not value Great Power agreements and that he would pursue unilateral policies within his sphere of influence.[214]

The alarmist group argued that Soviet behavior was the first signal of aggressive long-term intentions for three reasons. First, Soviet behavior was consistent with authoritarian tendencies to expand empire. Second, they argued that the way in which the Soviets expanded into Eastern Europe reflected a strong adhesion to Marxist ideology. Recent events made clear that "Stalin regards himself as the infallible interpreter of Marxism. To Bolsheviks Marx is almost as great a hero as Lenin.... His whole belief in the social revolution was based on the theory that the smaller must be merged

---

[211] Reynolds (1994, p. 169). See also Papp (1979).

[212] FO371/47897 Jul. 20, 1945.

[213] Ibid.

[214] The difference between the middle and the call for calm group is one of emphasis. For my purpose, they basically reach the same assessment. However, historians typically describe these as three different positions.

in the greater. It would therefore seem foolish for us to ignore the influence of Marx on Russian policy today."[215] Third, alarmists argued that "the internal history of Russia has been for centuries a fluctuating struggle between the European minded and the Asiatic minded schools... The idea of Russia's predestined role as a mother-state is a heritage from Byzantium... The Bolsheviks therefore have an historical motive or impulse for expansionist policies. It can be and is very easily harnessed to the Marxist motive."[216] As O'Malley explains, "When we consider the arrogant and aggressive character of the Soviet system... I think that we must conclude that this tension must end in a retreat by one side or the other in conflict with ourselves... the fact is that the Soviet Government has not hitherto been given any compelling reason to suppose that we should insist on it moderating its ambitions and behavior."

In June 1945, the PHPC presented these, and other alarmist assessments, to Cabinet in a single report.[217] The report argued that Britain should sustain defense spending and forward-deployed forces, and seek broad alliances with Germany and the United States to prevent Russian aggression. Yet even for the PHPC, "the tone of the paper was quite different from earlier studies. In all previous papers, it had always been stressed that the best defense against the Soviet Union was to maintain friendly and cooperative relations with her... Now the argument had been dropped, and the possibility of a global conflict with the Soviet Union was taken very seriously."[218]

At the other end of the spectrum, several analysts called for calm. While recent events concerned them, they argued that the Soviets "intend, however, to secure their own essential interests, and in particular to buttress the Russian frontiers against any possible renewal of German aggression..."[219] They argued that the Soviets do not care about British interests in Eastern Europe at all, "But this should not, I think, be interpreted as a sign of hostility to the west or as a danger signal for the future,"[220] because Soviet behavior was still consistent with security.

Responding to the alarmist claims, those that called for calm acknowledged that Soviet behavior was consistent with authoritarian and communist designs. However,

---

[215] FO/371/50912 Lockhart's Minute, Apr. 11 1945.
[216] Ibid.
[217] CAB81/46/PHP (45)29(0) (Final).
[218] Kitchen (1986, p. 261).
[219] Clark Kerr's opinion: FO 371/47076 Apr. 16, 1945.
[220] Ibid.

Soviet Russia now fears a world coalition of the liberal Powers and the revival of
Germany as a liberal Power... Stalin, however, does not necessarily intend to obtain
his security by territorial conquest, as Hitler wanted to. He may well prefer to
obtain it by creating what might be termed an ideological Lebensraum in those
countries which he considers strategically important.[221]

They further noted that Soviet behavior outside their immediate sphere
of influence supported this conclusion.

Russia policy, however distasteful it may be to us... has the air of remaining a policy
of limited objectives... in the case of Greece, they have refrained from intervention
and shown what is for them extreme moderation... [In Persia] they have in fact
refrained from reviving their demands for oil concessions and they seem to have
realized that the independence of Persia is a matter of vital importance.[222]

A few even argued that there may have been a genuine misunderstanding about the status of Poland in the Yalta Agreement. One interpretation
argued that Stalin and Molotov "may have got the impression that we might
be satisfied with their interpretation of the Yalta Agreement as a means of
cleansing ourselves of our commitments to Poland."[223] Therefore, Stalin's
new position reflected what he thought was a tacit understanding.

The balance of opinions lay between these two. Most analysts noted that
these actions did not rule out that the Soviet Union sought limited interests based on security. However, these analysts placed more emphasis on
what recent events meant for future negotiations. As Roberts outlined in a
discussion on Eastern Europe,

The realistic rulers of Soviet Russia, who are not used to compromise or concessions, as these are understood in the West, are determined to be the masters in
neighboring countries, and to ensure that there are no rival influences which the
local Governments can play off against them. We must, therefore, I fear, expect to
meet with many difficulties and disappointments even in securing and maintaining normal representation, and still more in making British influence felt in these
countries.[224]

Churchill, who also subscribed to this middle ground assessment, was
most alarmed by the intense secrecy that surrounded Soviet behavior in
Eastern Europe. In an outburst, over a private luncheon,[225] he argued that

---

[221] Orme Sargent's assessment: FO/371/50912 Jul. 11 1945. Affirmed by A. Cadogan, B.
Locheart.
[222] Clark Kerr's assessment: FO371/47941 Mar. 27, 1945.
[223] Ibid.
[224] Roberts's assessment: FO371/48928 Apr. 21, 1945.
[225] Churchill thought the discussion was private. It was later recounted by his lunch guest.
It was noted Churchill had been drinking.

the Soviets had caused some concern "by dropping an iron screen across Europe from Lubeck to Trieste behind which we had no knowledge of what was happening. All we know was that puppet governments were being set up about which we were not consulted, and at which we were not allowed to peep... All this was incomprehensible and intolerable."[226]

The dominant view, and the view held by the prime minister, reflected the average assessment before the Yalta Conference. Some Soviet behavior was concerning, but it was too early to tell what it meant. To make a proper assessment they needed more information. Ultimately, the prime minister and the Cabinet

regarded their Soviet comrades-in-arms with apprehension but without hostility... The British government was not unduly concerned. The Soviet Union appeared to be pursuing its legitimate security interests, albeit in an often-heavy handed way... The Soviet Union as seen as a pragmatic and autocratic power, obsessed with its security, and bent on attaining traditional Russian goals... For the British, this state of affairs gave little grounds for optimism, but also no reason for despair.[227]

6.5.2 From Divergence to Consensus: V.E. Day to the Iran Crisis

As more events unfolded, analysts came around to the alarmist view. As my theory expects, analysts adjusted their opinions about Soviet intentions following events that implied that the Soviet Union's interests were something other than security. In this section, I observe events that changed British assessments and those that failed to.

Continuity in assessments and leadership change Victory in Europe meant that the postwar international order was now starting to take shape. The Allies would soon occupy Germany, begin to normalize their relations with the other Axis powers, end their military occupations, and return sovereignty to most of Europe. Yet given the events after Yalta, the Western allies were deeply uncertain about how peace would be implemented. To complicate matters further, President Roosevelt died just before Germany's surrender. With all this uncertainty, the Big Three agreed to another meeting at Potsdam in July and August to clarify their postwar policy. Further uncertainty was thrust upon them the first day of the Potsdam Conference. Churchill was defeated in a general election and replaced by a new prime minister, Clement Attlee, and a new foreign minister, Ernest

---

[226] Prem 3 396/12.
[227] Kitchen (1986, p. 269).

Bevin.[228] Thus, Potsdam was the first time that Truman, Stalin, and Attlee met.

Ultimately, no British assessments of Soviet intentions changed following Potsdam. Stalin continued to push his position in Poland and Eastern Europe. However, he affirmed that he would withdraw from Iran, honor the German Zones of Occupation policy discussed at Yalta, and participate fully in the United Nations. He also committed to repatriate British prisoners of war promptly that the Red Army freed in Eastern Europe and Germany.[229]

One might wonder if the change in British leadership affected Britain's assessment of Soviet intentions. This may be the case because Attlee and Bevin had different strategies and assessment protocols from Churchill or Eden, or because they had not yet developed a rapport with Stalin, and therefore the new nature of their meeting affected their assessment. Put another way, if Churchill and Eden had represented Britain at Potsdam, would Britain's assessment have differed?

Three pieces of evidence suggest that leadership change had little effect. First, Churchill had gone to great lengths to coordinate his policy with Attlee in the event of a leadership change.

The change in the British representation did not mean a break in the continuity of British policy. At the prime minister's invitation Mr. Attlee had attended the earlier meetings of Conference; he and Mr. Bevin had been members not only of the War Cabinet but of the Armistice and Post-War Committee. They knew the background of the questions in dispute at the Conference and had approved of the general instructions and briefs given to the British Delegation.[230]

Second, British foreign policy remained almost constant. In the first foreign policy debate in Parliament following the election, in August 1945, Eden praised Bevin's performance at Potsdam. He then recalled serving on the War Cabinet with Bevin. "During that period, there were many discussions on foreign affairs I cannot recall one single occasion when there was a difference between us. I hope I do not embarrass the Foreign Secretary when I say that." Bevin agreed with Eden's assessment.[231]

Third, all four leaders had full access to the minutes and secret details of the Potsdam Conference. The assessment of all four leaders following Potsdam largely reflect their assessments before the conference. Thus, the

---

[228] Attlee arrived on July 26, the conference started on July 17.
[229] This was a reciprocal agreement. The British agreed to return Soviet prisoners they freed.
[230] Woodward (1970c, p. 409).
[231] Hansard Record of the House of Commons, August, 1945.

conference had the same impact on all of them (which is to say no impact). At lower ranks, Attlee retained the same foreign policy, intelligence and military staff. Consistent with the new leadership, none of these officials altered their assessments in the aftermath of Potsdam.

6.5.3 The Foreign Ministers Conference at London and Moscow

To implement the agreements reached at Potsdam and Yalta, it was decided that the foreign ministers of the five permanent members of the Security Council would to meet regularly and discuss the details of implementation. The first meeting took place in London in September 1945.

The London meeting ended in complete deadlock with Molotov on one side, and the Western ministers, Bevin and James F. Byrnes, on the other. The main issue was procedural. The Potsdam Conference specified that only the foreign ministers of the three Great Powers had a right to settle all questions. Other powers would participate either by invitation of the Great Powers, or on issues that directly related to them. At the first meeting, Bevin asked if the foreign ministers from France and China had a right to vote in addition to their right to "attend all meetings and participate in all discussions."[232] Byrnes and Bevin strongly supported the inclusion of France in the discussion on Europe. Molotov would not discuss it. Instead, he deferred the broader question about participation rights. At the thirteenth meeting, Molotov raised an objection to the French Minister attending a discussion on Finland. Following a protest from Bevin, the issue was not discussed.[233] French participation was revisited repeatedly over the following fortnight. Bevin was unwilling to continue without the French in the room and Molotov refused to yield. At this impasse, the foreign ministers concluded the conference with no agreement.[234]

Two other issues troubled Bevin. First, Molotov argued that Russia was vulnerable to port closures in the Mediterranean. Thus, to protect its interest in sea lanes on inland waterways, Russia required a naval base in Turkey on the Bosphorus/the Dardanelles.[235] Second, Molotov advanced Soviet claims for a trusteeship over the Italian colony of Tripolitania. Molotov argued that this would help safeguard Russian commercial interests in the Mediterranean. Further, he argued that Russia had suffered considerable

---

[232] Proceedings of the London Conference of Foreign Ministers, 1 Sep.–2 Oct. First meeting of the Council, 11 Sept. 4 pm.

[233] Ibid. Thirteenth meeting of the Council, 20 Sept. 11 am.

[234] Ibid. Thirty-third meeting of the Council, 2 Oct. 11 am.

[235] Roberts (2011, p. 81).

losses at the hands of Italian soldiers.[236] Thus, Russia was entitled to reparations from Italian interests. These issues were not resolved before the conference was completed.[237]

Disturbed by these issues, Bevin confronted Molotov about Soviet intentions on September 23rd. Bevin stated that "the whole European problem was drifting into the same condition as that which we had found ourselves in with Hitler. He was most anxious to avoid any trouble about our respective policies in Europe... He wanted to get into a position in which there was not the slightest room for suspicion about each other's motives. M. Molotov had quite rightly said that he wanted friendly neighbors and security in the east of Europe." The Secretary of State then made two points to illustrate the kind of doubts he felt. He noted that Stalin had specifically stated that Russia had no interest in the Mediterranean. But Molotov's policy differed. He could not understand Russia's claims over Tripolitania and the inland waterways. Molotov replied that there was "room for an agreement," at least as far as these issues went. However, Molotov would require more detailed discussions with Moscow before he could commit to an agreement.[238]

The foreign ministers met again at Moscow in December. All the same issues were raised and Molotov maintained a hard line on many of them. However, both Bevin and Byrnes were able to find much more common ground in their conversations with Stalin. In the end, Stalin acceded to all British demands that lay outside Eastern Europe and the Baltic States.[239]

Assessment of Soviet intentions   Public reports described the breakdown of the London Conference as a catastrophe. The events moved some in the FO and the IC over to the alarmist camp. These elites argued that during the war, Russia was reliant on the British. But now the war was over, Britain was left weak and Russia had a free hand. The demands in the Mediterranean therefore reflect true Soviet intentions unfettered by the constraints of war.[240]

However, many still called for calm. They pointed out that Molotov's demands for concessions in the Mediterranean may reflect Russian bargaining "tactics" rather than a deeper "strategy."[241] Some argued that

---

[236] Roberts (2011, pp. 94–95).

[237] Messer (1982, ch 7).

[238] All from Proceedings of the London Conference of Foreign Ministers FO 371/50992, Sep. 23, 1945 (afternoon session).

[239] Messer (1982, ch 8).

[240] Dixon's assessment: FO 371/47856 Sep. 24, 1945.

[241] FO 371/47856 Warner's Minute Oct. 3, 1945.

Russian demands in the Mediterranean were "put forward in order to strengthen their bargaining position in other directions."[242] Similarly, others argued that Russian claims were in direct response to "Anglo-American claims to interfere in Russian interests nearer home (Balkans)."[243] Others argued that Molotov was using the "classic Russian nuisance tactics" of stalling negotiations with difficult claims, "expecting that the Americans, as so often before, would toward the end of the conference start 'formula hunting' in order to prevent a breakdown."[244] They pointed out that this tactic was effective in the past. However, in this case Molotov had miscalculated.[245] In fact, many pointed out that Molotov was willing to drop the claims readily when pressed by Bevin as a sign he realized he had pushed too far.[246]

Another line of argument suggested that the atomic bomb had an unusual effect on Soviet threat perceptions.[247] Observing the power of the atomic weapon, the Soviets realized that, until they developed it, they were vulnerable to coercion by those that held it. Further, they were in a strangely weak position to use coercive threats of their own. This odd combination led them to believe that the Western powers were confident in their own security, and would understand that the Soviets were not. Thus, these increased demands were still broadly consistent with security.[248]

A third line of argument considered that Molotov's position may not reflect Stalin's or the Politburo's position.[249] Cables from Stalin suggest that these issues were not important to Soviet intentions. Molotov's performance at the London Conference was poorly received in the Soviet press and it may be that Russia would not pursue these interests seriously in future conferences.[250]

---

[242] FO 371/47856 Sargent's Minute Sep. 24, 1945.

[243] FO 371/47856 Cadogan's Minute Sep. 25, 1945.

[244] FO 371/47856 Warner's Minute Oct. 3, 1945.

[245] FO 371/47856 Sargent's reply to Warner's Minute Oct. 6, 1945.

[246] Frank Robert's raises this point FO371/57089 Sep. 28, 1945. Molotov was known as a ferocious bargainer, never to back down from a position. This was highly unusual for his style of diplomacy.

[247] Roberts raises this argument: FO371/47883 Oct. 26, 28, and 31. Affirmed by foreign minister on Oct. 31, 1945.

[248] The prime minister and foreign minister broadly agreed that Soviet behavior seemed consistent still with security in the context of nuclear weapons. See CAB128/4 CM(45)51, Minute 4 & Confidential Annex. The foreign minister and prime minister concur with statement "It was true that the Soviet Government were not at all present fully co-operative in world affairs; but that was due in large measure to their suspicion of Western democracies."

[249] FO/800/7997, Nov. 29, 1945.

[250] FO/800/5155 Nov. 29, 1945; FO/800/5260 Dec. 8, 1945.

6.5.4 Discussion

At first glance, the divergent assessments appear to challenge my theoretical expectations. I expect that all analysts should observe behavior that they believe is inconsistent with political reassurances, and then uniformly update their assessments. Why do I observe divergent assessments? Indeed, there was a tendency for military staff in the PHPC to grow alarmed and the FO to call for calm. Is not, then, the updating largely explained by organizational traits and interests?[251]

A closer inspection of the arguments that each side puts forward suggests their reasoning is largely consistent with my theory. Although the conclusions that analysts reach differ, their arguments are formulated around the idea of whether Stalin's rhetoric and actions were consistent with security. The alarmist pointed to how Soviet behavior was consistent with aggressive aims rooted in the interests of Marxist communism or authoritarianism. They argued that the way that Stalin pursued Soviet interests in Poland and Eastern Europe signaled aggressive long-term intentions because they extended beyond what was reasonable for security. By contrast, those who called for calm observed that nothing Stalin had done was inconsistent with security aims in terms of the specific territories that had been subjected to intense Soviet influence. They pointed to Stalin's restrained behavior in Finland, Persia, and Greece as positive signs.

The differences in conclusions hinged on what types of information analysts prioritize. Those who prioritized the method of administration as the primary indicator of true intentions were alarmed. Those who prioritized the areas that Stalin was willing to fight for called for calm. This distinction clarifies an underlying assumption of my theory about how analysts derive their prior beliefs. In my theory, each analyst uses their education, expertise, seniority and experience in government and institutional affiliation to inform their assessments. These experiences will form their underlying prior beliefs about the long-term intentions of Challengers (generally), and the indicators that they believe are the most important signals of shifting intentions. I cannot predict what these indicators are at an individual level. However, I argue that when an analyst observes inconsistent behavior in the areas that they think are most important, they will become alarmed.

Finally, it is important to note that two features of Soviet behavior did not influence British perceptions because it illustrates how my rationalist

---

[251] Although there is an organizational tendency, there is still considerable variation within both the PHPC and the FO on the intentions question.

theory can explain nuances of interest to scholars of sociology and psychology. First, is clear that Stalin's violation of the Yalta Accord (an international agreement) was not the primary reason that the PHPC or others grew alarmed about Soviet intentions. Their arguments focused on the implications of Soviet behavior for what its interests are. This is important because it distinguishes my logic of consistency with a principle, from the logic of honoring a promise (Sartori, 2005; Renshon, 2015). Similarly, the indifference to Soviet actions in Hungary emphasizes that norm violations are not perfectly correlated with threat perceptions. The case is especially puzzling for Goddard (2018) because British elites explicitly asked for Stalin's justification and Stalin did not provide it. Still this episode had little influence of British perceptions of Stalin's strategic aims.

This is not to say that Stalin's violation of the Yalta Agreement had no effect. It made clear to many that Stalin did not value formalized agreements. In discussing the value of signing onto an international organization with Russia, Eden asked, "How can we lay the foundations of any new world order when Anglo-American relations with Russia are so completely lacking in confidence?"[252] Interestingly, Eden sided with the call for calm camp on the question of Soviet intentions. He and others were able to separate out the implications for Soviet behavior on the possibility of future agreements, and the implications for Soviet intentions.

Second, there was wide variation in the assessments of Soviet intentions from the analysts that attended Yalta (and also within those that did not). Thus, it is difficult to argue that perceptions followed from face-to-face interactions, or vivid images (Holmes, 2018; Yarhi-Milo, 2014).

6.6 The Final Straw: The Iran Crisis and the Turkish Straits Crisis

During the war, Persia was a critical oil supplier of, and access point to, the Soviet Union. British and Soviet forces occupied Persia to safeguard access to the Soviet Union. However, with Germany demobilized, there was little reason to occupy Persia. Indeed, the JIC report explicitly judged that a permanent occupation of Iran was not consistent with Soviet security interests, and Stalin had disclaimed Soviet interests in territorial control over Persia. To that end, the British and the Soviets had agreed to withdraw their forces from Persia by March 1st 1946.

By the end of February 1946 Stalin and Molotov claimed in private interactions with Britain and through public statements that Persia was not yet

---

[252] FO/371/37584, Mar. 24, 1945.

stable, and indicated that they may not leave.[253] They pointed to insurgent and separatist activities, especially the Azerbaijan People's Government, in Northern Persia.[254] When the March deadline passed, Iran complained to the United Nations that the Soviets had violated their commitment. The Soviet Union tried unsuccessfully to remove Iran's claim from the Agenda. Under considerable pressure from Truman and threats of force, the Soviet Union agreed to remove their troops immediately. They did not. Only after military threats from the Americans did the Soviet Union exit.[255]

6.6.1 Assessment of Soviet Intentions Following the Iran Crisis

Witnessing events in February, the JIC began drafting a report that they released in March. They noted that "Our report of the 18th December, 1944,... [concluded that] Russia's policy after the war would be directed primarily towards achieving the greatest possible measure of security." However, they now believed that

Russia will seek, by all the above means, short of major war, to include within her "belt" further areas which she considers it strategically necessary to dominate. Turkey and the major part of Persia are such areas... Elsewhere she will adopt a policy of opportunism to extend her influence wherever possible without provoking a major war, leaving the onus of challenge to the rest of the world. In pursuing this policy she will use, in the way she thinks most effective, Communist Parties in other countries and certain international organisations. She will also use her propaganda to stir up trouble among colonial peoples.[256]

Before March 1946 the JIC assessed that the Soviet Union had limited interests in the Middle East. The Iran Crisis caused it to update its assessment. In a report on the implications of the Iran Crisis the JIC argued that

The Soviet Government have, in fact, resumed the traditional Russian policy of southern expansion, which was temporarily suspended between the fall of the Czarist regime and the war of 1939. The Soviet Government will implement this

---

[253] Yegorova (1996, pp. 18–20).

[254] In November 1945, a communist insurgent group in Northern Persia, the Azerbaijan People's Government, declared their independence from the Iranian government and fought off forces loyal to Tehran. At around the same time, Kurdish separatists rebelled against the Iranian government. The British suspected that these groups were supported by the Soviet Union but did not know it at the time. See Harper (2018, pp. 1–5), and Raine (1994, pp. 94–98).

[255] Fawcett (2009).

[256] Report of the Joint Intelligence Sub-Committee of Great Britain: "Russia's Strategic Interests and Intentions," Mar. 1, 1946.

historic policy by every means short of war. Their ultimate goal is clear, but the intermediate moves will be opportunist and their order of priority flexible... She will seek to extend her influence wherever possible in the world.[257]

The FO also changed its tune. Frank Roberts had remained calm in the face of unusually large Soviet demands in the Mediterranean in October 1945. However, starting in March, he wrote a series of assessments of Soviet strategic intentions that earned him the title of the British George Kennan. The thrust of Roberts's argument was that Soviet behavior could not be motivated by security. He pointed to Soviet support for communist forces outside their sphere of influence and Soviet behavior in Iran as clearly outside a security motivation. Roberts disagreed with the JIC on Soviet motives. He claimed that communism was driving their behavior. Nevertheless, he agreed with the JIC that the Soviet Union would exert their influence whenever the opportunity presented itself.

At the highest levels, both the prime minister and foreign minister had come to deeply mistrust the Soviet Union.[258] The prime minister called for weekly intelligence reports on Soviet intentions and the foreign minister commissioned a report on the possibility of a Soviet invasion of the Middle East.[259]

6.6.2 The Turkish Straits Crisis

One might wonder how permanent this shift was. Did these policy-makers confront future Soviet behavior with the assumption that the Soviets were aggressive, or did they revert back to uncertainty? To answer this question, I report evidence from the next major event in Anglo-Soviet relations. On August 8, 1946, Stalin further pushed Soviet demands into Turkey. Stalin demanded that Turkey revise the Montreux Convention in favor of the Soviet Union. Specifically, Stalin demanded control over the Turkish Straits. If granted, it would provide the Soviet Union considerable strategic influence in the Mediterranean.

In many ways, Stalin's demands were simply an extension of prior Soviet behavior. At the London Conference in 1945, Molotov had unsuccessfully raised the idea of Soviet Control over the Turkish Straits and Bering Strait. He had also asked to revise the Montreux Convention that governed

---

[257] JIC(46)38(0) Final, Jun. 14, 1946. "Russia's Strategic Interests and intentions in the Middle East."

[258] See Messer (1982); Fawcett (2009); Lomas (2016); Smith (1988) for discussion.

[259] JIC(46)24(0) Final March 16, 1946. "Implications of Recent Russian Movements in Persia."

Soviet–Turkish relations. As outlined above, Molotov's demands caused a great deal of concern among the War Cabinet. However, there was considerable debate about what they meant for broader Soviet intentions. Some thought Molotov had signaled aggressive Soviet intentions, others called for calm.

Even though Stalin's demands in 1946 were almost identical, they generated a different reaction. The consensus opinion in both Britain and the United States was well summarized by the Acting Secretary of State Dean Acheson a day after Stalin made his demands:

In our opinion, the primary objective of the Soviet Union is to obtain control over Turkey. We believe that if the Soviet Union succeeds in introducing into Turkey armed forces with the ostensible purpose of enforcing the joint control of the Straits, the Soviet Union will use these forces in order to obtain control over Turkey.... In our opinion, therefore, the time has come when we must decide that we shall resist with all means at our disposal any Soviet aggression and in particular, because the case of Turkey would be so clear, any Soviet aggression against Turkey. In carrying this policy our words and acts will only carry conviction to the Soviet Union if they are formulated against the background of an inner conviction and determination on our part that we cannot permit Turkey to become the object of Soviet aggression.[260]

In general, there was no debate about what Stalin's demands meant for Soviet intentions. British and American elites took as given that Stalin's intentions were expansive. As a result, they worked directly with their Turkish counterparts to protect Turkish independence and hinder any Soviet expansion.[261]

Unlike all the crises that had come before, it seems that the British and Americans had already made up their mind about Soviet intentions prior to the Turkish Straits Crisis. Because they had made up their minds, they chose to resist Soviet efforts to expand.

6.6.3 Inference

I infer from this evidence that each decision-maker carries their unique expertise and experience into the assessment process. This will lead each decision-maker to prioritize different pieces of evidence in their assessments. Organizational processes, too, may lead different analysts to gain access to different pieces of information. Thus, only those at the very top

---

[260] Acheson, The Acting Secretary of State to the Secretary of State at Paris, August 15, 1946. Foreign Relations of the United States, Vol. VII, 1946, pp. 840–842.
[261] For discussion, see Cohen (1978), Seydi (2006), Kuniholm (2014).

have a complete picture. As a result of high variance in how individuals interpret evidence, each comes to mistrust Soviet long-term intentions at different points in time.

Important for my theory, each analyst uses the evidence they are presented with to ask the same fundamental question: "If Stalin wants security, would I ever observe this evidence?" The critical point is that analysts justify their assessment using this framework in every case. Those that update their beliefs argue that the evidence suggests Stalin's behavior is inconsistent with his security claims. Those that fail to update argue that Stalin's behavior could be consistent with security. Thus, I infer from this evidence that consistency between words and deeds is the primary way that decision-makers structure their assessments and form beliefs.

6.6.4 Discussion of Alternatives

As others have argued, the Iran and Turkish Crises closely follow the basic logic of costly signaling, and provide compelling evidence that defensive realism explains the onset of the Cold War.[262] My theory provides two friendly amendments to this explanation. First, defensive realists suggest greedy Challengers compete when they can exploit surprise to cheat the Challenger. But Stalin indicated his intent to remain in February, the Allied forces stalled their withdrawal, and Stalin was unable to exploit them through a permanent occupation.[263] Under the defensive realist logic, Stalin either should have delayed his move until after the British withdrawal, or otherwise waited for a moment to reveal his motives, where he could exploit Western trust for significant gain. He did neither. My theory clarifies that greedy states opportunistically expand even if it will not afford them the opportunity to cheat a trusting rival. Second, the common applications of defensive realism struggles with a longer view of Anglo-Soviet relations. Notably, the standard logic is that costly signals are most informative when the stakes are high, and the costly actions are most violent (Yoder, 2019; Glaser, 2010; Edelstein, 2019). But the Polish Crisis was highly salient to Britain, and Stalin's decision to overturn governments in Romania was viewed as more violent than the decision to keep forces in Iran. And yet, only Iran caused mistrust. My theory clarifies that it is not the level of violence that matters, but how the Challenger's actions fit a principle. Overall, this clarifies why the Iran Crisis shifted British estimates, but prior costly actions had no effect.

---

[262] Kydd (2005, p. 101).
[263] Raine (1994, pp. 102–105).

These events are harder to explain from the perspective of face-to-face interactions (Holmes, 2018), persuasion (Goddard, 2018), or pretext (Rosato, 2015). Notably, Stalin and Molotov used both face-to-face meetings and multi-vocal messages to legitimate their decision to remain in Iran. They pointed out that Azerbaijan was a critical interest, that local rebels had complicated issues, and that Western powers were allowed to deploy occupying forces outside their sphere of influence. But the British were not persuaded to remain trustful. This event is especially surprising given that Stalin refused to justify events in Romania, and British elites did not update. Consistent with my theory, once the moment of truth had passed and Stalin had identified a single principle, British elites used their pre-crisis estimates of how issues fit with Soviet security to adjudicate Stalin's future actions, and were largely insensitive to Stalin's rhetorical pretexts.

6.7 Conclusions

In this chapter I traced my causal mechanism through a single case. I found evidence to support my theory at every step of my causal mechanism:

- British elites were initially uncertain about Stalin's motives because they did not understand what principle motivated Stalin. They theorized about different principles and then extrapolated to predict what Stalin would want if Stalin was motivated by each principle.
- British elites coordinated their beliefs based on a diplomatic exchange between Eden and Stalin. It was clear that the content of Stalin's message mattered: He declared that security motivated his limited foreign policy aims. Consistent with my coordinating logic, many British elites, especially those who did not attend, used this to coordinate their estimates.
- For several years, British elites tolerated Stalin's costly actions including territorial demands, coercive threats, and efforts to undermine liberal world order because they believed that his actions could plausibly serve his declared motives.
- British elites individually and collectively use the logic of qualitative inferences to justify why they eventually come to mistrust Stalin. Analysts grew alarmed when they could not reconcile Stalin's actions with his declared motivation. They therefore ruled out the possibility he was motivated by security, and inferred he wanted something much more.
- Britain's choice to compete with the Soviet Union followed closely after they realized Soviet intentions were vast.

As a result, I infer strong support for my theory from this case.

To be clear, I also found support for other theories at important moments. My theory advances defensive realist accounts by clarifying why costly signals work at some moments and not others, and how costless diplomacy can function. I also found evidence that elite perceptions and preferences deviate based on their institutional affiliations or among individual elites based on their personal backgrounds and world views. However, these deviations fall around the rational baseline that my theory predicts. When my theory predicts that all kinds of analysts should change their perceptions, I see movement across military, diplomatic, and intelligence analysts. In this way, I advance bureaucratic and personalist theories by providing a new rational baseline around which analysts should fall.

Finally, I found compelling evidence against social theories of diplomacy, psychological theories of misperception and vividness, and normative theories commonly used by social scientists to explain similar cases. While there were two moments–the *Pravada* incident, and Churchill's views on Stalin following the Tehran Conference–where the perceptions of important elites succumb to such mechanisms, the effects were short lived, and held no bearing on British behavior. Elite perceptions revert to my rationalist expectations quickly. In other cases that these scholars have used to evidence their theories, such as optimism following Yalta, I raise important questions they must reckon with.

Explaining the Origins of Great Power Rivalries since 1850: A Medium-*n* Analysis

Can qualitative inferences help us understand patterns of competition and peace across the cases that fill our history books? I answer this question with a medium-*n* analysis of fourteen major power rivalries since 1850. I present my findings in three parts. The first part provides a broad overview of my approach, predictions and findings. I predict that cases end in peace if the Challenger initially appeals to a limited aims principle, and from that moment on, the Defender can always reconcile the Challenger's violent actions with a single limiting principle. I predict competition otherwise. Of the cases that end in competition, I predict that competition will come shortly after the Defender cannot reconcile the history of the Challenger's actions with a limited aims principle. I find that my theory well predicts the instances and timing of competition in twelve of the fourteen cases.

This top-line summary is intentionally brief. At the end of it, you will likely have questions about how I coded my variables, and whether elite choices reflect the logic of my theory. The second part of this chapter addresses these questions through four case vignettes. The first two vignettes trace my coding and logic through typical cases that my theory well-predicts (one ends in competition and the other ends in peace). The second two vignettes analyze the two cases that my theory does not well predict. The vignettes show that my mechanism is at work in all four cases. The vignettes of the two cases I miss illuminate how other factors, such as power and regime type, impact decision-making in these cases. I show that these variables are important and complimentary to my theory for explaining the grand strategy that elites adopt.

The third part of the chapter explores the value-add of my theory relative to existing structural explanations.[264] I identify the ideal conditions for

---

[264] To be clear, the main alternative explanations in this chapter are structural theories that make precise predictions about the timing of competition, and shifts in threat perceptions in particular cases. These are mainly theories of power and military force (Powell,

competition and peace in all fourteen cases based on existing explanations about power and crisis behavior. If my theory is valuable, it will not only explain competition in the context of existing explanations. Rather, it will give us leverage on the timing of competition when other structural theories predict peace should persist. I find my theory performs well under a broad range of conditions. In fact, my theory compliments power-based explanation because it fits the dogs that don't bark: cases where power shifts rapidly but peace persists.

Putting it altogether, my theory outperforms other structural theories in explaining the overarching pattern of competition and peace at the origins of great power rivalries over the last 250 years. However, we can learn the most from an overarching framework that balances my motives-based explanation and the pressures caused by the rate of shifting power.

7.1 Part 1: Summary of Approach and Findings

My goal is to analyze the turn from hedging to competition or peace across powerful state dyads since 1850. To be clear, there is a large empirical literature that identifies rivalries, and compiles cases based on the frequency of militarized disputes within some pre-specified interval of time (e.g., Goertz and Diehl, 1995; Klein, 2006). But my theory begins in the prior period, where a rivalry has not begun, and one state perceives a potential rivalry on the horizon. I am interested in examining cases during the period of hedging, which may give way to either competition or peace. As Thompson (2001) (a leading figure within the rivalries school) argues, scholars risk incorrect inferences if they rely on existing datasets that selected cases based on a logic that does not match their theory (see also Fordham, 2020; Sechser, 2011). Thus, I used my theoretical scope conditions to select cases.

The cases I analyze are presented in Table 7.1. How did I arrive at these cases? Appendix F online details my coding rules and procedures. Here I summarize the overall approach. I started with my theory. My unit of analysis is a rivalry that includes a directed dyad of one Challenger and one Defender. My goal was to include cases where the Defender anticipates that the Challenger could demand regular and sustained foreign policy

1999; Organski and Kugler, 1980). I discuss a wide range of secondary alternatives that focus on particular moments in the vignettes. But the other chapters provide a more detailed analyses of these alternatives.

Table 7.1 *Universe of great power rivalry cases*

Defenders	Challengers	Onset
France	Germany (Prussia)	1866
Russia/USSR	China	1949
Russia/USSR	Japan	1978
United Kingdom	Germany	1890
United Kingdom	Germany	1931
United Kingdom	Germany (Prussia)	1866
United Kingdom	Russia	1941
United Kingdom	United States	1865
United States	Germany	1934
United States	Germany	1990
United States	India	1974
United States	Japan	1905
United States	Japan	1987
United States	Russia	1943

concessions for the foreseeable future.[265] Partly for simplicity, and partly for theoretical reasons, I restrict my case selection in two ways. First, I only included cases where the Defender was a great power. Second, I focused my analysis on cases starting after 1850.[266] As a result, I confine the inferences I draw from this chapter to great power relations from 1850 onward.

Starting with this definition, I developed a two-stage coding procedure to select cases. In the first stage, I use fifteen quantitative indicators to identify a short-list of forty-four plausible dyads. First, I used indicators to isolate well-established great powers in each decade. I took these as the states that could plausibly serve as status-quo Defenders. Next, I used indicators to identify states that would plausibly hold the ability to make repeated demands over a long period of time. I took these as the states that could plausibly serve as Challengers. My shortlist of plausible dyads is every Challenger–Defender combination from these two lists.

---

[265] This includes power transition cases. But it also includes cases (such as the rise of the United States) where a Challenger uses its growing economy for domestic projects for multiple decades, and then eventually turns to foreign policy. It also includes cases where a regional power vacuum or regime change creates opportunities for revision that were not previously there.

[266] In 1850, elites started to take citizen preferences more seriously, nationalism and identity started to be taught in school. As a result, the foreign policy motives started to vary along the lines that my theory predicts for at least most states in Europe.

In the second stage, I took each dyad on my shortlist and read historical accounts to identify whether the great power Defender was concerned that the Challenger could revise the status quo repeatedly in the near future. When I found evidence in the historical record that this was true, I included the case.[267]

Some readers may question the inclusion or omission of certain cases. This is an inevitable product of using a systematic case inclusion rule. The advantage of using a systematic procedure is that case selection is not biased by how the case ends, or other aspects of my predictions (Fordham, 2020). My reliance on theoretically motivated quantitative indicators also ensures that I cannot pick and choose cases from my reading of political accounts. One disadvantage is that I exclude some important cases. My coding rules assure that I miss cases that involve middle-power Defenders, or cases that start before 1850, or cases that historians focus on but where the Defender is not actually powerful based on objectives measures I use for case inclusion (such as GDP). For example, even though they would support my theory, I do not include Anglo-Russian competition during the Great Game, or events leading to the Crimean War, because these cases start before 1850. I also do not consider Germany a major power because it does not meet my requirement for force projection capabilities. I also include cases that scholars who use subjective inclusion rules omit. For example, I include US–India because India held revisionist demands, its economy and military were growing, and India sought nuclear weapons, which could trigger a massive power shift. In the years following the Indo-Pakistan War, the US increasingly worried that India was a capable 'friend' of Russia's (Kissinger, 1979, p. 901), and investigated India's strategic aims (Hess, 1992). I chose not to deviate from my coding procedure to preserve the credibility of my inferences. If I arbitrarily include cases that do not fit the coding procedure but are popular, one must wonder if I am rigging the case universe to fit my theory. By considering all cases that fit the rule, I am also forced to reckon with a few surprising cases that I may not be able to easily explain.

Still, I took two steps to increase my confidence in my construct validity overall. First, I verified that my cases were broadly consistent with existing datasets. As expected, my cases are a subset of notable datasets that use quantitative indicators to identify cases of emerging threats (Kugler and Lemke, 1996; de Soysa et al., 1997), and nearly identical to the case

---

[267] As I explain later, I used a similar procedure to code the start/end dates, and the variables in my cases.

universe identified by Allison (2017), and the strategic rivalry dataset proposed by Thompson (2001). This suggests that I did not inappropriately include cases. I also include the cases analyzed in recent cross-national accounts that select on their outcome variables (Goddard, 2018; Edelstein, 2019). This suggests that I did not inappropriately rule out many important cases.

Second, and as fully described in Appendix F online, I identified two key moments in history where status-quo Defenders faced a dramatic shift in the global situation, and engaged in a comprehensive review of the potential threats that they faced: US threat estimates at the end of the Cold War, and Britain's choice (circa 1930) to abandon the five-year plans given growing unrest in Europe. I reviewed primary sources surrounding these strategic reviews to make sure that the Challengers that were in my lists where the same states that weighed on the minds of real-life decision-makers. For example, when the Cold War ended, the White House ordered a new estimate of states which could threaten US interests. I interviewed an NSC official who played a prominent role in crafting that estimate. The list of states initially considered, and the list of potential threats provided to the White House match the cases identified in my initial quantitative coding, and then my final coding based on my review of qualitative sources.

Readers may also question the start years of particular cases. Some dates appear later because a Challenger must meet a capability threshold before I consider them (e.g., Russo-Japanese relations). In other cases, the inclusion is based on my analysis of when the Defender began to estimate the Challenger's motives amid a historical debate. Fortunately, these coding choices do not impact how I evaluate my theory. The reason is that other plausible start dates occur during the period of hedging. My theory simply predicts the Defender's policy continuity in this period, and that is what we observe. Consider the pre-Cold War period. We saw in Chapter 6 that it would not have influenced my analysis if I selected other plausible start dates because they all arise during a period where I expect continuity. A detailed historical analysis of the case would support my theory either way. Still, I code the onset of Anglo-Russian and Russo-American case differently. The reason is that my theoretically motivated coding rule asks me to start when I find the Defender's estimates of Russia's strategic intentions. These differ for Britain and the United States.

Finally, the Defender in 12/14 dyads is a democracy. One might worry that I can only say the evidence supports cases where the Defender is a democracy. This concern is partly alleviated by three factors. First, my theory is abstract. There is no regime-specific feature. Second, the two cases with an autocratic Defender both fit my theory. Third, the US is entering a period of relative decline against many states and is likely to serve in the Defender role over the next half century. I can still use the analysis to extrapolate to US cases in the future.

7.1.1 Predictions about Declared Principles

Before I can explain patterns of competition at the moment of truth, I need to verify that Challengers declare a principle in a way that matches my theory. In this section I code each Challenger's core interest claims at the moment of focus. Next, I will use these results to help me code costly actions that are consistent (or not) with a declared principle.

I report my coding of declared principles in Table 7.2. Column 4 asks did the Challenger assert limited intentions by tying her demands to a specific foreign policy principle? Column 5 asks if she did, what was the principle? Column 6 asks did the Defender understand what issues and territories would the Challenger want, if the Challenger's claims were honest? I review the coding procedure and the sources I used in Appendix F online.

Consistent with my theory, the Challenger justified revisionist desires by appealing to a specific principle. In 13/14 cases, the Challenger appealed to a principle that was tangible and reassuring for the Defender. That is, the Defender could easily understand (sometimes with a handful of ambiguities) the issues and territories that were associated with the Challenger's claim, and the number of issues were sufficiently small such that the Defender was willing to facilitate early concessions.

I code one case, Germany following the rise of Wilhelm II, as deviant because I could not substantiate expectation 1: Britain could not clearly identify what issues Germany would contest under Weltpolitik. This deviation highlights the relative specificity in other cases. In 13/14 cases, the Challenger clearly articulated a principle, and the Defender was reasonably confident that it understood whether many issues fit the Challenger's declared principle or not.

Looking across cases, Challengers appealed to seven distinct principles to explain their limited aims: ethnic/historical nationalism, security, restoring borders, trade rights, regional hegemony, support for communism, colonial resource extraction, and status.[268] Furthermore, the same state at different points in history use different justifications. For example, Hitler's

---

[268] Going further back in history suggests more. Russia, for example, claimed it sought to protect Orthodox Christians in the 1820s.

Table 7.2 *What principle did the challenge appeal to?*

D	C	Onset	Did C promise limited aims?	Nature of claim	D finds claim plausible	Scope of demands
FRA	GER	1866	✓	Ethnic	✓	Territory: France, Denmark, Austria
RUS	CHN	1949	✓	Communism	✓	Influence in Asia, nuclear weapons, spread of communism.
RUS	JPN	1978	✓	Peace, border claim	✓	Territory: 3 islands
UK	GER	1866	✓	Ethnic	✓	Territory: France, Denmark, Austria
UK	GER	1890		Status (Weltpolitk)		Unclear
UK	GER	1931	✓	Ethnic	✓	Territory: 6 European states
UK	RUS	1941	✓	Security	✓	Territory: 8 European states. + Germany dismemberment
UK	USA	1865	✓	Western hegemony	✓	Influence over Western Hemisphere /Caribbean
USA	GER	1932	✓	Ethnic	✓	Territory: 6 European states
USA	GER	1990	✓	Human rights	✓	Enforce international norm.
USA	IND	1974	✓	Security	✓	Accepted as nuclear power + Pakistan concessions
USA	JPN	1914	✓	Access to resources	✓	Territory: Korea, Taiwan, Pacific Ocean. Manchuria
USA	JPN	1987	✓	Peace + border claim	✓	Nothing
USA	RUS	1942	✓	Security	✓	Territory: 8 European states + Germany dismemberment

demands differed from Wilhelm II's, and again from post-Cold War Germany's. This cross-case variation provides very strong support for my underlying assumptions. My theory assumes that different Challengers can value different principles. If all Challengers claimed nationalism as their declared principle, then there would only be one limited-aims type, and no coordination problem to speak of. But as we can see, even the same Challenger alters its claim across history. This suggests that uncertainty about the Challenger's principle is a reasonable starting place.

7.1.2 Predictions about Competition and Peace

I predict that Defenders will turn to competition if and only if the Challenger takes costly military actions that the Defender cannot easily reconcile with the Challenger's declared principle, given the Defender's knowledge of the Challenger's history and culture.[269]

My dependent variable is the strategic orientation of the Challenger and the Defender. For the purpose of these tests, the most important and difficult strategic shift to code was the Defender's change from hedging to competition.[270] My analysis also requires me to code the shift to peace to determine when cases end. But, as stated above, this was less consequential for evaluating my theory in practice.

How do I measure these strategies? I start with my theory. Chapter 2 provides detailed conceptual definitions of competition and hedging. As stated, the main conceptual difference is what the Defender intends his strategy to achieve. Under hedging the Defender seeks to leave his options open. He wants to make most concessions that the Challenger demands to avoid war and leave open the possibility of achieving lasting peace. But the Defender also continues to arm, monitor the Challenger, and forward-deploy forces to put the Defender in the best position to compete. Under competition, the Defender seeks out opportunities to harm the Challenger, and prevent the Challenger's expansion.

The most direct evidence of the Defender's strategic goals lies in historical accounts of the Defender's strategic deliberations, and declassified archival materials. This is where I mainly focused my data-collection efforts.

---

[269] Assuming we get past the moment of focus.

[270] While I describe competition as a rivalry, it is different than the presence of a dyadic militarized disputes, or contested territorial claims that empirically orientated scholars use to code rivalries. See Thompson (2001) for the value in my approach.

A secondary indicator lies in the Defender's perception of the Challenger's incentive to misrepresent. The strategic dynamics of hedging mean that the Defender is uncertain if the Challenger's aims are vast, and hopes that they are not. Therefore, the Defender is trying to figure out if the Challenger wants more than what she claims. Once competition has started, the Challenger overstates her willingness to fight and the Defender is hopeful that the Challenger is less resolved in a specific case than she claims she is.

Finally, I partly relied on behavioral indicators (Edelstein, 2019). As stated in Chapter 2, behavioral indicators are imperfectly correlated with a shift in the Defender's strategic goals. For example, if the Defender is hedging in the sense I mean it, he will continue to arm, monitor the Challenger, and forward-deploy forces. Different still, when the Defender does turn to competition, there is often a long lag between when the Defender actually implements comprehensive sanctions, declares war against the Challenger, or takes other competitive policies. The reason for this lag is that Defenders must balance the pros and cons of military conflict in each specific situation, even if their overall goal is to thwart the Challenger.

My independent variable is whether the Challenger's actions are consistent or not with the Challenger's declared principle. To start, I used existing events datasets and historical accounts to compile a list of notable events. These events included the Challenger's choice to start or intervene in a crisis, seek to overthrow a foreign government through meddling in their domestic politics, produce offensive weapons, threaten military force, form an offensive or defensive alliance, join or leave an institution, violate a treaty or other commitment, build a shadow institution, make a territorial demand, or take territory.

Costly signaling theory predicts that these indicators should all raise mistrust. I predict that these indicators only trigger mistrust if they help rule out the Challenger's declared principle. Thus, to properly evaluate my theory, I coded these different events based on whether the Defender perceived these actions as plausibly consistent with the Challenger's declared principles or not. I code cases that end in competition as supporting my theory if the Defender turns to competition two years after the first inconsistent action. I code cases that end in peace as supportive if the Challenger does not take an inconsistent action.

Compiling a comprehensive list of costly events presents the toughest possible test for my theory. If I was to focus only on key crises (Goddard, 2018) and observed diplomatic episodes (Yarhi-Milo, 2014) identified by historians, I risk omitting events where I predict change in the Defender's strategy, but the case displays continuity. This would artificially inflate my confidence in my theory.[271]

I say my theory fails to predict a case in one of three conditions. First, the Defender turns to competition before the Challenger's first inconsistent action. Second, the Challenger takes an inconsistent action and the Defender waits for more than two years to compete (or never competes). Third, the Challenger does not declare a principle that is limited.

Table 7.3 summarizes the cases my theory predicts correctly, and not correctly. I find that my theory well predicts 12 out of 14 cases. As my theory expects, 6/8 cases that end in competition do so shortly after the Challenger's first inconsistent action. Also as my theory expects, 6/6 cases end in peace given that the Challenger never behaves in an inconsistent way.

Table 7.3 *Coding the timing of competition and instances of peace*

C fails to declare clear, limiting principle	UK-GER (1890s)
D competes before C's inconsistent action	FR-GER (1860s)
D competes soon after C's first inconsistent action	RUS-CHN (1949) UK-GER (1931) UK-RUS (1941) US-RUS (1942) US-GER (1942) US-JPN (1938)
D competes long after C's first inconsistent action	
C's actions are consistent and states achieve peace	RUS-JPN (1978) UK-GER (1866) UK-USA (1865) US-GER (1990) US-IND (1974) US-JPN (1987)

Note: I expect cases to fall into the grey boxes. The mispredicted cases fall into the white boxes.

---

[271] This is a core difference between how social scientists and historians should approach cases. Since social scientists intend to verify theories against cases, they should examine all relevant events.

7.2 Part 2a: Case Vignettes That My Theory Well Predicts

Under my coding rules, twelve cases fit my theory. I now detail vignettes for two typical cases from this set. One of these cases ends in competition shortly after the Challenger's first inconsistent action. The other ends in peace. I use these two cases to address three questions about my overall approach.

First, you may wonder about my coding choices. Specifically, how did I code the Defender's strategy (competition, hedging, and peace) given that strategies sometimes take years to implement? What do Challenger-actions look like in real life, and is it easy to know if the Defender perceives the Challenger's actions as ruling out a principle or not? The case vignettes help clarify how I apply my coding rules in typical cases.

Second, the medium-n analysis only codes a shift in the Defender's strategy. While the timing is supportive, the summary does not provide evidence for my mechanism. You may wonder if elites use the logic of my theory in these cases. I focus on critical moments in these cases that clearly illustrate the logic of my theory.[272]

Finally, there are many other theories that make predictions about patterns of competition and peace. For example, the last century of research into great power competition has focused on power (Blainey, 1988; Carr, 1945; Morgenthau and Thompson, 1948; Vasquez, 1993; Levy, 1998). Scholars argue that shifting power (Powell, 1999) the balance of power (Organski and Kugler, 1980), or the threat to use force (Mearsheimer, 2001; Waltz, 1979) are theoretically vital for explaining patterns of war and peace between great powers. If power concerns dominate my logic then I will observe cases that end in peace when the rate of shifting power is slow, or never achieves parity. I will instead only observe competition when the rate of shifting power is fast (or at parity). Alternatively, domestic political concerns could confound my theory. It is possible that certain regime pairs are prone to competition but others (i.e., pairs of democracies) are not. Different still, each new leaders may have a specific preference for her nation's strategy based on her unique personal experiences. As a result, Challengers may only take an inconsistent action when a new leader comes to power.[273] Defender may changes strategy when new leaders come to power and not

---

[272] Of course, there is only so much I can do in short vignettes. These cases only compliment the detailed accounts of Anglo-Soviet relations and Sino-American relations in later chapters.

[273] This would not be inconsistent with my theory, but it would call on me to think more about how leadership impacts my theory.

when the Challenger takes an inconsistent action. Throughout the analysis, I consider how my explanation intersects with these alternatives. I provide some analysis of the context surrounding leadership and regimes, and power.

7.2.1 Anglo-American Peace

In 1823, president James Monroe declared that the US held two overarching foreign policy goals: the ability to trade freely and peacefully with independent states; and to stop European powers from meddling in the Western Hemisphere so that the United States could exert influence. Although the claim to the Western Hemisphere was somewhat ambiguous, it was broadly understood to include the Americas, Caribbean Islands, and certain Pacific Islands (e.g., Hawaii). It did not include, for example, independent states or colonial possessions in East Asia or Australasia (Gilderhus, 2006, pp. 8–12).

Consistent with my theory, the Monroe Doctrine represents the declaration of an acceptably limited principle. To be sure, the second pillar clearly conflicted with British interests (May, 1975, pp. 39–41; Lawson, 1922, pp. 125–128). British elites occupied important positions across South American governments, and this gave Britain an economic advantage in trade. Britain also wanted to enforce contracts in South America. The Monroe Doctrine would prevent that. Finally, Britain maintained territorial claims in Alaska that conflicted with the Monroe Doctrine. However, the terms set–forth were acceptably limited to the British owing to their more pressing interests in Europe, and the fact that the Americas were geographically distant (Edelstein, 2019, p. 78). Indeed, as the United States was crafting the Monroe Doctrine, they consulted British diplomats in part to reduce the chance of ambiguity (Mowat, 1925, pp. 86–92). Britain was especially supportive of the Doctrine's anti-European (Spanish) terms (Lawson, 1922, p. 104). What the British did not know, however, was if the US's true intentions were confined to those set forth in the Monroe Doctrine, or if the US secretly held broader intentions. Britain's uncertainty over the US's true intentions drove Anglo-American tensions throughout the nineteenth century (Mowat, 1925, p. 94).

Even though the Monroe Doctrine was articulated in 1821, I start my analysis of events in 1865 (see Campbell, 1976).[274] Between 1821 and 1865

---

[274] I could have plausibly begun my analysis in 1890 owing to increased British attention. My conclusions are identical.

the US faced a series of domestic conflicts that sapped its resources and attention. The US Navy was too weak to enforce the Monroe Doctrine on its own. Indeed, the US relied on Britain to exert any influence. For example, Britain supplied ships so the US could contest Spanish influence in South America. Given Anglo-American collaboration during the 1850s against other European powers, it is unusual to consider it a rivalry. In 1865 the US Civil War ended. Peace brought a rapid increase in US economic productivity and a renewed interest in an expanding foreign policy. With it, Britain reinvigorated its hedging strategy. Notably, Britain devised new war plans to defend Canada against a US attack, and sustained military positions in Canada in case competition was necessary (Bourne, 1967).

Starting from 1865, Figure 7.1 summarizes how I code different aspects of the case over time. From the perspective of existing theories, there are severe pressures that should incentivize Anglo-American competition. The top of Figure 7.1 plots expectations about the future trajectory of US economic growth and military capabilities (Bell and Johnson, 2015). It shows that the US economy rose consistently and at a rapid rate from 1865 until 1907. In fact, the US economy rises faster in this case than any other Challenger in any other case that I study. Furthermore, US military spending came in punctuated bursts. This created sudden and steep increases in US military abilities.

Although it does not reveal itself in the quantitative summary, several events circa 1880 could have heightened Anglo-American tensions. First, the United States embarked on a more assertive foreign policy in the Americas. A staunch pan-Americanist, Blaine was appointed as Secretary of State in 1880. Blaine declared it the US mission "first, to bring about peace and prevent futile wars in North and South America; second, to cultivate such friendly commercial ties with all American countries as would lead to a large increase in the export trade of the United States."[275] This was clearly a more assertive version of the Monroe Doctrine later codified in the Roosevelt Corollary. Second, the British realized the "enormous reversal of economic fortunes" around 1880 (Dobson, 1995, p. 8). Thus, they appreciated that US power would rise enormously at a time of British decline. Third, the US announced its intention to build a "world class" navy over the next decade (Veeser, 2003). Britain saw the source of its power in its navy. In every prior case, (e.g., Germany naval arming) Britain perceived naval acquisitions as a direct threat.

---

[275] Quoted by State Department's Office of the Historian (2024).

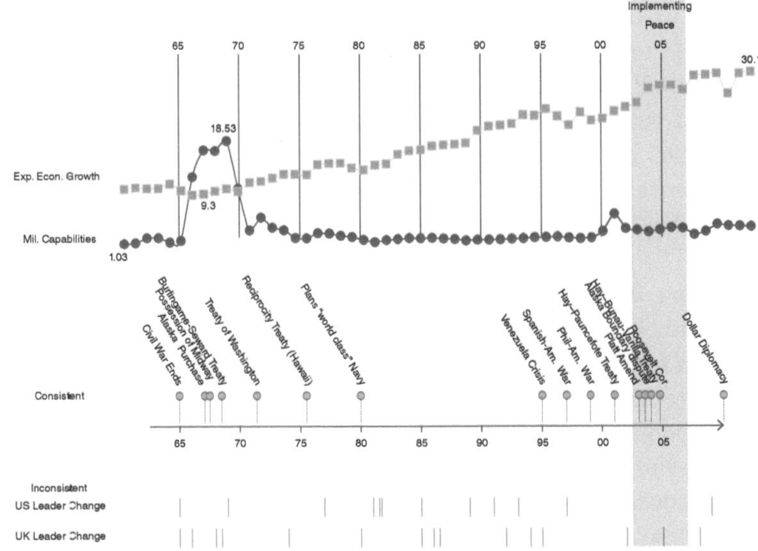

Figure 7.1 Time-varying events that could affect competition and peace during Anglo-American relations.

Figure summarizes factors that different theories believe could influence the UK's choice to compete with the United States over time. The top plots expected economic growth and military capabilities (Bell and Johnson, 2015). We label min/max values. Note these are statistically estimated values and the numbers are not substantively meaningful. The critical factor is the overall trajectory of economic growth and fluctuations in the rate of military spending. The bottom marks US and UK leadership changes. In the middle I plot salient US military, diplomatic and commercial choices. I code all choices as consistent with the US declared principle (Monroe Doctrine). By consistent, I mean that the British could not rule out the Monroe Doctrine as the US's principle as result of the action. There are no inconsistent choices. The grey bar represents the shift from hedging to Anglo-American peace.

The bottom of Figure 7.1 shows that this period was also dominated by frequent leadership changes.

The middle of Figure 7.1 plots salient diplomatic, military, and economic events. Under my coding procedure, I used quantitative indicators and broad historical accounts to develop a list of choices that the US made that could have theoretically triggered a shift in threat perceptions. This included all new commitments (such as treaties signed), diplomatic meetings with British elites, military deployments, crises and wars, and public declarations of foreign policy intentions.[276] The US fought multiple

---

[276] To be clear, Figure 7.1 does not plot every event. I exclude fifteen force deployments between 1865 and 1880 (including to Egypt and Japan). These deployments enforced commercial contracts or protected American citizens, and were consistent with practices

wars, directly threatened war against Britain twice, and announced naval expansion in the 1880s that directly threatened Britain's source of power.

Others predict that these events should engender mistrust and competition. And yet, competition did not come. I code a period of hedging between 1865 and 1903. Throughout this period I find British trust was roughly constant. I code the transition to peace as starting in 1903. I stop coding in 1907 because Anglo-American relations achieve stability and peace.

My theory explains this pattern of behavior because all these costly events could plausibly serve the Monroe Doctrine. Consistent with my theory, Britain understood this fact, and chose to deconflict its crises with the United States leading to a stable peace.

In what follows, I dig deeper into the case in three steps. First, I use US diplomatic and commercial expansion between 1865 and 1880 to illustrate how Challengers and Defenders coordinate during the period of hedging. Second, I detail how I wrestle with three difficult-to-code events during the period of hedging: the Venezuela Crisis, the American-Philippines War, and the Roosevelt Corollary. The additional detail is important to better understand how my theory applies in real life, and how I approach coding challenges in all of the cases. Third, I explain how I code the shift from hedging to peace. This helps clarify substantive differences between hedging and a stable peace in a typical case. After I detail these features, I explain how other theories fare in explaining this case.

How coordination during the period of hedging contrasts with bargaining under shifting power   As I conceptualize it, Challengers and Defenders should coordinate to diffuse tensions during the period of hedging. Modern scholars may wonder how this is different from bargaining in the shadow of power? One critical difference is that in my theory Defenders take extraordinary steps to avoid major war while they are hedging. They do not often exploit serious threats of major war to improve their bargaining position. Another difference is that I allow for misalignment between the distribution of territory and power. It is consistent with my theory if

of even weak European nations. I also exclude about thirty treaties that involve migration, commerce, citizenship, protection of medical staff, or related matters. I also exclude events that were secret, such as the 1907 US–Japan Treaty because Britain did not observe them. I include all force deployments to secure political objectives (i.e., non-commercial, or diplomatic security), all actions including treaties that involve shaping world order, or that expand and limit US territorial influence. I also include major statements of foreign policy intentions and all Anglo-American interactions.

the Challenger makes demands before it acquires the military capabilities to back them up. By contrast, scholars of shifting power predict that the US could only capture concessions after its expectation of victory in war shifts (Powell, 1999).[277]

The early period of the rise of the United States offers two examples of how hedging departs from the predictions of bargaining with shifting power. Between 1965 and 1878, the US Navy was too small to seriously compete with European powers in the Western Hemisphere. Although the US did increase military spending during the 1860s, they did not have the coercive power to push the Europeans out of the Americas (Bourne, 1967, ch 8). Despite a lack of coercive power, the US pursued the Monroe Doctrine in earnest. To do it, the US exchanged money and normative concessions for increased influence. The most extreme example is the 1867 Alaska purchase from Russia. The US did not have the military power to enforce this settlement should Russia refuse to leave, and they did not threaten invasion should Russia decline to sell (Luthin, 1937).[278] Despite the lack of the shadow of power, Russia accepted the terms of sale and withdrew from the Americas.

Negotiations surrounding the Treaty of Washington illustrate Anglo–American coordination over US influence in the Americas. The US, Canada, and Britain had longstanding grievances from the War of 1812 (Campbell, 1976, pp. 121–125). Some of these grievances related to the Canadian border, but others related to accusations about military conduct. The US complained that British naval vessels did not have the authority to stop or search American vessels that traversed waters in the Americas, and yet, British military vessels had fired on US commercial ships. On the surface, the Treaty of Washington settled these claims through reparations, but a subtle feature of this settlement was that Britain implicitly acknowledged US influence in the Americas. Specifically, by paying reparations, Britain acknowledged that the US had the main authority to police waters in the Americas. This was the first international recognition that the US had some legitimate influence over the Western hemisphere (Stuart, 1988, pp. 238–261; Smith, 1941).

---

[277] Strictly, these theories predict the US may make concessions initially to off-set the expectations of their future rise.

[278] Furthermore, it was well known that Russia would soon decline. Thus, the US could have expanded its military and contested the territory if it wanted to (Bolkhovitinov, 2003).

Three critical events for my theory   Reading the historical details of this case, I identified three events that illustrate plausible concerns for my explanation: the Venezuela Crisis; the American-Philippine War; and the Roosevelt Corollary. In the end, I found that US behavior during these episodes fits the Monroe Doctrine, and Britain's reactions fit my theory. I raise these three concerns here to help clarify my coding procedure and illustrate important nuances of historical and cultural context in real life.

First, my theory predicts that British elites avoid escalating in crises that are clearly consistent with the Monroe Doctrine. If anything, British elites should work hard to coordinate with the US and avoid spirals of mistrust. I find repeated evidence of this behavior. But during the Venezuela Crisis some British elites argued for escalation to war. One might wonder, how far can individual-level factors influence state choices in these cases?

To answer this question we need to know about the Venezuela Crisis. The story starts with a longstanding local dispute between Venezuela and Britain over the possession of Essequibo and Guayana Esequiba. In 1895, Britain escalated the dispute by dispatching naval forces. In response, the United States dispatched forces to support Venezuela. US President Cleveland did not intervene because he thought Venezuela held rightful possession. Rather, and consistent with my theory, President Cleveland explicitly invoked the Monroe Doctrine. He explained that if Britain won, it would amount to a new colony within the Western Hemisphere. As stated in the Monroe Doctrine, the US would fight to prevent any further colonization.

The staunchly imperialist British Prime Minister Salisbury saw the implications of American demands in the Venezuela Crisis, and he was angered by them. He argued for a strong response (Mathews, 1963). He believed that the United States would back down if Britain did not, but he also understood that his policy could escalate to war. As he put it, "a war with America...in the not too distant future – has become something more than a possibility" (quoted in Bourne, 1967, p. 339). Salisbury's rhetoric represents a deviation from my theory because he is calling for war. But consistent with my theory, his position did not translate into policy because he was met with strong opposition from members of his cabinet who wanted to avoid conflict with the United States at all costs. For instance, Colonial Secretary Joseph Chamberlain argued that a war with the US would be "the very worst thing that could possibly happen to us" (quoted in Orde, 1996, p. 11). In the end domestic institutional checks won out. The cabinet instead decided in 1896 to make the necessary concessions to the United States in Venezuela to avoid escalation to war.

A broader look across Anglo-American relations offers a puzzle for those who believe leaders hold persistent personal attributes that influence state behavior. Notably, Lord Salisbury was re-elected in 1901 and spearheaded Britain's withdrawal from the Americas to reach peace with the United States. Clearly, his leadership style and preferences were not consistent over time if he was the lone voice for war in 1895, and then the champion for total withdrawal in 1901.

The second critical event surrounds the Philippine-American War. In 1898, the US took colonial possession of the Philippines from Spain. Filipino Nationalists rebelled against colonial rule. The dispute led to a three-year civil war in which the United States tried desperately to hold onto the colony. As a researcher reading history in 2019, it was not initially clear to me that the US choice to fight in the Philippine-American War was consistent with the Monroe Doctrine. This episode is plausibly inconsistent because the Philippines is much further into the Pacific than Hawaii. It was not obvious to me why the US would colonize this area, much less repress local forces who wanted independence.

But my theory does not rely on whether I think US choices rule out a principle. It relies on how British and US elites perceived this episode at the time. To understand British perceptions, I must detail more of the historical context. The story starts when the US chose to support Cuban nationalists rebel against Spanish colonialists. US intervention in Cuba was clearly consistent with the Monroe Doctrine. However, it led Spain to declare war against the United States. The US easily pushed back Spanish forces in Cuba. At around the same time, Filipino nationalists also started to rebel against Spanish colonialists. The Philippines was a critical staging point for Spain to reach the Americas. Thus, ousting Spain from the Philippines was instrumentally important to keeping Spain out of the Americas. Consistent with the Monroe Doctrine, the US chose to expand the war to the Philippines to oust Spain, and thereby end Spain's influence in the Americas. In 1898, Spain conceded, and the parties convened in Paris to negotiate a settlement, leading the US to acquire the Philippines.

Indeed, the British recognized that the Philippines were more distant to the Monroe Doctrine. As Seed (1958, p. 259) notes, there was a concern that the episode evidenced broader US interests to pursue a 'moral duty' in expansion. Therefore, the "American intervention in the Philippines sparked rumors and international calculations" (Elizalde, 2016, p. 228) among the British public and lower-level elites. But consistent with my theory, and especially the extension that introduces ambiguous issues (Section 4.4.2), such concerns were "virtually ignored" (Seed, 1958, p. 260) by those at the highest levels of British government because they saw two reasons that the US occupation was consistent with the Monroe Doctrine.[279] First, Spain had used the Philippines as a staging point for their operations in the Americas. To assure the security of the Americas, the US needed to prevent Spain from regaining influence. The British believed that the US occupation was especially important for assuring Spain did not regain influence because local militant groups in the Philippines remained loyal to Spain (Pagunsan, 2010, p. 135), and Spanish institutions still dominated (Seed, 1968, p. 49). Second, the Philippines was vital for maintaining trade between the Americas, Asia, and Europe. British elites believed that a colonial occupier was necessary to sustain this trade, and giving this role to a European power would exert undue influence over the Americas. Thus, in their view, the role rightly belonged to the American hegemon (Seed, 1968; Ells, 1995). Thus, British elites "left no doubt that it favored an American presence in the Philippines" (Elizalde, 2016, p. 229), and even worked to ensure the US was awarded the Philippines under the Treaty of Paris.

A third event surrounds the Roosevelt Corollary. In my theory, I claimed that Challengers declare their intentions at the moment of focus. However, I also argue that they cannot credibly expand or change their claims later in the case without provoking mistrust. In 1904, right as Anglo-American peace was forming, the United States issued the Roosevelt Corollary.[280] Some historians argue that the Roosevelt Corollary was a major revision of the Monroe Doctrine (see Veeser, 2003, for review). The reason was that it formally changed US declared policy from preventing further European colonization to a clear statement that the US may intervene against European powers who meddled in the affairs of states in the Americas.

At first glance, this seems inconsistent with my theory. A closer look at Roosevelt's intent and the outcome shows that the episode supports my theory. The Roosevelt corollary does not alter what the US claims its interests are. It simply explains that the US is highly resolved to contest issues it perceives as within its core interests. In fact, the Corollary limits the scope of American aims because it focuses US interests to the Americas and not a broader conceptualization of the Western Hemisphere.

This episode illustrates how diplomacy plays a clarify role in real life. In the formal model, it is easy for states to clearly delineate their core

---

[279] The Americans saw them too (McHale, 1961).

[280] The US also registered the Platt Amendment (1903) expanded US control over Cuban foreign policy and established a military base there. But this is not as controversial.

and peripheral interests. But in real life ambiguity remains because historical and cultural context is complicated. This ambiguity may not present a problem as the Challenger is initially expanding. In practice, Challengers and Defenders are likely to focus on the major flashpoints first. But once the major flashpoints are resolved, and over time, ambiguous issues become salient. It is consistent with my overall theory that states can use diplomacy to clarify ambiguities as the case unfolds.

How the case ends: A shift to peace (1903–1907)   In 1907, Britain and the United States started to describe their relations as a special friendship. Anglo-American efforts to reach a stable peace start in the late 1890s. However, these efforts went through "fits and starts" (Goldstein, 2010, p. 9). Many of the peacebuilding measures were informal and Britain retained possessions in the Americas that created a risk of competition. I code the period between 1903 and 1907 as the turn from hedging to peace on the British side, and revision to stability and status quo on the US side. Illustrating the differences in state strategy on both sides helps illustrate how I code the shift to peace in other cases.

During the turn to peace, Britain unilaterally conceded issues that were consistent with the Monroe Doctrine, and did not wait for the United States to contest them. Britain agreed to the arbitration decision over Alaska and ceded it to the United States, and unilaterally acknowledged US possession of the Panama Canal. After the Roosevelt Corollary was announced, Britain unilaterally withdrew most naval forces and administrators from South American and Caribbean states. This, in effect, left no points of tension with the United States in the Western Hemisphere. 1903 also marked the beginning of efforts to "institutionalize" stability (Goldstein, 2010, p. 6).

While British concessions were not conditional on any explicit limits in American militarization, American naval spending and tonnage did slow down relative to Britain growth (Crisher and Souva, 2014), and relative to US growth in the decade prior (Kennedy, 1989, p. 203). This effectively limited the United States' ability to expand beyond the Western Hemisphere, consistent with how I characterize peace. The US continued to contest issues against other European powers in the Western Hemisphere and assert dominance over independent states.

Other theories   As discussed, this case is hard to explain in terms of shifting economic or military power (Powell, 1999), or power parity (Organski and Kugler, 1980). British perceptions during the case also offer little support for the standard costly signaling theory (Glaser, 2010).[281] The United States makes frequent demands, and inserts itself provocatively into crises against the British. But British elites do not infer that America held vast aims. In fact, Britain remains confident that American aims were limited throughout the case (cf. Edelstein, 2019, predictions).

It is important to note that the case is consistent with two other insights. First, some scholars argue that peace is more likely when states have large oceans between them. Indeed, the case does end in peace and there is a large ocean between the US and Britain. But this argument is not inconsistent with mine. It likely forms the parameters that determine the cost of competition. This partly explains why Britain was willing to view the Monroe Doctrine as acceptably limited even though it was reasonably large.

While a factor, geography cannot completely explain peace in this case for two reasons. First, water cannot explain why the United States decided to stop its expansion. If water prevents a British invasion, why didn't the US continue to militarize and take territory in 1907?[282] Second, Britain was willing to deploy forces over water to fight over relatively small issues in Burma and the Ottoman Empire in the 1850s. If the stopping power of water prevails, it is unclear why it didn't prevail in these other cases.

The case is consistent with regime theory. It is plausible that British elites were initially optimistic because the United States was a democracy. This argument is not inconsistent with mine because it describes a set of prior beliefs, and not how beliefs changes. Indeed, it is plausible that one reason British tolerated such a large initial principle (the Monroe Doctrine covered a huge land mass) is that they believed the United States was very likely limited.

7.2.2 Anglo-German Competition

In 1933, Adolf Hitler was elected as the Chancellor of Germany. In the six years that followed he rampaged across Europe, and the British did little about it. I have discussed anecdotes from this case in Chapters 2, 3, and 4. Figure 7.2 puts them altogether. The top of Figure 7.2 plots military spending and economic data. These data shows that Hitler rapidly increased military spending year on year. Although it does not reveal itself

---

[281] Even though Edelstein (2019) argues that time horizons will limit Britain's incentives for competition, his theory still expects that British perceptions of American interests should change in response to costly military actions.

[282] The Spanish–American War suggests that they were willing to extend at least as far as the Philippines.

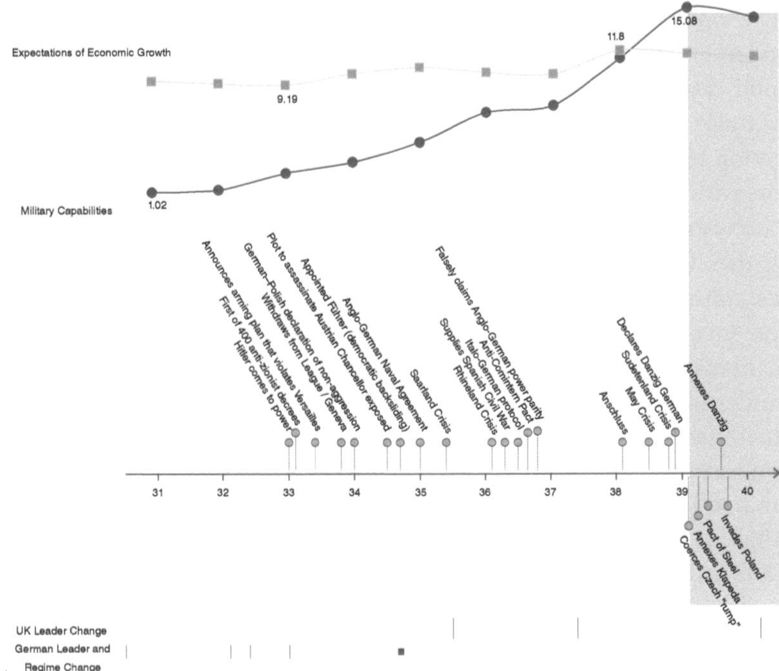

Figure 7.2 Time-varying events that could competition and peace during Anglo-German relations.

Figure summarizes time-varying events that different theories believe could influence the UK's choice to compete with Germany. The top plots expected economic growth and military capabilities (Bell and Johnson, 2015). Note these are statistically estimated values and so the scales are not substantively meaningful. The critical factor is the overall trajectory of economic growth and fluctuations in the rate of military spending. The bottom marks German and UK leadership changes. The black square represents a regime change in Germany when Hitler is appointed Führer. In the middle I plot Hitler's salient military, diplomatic and commercial choices. Choices above the line are consistent with Hitler's declared principle (ethno-nationalism). By consistent, I mean that the British could not rule out nationalism as Hitler's principle as result of Hitler's action. The shaded grey bar represents the shift from hedging to competition.

in the quantitative summary (which relies on correlates of war data), Wark (1985, app 6) argues that British elites were most concerned about Hitler's military spending in 1936. Despite the rapid increase in Germany's military spending, Britain avoided war. If the rate of shifting power causes conflict, then conflict should have come before 1936 (Powell, 1999). The bottom of Figure 7.2 describes leadership and regime changes. Most critically, Hitler eroded democracy in Germany in 1934 when he established the Third Reich and appointed himself as Führer. If regime type is an important indicator for trust, democratic corrosion should have heightened mistrust and caused competition in 1934.

The middle of the figure plots theoretically salient events.[283] Hitler engaged in frequent and extreme costly military actions that scholars argue should cause mistrust (Glaser, 2010; Edelstein, 2019). He orchestrated a failed plot to assassinate the Austrian Chancellor, took through force or coercion territorial concessions from six states, and supported other dictators with their expansive agendas. To the extent that either a reputation for honesty or a commitment to international norms influences competition, then Hitler should have first aroused suspicion circa 1934 by violating arms control agreements and withdrawing from the League of Nations. These inconsistencies between words and deeds demonstrated that Hitler was insensitive to consistency costs (Renshon, 2015), and that he intended to undermine established international norms and institutions. As a result of these factors, many different theoretical traditions believe that competition was inevitable in this case. What they cannot explain, is why it took Britain so long to compete. Indeed, the pressures for competition are severe in 1933, 1934, 1936, and 1938. But Britain delayed competition until 1939.

Delayed competition fits my theory well because Hitler's rampage was broadly consistent with his declared ethnic-nationalist claims. In the years before Hitler came to power, the British Government met with Hitler's emissaries and read his writings and speeches to better understand his plausible intentions. After a thorough review, they found that Hitler had expressed an acceptably limited claim grounded in extreme German nationalism (Blain, 1988). Hitler's limited claim covered territorial and normative revisions that worked against British interests. On the territorial side, they thought Hitler would seek possession of all German-speaking territories.[284] This included the Sudetenland, Austria, the Rhineland, and parts of Denmark among other territories.

On the normative and institutional side, Hitler rejected many principles set forth in the League of Nations including human rights and equity. Indeed, the fact that British elites viewed Hitler's hypernationalist vision as acceptably limited contrasts my theory with those who believe limited-aims principles must conform to prevailing norms (Goddard, 2018). Consider Hitler's 400 anti-Zionist decrees, which began in 1932. British elites found them repugnant. They saw them as a signal that Hitler was not committed

---

[283] Again, I use quantitative data sets and historical accounts to develop a list of all costly military actions, diplomatic encounters, institutional commitments, and other salient events that could influence trust and competition.

[284] Wark (1985) shows this with an analysis of the deliberations from the Defense Requirements Committee. But the War Cabinet documents also support that British elites internalized these estimates.

to international norms (Barros et al., 2009). But when it came to estimating Hitler's strategic intentions, British elites developed "complex" (Kushner, 1989, p. 153) views on the Jewish question that included both support and disgust. My theory explains these seemingly contradictory views. British elites were disgusted because they violated norms. However, they did not cause concern about Hitler's aggressive intentions because they were consistent with a nationalist principle. British beliefs that Hitler's aims were limited had little to do with their perceptions of whether he would comply with international norms, and more to do with how they understood what he would want if he was motivated by nationalism.

In what follows, I use details of the case to illuminate my theory, and clarify my case codings. First, I explore why Hitler's initial claims were limited given what Hitler had written in *Mein Kampf*. Second, I detail events that surround the Munich Agreement. These events provide strong support for my mechanism and illuminate some critical episodes in this case. Third, I describe my choice to code Hitler's turn to competition in March 1939 (about six months before war is declared). This choice helps clarify the difference between war and competition, and how I operationalize it in a typical case.

Mein Kampf: *Were Hitler's declared interests actually acceptable?* A condition for my theory is that the Challenger declares an acceptably limited principle. But Hitler's writing in the 1920s potentially extended well beyond what the British would have found acceptable. Many historians have argued that in *Mein Kampf* Hitler expressed a desire to provide ethnic Germans with living space by expanding eastward at the expense of Slavic populations when he writes, "If we speak of soil in Europe today, we can primarily have in mind only Russia and her vassal border states" (Shirer, 1990, p. 76). But the systematic estimate from the Defence Requirements Committee (DRC) in 1934 found that if Hitler's ethnic-nationalist vision was likely more limited (Hauner, 1978).[285]

Why did the British ignore Hitler's writings? One potential answer is irrational optimism. This is unlikely, given that even British elites, such as Vansittart, who deeply mistrusted Hitler from the start, downplayed *Mein Kampf* (Foster, 1941, p. 367). More likely, *Mein Kampf* "teem[ed] with

---

[285] To be clear, the DRC did not conclude Hitler held limited aims. Only that if he did, this is what they were. They described him as the "ultimate potential enemy," which illustrates that they were uncertain about whether his declared principle was genuine.

contradictions and misconceptions."[286] This created confusion among British elites about how to interpret it. Starting in 1932, Hitler's emissaries[287] explained that Hitler's earlier writings were designed to rally hypernationalist Germans around his cause and launch him to power. They pointed out that in the 1920s, Hitler faced severe obstacles to his political aspirations because he was not a German citizen (he was Austrian) and he was in prison. He realized it would be difficult to compete with moderate German-nationalists who had a more suitable background. Thus, his writings in the 1920s reflected his desperate position, and not his true interests. All but one chapter of *Mein Kampf* discussed domestic politics. It is plausible that British audiences believed the short foreign policy chapter was to arouse domestic support. To support this interpretation, British elites pointed to the fact that Hitler's claims moderated once he was appointed as administrator for the state's delegation to the Reichsrat in Berlin and his political aspirations were more secure.[288] British elites were persuaded by these arguments.

The moment of truth: The Munich Crisis   The Munich Agreement is a critical moment in this case because it was the last major concession Britain made before turning to competition. Three features surrounding how the agreement was forged are well explained by my theory.

First, my conceptualization of hedging well fits British efforts to negotiate the Munich Agreement. Britain was not involved when the crisis started. Rather, Britain was brought in to negotiate with Hitler on Czechoslovakia's behalf. In the end, Czechoslovakia did not even attend the Munich Conference. In bargaining theory, negotiators try hard to extract as much of the surplus as possible. But Britain did the opposite: They gave away so much that they were unsure that Czechoslovakia would accept the terms. Indeed, the Czech leadership was upset and branded British concessions a betrayal (Barooah, 1966). Why would Britain give away the surplus? Consistent with how I conceptualize hedging, Britain's negotiations clearly illustrate their desire to deconflict with Germany in the hopes of reaching a stable peace.

---

[286] US Amb. to Germany Rumbold Apr. 13, 1933 dispatch. Quoted in Gilbert (1966, pp. 377–378).

[287] Although Hitler took power a year later, his confidants met with British elites in London starting in 1932.

[288] Stone (2008) also argues that English translations were less expansive then the original German text.

Second, the Munich Settlement partitioned Czechoslovakia in an oddly drawn way. The division was not a straight line. It did not reflect the distribution of power, or strategic or administrative boundaries. Consistent with my theory, the border included all of the territories that are majority German and nothing more. The fact that this was the last concession Britain was willing to tolerate clearly fits with how I conceptualize the moment of truth. It is everything Hitler would want if he desired Germanic territories.

Third, my theory assumes that the Challenger knows that the Defender employs the logic of principles. If my theory is correct, a greedy Challenger should therefore publicize their intent to take actions that match their declared core interest, and conceal their intentions to violate this claim. Hitler's public and private statements leading up to Munich clearly show he understood the strategic game that my theory illuminates. Consistent with this logic, a week before taking the Sudetenland, Hitler publicly declared, "I am asking neither that Germany be allowed to oppress three and a half million Frenchmen, nor am I asking that three and a half million Englishmen be placed at our mercy. Rather I am simply demanding that the oppression of three and a half million Germans in Czechoslovakia cease and that the inalienable right to self-determination takes its place."[289] But this claim was not genuine. Only one year earlier, Hitler called a secret meeting of Nazi leadership where he detailed his true foreign policy vision. No minutes were taken. However, attendees later wrote down their recollection of Hitler's desires in the Hossbach Memorandum (which they kept secret). From their recollection, Hitler explained his desire to take Eastern Europe and exterminate the Slavic populations, then expand across Western Europe (Weinberg, 1980, pp. 39–40).

Why keep these specific interests secret but publicise a desire to take the Sudetenland? Consistent with my theory, Nazi elites understood that British elites were only willing to hedge while Hitler could plausibly claim to be motivated by limited ambitions. Debate between Hitler and other leading Nazi officials shows that they know the invasion of Eastern Europe would trigger "major war" with Britain (Hillgruber, 1974, pp. 5–22).

Hitler's inconsistent action came in March 1939 when he gave Czech President Emil Hácha an ultimatum: cede the remainder of Czechoslovakia, or face invasion. Hácha conceded, and German forces entered the rump of Czechoslovakia on March 15th without resistance. Since the Munich Agreement characterized the territories that plausibly fit Hitler's nationalist interests, this ultimatum represents the first inconsistent action.

---

[289] Speech at the NSDAP Conference at Nuremberg, September 12, 1938.

Hitler's costly military actions in the next three months further support my theory. Specifically, once Hitler violated the Munich Agreement, he took several actions noticeably unconstrained by nationalist aims. He demanded Klaipėda from Lithuania, which had no Germanic connection. He also signed the Pact of Steel with revisionist powers, which further indicated a broad interest in expansion. Hitler then invaded Poland. To be sure, Germany held a strong ethnic attachment to parts of western Poland. However, Hitler chose to advance into territories, such as Czestochowa, that are hard to justify under his nationalist agenda. This stands in stark contrast to the careful borders he accepted at Munich. Why would Hitler take so many inconsistent actions after five years of taking careful actions that fit within a limiting principle? Indeed, Yarhi-Milo (2014), Jervis et al. (1989), and others who conceptualize indicator theory, suggest that each costly action should incrementally deepen mistrust. If true, then Hitler should have avoided these repeated signals. My theory suggests an alternative story. The first action that cannot be reconciled with a principle sends a very strong signal. Consistent with this insight, Hitler initially avoided all these actions to avoid British learning his motives. Once Hitler violated the Munich Agreement, he revealed his intentions. At that moment, the die was cast. He had no incentive to hold back over other demands. This incentivized Hitler to take the territories that were easy to take but that he deferred because it would communicate his vast aims.

How the case ends: Britain turn to competition, March 1939   I code this case as ending in competition in March 1939. To be clear, this is six months before Britain declares war. Coding competition in March or September 1939 does not affect my finding. In what follows I explain my coding choice to clarify what I mean by competition and how it is different from hedging.

In my theory, competition is a grand strategic orientation. Therefore the coding is based on the Defender's intention about how to manage the Challenger in general, and not highly situation-specific choices, such as how the Challenger responds in a particular crisis. In the British case, I code competition in March because this is when the British Government decided to start confronting Hitler at every turn. To be clear, British elites had started to militarize long before 1939 in case war was necessary. They also held longstanding alliance commitments across Europe that they knew would cause tension with Hitler even if his aims were limited. Furthermore, they had taken limited steps to isolate Hitler diplomatically. However, pre-1939

Britain's strategic goal was to avoid escalation and preserve the opportunity for peaceful coexistence in the future.

As Strang (2008, abstract) describes, British policy changed starting in March 1939:

After Munich, continued German belligerence, the Kristallnacht, and British intelligence assessments indicating that Hitler was prepared to attack the Western powers led to a reassessment of appeasement. The British government gave security guarantees to several European countries, seeking to deter future aggression and to lay the groundwork for a successful war against Germany should it prove necessary. While most of the British elite detested communism, anti-communist views did not govern British policy; security considerations required Soviet support in Eastern Europe, and Britain and France made a determined effort to secure Soviet support for the Peace Front.

To be clear, Britain's observed actions did not always match their strategic goals. Britain and Germany experienced crises before 1939, and Britain did not escalate to war in key crises that start after they chose to compete. However, these situation-specific choices were based on weighing the instrumental costs and benefits in each case. To appreciate this nuance it is helpful to contrast British thinking during two crises: the Rhineland Crisis (1935) and the Danzig Crisis (1939).

In 1934, British elites realized that Hitler would soon remilitarize the Rhineland. Even though this was during the period of hedging, and the Rhineland clearly fit within Hitler's declared principle, many British elites were concern that remilitarization would trigger war (see Yarhi-Milo, 2014, pp. 63–65). However, that concern was based on Britain's longstanding commitment under the Treaty of Locarno. Under the treaty, Britain promised to intervene if German forces entered the demilitarized zone. Consistent with how I conceptualize hedging, once Britain realized that Hitler would likely remilitarize the Rhineland, they took steps to avoid escalation. In the end, they did not intervene, despite their treaty commitment. They realized that this would weaken their reputation for resolve, but their priority was avoiding broader conflict with Germany (Edelstein, 2019, pp. 99–101). In fact, as the crisis unfolded, they took additional steps to reassure Hitler and avoid any chance of a spiral of mistrust that could inadvertently trigger competition. The British War Secretary told the German Ambassador, "through the British people were prepared to fight for France in the event of a German incursion into French territory, they would not resort to arms on account of the recent occupation of the Rhineland. The people did not know much about the demilitarization provisions and most of them probably took the view that they did not care 'two hoots' about the Germans reoccupying their own territory."[290]

In October 1938, right after the Munich Agreement was signed, German Foreign Minister Ribbentrop declared Germany's intent to possess the Free City of Danzig. One month later, Hitler told the Polish foreign minister that Danzig was German. However, Hitler did not threaten Poland, or explicitly demand Danzig at the time. Hitler's claims were consistent with Germany's declared principle because Germany had possessed Danzig prior to World War One, and there was a considerable Germanic population that still lived there (Watt, 1989).

In April 1939, after Britain had turned to competition, Hitler made coercive threats against Danzig. Hitler's limited demand put Britain in a tough diplomatic position. Two months earlier, Britain had committed to defend Poland from German invasion. But Danzig was a free city controlled by Poland. Technically, Britain had no obligation to support Poland if Hitler invaded Danzig. Furthermore, Britain had strategic incentives to stay out of the crisis. Britain was not well prepared for war in April (but Hitler did not know that) (Overy and Wheatcroft, 2009, p. 18). As a result, Britain was not willing to fight over Danzig if Hitler did invade. Despite this fact, Britain extended its security commitment to cover Danzig in an effort to force Hitler to back down.[291] This choice is consistent with how I conceptualize competition. Even though Britain was not yet prepared to fight, and their core interests were not at stake, Britain tried hard to prevent Hitler's advances (Watt, 1989).

The difference in Britain's intent in these two crises is clear. In the Rhineland Crisis, British elites wanted to avoid escalation and mistrust. Therefore, they looked for potential flashpoints, and sought to minimize them, even if it meant making concessions and signaling weakness. In the Danzig Crisis, British elites wanted to prevent Hitler's expansion by extending their alliance commitments. They did not care that their new commitment could trigger war, or that Danzig was not strategically important. The reason was that their aim was competition (for a similar comparison between Danzig and prior crises, see Taylor, 1961, pp. 302–303).

---

[290] Quoted in Weinberg (1980) p. 259.

[291] In the end, Hitler took Danzig and Britain did not honor their security commitment completely. They sent materiel to Poland, but did not declare war. But this choice was based on strategic factors. Their decision to extend the security guarantee exemplifies what I mean by an attempt to thwart Hitler.

Other theories As discussed above, existing theories of power, costly signaling, institutional commitments, and regime type struggle to explain delayed competition in this case. There are three other explanations that isolate particular moments in this case. But like the explanations previoulsy outlined, they struggle to comprehensively explain the case as a whole.

First, some argue that Britain delayed competition because they were unprepared (Ripsman and Levy, 2008). It is undoubtable that Britain was not well prepared in 1934, and this explains why Britain armed substantially during the period of hedging. However, it cannot explain why British perceptions of Hitler's intentions remained hopeful, why they shifted in 1938, and the clear relationship between the shift in perceptions and the shift from appeasement to competition.

Second, some argue that British elites were irrational (see Gilbert, 1972; Barnett, 1986). It is plausible that Britain's prior beliefs about Hitler were partly motivated by wishful thinking. It is also plausible that specific elites succumb to personalist impressions. However, these theories cannot explain the rapid shift in estimate after Hitler violated the Munich Agreement. Hitler's coercive threats for the rump of Czechoslovakia were no more vivid or egregious than his past actions (cf. Yarhi-Milo, 2014). Hitler had broken promises before. It is hard for any of these theories to explain why British mis-impressions did not persist through 1939 given that they previously persisted.[292]

Third, Goddard (2018, ch 5) argues that Britain shifted perceptions and turned to competition because Hitler could no longer use rhetoric to persuade British elites that he would comply with prevailing international norms, especially the sovereignty norm. However, she only analyzes 1938–1939. She cannot explain British indifference to perceived norm violations between 1933 and 1938. As stated, British elites believed that the racist components of Hitler's declared intentions in 1933 clearly violated international norms. In another example, Hitler explicitly violated the sovereignty norm by orchestrating a coup plot in Austria in July 1934. Hitler never talked about the plot, and thus made no effort to persuade British elites

---

[292] As discussed in Chapter 3, Yarhi-Milo (2014) also argues that the British irrationally over-relied on specific events that she called litmus tests. But she provides no theoretical reason that these are irrational, and no way to identify which events will constitute litmus tests, and no evidence that litmus tests are irrational. She only shows that some events matter more for British perceptions than others.

that this clear violation was anything else. Goddard (2018) cannot explain why British elites remained trustful given Hitler's clear norm violation that he did no seek to offset through rhetorical persuasion.

7.3 Part 2b: Vignettes for Cases That My Theory Does Not Neatly Predict

Under my coding rules, two cases do not fit my theory. In one case, France competes with Prussia even though Prussian actions were clearly consistent with Prussia's declared principle. An interesting quirk of this case is that Britain also closely watched Prussian unification, observed Prussia's behavior, and (consistent with my theory) chose not to compete. I exploit the difference in France and Britain's strategic response to illuminate my theory. In the other case, Germany declared a principle that was at best ambiguous and at worst unacceptably greedy to British elites. Then Britain took a long time to turn to competition. I expected Germany to make a clearer statement of its interests. Given that it did not, I expect Britain to turn to competition earlier than it did.

These cases illustrate how my theory interacts with power transition theory and defensive realism. I show that even though my theory fails to explain the exact timing of competition in these cases, that the logic of my theory is at work. That is, Defenders still care about the Challenger's true principle, and interpret the Challengers words and actions to estimate what the Challenger's long-run interests are. However, both of these cases lie outside the scope conditions of my theory for different reasons. As a result, shifting power (Powell, 1999) explains the precise timing of competition in one case and an arms spiral better explains the other (Glaser, 2010).

7.3.1 Contrasting a Supportive and Non-supportive Case: British and French Divergent Responses to Prussian Unification

In 1862, Prussian Prime Minister Otto von Bismarck articulated a new foreign policy principle: the unification of Germanic territories under Prussian government (Pflanze, 1990b, p. 3; Steinberg, 2011, ch 8). France understood that Bismarck's claims held clear normative and territorial implications for France (Wawro, 2023, p. 17). Although Bismarck did not explicitly state it, unification would inevitably create territorial disputes over villages and cities including those in Bas-Rhin and Haut-Rhin, Moselle, Meurthe, Saales, and Schirmeck. Prussian demands also created normative tensions for Britain. Britain's Queen Victoria held close relations with the Austrian monarchs. However, Prussia wanted broad recognition (including Britain's blessing) that it was the legitimate representative of German people (Mosse, 1951, pp. 206–208).[293]

Beyond what Prussia had claimed, Britain and France also realized that Bismarck could hold ambitions beyond Germanic territories. Even in 1862, they knew that German unification would dramatically affect the balance of power in continental Europe, making further German expansion harder to stop. Thus, if Prussia's goals were to extend beyond German unification, it would pose an enormous threat for stability in Europe (Wawro, 2023, pp. 16–20).

Over the next decade, Prussia slowly consolidated power through wars against Denmark (1864), Austria (1866), and France (1870).[294] This culminated in German unification in 1871. I code Prussian actions during this period as consistent with Prussian ethnic-nationalist agenda. Therefore, my theory predicts that this case should end in Anglo-Prussian and Franco-Prussian peace.

Consistent with my prediction, I code Anglo-Prussian peace shortly after German unification.[295] In contrast, and inconsistent with my predictions, I code France as starting to turn to competition soon after the German invasion of Königgrätz in 1866 and culminating in the Franco-Prussian War.[296]

Why did France turn to war when Prussian behavior was consistent with its limited principle, and what explains the differences in French and English reactions? The difference lies in what France and Britain considered as acceptably limited. Recall, I defined an acceptably limited Challenger based on the Defender's cost-benefit calculus. The Defender would weigh (i) conceding everything implied by the Challenger's declared

---

[293] As Pflanze (1990a) notes, Prussia was careful to explain why Austria did not fall within the principle of unification. But the claim was ambiguous. As de Mesquita and Lalman (1992, ch 7) argue, the ambiguity was over a single issue and not broader ambitions. I showed that my theory survives given a confined ambiguity.

[294] There are other notable events. For example, in 1866, Prussia secretly negotiated Britain aid to fight France if France invaded Belgium. In 1866, Prussia sent supplies to Italy in aid of Italian unification.

[295] As I explain later, this is consistent with Stafford (1982) and Kennedy (1988). Mosse (1958, p. 295) sees the origins of peace as starting even earlier, and Raymond (1921) argues it begins right after the Austro-Prussian War. Any coding supports my theory given that Prussian actions fit unification and Britain peacefully engages.

[296] Wawro (2023, pp. 17, 30) argues France was shocked by German success at Königgrätz and began diplomatic efforts to isolate Prussia in 1866. Howard (1961, pp. 29–39) argues that France's build-up until 1870 was designed to sue for a stable peace. My theory mispredicts this case either way, and so I omit a full discussion.

principle against (ii) first-period competition. A principle was acceptably limited if the Defender preferred to concede those issues, rather than turn to competition.

Prussia's declared principle was acceptably limited for Britain but unacceptably greedy for France. Notably, if Prussia genuinely wanted German unification, then it would demand territories that France viewed as part of its sovereign land. Since these territories were highly salient to both France and Prussia, there was no room to achieve a stable peace. In contrast, German unification was far less salient for England. As stated, London favored Austria as the primary representative of Germans. It also held relations with several principalities that Prussia would capture. However, these issues were small relative to the costs of competition with Prussia.

Bismarck explicitly acknowledged how Prussian interests differently conflict with Britain and France. For France, he noted that given Prussia's declared interest that he "did not doubt that a Franco-German war must take place before the construction of a United Germany could be realised."[297] He also realized that Britain would not come to France's aid in a war because "France, the victor, would be a danger to everybody—Prussia to nobody."[298] In short, Bismarck realized that so long as his interests remain targeted at unification, Britain would not perceive Prussia as a threat.

Britain also distinguished its limited interest in supporting Austria with its broader interest of finding a path to long-term peace. Indeed, the British "were shocked and disillusioned by Bismarck's methods" (Stafford, 1982, p. 250). This disdain for Prussian methods drove Queen Victoria to remark that "Prussia seems included to behave as atrociously as possible, and as she always has done! Odious people the Prussians are" (quoted in Kennedy, 1988, p. 16). However, with a broader perspective, and "despite this indignation, their was no thought of actual intervention on London's part" (Kennedy, 1988, p. 16). Why did London take on this policy? According to Kennedy (1988), and consistent with my theory, a major reason was that Britain perceived that Prussia's broader interests were limited despite Prussia's repeated military actions. "What was clear about 1866, however, was virtually no Briton felt that way [threatened] by the rise of Prussian dominance" (Kennedy, 1988, p. 18). Indeed, Taylor (1954, pp. 176–200) argues that Britain viewed France as more of a threat than Germany, and Raymond (1921) suggests Britain realized that post-unification Germany would prove a sound trade partner.

---

[297] Translated in Butler (1989, p. 58).
[298] Quoted in VonPoschinger and Whitman (2007, p. 97).

Even if my interpretation is reasonable, it raises two questions. First, why didn't France fight right after Bismarck's 1962 "Blood and Iron" speech? Several situation-specific factors motivated France's choice to delay war.[299] But the long-term cause was a shift in France's perception about Prussian capabilities between 1866 and 1870 (see Howard, 1961). First, in 1866 Prussia easily defeated Austria. Prussia's performance alerted France that Prussia was a skilled military foe (Wawro, 2023, p. 17). Second, France assessed that Prussian power was growing with each military victory because each time Prussia won it took possession of highly productive Germanic territory (Howard, 1961, pp. 30–35). Third, in 1870 a close friend of Bismarck, Amadeo I, was crowned as the Spanish King.[300] France feared that if it did not act soon, Prussia and Spain would forge an alliance that encircled France. Putting these three factors together, France faced the classic problem: it anticipated power would soon shift against her, and turned to war to prevent it.

This discussion helps clarify how my theory fits with theories of shifting power and war (Powell, 1999). In this case, France knew that Prussia was unacceptably greedy from the start because France was unwilling to tolerate Prussia's limited aims. Therefore, France did not start out uncertain about Prussian intentions. Rather they thought about the problem as a classic bargaining problem against a greedy rival. They did not compete initially, because they perceived Prussia as too weak to make demands against them. In contrast, Britain perceived Prussian claims as acceptably limited. Since Britain believed that there was a plausible chance Prussia would stop at German unification, Britain worked hard to avoid competition so that they could forge peace with Prussia once it unified. For Britain the critical question was not Prussian capabilities, but Prussian intentions.

Second, why did Prussia provoke France with an unacceptably greedy claim? If the logic of salami tactics is reasonable (Mearsheimer, 2001), or if it is easy for Challengers to exploit pretexts (Rosato, 2015), then Bismarck should have declared a modest interest in a few territories first, revealed additional interests slowly over time, and then only express an interest in French territories at the last possible moment. My theory suggests two plausible reasons Bismarck started with a larger claim that caused tension with France. First, Bismarck understood that it would appear suspicious if he asserted an interest in fewer territories without tying them to a principle. The fact that Bismarck articulated a principle and that British and French elites knew what it implied, substantiates my core assumptions detailed in

---

[299] Including domestic politics and Prussian provocation.
[300] Wilhelm I invested Amadeo into the Knight of the Order of the Black Eagle in 1868.

expectations 1 and 2 (cf. Rosato, 2015; Goddard, 2018). Second, my theory shows that speech acts are especially powerful at the onset because the coordination problem is most severe. If Bismarck genuinely valued Prussian unification, and hoped to retain peace with London in the long run, it would have been unwise to make a different claim and then revise it. Given that Bismarck sought multiple alliances with England right after Prussian unification suggests he was genuine about cooperation with London (Valentin, 1937). Since Britain was willing to tolerate Prussia's actual principle, declaring that true principle was important for Anglo-Prussian peace.

7.3.2 British Assessments of German Intentions (1890s)

In 1890, the new German Emperor, Wilhelm II,[301] announced a new foreign policy doctrine of *Weltpolitik*. Broadly speaking, this was a status claim. Some argue that Weltpolitik was clearly designed to secure Britain's recognition and nothing more (Murray, 2018, pp. 88–89). In this telling, the case would fit my theory because Weltpolitik could be seen as a limited status-seeking claim.

However, several British elites were suspicious of Wilhelm's intentions because they found Weltpolitik incredibly ambiguous, and believed Wilhelm could use it to justify anything (Seligmann and Nägler, 2015, p. 137; Press, 2022). Wilhelm could have viewed a powerful navy as key to great power status (Kennedy, 1988), or used the doctrine to justify colonial possessions that would conflict with British interests (Press, 2022, p. 16). Thus, I code Weltpolitik as an instance where the Challenger did not declare a clear principle because Britain could not neatly map it onto a small number of issues. Thus, the case fails expectation 1 and 2 (which validate my assumptions), falls out of my theory's domain, and into the domain of Rosato (2015) and Goddard (2018).[302]

It is also important to note that while I expect that the Challenger will clearly articulate limited aims through a principle, if they don't, I expect (off-path) that the Defender will respond with competition. Further surprising for my theory, Britain did not react this way. Rather, I code Britain as turning to competition in 1898 with the onset of the Anglo-German naval race (Kennedy, 1988). In 1897, Germany announced that it would

---

[301] Not to be confused with Wilhelm I mentioned previously.

[302] To be clear, I can easily establish expectations 1 and 2 in all other cases, meaning they are in scope for my theory, but violate a core assumption of those who assert Defenders cannot use their knowledge of the Challenger's history to know how issues fit principles.

start to construct a blue-water navy. At that time, Lord Salisbury grew alarmed that this was Germany's first step towards threatening British core interests. As a result, Britain turned to competition. Inconsistent with my theory, this was nearly a decade after Weltpolitik was announced, and before Germany had threatened British interests in any way.

Why did Britain not turn to competition once Wilhelm announced Weltpolitik, and what explains the sudden turn in the late 1890s? A plausible interpretation for delay is that Germany behaved like a de facto status-quo power during the early 1890s. Germany had a small navy, and made no effort to expand it initially (Woodward, 1935; Steinberg, 1966). While it pursued colonial interests, it did not interfere with British colonies, and comported with standards at the time. It did not interfere in European affairs. In my theory, Challengers make at least one demand. However, if a Challenger made no demands, and did not expand its military to make future demands viable, then peace would persist no matter what its diplomatic statements were. In short, it is most plausible that the early period of this case falls outside my scope because Germany's rise was too slow.

From Britain's perspective, events starting in 1897 reflect the classic spiral model (Glaser, 2010, pp. 238–240). Britain conceptualized German status claims as possibly a desire for normative recognition and nothing more. In which case, Germany was a status-quo power. Alternatively, Germany's status claims could drive expansive interests. Since British elites did not understand how expansive, they treated them effectively as unacceptably greedy. British elites used Germany's costly arming as a signal of Germany's intentions along this one dimension.[303] When Germany chose to arm, they turned to competition.

However, one feature of this case is somewhat puzzling for the spiral model. What explains Germany's choice to initiate a naval build-up and trigger the spiral of mistrust in the first place? After all, Germany did not perceive a threat from Britain. They had no security reason to expand their navy. My theory clarifies and refines the spiral model by introducing normative preferences. Germany chose to kickstart the spiral because they needed to arm to secure their status motivations. For Britain, this act was ambiguous. It was unclear if a large military was a status symbol, or an instrument to demand much more. Therefore it posed a security threat in the sense that defensive realists mean it.

---

[303] Further supporting Glaser's (2010) account, British elites articulated this basic test as early as 1866 (Kennedy, 1988).

7.4 Part 3: My Value-Add to Existing Explanations

In this section, I address two broader questions: How much do different theories contribute to explaining the overarching patterns of competition and peace across observed cases? If multiple theories contribute to explaining the timing of competition and peace, then how should we best understand where my theory fits in this multicausal process?

To address these questions, I code each case for years in which theories of power suggest competition is likely. Table 7.4 summarizes my codings for these cases. Columns 4 and 5 focus on pressures caused by conflict. Some argue that if power shifts rapidly, the first crisis over territory triggers competition (Powell, 1999), others argue that the largest and most violent crisis that the Challenger initiates creates the largest pressures for mistrust and competition (Glaser, 2010). Consistent with these theories, column 4 identifies the Challenger's first threat of force to take territory (if they did); and column 5 identifies the year in which the Challenger uses the most force to take territory.

Columns 6 and 7 focus on pressures caused by the rate of shifting power. Research suggests that a threshold emerges on the rate of shifting power (Spaniel, 2019; Debs and Monteiro, 2014). If power shifts faster than the threshold in a given period, then war occurs at the point at which the rate of shifting power is most rapid. If the rate of shifting power never exceeds the threshold, then the power transition passes peacefully. Based on this insight, I identified cases that experience at least one year of unusually rapidly shifting power.[304] When I find it, I record the year in which power shifts the fastest in that case. If the rate of shifting power is never extreme, I omit the year. If shifting power confounds my theory, then we should observe most cases that end in competition surrounding the year I record. Further, we should rarely observe competition when power shifts are never rapid (I do not record a year).

Columns 8 and 9 focus on pressures caused by power parity. Research suggests that when the Challenger achieves power parity, that the pressures for war are most severe (Organski and Kugler, 1980). Based on this insight, I identified cases in which the Challenger achieves power parity in at least one year. When I find it, I record the year in which the Challenger achieves parity. When I do not find it, I omit the year. If power parity confounds my theory, then we should only observe cases that end

---

[304] As I explain in Appendix F online, I define power as shifting unusually fast based on the average rate of shifting power across all cases and years. Unusually fast shifts are two standard deviations outside of the norm.

Table 7.4 *The timing of competition during great power rivalries*

Case			My Mechanism	Confounder: Use of Force	Confounder: Shift Power[†]		Confounder: Relative Power		Outcome
Def	Chal	Year	First Inconsistent Behavior	First Use of Force to Take Concession	Max Expected Future Power	Max. Shifting Capabilities	First Mil. Parity	First Econ. Parity	Shift to Competition
FRA	GER	1866		1866		1868		1866	1869
RUS	CHN	1949	1957	1968	1950			1949	1961
RUS	JPN	1978							
UK	GER	1866		1866	1871	1868	1869		
UK	GER	1890		1914	1914	1914	1890	1898	1897
UK	GER	1931	1938	1934	1939	1938	1933	1931	1939
UK	RUS	1941	1946	1945	1945	1946	1941	1941	1946
UK	USA	1890		1898	1898	1868	1898	1890	
USA	GER	1934	1938	1934	1941	1938	1933		1939
USA	GER	1990							
USA	IND	1974		1984				1985	
USA	JPN	1905	1915	1910			1906		1916
USA	JPN	1987						1987	
USA	RUS	1942	1946	1945	1945	1946			1946

Missing years imply the event did not occur.

235

in competition in the cases where I record a year. We should expect those pressures to be most severe in the year that power shifts are fastest. Further, we should never observe competition or war in cases where power shifts slowly.

As a first cut, Figure 7.3 summarizes the predictive accuracy of each variable on its own terms. My theory is reported in the first row. The power variables appear in the remaining rows. The cases are broken out by whether the case ends in competition or peace (and then the total predictive accuracy). The black shaded region in each pie represents the proportion of cases that are correctly predicted. To be clear, I constructed the case universe and coded variables to test my theory while factoring in potential confounds. Therefore, we should not draw strong inferences against other theories from this plot. However, there are two interesting results that we can derive from this summary plot.

First, my theory well predicts many cases. However, it does better (and remarkably well) at predicting cases that end in peace relative to cases that end in competition. As we saw in the case vignettes, the only two cases I mis-predict end in competition. In one, my theory expected peace. In the other, my theory expected competition would come earlier.

Second, one alternative theory: shifting military capabilities also predicts many cases (almost as many as my own). However, this alternative theory does better at predicting the cases that end in competition than in peace. That seems to be a trend across the power based explanations that do not perform as well: they tend to better predict cases that end in competition than cases that end in peace.

This trend matches what we learned from the case vignettes. Recall that power shifts rapidly in Anglo-American relations. The United States achieves and exceeds power parity with Britain, but competition never comes. Similarly, Prussia rapidly expands its military and economic power during unification. Britain refrains from competition and actually promotes Prussia's power by expanding commercial ties.

Figure 7.4 reports the correlation between the predictive accuracy of all of the variables that I test. If the correlation is close to 1 it means that the two theories well predict the same cases and fail to predict the same cases. Numbers close to -1 mean that when one theory makes a correct prediction, when the other makes an incorrect prediction. Notice that my theory is not well correlated with any of the power-based explanations. The correlation is noticeably weak when compared to shifting military capabilities (0.19). This is surprising because shifting military power correctly predicts the outcomes of many cases.

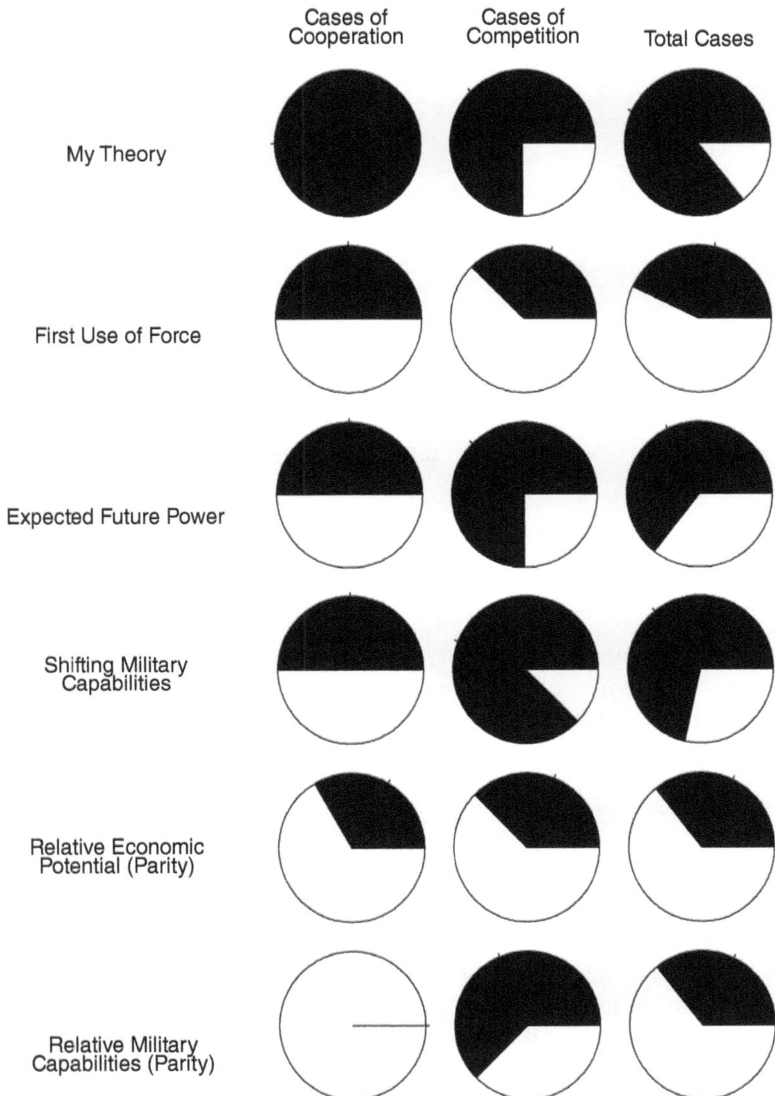

Figure 7.3 Testing theories that predict a shift to competition.

Note: Shaded in black are the proportion of correctly predicted cases.

A closer look at the cases shows that the two cases that my theory fails to predict are well predicted by rates of shifting power. The four cases that shifting power fails to predict, are well explained by my theory. There are eight cases that both theories correctly predict. These results confirm that

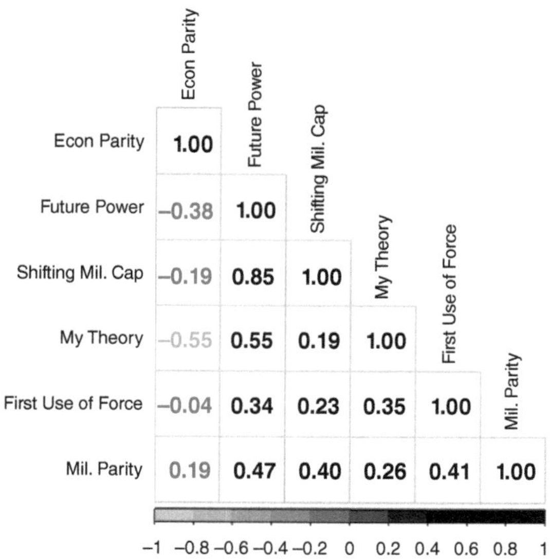

Figure 7.4 Correlations between theoretical explanations.

my theory not only explains many cases, the cases that it well explains are
the cases that theories of power struggle with. As a result, I view my theory
as especially valuable because it explains the cases that existing theories
cannot.

7.5 Discussion

Taken together, the case vignettes and the comparative medium-n analysis suggest that my theory and theories of shifting power complement
each other. The vignettes of outlier cases confirm that power provides two
scope conditions for my theory. First, if the Challenger's declared principle
includes many highly salient territories that the Defender cares intensely
about, then the Defender wants to compete even if the Challenger's aims
are limited. In a case like this, competition is governed by the rate of shifting power. Second, if the rate of shifting power is incredibly slow, then the
Defender will delay competition even if he perceives the Challenger has
expansive aims. In the fourteen cases I study, only two of them fall into
these extreme ranges.

For the twelve cases that fall between these extreme ranges, the analysis shows that perceptions of the Challenger's motives play a critical role
in the Defender's choice to compete or not. As all four vignettes show,
the Defender relies on principles to develop an assessment framework,

then exploits the logic of qualitative inferences to update beliefs. In the two vignettes that represent typical cases, the Defender also conditions competition choices on those beliefs.

For these twelve cases, theories of power are less accurate mainly because they fail to predict the dogs that don't bark: cases that end in peace despite rapidly shifting power. Indeed, this seems consistent with the core logic of my theory. My theory explains why trust persists for long periods as the Challenger rapidly militarizes, takes territory, and commits unspeakable abuses to serve a limited principle. The existing literature does not have a good explanation for inaction during these periods. My theory fills this important gap. It explains the timing of competition and peace for many cases of great power competition since 1850.

8

Evaluating the US's China Policy and Intelligence
(1990–2020)

US post-Cold War strategy towards China is often described as hedging. The US created opportunities for long-term cooperation hoping that China was peaceful. It deepened commercial ties, promoted technological exchange, and supported China's bid to join international institutions. The US also maintained forward-deployed bases across Asia, focused intelligence collection on China, and invested in naval capabilities that would be important if the US discovered that competition was necessary. Although each president had pet projects, this basic hedging strategy persisted for two decades (Steinberg, 2020).

US policy started to change under the Obama Administration's "strategic pivot" (Kitfield, 2012). Obama developed the Trans-Pacific Partnership to minimize China's influence in Asia's economic order (Naughton et al., 2015), promised diplomatic support to states vulnerable to China's economic coercion, and incentivized US firms to invest in Asian states other than China. On the security front, Obama promised to station 60 percent of US air and naval forces in Asia over the coming decade (O'Callaghan and Mogato, 2012), focusing on states most at risk of Chinese military coercion (Tan, 2016, pp. 12–14). US forces began refusing to sail away from Chinese patrols in the South China Sea (Glaser, 2012). But Obama's strategic pivot was incomplete, and certainly short of competition (Blackwill and Fontaine, 2024). Most notably, Obama avoided public rhetoric that suggested Sino-American relations had soured, even though many analysts have characterized his policy as anti-China in spirit (Ross, 2013). Obama avoided politically sensitive decisions such as imposing commercial barriers that were disliked by American firms, and cautioned staff who publicly suggested competition was looming (Gentile et al., 2021, p. 24). Further, following concern from European partners (Ford, 2017), he expended considerable resources on affirming the US commitment to Europe, which distracted him from Asia (Blackwill and Fontaine, 2024).[305]

The first Trump Administration clearly shifted US's China policy towards competition. The 2017 National Security Strategy (White House, 2020) explicitly directs the United States to counteract China through renewed military capabilities (pp. 28–32) and expanded diplomatic and commercial influence (pp. 33–35) because China is a revisionist power, that "seeks to displace the United States in the Indo-Pacific region, expand the reaches of its state-driven economic model, and reorder the region in its favor" (p. 25). The administration reaffirmed the shift in the 2018 National Defense Strategy, and followed through with tangible policy changes (White House, 2020). The president started a trade war with China, accused China of currency manipulation, extradited and prose-cuted executives from Chinese-owned firms, and promoted US military patrols in East Asian waters that confronted Chinese ships directly. Trump also focused US military spending on platforms necessary to compete with China. President Biden largely continued the policies Trump implemented (Bader, 2020).

Why, after two decades of cautious hedging, did competition suddenly and rapidly intensify under Trump and remain that way? This pattern of behavior is puzzling for two reasons. First, China experienced rapid economic growth and military spending across this whole period. Thus, scholars would expect a gradual shift in US policy to account for China's growth. They are puzzled by long periods of inaction, followed by an extreme policy change (Johnston, 2013, 2019).

Second, each president faced different China-specific challenges that many believe they did not deal with appropriately. Critics argue that H. W. Bush and Clinton should have, but did not, respond to China's human rights abuses and autocratic consolidation (Nakatsuji, 1999; Skid-more and Gates, 1997). Critics also believe that these presidents improperly enabled China's rise by deepening commercial and diplomatic ties (Allison, 2017; He, 2016). Critics of Obama argue that the Pivot to Asia was both ineffective and unnecessarily provocative because it was poorly resourced (Gilder, 2010; Lieberthal, 2011). Critics of President Trump argue that his rhetoric was unsophisticated and extreme (Swaine, 2018), and that his pol-icy changes were so rapid that they harmed American firms and workers (Johnson, 2019). In each case, critics attribute the history of US policy to a series of individual and bureaucratic blunders, each worst than the last.

---

[305] Klau et al. (2016) provide the range of perspectives on Obama's European legacy.

They argue that our leaders are inexperienced (Gilder, 2010), ignorant of East Asia (Bader, 2020), or captured by personal preferences (He, 2016) or encounters with Chinese elites (Engel, 2010). But these individual-level explanations are puzzling given continuity across presidents. For example, Presidents Biden and Trump agreed on little. Their differences could plausibly follow from differences in experience, political party, world view and many other attributes. However, "when it comes to the greatest foreign policy challenge facing the United States – how to deal with the rise of China – Biden's team have continued and mimicked Trump's destructive approach" (Bader, 2020). Similarly, H. W. Bush, Clinton, and W. Bush vary extensively in terms of their foreign policy experience, age, upbringing, world view, partisan affiliation, and adviser pool. But "in the end, most observers have argued that the similarities in each administration's China policy were greater than the differences" (Steinberg, 2020, p. 128). If partisan or individual differences matter, what explains these two periods of remarkable continuity?

In this chapter, I use my theory to help systematically collect, organize, and interpret the publicly available information on this case. Part of my contribution is to fill in the gaps in public knowledge in two ways. First, I contribute new data on US perceptions of China. I utilize over 200 interviews with US China-watchers in Washington DC, and a policy analysis to answer the question: when and why did the consensus view shift on China's intentions? Second, I use my theory to fill gaps when data is not available. For example, the most recent national estimates on China's intentions remain classified, and senior National Intelligence Estimate (NIE) authors were not available to interview.[306] But through a combination of interviews with their political masters and other IC employees, and a theoretical analysis given the information we have, I can estimate a fuller picture of what transpired. This will help public intellectuals better evaluate the quality of elite decisions. As we shall see, much of what we can observe and infer from secondary sources, is largely consistent with what I expect. Which suggests my theory provides a useful benchmark.

This chapter also critically evaluates US policy and intelligence towards China. It is important to scrutinize the US's China policy because China is the most substantial threat to US national security. We must get this

---

[306] Specifically, the long-serving Central Intelligence Officer and Defense Intelligence Officer for East Asia. However, I did interview one Director of Analysis at the CIA, several Directors of National Intelligence (DNIs), IC customers on the NSC, and important contributors to several National Security Strategies and National Defense Strategies.

policy right. But any criticism makes an assumption about what a president should have done. These are difficult claims to make because Sino-American relations are multifaceted, and the details of US intelligence and decision-making on China are closely guarded secrets. Thus, even pundits with access to the White House only get a narrow view of what transpired, and usually for a small period of time. Following Glaser (2010), I argue that rationalist theory presents the normatively correct benchmark to evaluate policies against because the predictions from a rationalist theory assume that decision-makers make optimal policy choices based on their desire to serve the national interest. To be clear, others who evaluate US–China policy implicitly rely on a rationalist baseline when they say, for example, that analysts should respond to a rival's costly signals or illiberal actions. But these critics rely on a more stylistic rationalist theory to serve as the benchmark. My basic claim is that these rationalist benchmarks are too simplistic to accurately reflect what decision-makers are supposed to do. Therefore, we must be cautious to criticize policy-makers who deviate from their predictions.

Using my rationalist theory as the benchmark, I argue that the period of continuity and sudden change in US policy was a rational response to a sudden change in information about China's motives circa 2011, with power shifting constantly in the background. I infer from novel elite interviews and recently declassified data that the IC alerted US policy-makers to the fact that China's intentions were clearly expansive circa 2011. Before this estimate, the IC was deeply uncertain if China's intentions were limited or expansive. I find that policy-makers believed this estimate was a vital piece of information they used to form their overall strategy. Consistent with my policy predictions, I find that presidents from H. W. Bush to W. Bush were right to pursue hedging, largely because they were uncertain about China's motives and were hopeful that cooperation was possible. My theory suggests that President Obama should have turned sharply towards competition during his second term, given revised intelligence estimates. President Obama's Pivot to Asia was somewhat consistent with my prediction. But from the perspective of my theory, this shift was not as strong as it should have been given the revised estimates that Obama received. In parts of this chapter I explore Obama's reasoning and performance in detail. Notably, Obama's partial turn was short lived. Consistent with my policy predictions, President Trump turned sharply towards competition with China even in the face of commercial opposition, and concern among European partners. Once implemented by Trump, President Biden did not revert to the policy he supported as Obama's Vice President. Rather, Biden continued with Trump's policy despite their different political views and personal backgrounds.

Even if we accept competition with China was right given the intelligence, it does not mean that the intelligence was right. In fact, a second group of critics has argued that the intelligence community ignored clear indicators that China's intentions were vast.[307] They attribute these failures to bureaucratic pathologies inside the IC (Herkert, 2017). Our Congressional leaders are now calling for intelligence reform (Schiff, 2020).

Through a series of interviews with intelligence and national security elites, and a review of declassified information, I find that intelligence estimates of China's motives closely follow the logic of my rationalist theory, and therefore represent ideal estimates. Long before the Cold War ended, US diplomats met with Chinese elites to better understand their intentions. During these meetings, China declared its interest in a variant of nationalism that would restore China's position in Asia. From that moment forward US intelligence analysts sought to verify if China's declared motives were genuine. Much changed in the post-Cold War world. This enabled China to pursue several violent actions. But analysts did not alter their long-term estimates because China's actions plausibly fit with China's declared motives. It was only circa 2011 that analysts observed actions that they could not reconcile with China's narrow nationalist agenda. At that moment, they sounded the alarm.

This interpretation is vital for future policy because it pushes back against extensive criticism of US policy and intelligence performance. If the critics are right – our policy and intelligence was the result of individual and bureaucratic failures – then we need to fix our bureaucratic problems (Schiff, 2020), repair our relations with China (Bader, 2020), and enact a China policy that fits their version of what we should be doing (Johnston, 2019). I argue that these criticisms are based on a faulty premise. As a result, the reforms they call for will damage our ability to provide reasonable intelligence, and potentially cause us to embark on the wrong China policy. To make these concerns clear, I focus on alternative arguments in the modern policy debate on US policy and intelligence towards China. As we shall see, these arguments implicitly follow the logic of defensive realism, power transition theory, and regime theory to explain what the US should have done. But they focus mainly on partisan politics,

---

[307] The House Select Committee on Intelligence recently chastised the IC in "The China Deep Dive: A Report on the Intelligence Community's Capabilities and Competencies with Respect to the People's Republic of China."

bureaucratic politics, and the power of individual elites to explain what happened. I take these case-specific arguments head on.

To be clear, my coding is similar to others who informally observe a shift in estimates circa 2011. But these scholars either argue that the shift was a mistake (Johnston, 2013, 2019), or suggest it followed from the rise of Xi (Campbell and Blackwill, 2016; Shuman, 2021). My novel data gives both a precise timing of the shift, and more detailed information about what drove it. This data supports my theoretical explanation that the IC responded rationally to qualitative differences in China's actions. Therefore their inferences reflected a high quality estimates, given the information they had.

Also to be clear, my analysis emphasizes the reassurance problem in Sino-American relations. Others emphasize deterrence and resolve (Zhang, 2023), usually over specific territories that indisputably fell within China's core interests; such as China's resolve to fight for Taiwan (Henley, 2023). While the Taiwan question is important, it has always been clear that China and the US hold divergent preferences over Taiwan. I am interested in estimates about China's broader interests, which were less clear in the post-Cold War era.

I proceed as follows. First, I analyze US intelligence estimates of China's strategic intentions. Second, I analyze US policy towards China from H.W. Bush to Biden. At the end, I speculate about the future: what will come next, and what policies should we implement to best prepare for competition with China.

8.1 US Intelligence Estimates of China's Intentions

We now know that the IC remained uncertain about China's motives for decades. Why did it take the IC so long to realize that China's intentions were vast? The conventional wisdom is that they made a mistake. In a recent inquiry, the bipartisan House Select Committee on Intelligence reviewed all intelligence products on China written since the post-Cold War period. The year-long review culminated in a report (House Permanent Select Committee on Intelligence 2020), aptly titled "The China Deep Dive: A Report on the Intelligence Community's Capabilities and Competencies with Respect to the People's Republic of China." In this report, Congress chastised the IC for its poor performance and incompetence.[308]

---

[308] The criticism was far reaching. Congress argued that the IC: did not dedicate enough collection resources to monitoring China; did not predict crises that China instigated; and did not properly attribute cyber operations to China even months after attacks occurred.

Their most damning criticism relates to how the IC has evaluated China's intentions. Notably, the Committee found that the IC waited about a decade too long to learn that China's intentions were vast. The Committee laid out a clear statement of what the IC should have estimated, and then what they actually did estimate. The report states:

China's ascendance has been spectacular in its scale and far less benign than initially expected. During the 1990s and 2000s there was a consensus in the West that, as China became more prosperous and developed, it would also become freer and play a constructive role in international relations in the 21st Century. Observers convinced themselves that the leadership in Beijing learned the "right" lessons from the international and domestic reaction to the Tiananmen Square crackdown in 1989. As a result, the broad trend as one of convergence between China and the West was assumed. Confidence that China would choose to liberalize was central to the decision to admit China to the WTO and to award the 2008 Summer Olympics to Beijing. This optimism was not entirely unfounded. Indeed, the introduction of village elections within China was considered by some to be a harbinger of liberalization.

However, the last decade has shown those expectations to have been deeply misplaced. Western policy-makers' belief that our own democratic systems were globally inevitable blinded observers to the Chinese Communist Party's overriding objective of retaining and growing its power. In the interim, the People's Republic of China (PRC) has increasingly sought to revise the international order and global norms in a way that furthers its own strategic interests and undermines those of the United States specifically, and the West generally. Beijing has sought to expand its economic and political influence through its "One Belt, One Road" Initiative and the large-scale co-option of media outlets throughout the world. Militarily, China has embarked on a massive modernization drive - creating a "blue water" navy, investing heavily in hyper-sonic weapons, developing its own fifth-generation fighter, militarizing a series of atolls and islets in the South China Sea to strengthen its claims in the region, and building its first overseas military base in Djibouti. (House Intelligence Committee, 2020, pp. 5–6)

Clearly, two academic findings have crept into the Committee's thinking about the ideal inferences the IC should draw. First, consistent with the democratic peace, the Committee assumes that autocratic, and illiberal regimes are war-prone. Based on this theory, the Committee believes that autocratic behaviors dating back to the Tiananmen Square Massacre (1989) should have convinced the IC that China was an illiberal regime, and not capable of liberalizing.

Second, consistent with defensive realism, the Committee assumes that all costly actions communicate expansive aims. Based on this theory, the Committee believes the IC should have drawn an inference from China's spending on offensive military weapons, China's efforts to undermine the liberal order in East Asia, military crises that China started, and China's territorial demands. The Committee asserts that the IC did not appropriately update following these indicators.

The Committee blames the error on pathologies well-known to researchers. Specifically, it argues that the IC relied on wishful thinking that interdependence would change China's preferences. Elsewhere, Congressional leaders find that bureaucratic incentives and group-think amplified these pathological estimates. Based on this finding, they demand intense intelligence reform so this alleged failure does not happen again (see the policy op-ed released by the ranking Committee Member at about the same time (Schiff, 2020)).

I agree with the basic claim that the IC should monitor China's costly actions. However, it is not the case that the IC should update in each case. Rather, the inferences that the IC should draw depend on China's historical and cultural context. When I take China's historical and cultural context into account, I find that the IC rendered near-perfect estimates of China's strategic intentions throughout the entire case.

Table 8.1 summarizes what my theory expects high-quality analysts to do in this case. The table is broken down into the three periods that my theory identifies. I code the moment of focus as following from Henry Kissinger's 1970 diplomatic visit to China. Consistent with my theory, the IC exploited Mao's statements about China's declared motives to develop an assessment framework. I code the period of consistency between 1970 and 2011. I agree with Congress that China consolidated an illiberal autocratic government, and took many costly military actions. However, China's behavior is clearly explained by China's declared principles. As a result, the IC was right not to update their estimates. Finally, I code the moment of truth starting in 2011. I find that at this moment, the consensus view on China's intentions shifted. Although analysts disagree about the event that triggered the shift, they all use the logic of my theory to explain why the shift occurred. Specifically, they could not reconcile China's behavior with its declared principle, and therefore they concluded that China's aims were not limited. In what follows, I substantiate these claims one period at a time.

8.1.1 The Moment of Focus

In 1969, the US realized that Sino-Soviet relations were unusually tense. Henry Kissinger reasoned that if the US extended diplomatic and commercial support to China, that the US could feasibly coax China out of the

Table 8.1 *Theoretical expectations*

My Theory Predicts	Dis-confirming Evidence
The Moment of Focus	
Nixon's visit to China, the first diplomatic exchange in decades, prompts the IC to write an estimate of China's intentions. In their estimate, the IC: - Explains China could hold limited or expansive aims - Explicitly ties China's limited aims to a principle - Details China's history and culture surrounding its declared principle - Explains what specific issues and territories China will want if China is motivated by its declared principle	The IC do not write an estimate, or otherwise communicate, an estimate about China's motives to the Executive. In their estimate, the IC: - Are certain China has limited/unlimited aims - Assume that China is motivated by security if not greedy - Discuss limited aims without reference to a principle - Cannot tie specific issues to China's declared principle for most issues, possibly because of irreconcilable ambiguity
The Period of Consistency	
The IC does not update their estimate about China's strategic intentions so long as China's behavior fits with its declared principle. This includes if China: - Rapidly militarizes - Builds/purchases offensive weapons - Demands territory - Instigates a crisis /deploys forces	The IC alters their estimates after China takes consistent actions. The IC does not evaluate China's intentions. Instead, relies on optimism about China's shifting intentions. The president ignores the IC estimates and makes choices based on personal characteristics or electoral incentives.
The Moment of Truth	
When the IC observe China take actions that cannot be explained by their declared principle, IC update estimates that China's intentions are vast.	IC observe China do something inconsistent. Do not update their beliefs. IC update their beliefs because of the scope of China's actions and not because they cannot reconcile China's actions with assessment framework. Leaders turn to competition for personalist reasons/based on inexperience.

Soviet-led Communist Bloc. Kissinger's goal was to meet with Mao and determine if a compromise was possible.

In 1970, Henry Kissinger secretly visited China to express American intentions and obtain a clear statement of China's strategic intentions from China's leadership.[309] Kissinger's historic visit well fits the moment of focus in my theory. Notably, the US had cut off high-level Sino-American diplomacy in the two decades prior. Therefore, in 1969 the IC did not have a clear statement from Mao about what China's intentions were. But Kissinger discussed China's strategic aims in great detail during the visit.[310]

Taking Kissinger's visit as the moment of focus, I make clear predictions about estimates of China's motives before and afterwards. Before Kissinger's visit, I expect that CIA will speculate about China's motives with low confidence. This is what we observe. The CIA knew little about the inner-workings of Communist China or its foreign policy goals.[311] Even though the US knew very little about China, it did not stop the CIA from theorizing about China's strategic intentions. For example, in 1969 the CIA assessed that China's objectives could include "treatment as a major world power and as a primary source of revolutionary leadership; accommodation of its policies by other Asian states; and control of Taiwan."[312] But even this report was not sure which of these interests China would prioritize. It also discussed the possibility that China wanted recognition as a nuclear power, among other objectives.

My theory suggests that CIA estimates should crystallize after Kissinger's visit. I make four specific claims about ideal estimates. First, I expect the IC to write a comprehensive national-level estimate of China's strategic intentions shortly after Kissinger's visit. That estimate should be motivated by

---

[309] The fact that Kissinger went to China to learn about China's motives and communicate US policy is also supportive of my theory. If diplomacy did not provide vital information, Kissinger would not have gone.

[310] I start the policy analysis in the post-Cold War period because this is where policymakers broaden their focus. However, the estimates during this period have not changed much since 1970. Starting with the earliest CIA estimates (1950s) shows a long period of deep uncertainty and disagreement amongst analysts. This is consistent with my theory because we are in the pre-diplomatic period.

[311] One reason was that the US did not think about China as an independent actor. Before 1969, the US had several analysts dedicated to understanding China's intentions. But they typically analyzed China in the Cold War context. Thus, estimates usually thought about China as a member of the Communist Bloc, and not an independent actor with a grand strategy. There were some exceptions. For example, the US analyzed China's intentions over Taiwan. But this was limited to a single issue.

[312] Summary of the CIA Response to NSSM 14. National Archives, RG 59, S/S Files: Lot 80 D 212, NSSM 14. Date still classified.

information gathered during Nixon's diplomatic exchange. This is exactly what I find. In November 1970, two months after Nixon's visit, the CIA produced National Intelligence Estimate (NIE) 30-7-70 titled "Communist China's International Posture," and circulated it to the White House and NSC. Consistent with my theory, NIE 30-7-70 is explicitly motivated by information gleaned from "China's return to active diplomacy" (p. 1).

Second, I predict that the CIA should focus on two potential outcomes. One is that China's interests are limited to a specific principle that is consistent with Mao's diplomatic statements. The other is that China could be driven by more expansive aims. This is exactly what NIE 30-7-70 does. The second paragraph explains that China's "basic goals" are determined by one of two principals. Either China sees itself as "a great power and leader of the world revolution or as a more traditional but highly nationalistic country concerned primarily with Asian interests." In short, NIE 30-7-70 makes clear a plausible reason that China could seek some revisionist territory and then stop: China could be a highly nationalist country that cares about its nationalist history.

To be clear, this nationalist estimate is cautious. NIE 30-7-70 (p. 8) also estimates that China could be motivated by principles that imply broader foreign policy aims. The section on contingencies (i.e., potential alternatives) warns about "Peking's Activist Foreign Policy," as a potential alternative motivation that would drive more expansive aims.

Third, I expect that the CIA will detail the historical context that surrounds these principles. NIE 30-7-70 does that. It devotes two pages to fleshing out what nationalism means for China. It notes that the "Sino-centric view of the Middle Kingdom," is the dominant narrative of China's nationalism. And that "The past century has left a residue of bitterness and frustration among those Chinese whose sense of nationalism and patriotism has been outraged by what they see as unfair treatment of China by foreigners [this likely refers to both Europeans and neighboring Asian states]" (p. 4). NIE 30-7-70 goes on to distinguish between the principle of nationalism and other potential motivating ideologies that would likely drive broader ambitions. Consistent with my theory, the CIA believes that their assessment is not leader-specific. Rather, their assessment framework is valuable for understanding China's long-term aims. It states, "Unlike the ideology of Maoism, which may not long survive its creator, the traditional sense of China's privileged role in the world will probably remain a consistent theme in this and any foreseeable Chinese government" (p. 4).

Finally, my theory expects that the CIA will use historical and cultural context to explain to policy-makers the issues and territories that fit and do not fit with China's conceptualization of nationalism. NIE 30-7-70 does that. It states that territorial control of Taiwan, Tibet, and Hong Kong unambiguously fit China's long-term interests. It also explains that China would like to resolve border disputes with India and the Soviet Union, noting that China views these territories as part of its sovereign territory. However, it assesses these as less important because they have less salience to nationalism.

NIE 30-7-70 provides additional nuances that illustrate the CIA understood the difference between China's underlying principles and the strategy it could use to serve those principles. Specifically, NIE 30-7-70 clarifies a difference between China's actual interests and additional military actions China might take given the regional security situation. For example, NIE 30-7-30 states that China may make "defensive" military deployments if US or Soviet forces threaten to disrupt peace along China's borders. But the report clearly distinguishes between these military deployments which depend on the strategic situation, and China's core interests, which China will pursue in any strategic situation (pp. 5–6).[313]

One concern is that China's nationalist ambitions are somewhat ambiguous. There are several specific territories and normative issues that could fit (or not) within China's core interests. Indeed, if the CIA cannot identify the ambiguous issues, and render at least a moderate confidence judgment over whether they fit, then they may have trouble exploiting historical context as my theory expects. However, NIE 30-7-70 explicitly deals with ambiguous claims by showing that they map onto slightly different interpretations of China's nationalist identity. Specifically, the Middle Kingdom refers to a pre-Westphalian period where China exerted broad influence and not direct control over surrounding territories. It was not exactly clear what level of control China would want over Southeast Asia and Korea under a nationalist ideology. Consistent with my theory, NIE 30-7-30 renders a moderate confidence estimate on ambiguous issues, and explains the exact indicators that could help resolve this sort of ambiguity. It claims that if China's desire is for minimal control then "China is likely to persist in encouraging local revolutionaries, but... significant material assistance is unlikely to be provided" (p. 12).

---

[313] This insight is far more nuanced than many realist theories allow for. It shows that the CIA can distinguish between territories of intrinsic value, and instrumental objectives that states seek to achieve their true aims. See Glaser (2010) for a description of the differences.

From the perspective of my theory, this assessment framework is first rate. It identifies different principles that could motivate China, then uses an analysis of China's history and culture to detail what China wants depending on what principle motivates it.

8.1.2 Did This Assessment Framework Persist?

One complication in this case is that the US meets with China to discus China's motives in the 1970s. However, the Cold War remains the focus of US policy until 1990. In between this time, China experiences serious political and strategic changes. Notably, in the late 1970s, Mao died and the Cultural Revolution ended. These changes brought about major governance reforms in China. It is plausible that the incoming CCP leadership held entirely different intentions.[314] At the end of the Cold War China's strategic position changed by so much that it could have affected their intentions.[315] It is plausible that China reformulated its intrinsic motives at this moment. If they did, then I should focus on the (still classified) estimates of China's intentions that followed these more recent events.[316] To be clear, my theory does not expect that if the IC does not change their estimates, that they will furnish the same estimate regularly. However, one might imagine that after major events, they may report to policymakers that their estimate has not changed and clarify why.

Still to evaluate the IC's performance using my theory, I must code the assessment framework it used starting at the end of the Cold War. The NIEs in this period remain classified. Fortunately, the evidence I have suggests that the US relied on the same basic assessment framework that is laid out in NIE 3-7-70. Whether or not this followed from an entirely new assessment effort in 1976, or 1990, or was a continuation of NIE 3-7-70 does not matter. What is important is to understand the basic contours of the framework they relied on in the 1990s.

---

[314] There is also good reason to suspect that they didn't. Notably, they were mainly Mao loyalists.

[315] For example, the fall of the Soviet Union could have de-legitimized the principle of global communism. It also changed China's largest threat. It also created normative space for China to legitimately pursue regional influence in the area previously occupied by the USSR.

[316] In Section 4.4.3, I showed that my overall theory is robust to expectations of leadership changes so long as they occur reasonably infrequently, or that new leaders are likely to hold similar preferences from their predecessors. Therefore, I do not necessarily expect US estimates to change.

Here are some examples that illustrate continuity in the assessment process. In 1982, President Reagan ordered two National Security Study Directives (NSSD 1, 12) that caused the IC to provide a holistic assessment of China's strategic intentions. Both studies remain classified, but the initial outline and study plans are declassified. Consistent with NIE 30-7-70, these documents reveal that the US appreciated that China could pose a strategic threat to US security interests. However, it could also hold regional aims grounded in nationalist ideology.

In 1989 President H. W. Bush ordered a National Security Review (summarized in his executive orders NSR-12 and NSR-29) to assess any and all threats to US interests in the post-Cold War world. These far-reaching reviews took two full years to complete (there was no National Security Strategy in 1990). Most of the study documents remain classified. However, I interviewed the Deputy Assistant Secretary of State, Ambassador Robert Kimmitt, who coordinated these reviews. Kimmitt acknowledged that the study teams considered China as a potential threat based on the trajectory of its economic growth and population. However, the study team was uncertain about China's strategic aims. Since they were uncertain about China's aims, they where uncertain if China would pose a long-term threat to US interests.[317]

Published interviews also suggest that the National Security Council up until the Obama Administration held the same core impression of China. For example, Obama's Deputy National Security Adviser for East Asian Affairs, Jeffery Bader, has noted, "we were, for the most part, inheriting a general framework for dealing with China that went back decades" (Barboza and Bader, 2020).

Publicly available documents published since 2000 further suggest that the IC continued to follow this assessment rubric. For example, the 2005 Report to Congress on the "The Military Power of the People's Republic of China," included a ten-page declassified assessment of China's future strategic intentions. It started by noting that "Direct insights into China's national strategies are difficult to acquire. To assess China's intent, analysis of official Chinese strategy documents and White Papers must be augmented by examination of what China has accomplished in recent years and is attempting to accomplish in the future" (p. 9). In other words, the best estimate must take China's actions in the context of its stated aims.

---

[317] He did state that the US and China were destined to compete over Taiwan and Hong Kong. This indicates a broader view that the IC realized what specific issues fit within China's nationalist aims.

The report then goes on to outline two potential strategic orientations that are consistent with NIE 3-7-70. In another example, a 2010 Department of Defense Report to Congress that included an assessment of China's strategic aims affirms a statement made by President Obama earlier that year, "[the US–China] relationship has not been without disagreement and difficulty. But the notion that we must be adversaries is not pre-destined."[318] While the public report does not go into as much detail about the basis of the estimate as the classified NIE 3-7-70, it is clear that the Department of Defense's strategic estimate is that China could prove to be either a "partner" or an "adversary."

Interviews I conducted suggest that this basic framework was consistent with how the IC approached China analysis up until 2012. Notably, when I asked the DNI how the IC went about understanding China's interest, he explained that "Determining core interests has a long and honorable place in analysis, [however] that's not that difficult. You ask any 50 China-analysts and they'd give you that same list of things that I came up with."[319]

In other interviews, I showed intelligence analysts and former NSC staff NIE 3-7-70 and asked them if much has changed about how the US viewed the plausible outcomes with regard to China before 2010. While their answers were carefully worded so as not to violate classification rules, it was clear that this was how they thought about the problem.

8.1.3 The Period of Consistency: Was the IC Right to Ignore Costly Signals?

One of the central criticisms levied against the IC is that they missed key indicators that China's aims were vast. Like these critics I take two sets of facts as given. First, China displayed many violent actions that clearly signaled it was an illiberal regime that desired revision of the status quo. In 1989, China brutally suppressed student protesters leading to the Tiananmen Square Massacre. In 1995, China dramatically escalated in the Taiwan Strait leading to a military crisis with the United States. In 2005, China embarked on an aggressive military modernization program. Military analysts assessed that China's modernization would help China conduct offensive military operations in Taiwan and its near abroad, while deterring a retaliatory strike from the United States in mainland China.

---

[318] Military and Security Developments Involving the People's Republic of China (Department of Defense, 2010, p. I).

[319] Author's interview with Denis Blair.

Second, I also take as given that the IC did not alter their estimates of China's intentions during this period.

Consistent with a large literature on costly signaling and the democratic peace, critics argue that these two facts evidence an intelligence failure (House Intelligence Committee 2020). The existing signaling literature suggests that China's choice to militarize, purchase clearly offensive weapons, demand territory, instigate crises, and brutally suppress all efforts at democratization should cause the US to grow alarmed.

My theory expects something different. I argue that the IC should conduct a qualitative estimate of China's actions and ask: "can I look at the history of China's actions and say that they plausibly serve China's declared aims? If I can, I will not update my estimate of China's strategic intentions." Thus, unlike theories that focus on indicators alone, the fact that the IC did not update their estimates during this period is not inconsistent with my theory.

Upon review, it is quite obvious that the foreign policy actions highlighted by the House Intelligence Committee (2020) are broadly consistent with China's declared *limited* aims. Perhaps the most extreme example is the 1995–1996 Taiwan Strait Crisis. In 1995 China sought to revise the status quo over Taiwan. China initiated an invasion plan, concentrated 150,000 troops on its coastline, and executed live-fire drills (Scobell, 2003, pp. 176–177). China backed down only after the United States sailed a carrier through the Taiwan Strait. But even then China did not stop. In 1996, China invested in offensive battleships and used live-fire exercises to influence Taiwan's election. American foreign policy elites acknowledged that they had underestimated China's interest in violent territorial revision over Taiwan. The IC understood the importance of these actions and used them to update their inferences about China's resolve to fight for Taiwan. A declassified assessment from the Office of Naval Intelligence, affirmed by the CIA, reads "China is likely to conduct similar, politically motivated exercises in the vicinity of Taiwan in the near future." However, analysts drew a different inference about China's strategic intentions. Most analysts did not alter their estimates in response to the Taiwan Strait Crisis. Surprisingly, a handful of senior analysts even raised their confidence that China's long-term intentions were limited to peaceful reunification (Qimao, 1996).

Consistent with scholarship on trust (Kydd, 2005), the House Permanent Select Committee on Intelligence (2020) argued that violent territorial demands and offensive arming signal aggressive motives. Thus, the IC was wrong to sustain uncertain estimates about China's motives. But this does not account for China's historical context and the IC's prior estimate about what China would want if it held limited aims. As my theory illuminates, it is appropriate to sustain uncertain estimates following this militaristic behavior because China could have plausibly behaved this way either if China held expansive aims, or if China was intensely motivated by limited nationalist objectives.

Of course, just because the IC failed to alter their estimates in response to the 1995 crisis does not directly suggest my theory is at work. It could be that the IC failed to update for a different reason. In fact, the Select Committee on Intelligence presents an alternative story. They argue that the IC's optimism was based on a naive hope that China would liberalize, and therefore China's intentions would change.[320]

This argument is largely misplaced for two reasons.[321] First, it assumes that China's regime type almost completely determines foreign policy aims. Second, it assumes that the main reason that the IC was unsure about China's strategic aims was that the IC could not predict whether China would liberalize. However, and as we just detailed, this is not true. NIE 30-7-70 made no mention of the fact that China could liberalize. And yet, NIE 30-7-70 still estimated that *autocratic* China's could hold limited strategic intentions. The reason is that it was plausible that autocratic China was motivated by restoring its historical position in Asia.

A closer look at China estimates at two critical periods shows that uncertainty about China's future behavior did not rest on beliefs that China's true intentions could change. The first period comes in the wake of the Tiananmen Square Massacre. We now know from declassified documents that Chinese leaders viewed liberalization and democratization as an extreme threat to their rule (Nathan, 2019). During private deliberations, the PRC agreed that economic and political isolation was better than risking enmeshment. The IC was aware of these deliberations and still estimated that China's intentions could be limited. The second period comes in 2018. As stated, the NSS reports a new, alarmist estimate of China's intentions. This revised estimate still includes the caveat that if China democratized that cooperation could be possible.

---

[320] A related criticism is that they believed China would become so enmeshed in the US economy that they would prefer to live in a compromise over Asia, rather than compete with the US and lose the economic benefits (Campbell and Ratner, 2018).

[321] Medeiros and Blanchette (2021) convincingly argued that a similar criticisms levied against policy-makers is also misplaced.

Putting these two estimates together, it is clear that IC beliefs about whether China's intentions *could change* did not determine their estimate about whether China's interests would cause a problem. In the 1990s, the IC believed that China would not liberalize and still thought long-term cooperation was possible. In 2018, the IC revised their estimate that China's intentions were aggressive but continued to note that if China changed their regime that cooperation could follow.[322]

8.1.4 The Moment of Truth: When Did Perceptions on China Change?

Public intellectuals now agree that the IC is gloomy about China's strategic intentions. But they do not know exactly when and why we got here. One challenge is that the intelligence community is broad and compartmentalized (Lowenthal, 2019). Analysts across different agencies have access to different information, come from different backgrounds, and do not always share their estimates. One might wonder, did the consensus shift at the same time, or was there wide spread disagreement across individual analysts? Second, the aggregation of intelligence in the US can follow many pathways. We want to know when alarmist estimates started to reach the White House.

In what follows, I present new evidence to answer these questions. I find that the consensus view shifted suddenly between 2010 and 2012, and that many analysts across the IC shifted at the same time. I find that the view of several NSC officials responsible for whole-of-government estimates shifted between 2011 and 2013. As a result, I find that revised estimates were likely communicated to the president between 2011 and 2013.

I used two types of evidence to arrive at this finding. First, between 2014 and 2019 I interviewed 207 mid-level national security professionals who focused on China issues. Interview subjects included congressional staff, employees at national security-affiliated agencies and the military, and think-tank employees. The opinions of mid-level China experts is important for two reasons. First, evidence shows that the mean of group responses is close to the true estimate (Horowitz et al., 2019). Second, the IC uses a consensus model to write NIEs. As a result, the views of intelligence professionals as a whole are largely reflected in national-level

---

[322] In my interviews, no subject argued that they were optimistic because they thought China's motives would change. Recall these interviews were conducted as early as 2014.

estimates (Lowenthal, 2019).[323] As a result, the responses help me appreciate how the consensus view shifts among professional China experts within the United States.

During these interviews I asked subjects some variant of the following questions.[324]

1. Among those who think about China's strategic ambitions, is the consensus view that China has limited aims in East Asia, or that China has expansive aims that are unacceptable for US policy in the long run?
2. If the consensus is that China is a competitor when did that consensus form?
3. What is your personal view on China's ambitions?
4. If pessimistic, what event caused you to change your estimate?

Figure 8.1 visualizes perceptions about when the "consensus view" shifted. The majority of analysts (91 percent) believed that the consensus view had shifted. Some subjects (n=137) provided a specific year or episode that they believed drove the shift in US assessments. However, a large portion were uncertain about exactly when the shift took place (n=51). The most common answer was some time between 2010 and 2012. But many subjects said some time during the Obama Administration.[325] Consistent with my theory, these estimates changed quite suddenly (especially once we account for the fact that I distribute uncertain answers across Obama's entire term). Over 70 percent of analysts who believe that change happened, pin point a three-year window where perceptions change. 90 percent of analysts who believe change happened suggest that it took place during the Obama Administration. Notice that the earliest year any analysts suggested a change took place is 2008. No analyst suggested that perceptions began to change during the 1990s. Indeed, the complete lack of updating in the 1990s seems inconsistent with Congressional thinking.

---

[323] The IC also regularly consults outside experts to forming their strategic estimates. For example, in Global Trends 2030, the National Intelligence Council explicitly acknowledged that they circulated classified documents with several experts out of government and took their opinions seriously into the final report.

[324] At the conclusion of each interview, I summarized that subject's answers to these questions in an Excel spreadsheet. After collecting all of the interview data, I normalized the answers to reflect the timing of when they believed the consensus view shifted.

[325] I average out range answers across the range. E.g. if a subject stated between 2010 and 2014, I added 1/5 to each of those four years.

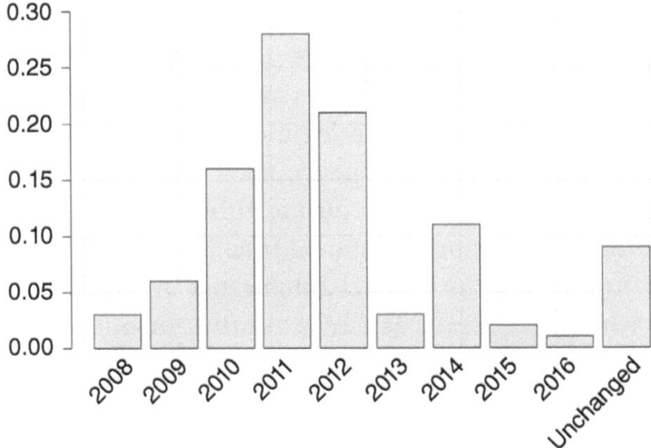

Figure 8.1 When China experts think the consensus view shifted about China's strategic intentions.

Personal assessments follow a similar pattern. There is a strong but imperfect correlation between personal estimates and individual perceptions of the consensus view. More individuals could pinpoint the year that they changed their personal assessment (and often the event that triggered their shift in beliefs). If we use personalist estimates we arrive at stronger confidence that perceptions shifted in 2011.

Second, I analyzed publicly available estimates of China's intentions to identify shifts in assessments at the national level. The documents I reviewed included unclassified, whole of IC estimates of China's motives. These included short estimates written in the National Security Strategy, the five-yearly Global Trends Reports, and the Annual Report to Congress on Military and Security Developments in the People's Republic of China. I also reviewed testimony and public writings by the most senior NSC staff who command vast intelligence agencies notably the Director of Central Intelligence, the Director of National Intelligence, and the Secretary of Defense.

Using these documents, I identified a change in the tone and content of publicly available, whole of government estimates of China's intentions around 2011.[326] In 2011, intelligence reports no longer emphasized the

---

[326] Obama's Adviser on East Asian policy, Ambassador Jeffery Bader, has recently stated that while Obama was in office, he received "the first indications that Beijing was moving away from Deng Xiaoping's mantra about prudence and modesty in their international profile. In fact, that mantra and approach came into debate internally in China, and some

prospect of cooperation under the current Chinese regime. The tone of these estimates started to shift towards revisionist China.[327]

The publicly available documents were subtle. They certainly do not provide sufficient detail to explain the logic of change. To supplement my coding, I interviewed senior intelligence elites who were responsible for publishing the documents written during this period. These interviews included the former Director of National Intelligence, and former Deputy Director for Analysis at the Central Intelligence Agency, and five other senior elites who either served as CIA executives or on the NSC. Several respondents confirmed that I accurately identified the shift in net assessment as occurring around 2011. I discuss these interviews in the next section.

Before moving on, it is important to compare my coding with Johnston (2013). At one level, our coding complements each other. He similarly codes a shift in US estimates based on anecdotal encounters, and an analysis of temporal shifts of publicly available China blogs. Specifically, he searches for blog entries where the word "assertiveness" appeared within five words of China and counts them over time. He finds a linear increase beginning in 2010, and scaling up until 2012 (where his study ends). This similar result provides face validity to my elite-based study. However, my findings suggest a more punctuated shift by focusing more directly on elite perceptions of the consensus view.

Where we depart is how we evaluate IC performance. Johnston argues that China's behavior circa 2010–2011 was not that different from China's behavior in the decade prior. Thus, he argues, that US analysts were wrong to update. However, his analysis follows from examining the frequency of costly indicators. For example, he notes that China had sustained the same level of militarization, crisis instigation and assertive rhetoric from 1990

---

of that spilled out. It was clear that it was being challenged by some who thought that China's growing power deserved a different approach" see Barboza and Bader (2020).

[327] For example, the Director of National Intelligence (Denis Blair) discussed China's strategic intentions during his confirmation hearing (2009) and then annually through reports to Congress. During his confirmation hearing, DNI Blair expressed "optimism" for "enduring" cooperation with China. In his capacity as DNI, his 2010 report to the Senate no longer expresses optimism. Instead, he notes "Beijing has tempered its cooperation, however, in areas where China views its interests or priorities as different from ours" (p. 27). He describes China's intentions as including "international status and influence." Blair was succeeded by James Clapper in late 2010. Clapper's (2011, p. 11) report to Congress is even more grim, claiming, "China's rise drew increased international attention of the past year, as several episodes of assertive Chinese behavior fueled perceptions of Beijing as a more imposing and potentially difficult international actor."

to 2011. Since the count of events did not change much, analysts should not have suddenly updated their estimates. I argue that the frequency of events is not especially important. What matters is whether China's actions fit with a principle. Thus, if the IC is using all the information available to them, the critical question for their estimate is not: did China raise their violent actions. Rather, the key question is: were China's costly actions circa 2011 hard to explain given China's declared aims?

8.1.5 The Moment of Truth: Why Did Perceptions of China Change?

My theory predicts that intelligence analysts will update their estimates of China's intentions because they cannot reconcile China's specific actions with China's longstanding justification for how they could act in an expansionist way today, but still hold long-run cooperative intentions. I've already argued that China's actions between 1990 and 2010 were largely consistent with China's declared aims. For my theory to reasonably explain the sharp shift in estimates circa 2011, I need to know if China's actions circa 2011 represent a qualitative departure. That is, were China's actions at this time difficult to explain in the context of China's declared principles. My review of China's actions suggests that there was. Notably, and as stated in the 2010 NSS, China extended its claims over islands in the South China Sea, expanded its military footprint in South and Central Asia and Africa, and built shadow institutions to subvert the international order in Central Asia. China also exploited predatory loans to gain political leverage over several states that did not fit its nationalist agenda.

It is important to note that many of these actions were less violent than China's behavior during the 1990s. For example, China's live-fire exercises over Taiwan in 1995 was more violent than China's actions in the South China Sea in 2012. Furthermore, China's rate of military investment was faster in 2006 than it was in 2012. However, my theory suggests that differences in the magnitude of military choices is less important than what China is using its military for. In my theory, what matters is whether China's actions are consistent with its stated aims.

There is also a notable change in how China described its strategy. During the 1990s and 2000s, China used two statements to describe its foreign policy: "Hide your brightness, bide your time," and "peaceful rise." The former referred to China's policy of slow shifts in its demands despite large shifts in China's economic influence and coercive abilities. The latter declared China's goals were limited (Economy, 2010). As a result, China would eventually seek a compromise with the Liberal Order generally, and with the US in Asia specifically. To be clear, these positions did not prevent China from contesting its core interests (e.g., the 1995 Taiwan Strait Crisis). But they did reflect China's overall approach to try to ease tensions with the United States through piecemeal concessions, and to focus only in areas that clearly fit within China's declared core interests. It was China's declared strategy that led Robert Zoellick to describe China as a "responsible stakeholder" as late as 2008. Starting around 2010–2011, China dropped peaceful rise and hidden power from its lexicon (Economy, 2010).

To be clear, this summary is largely based on my interpretation of China's actions. The more important question is whether the IC used a similar logic to draw their inferences. The public estimates of China's intentions are not sufficiently detailed to explain why analysts updated their beliefs. However, through a combination of interviews and policy analysis I arrive at two tentative conclusions. First, available information suggests that the IC changed estimates followed the logic of qualitative inferences. Second, discrepancies between the estimates of individual analysts reasonably followed different interpretations of China's limited-aims claims.

Reasonably direct evidence for these findings comes from a one-hour interview with the former Director of National Intelligence responsible for national-level assessments between 2009 and 2011. As described, this period is critical because it is when the consensus view of China's intentions likely started to change. During the interview, I asked the DNI the following question:

Question: I want to talk about differences in the National Level Intelligence products published during your tenure between 2009 and 2010. I notice that there is a change in your language. In my reading, you are cautiously optimistic about China's strategic intentions and US–China cooperation during your confirmation hearing and in your 2009 report to Congress. But you are considerably more pessimistic in your reports during 2010. Am I correct in thinking that you changed your estimate during this period? If you did, is there something that China said or did in about 2010 that led you to reduce your confidence that they are peaceful?

Answer: Part of it was, speaking honestly, there was still good reason to leave room for China to develop in a benevolent fashion and not to drive them to believe that the United States was inevitably hostile. I believed in 2009, and I sort of believe it now that an overly aggressive policy would have been a self-fulfilling prophecy. And that it would be a mistake. When you look at the harder line that they have taken in the south China Sea since 2010. In that particular area at least they are pushing pretty hard to take control of that area. Pushing the US out. *It* *was out of character for what they'd been doing up until that point. It was different and it would be hard to interpret their actions in any way other than their intentions were aggressive.* That sort of made me think about this dual path that China could follow – we are beyond that point. They had chosen to take a hard line.

His response clearly indicates that his logic, which supports different estimates reported to the highest levels of government, closely matched my theoretical ideal. Critically, the DNI correctly draws an inference by interpreting China's actions in the context of China's plausible motives.

Of course, it is possible that the DNI would have derived the same inference following any violent action over any issue. To verify this was not the case, our next exchange unfolded as follows.

Question: Let me asked you as a hypothetical – if China had behaved the same way against Taiwan. So rather than go to the South China Sea and do these very provocative actions in the South China Sea, if they had instead ran the same bellicose and aggressive missions around the Strait of Taiwan would you have updated your assessment in the same way?

Answer: No – I don't think it would have been the same. I would have seen that as speeding up the time-table on something they had long-declared that they had been serious about. I think it has been the taking on a new area that was not mentioned as a core interest that influenced the assessment.

Again his answer clearly demonstrates how his estimate was mediated through how he understood China's limited aims. In fact he clearly explains that what distinguishes the two issues is that China had no longstanding historical or cultural claim to the South China Sea in his view, and this drove the shift in his estimate.

To be clear, this was not the only event that drove the shift. Later in the interview I asked how the US would know if China held global or regional ambitions. He explained that "The pieces of evidence that I think I've written about that do show a global interest rather than a regional interest are their space systems. If you are just interested in knowing what goes on up to the second Island chain you don't need satellites for intelligence and military applications. That's the one piece I've seen – but I haven't seen any other pieces." Again, this insight draws a clear link between China's choices, what kinds of objectives that those choices could plausibly serve, and then an appreciation of how to reconcile those choices with China's strategic context.

My recorded interviews with other intelligence elites rendered a similar result. For example, I interviewed the former Deputy Director of the

CIA who was responsible for analysis and production, Mark Lowenthal.[328] I asked him how analysts should go about evaluating the strategic intentions of long term rivals "like China." He responded that "Inferring China's strategic intentions was the single most difficult and important challenge that we faced." Then consistent with the logic of my theory he explained that "analysts need deep historical knowledge of China to properly appreciate China's interests." He also explained that, "you can't just rely on indicators like military spending ... analysts need detailed historical knowledge to understand the context that surrounds China's actions." While he did not go into specifics about the US estimates, he generally agreed that the CIA analysts followed these practices.

In addition to long form interviews with intelligence elites, I also conducted short, informal interviews with 207 mid-level national security professionals who worked on China issues. I asked 171 of these subjects why they altered their personal estimates of China's intentions. Figure 8.2 summarizes their answers. Different analysts disagree about exactly what event drove their pessimism. As a result, different analysts changed their beliefs at different points in time. However, the source of their disagreement usually hinged on a common logic: They all realized that China's behaviors could not be explained by a limited pursuit of historically salient territories. China's behavior therefore signaled a broader shift.

Although it is not easily seen in the quantified data, my discussions about how analysts saw the South China Sea dispute is instructive. Some analysts argued that China's claims in 2010 concerned them because the Senkaku islands were not previously part of China's nationalist project. Other analysts grew concerned in 2012 when China began to erect islands on the Scarborough Shoal. In their view, China's decision to extend its territory was a qualitatively different demand from what it had historically held, and therefore signaled China wanted to extend beyond its historical borders. Others still argued that China held longstanding cultural claim over the islands that it simply did not express. As a result this incident did not affect them. What this example illustrates is that analysts interpreted this event differently. However, the differences hinge on the correct distinction: How should the US interpret China's actions in the context if its historical and cultural claims?

In a different example, several analysts suggested that a range of factors influenced their estimate. On the surface, these analysts seem like they are

---

[328] Lowenthal was responsible for overhauling the CIA analytic training program (CAP) in the 1990s, and therefore had an oversized impact on how our largest intelligence agency processes information to form beliefs.

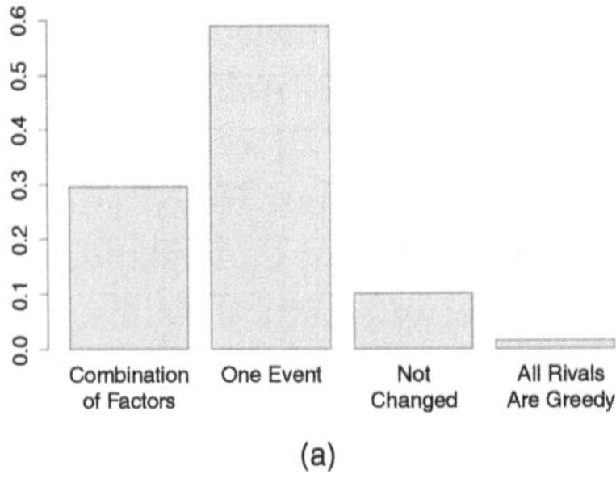

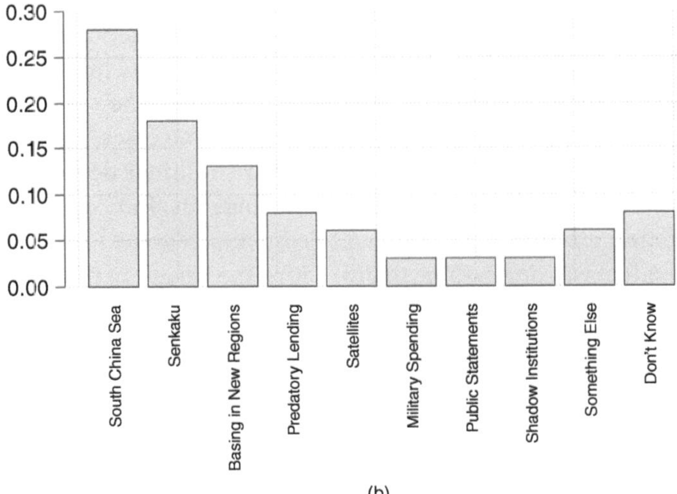

Figure 8.2 Why US–China experts think the consensus view shifted about China's strategic intentions. (a) Summary of total. (b) Most common answers for those who believe a shift has happened.

not correctly following the logic of qualitative inferences. But when they explain their reasoning, it is clear that they are correctly used my logic of cumulative qualitative inferences in the extension of the theory that accounts for the possibility of ambiguous issues and imperfect estimates.

For example, one analyst noted that it was a combination of China's expansion into the South China Sea; China's push to establish shadow institutions (One Belt One Road) in Central and South Asia;[329] China's expanding military presence in the Strait of Malacca, Sri Lanka, Pakistan,

---

[329] Strictly, BRI was not titled that until 2013. However, China's regional lending dates back to 2000, and many notable analysts describe the following period as BRI. See Parks et al. (2023).

and Bangladesh. The analyst acknowledged that he did not have a complete picture of China's strategy. He could imagine a situation in which any one of these actions could be part of a broader security strategy that was consistent with China's limited aims. However, when he looked at all of these choices together, he could not understand how China's actions were consistent with its historical and cultural claims.

Summing up, all of the evidence suggests that intelligence analysts thought about inferring China's motives as a puzzle. They looked at China's actions and asked, "given what I know about China's history and culture, how do these actions fit together in service of a specific strategy towards a specific principle?" Consistent with my expectation, so long as China's actions fit its declared core interests grounded in China's historical experiences, analysts did not alter their estimates. But once they found a piece that did not fit, they revised their estimates. In some cases, analysts were uncertain about whether particular issues fit with China's declared principle because the historical connection was ambiguous. But consistent with my theoretical extension, they did not tolerate much pretext creep. Rather, each individual was only willing to give China the benefit of the doubt over a small number of ambiguous issues.

This evidence also highlights something surprising about China's actions. Within a period of a few years, China engaged in many violent actions that were inconsistent with their declared motives. Even if my theory well explains shifts in perceptions, one might wonder: Why did China take so many provocative actions at the same time?

Others have sought to explain why China's rhetoric and actions became provocative circa 2012. The dominant explanation is that Xi Jinping held unusually hawkish goals, and quickly consolidated power when he was appointed General Secretary of the CCP (Campbell and Blackwill, 2016; Shuman, 2021).[330] These accounts convincingly show that Xi is more hawkish. But there are limits to what they explain. First, and as others have argued, Xi was chosen by a small group of Party elites who knew of his hawkish preferences, and who shared them. As Doshi (2021) has argued, "Many aspects of an increasingly assertive Chinese policy that the United States finds disagreeable are not 'bugs' introduced by Xi's unique power consolidation and aggressiveness but enduring 'features' of that consensus."

Second, Xi was appointed General Secretary of the CCP in 2012. But as I just showed, US perceptions of China mainly changed in 2010 and

---

[330] As discussed in Section 4.4.3, my results are robust to the expectations of new, more aggressive intentions.

2011. The reason for this change was that US analysts inferred qualitative differences in China's strategy before Xi came to power.

If Xi does not explain a sudden increase in highly provocative actions after two decades of peaceful rise, then what does? My theory provides the following answer. While the US was uncertain about China's strategic intentions, China avoided costly actions that implied its motives extended beyond what it had declared. Once China had tipped its hand to US analysts, then it had no incentive to hold back.[331]

8.1.6 Discussion

Against the findings of Congress and many recent pundits, I find that the IC did a great job in using the information it had to estimate China's intentions. At the earliest possible moment, the IC exploited China's diplomatic statements and their knowledge of China's history and culture to develop a rigorous assessment framework. They used that framework carefully from 1970 onward. They applied it despite political pressure to respond to China's aggressive behavior. In my opinion, their estimates were first-rate and consistent with my understand of what a rational intelligence community would do if it was interested in serving the national interest (and not some bureaucratic interest).

As a result, Congress's choice to chastise the IC and demand reforms for its low-confidence estimates risks damaging the IC's rigorous process. After all, if Congress tells the IC that they did a bad job, and forces them to reform, they are likely to conform to Congress's mistaken impression of what high-quality estimates would have looked like.

This does not mean the IC does not need to shift focus. Now that we know that China is a competitor with the United States, the IC must ask itself different questions including: What tools will China use to expand its influence, what will China target and what are the implications for our security, and how can we quickly identify China's revisionist behaviors in cyber and covert operations? These different questions generate different intelligence requirements, and new demands on current and strategic intelligence priorities. My interviews suggest that the IC is aware of these new requirements and has chosen to reconfigure itself to meet these challenges. If we demand that they address Congress's faulty criticisms, we will prevent them from making meaningful changes to address important questions they need to address.

---

[331] This echoes Hitler's behavior once he violated the Munich Agreement.

8.2 US Policy towards China

The puzzle I started this chapter with is common among China watchers: Why did US competition with China start under the Obama Administration and then rapidly intensify? My theory provides a clear answer. US policymakers should condition their strategy on perceptions of China's motives. Intelligence estimates correctly shifted circa 2011. US policy soon followed.

Table 8.2 summarizes my predictions and findings. Given what I found about US intelligence estimates, I expect that President Obama would turn to competition. All those that came before him should have hedged, and all those that came after him should have pursued competition.

In what follows, I use my theory to illuminate unappreciated features of three periods: hedging, the Pivot to Asia, and the complete turn to competition.

8.2.1 Hedging: H. W. Bush to W. Bush

My theory predicts that presidents before Barack Obama should have pursued a policy of cautious hedging. Consistent with the historiography, this is what I find. While each president before 2012 introduced personalist nuances into their China policy, "in the end, most observers have argued that the similarities in each administration's China policy were greater than the differences" (Steinberg, 2020).

Across this period, central features of US strategy matched my theoretical ideal. Each administration:

- Sought to raise the value of peaceful exchange through economic cooperation and reduce the risk of unnecessary conflict.
- Minimized concessions over issues of core interest to the United States, such as democratic freedoms in Taiwan.

Table 8.2 *Summary of predictions and findings*

President	Prediction	What Happened
H. W. Bush	Hedging	Hedging
Clinton	Hedging	Hedging
W. Bush	Hedging	Hedging
Obama	Competition	Weak Turn to Competition
Trump	Competition	Complete Competition
Biden	Competition	Complete Competition

- Strengthened US alliances in East Asia and the Pacific with states outside of China's declared core interests.
- Used diplomatic and economic exchange to bind China to long-term institutions that had the greatest chance of securing peace, such as getting a commitment for the Nonproliferation Treaty (NPT).
- Worried about spirals of mistrust, and backed out of contests that could have caused them.

While past scholars agree that this is what happened, many criticize each president for their choices. The critics pejoratively refer to post-Cold War China strategy as appeasement (Medeiros, 2005; Shambaugh, 1996). Successive administrations have been criticized from different perspectives. Some argue that the US position was too soft. By providing China such substantial economic opportunities, the US facilitated the rise of our greatest adversary (Kagan, 2005). Others suggest that the US was too tough. By imposing some sanctions on China, engaging in arms races (Zhang, 2011), and by refusing to negotiate over core claims like Taiwan, the US created a dynamic of mistrust (see Glaser, 2015).

Many of these critics explain the president's choice in terms of the president's unique style. They argue that the policies followed because of unique features of the president, and not because it was the right thing to do. If these critics are right, then my theory does not explain this case because the intelligence estimates did not factor into policy choices.

Consider reactions to China's human rights violations. With the fall of the Berlin Wall, liberal Chinese citizens had hoped for better democratic representation. When it did not come, protesters took to the Beijing streets. The Chinese Government responded with brutal repression. But unlike past crackdowns, this repression was broadcast across the globe. Most famously Americans saw footage of a Chinese tank slowly crushing and killing a defiant student in Tiananmen Square. The image outraged the American public and many members of Congress. On the question of whether the US should develop economic relationships with China, support dropped from 78 percent to 32 percent (Wike, 2014). Picking up on this public sentiment, then-Junior Senator Nancy Pelosi rallied bipartisan Congressional support for fierce sanctions against China and a firm statement of condemnation (Nakatsuji, 1999).

If the president was sensitive to public preferences or Congressional support, he would have adopted Congress's policies. But Bush took three steps to undermine efforts to punish China for its human rights abuses. First, Bush refused to support sanctions legislation that made it to his desk. Second, Bush refused to openly chastise the Chinese regime. Third, after

Congress passed sanctions that formally paused high-level Sino-American diplomacy, Bush continued diplomacy with China in secret. Bush had several phone conversations with Chinese Premier Deng Xiaoping in which Bush reassured Deng that the US sought a prosperous long-run relationship with China, despite the current outrage. He also secretly sent his most trusted Advisers, Brent Scowcroft and George Shultz, to deliver the message in person.

Historians agree that "President Bush's conciliatory approach to dealing with Chinese authorities was deeply unpopular at home within both Congress and the public at large" (Skidmore and Gates, 1997, p. 7). Thus, many wonder why Bush pursued these policies against the wishes of Congress and the American public? One important factor was that Bush believed that his China policy would form part of his legacy, that the policy he pursued was the best one, and would be thought of favorably in the long term.[332]

Those who believe that Bush made the wrong choice locate the source of his error in his unique experiences. Some argue that Bush was overly optimistic that China would change as a result of personal impressions he formed. Critically, Bush served as Special Envoy to China during the historic thaw in Sino-American relations (1974–1975). While in China, he developed a close relationship with Deng Xiaoping; the man who would become China's Premier in 1989 (Engel, 2010). Compounding this personal experience, Bush served as the CIA Director, and had high confidence in his own ability to draw inferences. It is plausible that his overconfidence in his own estimates and vivid personal interactions influenced his perceptions, causing him to pursue a suboptimal policy.

I argue that Bush chose the optimal policy because the intelligence estimates he received were uncertain about the scope of China's aims, and avoiding a long-term spiral of Sino-American mistrust was more important than China's human rights violations to US policymakers.[333] If Bush imposed crippling sanctions in 1989, it could have irreparably harmed Sino-American relations. Bush prioritized the potential benefits of long-term cooperation with China, over the short-term benefits from punishing human rights abusers.

---

[332] See claims made by George H. W. Bush Foundation for U.S.-China Relations (2025).

[333] Furthermore, the assessment framework they developed suggested that (1) China's violent human rights behavior was not necessarily inconsistent with long-term cooperation; (2) China's willingness to work with the United States hinged on the possibility of benefits from long-term peace.

Indeed, Bush describes this exact logic on page 12 of the 1990 National Security Strategy,

The relationship between the United States and China, restored in the early 1970s after so many years of estrangement, has also contributed to regional stability and the global balance of power. The United States strongly deplored the repression in China last June and we have imposed sanctions to demonstrate our displeasure. At the same time, we have sought to avoid a total cutoff of China's ties to the outside world. Those ties not only have strategic importance, both globally and regionally; they are crucial to China's prospects for regaining the path of economic reform and political liberalization. China's angry isolation would harm all of these prospects.[334]

Given what President Clinton did next, personalist or regime explanations for Bush's policy seem especially unlikely. In 1991 then presidential candidate Clinton hammered Bush on his disregard for human rights. Clinton called Chinese Premier Li Ping the "Butcher of Beijing," and used the incident to question Bush's commitment to US values (He, 2016). Even though candidate Clinton's preferences differed from Bush's, President Clinton followed Bush's policy anyway. When Clinton first came to power, he explicitly tied China's MFN status to human rights. But after a year of hearing active intelligence and expert advice, he reversed course and deepened Sino-American economic cooperation beyond even what Bush had envisioned. Notably, Clinton facilitated China's accession into the World Trade Organization. This policy was especially controversial because it allowed China to rapidly grow its economy and generate leverage over Asian democracies through economic dependencies. Consistent with leader and regime theories, Bush and Clinton held different true *preferences* likely because of their different personal characteristics and advisers (e.g., variation in foreign policy expertise, knowledge of China, world view, age). But inconsistent with these theories, Clinton's policy converged with Bush's once he had access to the necessary intelligence. Clinton reversed his own decision and deepened Sino-American economic cooperation beyond what Bush had even envisioned.

Second, theories of domestic institutional constraints suggest that leaders should be sensitive to audience costs or ex-post efficiencies. However, the leading theories in this tradition struggle to explain each of these

---

[334] It is plausible that Bush's experiences as a key figure in Nixon's China-policy team could have driven him to pursue policies that diverged from the public and Congress (Engel, 2010; Skidmore and Gates, 1997). In these roles, Bush was asked to ignore short-term normative issues and instead focus on the long-term security and prosperity of the United States. But this does not detract from the fact that Bush pursued the correct policy at considerable political costs.

president's choices. Some of these theories argue that leaders face incentives to pursue competitive policies if the leader is skilled at foreign policy, competition is popular, and the president is likely to lose re-election (Downs and Rocke, 1994; Goemans et al., 2009). This exactly describes Bush. And despite these electoral incentives, he chose to continue with cooperation.

A second set of theories suggests that the public imposes audience costs when leaders say one thing and then do another.[335] Clinton's decision to reverse his policies and to bolster China's influence came with personal costs. Members of his own party, especially Nanci Pelosi, fiercely criticized him (He, 2016). Theoretically, it is surprising that a self-interested policymaker would select a policy against his personal preferences, and for which he would suffer criticisms from his own party and the public. But through the lens of my theory, Clinton's decision to seek cooperation with China demonstrates strong leadership because Clinton was willing to continue with the optimal strategy (hedging) in spite of these costs. It is somewhat unreasonable to expect a candidate with limited access to top-secret national security advice, little foreign policy experience, and almost no knowledge of China to know the right policy. So it is reasonable for Clinton to come to power without appreciating the complexities of long-term China policy. Not only did Clinton quickly learn, he also was willing to suffer sharp criticism within his own party to put the US back on track.[336]

My theory also illuminates two other notable episodes of high-quality policy-making. Where past work suggests leaders only rely on diplomatic encounters in trust scenarios because of irrational select attention (Yarhi-Milo, 2014), my theory suggests high-functioning and rational policymakers will use diplomacy to resolve ambiguities over the Challenger's declared core interests over time. Recall, that the 1970 NIE identified some ambiguities in China's historical connection to a handful of territories. This created uncertainty about what China would want even if China held limited aims. Specifically, China repeatedly referred to a desire to restore the Middle Kingdom and to right a century humiliation. What did this mean? Did restoring the Middle Kingdom mean loose influence over Mongolia, and the East Asian seas, or did it mean direct control? Would China slowly increase its influence over Taiwan using coercion short of war, or would it revert to an all-out unprovoked military assault? In the 1990s, these

---

[335] For exception see Levendusky and Horowitz (2012).

[336] My finding that Clinton's policy served American interests given what he knew at the time is consistent with recent arguments that vindicate Clinton (Steinberg, 2020; Johnston, 2019).

ambiguities were not important because China was focused on issues that unambiguously fell within its core interests: increasing influence over Taiwan, Tibet, Hong Kong, and its recognition as a nuclear power. It did not pursue policies to serve the handful of issues that ambiguously fell within its declared core interests.

Things started to change circa 2004. A 2005 report from the Department of Defense to Congress observes that "The Chinese People's Liberation Army (PLA) is modernizing its forces, emphasizing preparations to fight and win short-duration, high-intensity conflicts along China's periphery. PLA modernization has accelerated since the mid-to-late 1990s in response to central leadership demands to develop military options for Taiwan scenarios."[337]

Under the assessment framework that the IC used to judge China's ambitions, militarization to take Taiwan was not alarmist. However, the report also noted that,

A second set of objectives includes building counters to third-party, including potential U.S., intervention in cross-Strait crises. PLA preparations, including an expanding force of ballistic missiles (long-range and short-range), cruise missiles, submarines, advanced aircraft, and other modern systems, come against the background of a policy toward Taiwan that espouses "peaceful reunification." China has not renounced the use of force, however. Over the long term, if current trends persist, PLA capabilities could pose a credible threat to other modern militaries operating in the region.[338]

In short, military modernization would put ambiguous issues within China's striking range. The Department of Defense (DoD) judged that China's new forces created several opportunities for "misperception and miscalculation" to start and then escalate crises.[339]

Through the lens of my theory, ambiguities about China's core interests are part of a coordination problem that can be resolved through diplomacy. Indeed, under my evaluation metrics, a nuanced US strategy would explicitly seek to resolve these ambiguities through asking China to clarify its exact strategic intentions. The point being that a clear statement of intentions could prevent a situation where China's legitimate attempts to take core interests were perceived as opportunistic land grabs.

---

[337] Military and Security Developments Involving the People's Republic of China (2005, Executive Summary).

[338] Ibid.

[339] Ibid.

This is exactly what the Bush Administration set out to do. In 2005, Robert Zoellick visited China to better understand China's intentions. He did not get a straight answer. Returning to the United States frustrated, Zoellick publicly explained:

China needs to recognize how its actions are perceived by others. China's involvement with troublesome states indicates at best a blindness to consequences and at worst something more ominous. China's actions – combined with a lack of transparency – can create risks. Uncertainties about how China will use its power will lead the United States – and others as well – to hedge relations with China. Many countries hope China will pursue a 'Peaceful Rise,' but none will bet their future on it.

For example, China's rapid military modernization and increases in capabilities raise questions about the purposes of this buildup and China's lack of transparency. The recent report by the U.S. Department of Defense on China's military posture was not confrontational, although China's reaction to it was. The U.S. report described facts, including what we know about China's military, and discussed alternative scenarios. If China wants to lessen anxieties, it should openly explain its defense spending, intentions, doctrine, and military exercises. (Zoellick, 2005)

More broadly the 2008 Bush Administration made several public overtures calling on China to be a "responsible stakeholder" in the international community. Part of that responsibility meant explaining its interests (Powaski, 2018).

I have no direct evidence that this pressure led China to make a clearer statement of its aims. However, China did release a clearer picture of its core aims shortly after. Consistent with what I believe is the best estimate, the IC used this information to report clearer picture of China's intentions. Unlike the 2005 DoD report to Congress described previously, the 2010 report stated,

Chinese State Councilor Dai Bingguo in July 2009 defined China's "core interests" as safeguarding the basic system and national security, national sovereignty, and territorial integrity, and sustained and stable economic and social development. China's current strategy remains one of managing the external environment to ensure conditions are conducive to its own economic development. This strategy appears to be accepted widely by Beijing's foreign and security policy establishment. However, differences of opinion within China occasionally surface, particularly in academic circles, about how China can achieve these goals and how it can best do so over time without conflict with its neighbors or the United States. (pp. 17–18).

From the perspective of realists, Zoellick's diplomatic efforts were puzzling (Mearsheimer, 2001). Why would he spend so much time soliciting these cheap-talk statements of China's strategic aims? My theory illuminates that diplomatic clarification can credibly (and rationally) reveal information. Thus relying on diplomacy is not a function of misperceptions (Snyder et al., 1987), it is a mechanism that high-functioning policy-makers use to avoid ambiguities in future crises.

8.2.2 The Pivot to Asia

My theory predicts that once the IC revised its estimates of China's intentions, that the president should turn sharply to strategic competition. While Obama's policy departs from the period of hedging, it is not as sharp as my theory expects.

Obama's Pivot to Asia is often criticized because its fell somewhere between competition and hedging (Shambaugh, 2013; Blackwill and Fontaine, 2024). One variant of this criticism is that Obama wanted to contain China, but the Pivot was poorly executed because the Obama Administration did not put the necessary diplomatic and economic resources into it (Lieberthal, 2011; Cha, 2016). Another was that calling the strategy a pivot caused alarm among European allies and partners in the War on Terror. To preserve these relations, Obama had to resource these older objectives more than what he would have liked (Klau et al., 2016). Others argue that the Pivot to Asia was poorly executed because the military and diplomatic arms worked against each other (Kitfield, 2012). On the one hand, the policy sought to keep trade relations with China, but on the other it sought to promote military competition and exclude China from major institutions (Gilder, 2010).

In all of these accounts two things are clear. First, and consistent with what my theory predicts, Obama implemented more competitive policies than prior presidents. Second, and inconsistent with what my theory predicts, there are several cooperative elements that do not fit neatly into a strategy of competition as I defined it. Like other critics in this episode, I agree that Obama's policy falls short. Also like these critics, the documents one needs to fully evaluate the Pivot are still classified. But my theory can help us evaluate the policy with circumstantial evidence because it illuminates that the theoretical ideal policy was to shift fully to competition. Thus, the best way to investigate Obama's choice is to ask, what explains why Obama did not fully shift?

One plausible reason was that Obama did not want competition because he was incredibly optimistic about collaboration under the Liberal Order. Thus, the half-Pivot could represent his design. While this may have been initially true (Cholet, 2016, p. 42), the circumstantial evidence suggests that Obama's strategic goals may have shifted over the course of his tenure. This shift is consistent with my theory given that he likely received revised intelligence estimates about China circa 2011. By contrasting two speeches Obama gave in Australia (in 2011 and 2014), others have argued that Obama likely repurposed the Pivot. During the 2011 speech, Obama only mentions China four times, promotes China's recent history of cooperation over Korea, and limits concerns to US efforts to "speak candidly to Beijing about the importance of upholding international norms and respecting the universal human rights of the Chinese people." Many view this as part of the carrot and stick approach designed to reach a stable bargain in Asia.

The 2014 speech is more provocative. In it, Obama (2014) directly questioned China's intentions, asking, "By virtue of its size and its remarkable growth, China will inevitably play a critical role in the future of this region. And the question is, what kind of role will it play?" Obama then explained that the US is

encouraging China to adhere to the same rules as other nations – whether in trade or on the seas. And in this engagement we will continue to be frank about where there are differences, because America will continue to stand up for our interests and principles, including our unwavering support for the fundamental human rights of all people. We do not benefit from a relationship with China or any other country in which we put our values and our ideals aside. And for the young people, practicality is a good thing. There are times where compromise is necessary. That's part of wisdom. But it's also important to hang on to what you believe – to know what you believe and then be willing to stand up for it. And what's true for individuals is also true for countries. (Obama, 2014)

Off-record interviews I conducted with two mid-level staff in Obama's Administration further suggest that the strategic objectives of the Pivot started to shift circa 2012–2013.[340] Interview subjects explained that the NSC increasingly be came of the view that cooperation would hurt US interests in the long run, and the best course was to emphasize the competitive aspects of the strategy. This is what I observed. Circa 2012, the US military started to ramp-up patrols in the South China Sea, approved highly controversial weapons sales to Taiwan and Japan, and

---

[340] One subject stated that military and NSC staff responsible for military deployments drove increased military policies as early as 2012. However, one subject pointed out that National Security Adviser Thomas Donilon prevented economic policy from shifting to competition until he left office in 2013.

permanently stationed forces across the Asia-Pacific region.[341] Also in 2012, the Trans-Pacific Partnership (TPP) took shape as an economic agreement that would exclude China. This departs from talk of economic partnership in Obama's 2011 speech.

If we accept that in his second term Obama desired a stronger turn to competition, then the next question is: Why was he unable to achieve it? As stated above, many argue that the Pivot was poorly resourced. But this does not explain why. China was clearly a priority. Why would Obama not better resource a policy priority? The circumstantial evidence suggests he found it difficult to fully implement his revised vision because his administration had spent years crafting a cooperative policy and he had already announced the Pivot in this spirit. Indeed, Obama's National Security Advisor, Thomas Donilon, had been crafting a China policy since the day he took office (2010). Donilon was dovish on China and wanted to build an East Asia strategy to maximize the chance of cooperation with China. He was also known for overruling dissenting voices within the NSC. Indeed, it is consistent with my theory that Obama would appoint a China dove as the National Security Adviser in 2010 because the consensus view on China had not yet shifted. It could be consistent with my theory that Obama would roll out a China policy that was an intense version of hedging in 2011 because he may not have received revised estimates of China's intentions just yet. Thus, a likely explanation is that Obama found it difficult to change to a more competitive policy because he had already started to implement Donilon's vision when intelligence estimates began to change.

Supporting this account, there is evidence that fissures started to emerge among Obama's senior advisers circa 2011. The NSC Director for East Asian Affairs, Kurt Campbell (2016) pushed to make the Pivot to Asia more hawkish starting in late 2011. Furthermore Donilon, who remained dovish on China until the end, was replaced with Susan Rice in 2013. Rice was not an Asia expert. Off-record interviews I conducted suggest that Rice was open to the growing consensus that China's aims were vast, and the US strategy should be competitive, in a way that Donilon was not. How the TPP unfolded provides another piece of suggestive evidence. When Secretary of State Hillary Clinton (2011) initially announced the TPP, she left ambiguous the possibility of collaboration with China. Only in 2012 did the administration reveal that the TPP would seek to exclude China. It is

---

[341] One notable deployment was nuclear-capable B52 bombers to Northern Australia that are capable of striking China's mainland.

also plausible that Obama was hamstrung by domestic-interest groups, and the costs of a rapid shift to competition.[342]

Thought of in this way, my theory provides a new account for why the Pivot to Asia failed. Part of it was bad timing. Obama developed the Pivot to Asia as a comprehensive strategy to achieve hedging. He unveiled this strategy right at the time he was learning that China's intentions were vast. Part of it was a lack of political dexterity. Obama was unable to unwind the Pivot after a major announcement that took a more cooperative approach, his concerns over domestic groups, and given the advisers he had selected. All he could do was exploit the ambiguities in the policy, and under-resource the parts that related to promoting China.

One might wonder what this means for my theory. After all, if my theory is predictive, shouldn't Obama have turned sharply to competition in spite of these domestic constants? It is worth making two points. First, even though Obama's NSC failed to shift top-level policy, those responsible for policy development and implementation within the Department of Defense were laying the groundwork for change. Perhaps the most critical issue was that China was closing the gap in military technologies because the Obama Administration had underinvested in new military innovations or controls to prevent China from stealing US technology. Starting in 2012, Under Secretary of Defense Robert Work developed the Third Offset Strategy to reorientate US military investments. Work was sidelined by Obama's NSC, but his efforts facilitated rapid change (rare within a bureaucracy the size of the DoD) once President Trump came to power (Gentile et al., 2021), and were integral for the 2018 NDS. Second, and fortunately for my argument, Obama's "policy is widely believed to have failed, and [in 2016] strong arguments are being presented for a tougher U.S. policy toward Beijing," which Obama should have considered (Harding, 2015). In other words, even in the worst case, political factors only derailed the structural pressures that my theory highlights for the remainder of Obama's presidency. As we shall see in the next section, President Trump did exactly what my theory expects the president to do: a sharp turn to competition.

8.2.3 Trump's Sharp Turn to Competition

In the face of Obama's failed policy, it was tempting for incoming President Trump to revert to hedging. By doing so, Trump could have argued that

---

[342] Next we will discuss President Trump's capacity to navigate or accept these costs contributed to his success.

Obama's efforts were misplaced. He could also have learned from Obama's efforts that competition would be difficult. Finally, if Obama was wrong to Pivot, then Trump may have reverted because it was the right thing to do.

I argue, however, that the best policy was to double down: expand Obama's policy by an intensified effort to compete with China. Consistent with this expectation, the Trump Administration turned US strategy sharply towards competition.

This shift was stark. Swaine (2018, p. 1) has noted that in Trump's 2017 National Security Strategy

Beijing is apparently seen as a near-existential threat to the United States and the West in general, engaged in a concerted effort to realize a "repressive vision of world order" by overthrowing the long-standing "free" vision of world order led by Washington. Unlike their predecessors, the strategies entirely "neglect to portray China as a potential contributor to regional or global stability and prosperity, or as a possible collaborator on common global and regional security (and other) problems."

In fact, Swaine believes the shift was so stark that Trump and Secretary of Defense Mattis unnecessarily risked war with China because they "seek to pit the United States and other democracies against China in a zero-sum competition" for dominance (Swaine, 2018, p. 1). Others argue that the sharp shift in Trump's economic policy against China caused backlash among the president's base (Hass and Denmark, 2020). Specifically, Trump's trade war only hurt American farmers and manufacturers who lost customers in China during the trade war. To the critics, Trump's heavy hand is an aberration. Searching for an answer, the critics argue that Trump's policies are the result of partisanship, hawkish preferences, inexperience, and leader-specific world views (Panda, 2018; Hamilton, 2017; Bisley, 2017; Dollar et al., 2019). Indeed, if these criticisms are correct, then Trump's decision to double down during his first term may not be the result of good choices, but of leader-specific preferences. However, statements from the president and his key advisers suggest that the administration thought the policy was appropriate for competition to be effective. For example, Trump argued that short-term costs were necessary to cultivate a lasting change in US-Sino economic relations that favored America's position (Johnson, 2019).

A more detailed look at the policy development demonstrates that it is unlikely driven by Trump's inexperience. Rather, it appears to be a thoughtful, whole-of-NSC effort. Specifically, the 2017 NSS was directed by Trump's national security advisor H. R. McMaster, and the 2018 NDS was directed by Mattis. Interviews I conducted with career staff suggested that both Mattis and McMaster encouraged their staff to regularly meet and collaborate, and to collaborate with the Department of State and CIA, among other key stakeholders. With so many stakeholders, it is hard to argue that a few actors drove change. What is more, the drafters skillfully reckoned with internal dissent to overcome barriers that the Obama Administration could not. Specifically, the turn to competition with China was resisted from those invested in combating terrorism – the Chairman of the Joint Chiefs of Staff (CJCS), CENTCOM, and the National Counter – terrorism Center, and the army; which worried that a China focus would promote air and sea platforms. Interviews I conducted with senior staff on the NDS revealed that the final document balanced the need to make a strong statement that would reorientate US national security towards China (their priority), and build broad consensus among those who would implement the policy. Thus, the NDS is careful to emphasize broader great power competition (which included Russia), and not China specifically. This seemingly small change won over the Army, and to some extent the CJCS because it implicated land-based assets necessary to combat Russia.

Similarly, given that President Biden consolidated competition, it is also unlikely that Trump held extreme policy preferences (Pesek, 2021). As Biden has acknowledged, he and President Trump agree on very little. However, even democrats who remain dovish on China policy have noted that "when it comes to the greatest foreign policy challenge facing the United States – how to deal with the rise of China – Biden's team have continued and mimicked Trump's destructive approach" (Bader, 2020). Indeed, many argue that Biden has further deepened military and economic competition with China (Pesek, 2021). These presidents differ in their partisanship, world views, leadership styles, and preferences for hawkishness. And yet, both have taken the US down the same path to competition. This is highly puzzling for anyone who suggests individual leaders matter. But from the perspective of my theory there is a simple explanation: It is the correct choice to make.

8.2.4 Discussion

US policy towards China is a story of long periods of continuity, punctuated by a sharp change. Analysts have long wondered why some presidents failed to adapt China policy to specific crises that they faced, and why others changed so sharply. They typically attribute both continuity and change to partisan differences, the structure of the NSC, or the president's abilities, world view, and experiences.

I argue that the US China policy is mainly a story of well-executed policy response to constant structural pressures and changes in information about China's motives. My structural story predicts long periods of continuity, punctuated by a shift to competition as soon as the president learns that China's intentions are vast. While I see differences across presidents in the details, and a suboptimal delay in the shift to fierce competition during the Obama Administration, overall the US strategy seems to serve the national interest, given the information available at the time.

8.2.5 Speculative Claims: My Theory and the Future

This holds important implications for the future of Sino-American relations that depart from some conventional wisdoms. Optimists argue that current tensions are temporary. For example, those who believe that leaders play a critical role note that Xi Jinping is notoriously hawkish. They hold out hope that a new leader will alter China's military trajectory. These scholars point out that Sino-American relations have overcome tensions following the Tiananmen Square Massacre and the Taiwan Strait Crisis. Pessimists argue that China and the US are destined for war so long as China's rise persists. They believe that absent a collapse of the Chinese economy that war will come.

Relative to the optimists, my theory predicts grim news: this time competition is here to stay. In the coming years, the US will see a dramatic rise in tensions with China. The US Government must prepare for Sino-American relations to look much more like the Cold War than a collaborative effort to mutually benefit from peace.

One might wonder, why is this time different? Why won't this tense period revert to cooperation as it did in the 1990s? The reason is that past tensions were driven by questions of resolve in a specific crisis over specific issues. After these crises resolved, the US remained optimistic that China's territorial aims were limited to historical and cultural claims in East Asia, and that China saw the value of integrating within the US-led order. For example, months after the Taiwan Strait Crisis brought the US and China to the brink of war, American policymakers called for stronger commercial ties with China because they were optimistic that long-term cooperation was possible. The reason for this optimism was simple: China had repeatedly claimed that its foreign policy was motivated by restoring its historical legacy. CIA assessments judged that China's choice to escalate over Taiwan matched their longstanding claims. Thus, China's actions in Taiwan said nothing about China's interest in Africa, the Pacific, or Central

Asia. When the crisis eased, American policy-makers still believed that long-term cooperation was possible.

This time, tension is driven by a fundamental shift in US beliefs about China's strategic aims and not a specific dispute over a specific issue. This fundamental shift has caused the US to dramatically reorientate its peacetime strategy. As the 2017 National Security Strategy makes clear, the US now estimates that China is an adversary. This fundamental shift in beliefs alters how the US should interact with China outside of periods of crisis.

Pessimists argue that the US and China are destined to war (Allison, 2017). Relative to the pessimists my theory predicts mixed news. I am more optimistic because I do not believe that war is inevitable. In fact, given that China and the United States both hold large nuclear arsenals, I believe that war is unlikely. Rather, Sino-American competition will look more like the Cold War. But I am more pessimistic because I do not think that variation in China's economic or military growth will moderate strategic competition (Beckley, 2018). If China's rise slows down but the regime remains in place, great power competition will persist.

Even though a Cold War is better than a World War, it is still a very bad outcome. The last Cold War was incredibly costly and dangerous. It lasted five decades. During that time, the US fought three proxy wars and several covert wars. The economic burden of five decades of competition was immense. The future Sino-American Cold War will likely be worse. When the Cold War started, the US did not depend on the Soviet economy in any way. As relations sour with China, the United States risks economic recession because of extreme Sino-American economic interdependence. To illustrate the scope of our vulnerability, the Director of Citigroup has pointed out that the US economy is beholden to microchips produced in Taiwan. If China decided to fight for Taiwan, the US would instantly plunge into an enormous recession because it could not generate the microchips necessary to produce its consumer goods.

In spite of these inefficiencies, competition is still the best strategy for the United States now that the US estimates that China holds vast aims. The reason is that the longer the US waits to compete, the more formidable China becomes. What is more, defeating China in a Cold War is a harder task than defeating the Soviets was. When the US began the Cold War against the Soviet Union, the Soviet economy was in ruins at a time when the US economy was flourishing. Early on, the US contained the Soviet Union, cut it off from US allies, and denied it technological advances. China is deeply integrated into the global economy. It leads innovation in several important areas. It is the largest trading partner among US allies including Japan, Taiwan, Australia, and South Korea. This makes it hard to convince allies to cut off ties.

On the normative front, China's view of world order is a more plausible alternative than the Liberal Order to developing and unaligned states today than Soviet communism was during the 1960s. Part of the problem is that the US-led order has lost some luster. In the 1950s, the promise of liberal values was attractive to many. However, after decades of stalled economic growth in the Global South, and the US meddling in the affairs of liberal and illiberal states, the Liberal Order is facing resistance. In contrast, the China Model brought 1 billion people out of poverty. This is attractive to states that have been stuck in poverty for decades. Furthermore, China's world order does not ask autocrats to liberalize domestically and completely accepts repression. This is highly attractive for Iran, Venezuela, Nigeria, Egypt, Saudi Arabia, and Turkey.

On the security front, the dynamics of modern war afford China several advantages. First, China is innovating in modern methods of fighting, such as cyber warfare. Second, the dynamics of modern warfare create risks that disadvantage status-quo powers. Most notably, the ambiguity of gray zone technologies makes it harder for the US to deter Chinese advances through forward-deployments. Third, specialist technologies mean that US advantages may be lost on the battlefield. For example, US forces rely heavily on satellite coverage. China has a formidable anti-satellite system that it would likely deploy in battle, in conjunction with cyber weapons. Putting it altogether, it is not clear that the US will win a Cold War. The chances against China are likely lower than they were against Russia in the 1960s.

9

Conclusion

For nearly a century, scholars of great power competition have faced a series of puzzles (Carr, 1945). They believe that power and uncertainty about motives generate enormous tensions at the origins of great power rivalries. However, the predictions that these variables yield about the timing of competition and threat perceptions do not bear out in many critical cases (Glaser, 2010). These scholars also know that states really hold more complicated foreign policy motivations than their theories allow, and that each state's historical and cultural context determines its foreign policy objectives (see Finnemore, 1996a). But this historical context is both nuanced and case-specific. As a result, it is hard to utilize this variation to draw predictions that generalize across cases. It is even harder to account for it in a strategic model that includes uncertainty and learning.

I developed a structured way to analyze how a Defender can exploit information about a Challenger's historical and cultural context to learn about the Challenger's intrinsic motivations. The theory celebrates the fact that Challengers can hold one of many diverse motivations that include nationalism, status, security, revenge, and so on. It also celebrates the fact that each of these intrinsic motivations will drive specific foreign policy objectives for different states. Despite this seemingly chaotic process, a relatively simple signaling dynamic emerges that compliments and expands rationalist theories of threat perceptions. Like standard signaling arguments, when a Challenger incurs costs over a specific issue, the Defender increases his confidence that the Challenger cares about that specific issue. But unlike standard arguments, what the Defender infers about the Challenger's strategic intentions depends on the historical and cultural context that surrounds that issue. Thus, when CIA analysts learn that China is willing to fight for Taiwan, they draw a different inference about China's strategic intentions than if they learn China is willing to overthrow a government in Africa.

I embedded this core insight into a strategic theory of great power politics that takes seriously the strategic difficulties created by shifting power, and uncertainty about the Challenger's motives. Against the conventional wisdom I find that great power relations unfold as either delayed competition or delayed peace. Which way they unfold depends on the Challenger's true motives, how the Challenger leverages costless diplomacy to initially communicate those motives, and then the pattern of costly military actions during the early revisionist period.

I supported my theory with a multimethod research design. First, I used an elite survey experiment to show that real-world national security elites use the logic of qualitative inferences to form and update their threat perceptions about a rival's motivations. The evidence shows that real-world national security experts do not simply rely on a single indicator. Rather they use a combination of indicators differently depending on the historical context.

Second, I traced my theoretical mechanism through British reasoning at the onset of the Cold War. My theory fits this case, and illuminates how British elites exploited diplomacy with Stalin, their historical knowledge of Russia, and Stalin's costly military behavior to coordinate their estimates of Stalin's strategic aims. The case also illuminates how each elite's unique experiences drove them to differently interpret Stalin's behavior as consistent (or inconsistent) with his declared principle. But almost all agreed that the right way to draw inferences was to use the logic of qualitative inferences. In the end, this common framework clarified when individual differences emerged, and why they were short lived.

Third, I used a medium-n analysis to show that my predictions about the timing of competition and peace well fit critical great power cases that fill our history books. I pit my theory, which complicates how motives can vary, against standard structural theories that complicate how power shifts and the range of costly actions states can take. Overall, I find my theory significantly compliments and advances power-based explanations because it explains many critical cases, and also explains the cases that power-based theories struggle with.

I used my theory to better understand US responses to the rise of China. My theory exposes overlooked issues with important critics, who argue that different presidents and the IC deviated from the rationalist ideal in how they managed China's rise. For example, if individual differences across administrations explain US policies, it is hard to understand why presidents with radically different world views, levels of experience, and from different political parties (e.g., Trump and Biden; or Bush and Clinton) chose remarkably similar policies. This difference is especially stark given that presidents from the same party and with similar backgrounds pursued very different policies (e.g., Biden and Clinton).

Instead, my rationalist theory explains two periods of a constant US grand strategy and threat perceptions punctuated by a shift to mistrust and competition circa 2011. It also explains why the IC rationally ignored China's autocratic consolidation, terrible human rights record, and militaristic behavior for decades. In the end, I find that the IC performed optimally in evaluating China's strategic intentions, and most administrations[343] performed optimally in the policies that they implemented given the information they had.[344] This finding holds important policy implications given fierce criticism and calls for reform (e.g., Schiff, 2020). It will prevent us from spending scarce resources on the problem of bureaucracy and free those resources to focus on the problem of China.

Beyond China, my theory has important implications for other US rivals. For example, at the onset of Russia's invasion of Ukraine, Vladimir Putin made expansive territorial claims that extended to all previously Soviet states. Many have wondered why Putin didn't say "I want Ukraine and nothing else"? My theory suggests that this claim would have been implausible because Russia has a high historical and cultural attachment to many post-Soviet states. By invading Ukraine, Putin made clear he was willing to bear large situation-specific costs to fight for historically salient territories. Russia experts in NATO would have quickly realized that Ukraine was not the end of Putin's ambition precisely because they know that there are many other territories with similarly high historical value. In effect, the world's knowledge of Russia's history bounded what Putin could claim.

My theory likely extends beyond great power relations. It likely explains regional contests such as Middle Eastern conflicts during the 1900s between Iran, Israel, Saudi Arabia, and Turkey. It also likely explains why newly formed Central Asian states found a path to peace, but certain South American dyads did not at the end of the Cold War. It also likely explains why the US was willing to tolerate nuclear proliferation in some cases (e.g., Pakistan) but not others (Iran). Even though these states are strategically similar from the US perspective, Pakistan could tell a plausible story to

---

[343] See Chapter 8 for some concerns about Obama's policy.

[344] I make no comment about how they executed this strategy.

explain why it held limited aims and desired nuclear weapons. Iran could not. But there are limits. For example, my insights do not help us better understand minor powers which only contest a single issue. The reason is that a one-issue dispute boils down to whether you want it or not. Thus, variation in historical context will not explain much beyond what standard theories of bargaining or signaling explain.

While I have focused on the strategic problem at the origins of great power rivalries, my method for conceptualizing motives is general. I believe we can yield novel insights about critical strategic problems beyond trust during great power rivalries by assuming that states' motives are attached to principles. As the Sino-American rivalry intensifies it is essential that scholars develop a more precise understanding of three specific interactions. First, in the coming decades the US must effectively cultivate a reputation for resolve over the issues and territories it is willing to fight wars over. If it doesn't, it risks accidental escalation with China. We know from recent evidence that how reputation transfers across issues likely depends on a more complex understanding of state motives (Weisiger and Yarhi-Milo, 2015; Crescenzi, 2007). My theory provides a structured way to understand exactly when reputations will transfer. For example, China carefully watched President Trump's forceful push to compel Ukraine to the bargaining table. Some worry that this signals his interest in isolationism, which in turn would communicate low resolve in general. If true, it could entice China to attack Taiwan. But this takes on a simplistic view of reputation. Trump's actions could also communicate that we care about Asia more than Europe, and are conserving our resources for that theater. We need more research to understand when decisions to withdraw signal low general resolve, and when they signal high resolve for an alternative priority.

Second, as we start to prioritize competition with China, we must consider the value of reconciling with other rivals. If we don't, we will be forced to split our resources and may face a large block of dissatisfied states that align with China. But who can we reconcile with cheaply? My framework offers a method to systematize Walt's (1992) insights about balancing threats. This will help us evaluate threats to US interests based on their historical and cultural context and not only their military capabilities, and economic and strategic position. We can use the overall framework to better estimate the scope of rivalry with others, and understand the minimal necessary concessions to entice them away from China's sphere of influence. My framework also explains which of our existing allies are most at risk of defecting to China's side. For example, it suggests that autocratic regimes with ethics that do not fit ours, and fungible assets (such as Saudi Arabia) are at a high risk of defection to China's side.

Third, eventually (i.e., many decades from now) domestic politics may change so much in either China or the United States that our preferences may align, and reconciliation may be plausible. At that moment, trust will be very low. We will want to communicate our compatible motivations, but will be reluctant to unilaterally disarm or send other trust-building signals necessary to rekindle cooperation (Jervis, 1978). My theory provides a blueprint for sending qualitatively distinctive signals that will help us escape enduring rivalries. These signals may allow us to communicate a deep interest in a specific issue area without leaving ourselves vulnerable in the overall military balance.

In my opinion, the future looks gloomy relative to unipolarity of the 1990s and 2000s (Monteiro, 2014), and relative to the Cold War. But if researchers can help the US better understand the dynamics of the situation it is in, we can reduce the harm the US suffers in Sino-American competition, shorten the time it suffers for, and raise the chance that it comes out the other side victorious.

References

Abdel-Khalik, A. R. (2014, September). CEO risk preference and investing in R&D. *Abacus 50*, 245–278.

Alanbrooke, Field Marshal Lord (2003). *War Diaries 1939–1945*. University of California Press.

Aldrich, R. J., R. Cormac, and M. S. Goodman (2014). *Spying on the World: The Declassified Documents of the Joint Intelligence Committee, 1936–2013*. Edinburgh University Press.

Allison, G. (1971). *Essence of Decision: Explaining the Cuban Missile Crisis*. Little, Brown and Company.

Allison, G. T. (2017). *Destined for War: Can America and China Escape Thucydides's Trap?* Scribe Publications.

Arber, S., J. McKinlay, A. Adams, L. Marceau, C. Link, and A. O'Donnell (2004, September). Influence of patient characteristics on doctors' questioning and lifestyle advice for coronary heart disease: A UK/US video experiment. *The British Journal of General Practice: The Journal of the Royal College of General Practitioners 54*, 673–678.

Arber, S., J. McKinlay, A. Adams, L. Marceau, C. Link, and A. O'Donnell (2006, January). Patient characteristics and inequalities in doctors' diagnostic and management strategies relating to CHD: A video-simulation experiment. *Social Science & Medicine 62*, 103–115.

Ardanaz, M., M. V. Murillo, and P. M. Pinto (2013, April). Sensitivity to issue framing on trade policy preferences: Evidence from a survey experiment. *International Organization 67*, 411–437.

Art, R. J. (1998). Geopolitics updated: The strategy of selective engagement. *International Security 23*, 79–113.

Bader, J. A. (2020). *Biden's China Policy Needs to Be More than Just Trump Lite*. Brookings Institute.

Barboza, D. and J. A. Bader (2020). Obama's past and Biden's future with China. https://www.brookings.edu/articles/obamas-past-and-bidens-future-with-china/.

Barnett, C. (1986). *The Collapse of British Power*. Humanities Press International.

Barnett, M. and R. Duvall (2005, February). Power in international politics. *International Organization 59*, 39–75.

Barnett, M. and M. Finnemore (2004). *Rules for the World: International Organizations in Global Politics*, Volume 9. Cornell University Press.

Barooah, D. P. (1966, November). Munich reconsidered. *Proceedings of the Indian History Congress 28*, 470–480.

Barros, A., T. C. Imlay, E. Resnick, N. M. Ripsman, and J. S. Levy (2009, November). Debating British decisionmaking toward Nazi Germany in the 1930s. *International Security 34*, 173–198.

Batatu, H. (2012). *Syria's Peasantry, the Descendants of Its Lesser Rural Notables, and Their Politics*. Princeton University Press.

Bates, R. H., A. Greif, M. Levi, J.-L. Rosenthal, and B. Weingast (1998). *Analytic Narratives*. Princeton University Press.

Battaglini, M. (2002, July). Multiple referrals and multidimensional cheap talk. *Econometrica 70*, 1379–1401.

Beaumont, J. (1980). *Comrades in Arms: British Aid to Russia 1941–1945*. Davis-Poynter.

Beckley, M. (2018). *Unrivaled*. Cornell University Press.

Bekkevold, J. I. (2022, December). 5 ways the U.S.-China cold war will be different from the last one. *Foreign Policy*. https://foreignpolicy.com/2022/12/29/us-china-cold-war-bipolar-global-order-stability-biden-xi/.

Bell, M. S. (2015, July). Beyond emboldenment: How acquiring nuclear weapons can change foreign policy. *International Security 40*, 87–119.

Bell, S. R. (2017, March). Power, territory, and interstate conflict. *Conflict Management and Peace Science 34*, 160–175.

Bell, S. R. and J. C. Johnson (2015, March). Shifting power, commitment problems, and preventive war. *International Studies Quarterly 59*, 124–132.

Berthon, S. and J. Potts (2007). *Warlords: An Extraordinary Re-creation of World War II through the Eyes and Minds of Hitler, Churchill, Roosevelt, and Stalin*. Da Capo.

Bisley, N. (2017). Donald Trump serves up clumsiness, inexperience and realpolitik in Asia. *The Guardian*. www.theguardian.com/world/2016/dec/04/donald-trump-serves-up-clumsiness-inexperience-and-realpolitik-in-asia.

Blackwill, R. and R. Fontaine (2024, June). Obama tried to pivot to Asia in 2011. We must succeed this time. *Washington Post*. www.washingtonpost.com/opinions/2024/06/10/trump-obama-biden-asia-pivot/.

Blain, M. (1988, November). Fighting words: What we can learn from Hitler's hyperbole. *Symbolic Interaction 11*, 257–276.

Blainey, G. (1988). *Causes of War*, 3rd Ed. Simon and Schuster.

Blair, D. (2010, December). Annual threat assessment of the US Intelligence Community for the senate select committee on intelligence.

Bolkhovitinov, N. N. (2003, July). The sale of Alaska: A Russian perspective. *Polar Geography 27*, 254–267.

Bourne, K. (1967). *Britain and the Balance of Power in North America, 1815–1908*. University of California Press.

Braumoeller, B. F. (2008, February). Systemic politics and the origins of great power conflict. *American Political Science Review 102*, 77–93.

Brooks, S. (1999, October). The globalization of production and the changing benefits of conquest. *Journal of Conflict Resolution 43*, 646–670.

Brooks, S. G., G. J. Ikenberry, and W. C. Wohlforth (2013, January). Don't come home, America: The case against retrenchment. *International Security 37*, 7–51.

Bryant, A. and A. B. Alanbrooke (1974). *Triumph in the West: A History of the War Years Based on the Diaries of Field-Marshal Lord Alanbrooke, Chief of the Imperial General Staff.* Greenwood Press.

Buhite, R. D. (1986). *Decisions at Yalta: An Appraisal of Summit Diplomacy.* Scholarly Resources.

Bull, H. (2002). *The Anarchical Society: A Study of Order in World Politics.* Columbia University Press.

Bush, R. C. (2019). 30 years after Tiananmen Square, a look back on Congress' forceful response. Brookings Institute. www.brookings.edu/articles/30-years-after-tiananmen-square-a-look-back-on-congress-forceful-response/.

Butler, A. J. (trans.) (1989). *Bismarck: The Man & the Statesman.* Harper & Brothers.

Campbell, C. (1976). *The Transformation of American Foreign Relations, 1865–1900.* Harper Row.

Campbell, K. M. (2016). *The Pivot: The Future of American Statecraft in Asia.* Twelve.

Campbell, K. M. and R. D. Blackwill (2016). *Xi Jinping on the Global Stage.* Council on Foreign Relations.

Campbell, K. M. and E. Ratner (2018). The China reckoning: How Beijing defied American expectations. *Foreign Affairs. 97, 2*, 60–70.

Carley, M. (1999, July). "A situation of delicacy and danger": Anglo-Soviet relations, August 1939–March 1940. *Contemporary European History 8*, 175–208.

Carr, E. H. (1945). *The Twenty Years' Crisis, 1919–1939.* Harper & Row.

Carter, D. B. and H. E. Goemans (2011, April). The making of the territorial order: New borders and the emergence of interstate conflict. *International Organization 65*, 275–309.

Cen, W. and J. A. Doukas (2017, October). CEO personal investment decisions and firm risk. *European Financial Management 23*, 920–950.

Cha, V. D. (2016, September). The unfinished legacy of Obama's pivot to Asia. *Foreign Policy.* https://foreignpolicy.com/2016/09/06/the-unfinished-legacy-of-obamas-pivot-to-asia/.

Chakraborty, A. and R. Harbaugh (2007, January). Comparative cheap talk. *Journal of Economic Theory 132*, 70–94.

Chakraborty, A. and R. Harbaugh (2010, December). Persuasion by cheap talk. *American Economic Review 100*, 2361–2382.

Chiozza, G. and H. E. Goemans (2011). *Leaders and International Conflict.* Cambridge University Press.

Cholet, D. (2016). *The Long Game: How Obama Defied Washington and Redefined America's Role in the World.* Public Affairs.

Churchill, W. (1948). *Triumph and Tragedy.* Houghton Mifflin.

Churchill, W. (1956). *The Second World War*, Volume 6. Time.

Churchill, W. (1966). *Russia and Poland the Soviet Promise.* D. C. Heath & Co.

Clapper, J. (2011, March). Worldwide threat assessment of the US intelligence community for the Senate Committee on Armed Services. Office of the Director of National Intelligence

Clemens, D. (1970). *Yalta.* Oxford University Press.

Clinton, H. (2011, October). America's pacific century. *Foreign Policy*. https://foreign policy.com/2011/10/11/americas-pacific-century/.

Coe, A. J. and J. Vaynman (2015, October). Collusion and the nuclear nonproliferation regime. *The Journal of Politics 77*, 983–997.

Coe, A. and J. Vaynman (2019, December). Why arms control is so rare. *American Political Science Review 114*(2), 342–355.

Cohen, R. (1978). Threat perception in international crisis. *Political Science Quarterly 93*, 93–107.

Collett, J. L. and E. Childs (2011). Minding the gap: Meaning, affect, and the potential shortcomings of vignettes. *Social Science Research 40*, 513–522.

Copeland, D. C. (2000). *The Origins of Major War: Hegemonic Rivalry and the Fear of Decline*. Cornell University Press.

Copeland, D. C. (2015). *Economic Interdependence and War*. Princeton University Press.

Crescenzi, M. J. C. (2007, April). Reputation and interstate conflict. *American Journal of Political Science 51*, 382–396.

Crisher, B. B. and M. Souva (2014, August). Power at sea: A naval power dataset, 1865–2011. *International Interactions 40*, 602–629.

Dafoe, A., J. Renshon, and P. Huth (2014, May). Reputation and status as motives for war. *Annual Review of Political Science 17*, 371–393.

Dafoe, A., B. Zhang, and D. Caughey (2016). Confounding in survey experiments. https://api.semanticscholar.org/CorpusID:149016983.

Daly, R. (2022). China and the United States: It's a cold war, but don't panic. *Bulletin of the Atomic Scientists*. https://thebulletin.org/premium/2022-03/china-and-the-united-states-its-a-cold-war-but-dont-panic/.

de Mesquita, B. B. and D. Lalman (1992, July). *War and Reason*. Yale University Press.

de Mesquita, B. B., J. D. Morrow, R. M. Siverson, and A. Smith (1999). An institutional explanation of the democratic peace. *The American Political Science Review 93*, 791–807.

de Soysa, I., J. R. Oneal, and Y.-H. Park (1997, August). Testing power-transition theory using alternative measures of national capabilities. *Journal of Conflict Resolution 41*, 509–528.

Debs, A. and N. P. Monteiro (2014, January). Known unknowns: Power shifts, uncertainty, and war. *International Organization 68*, 1–31.

Debs, A. and N. P. Monteiro (2016). *Nuclear Politics: The Strategic Causes of Proliferation*. Cambridge University Press.

Department of Defense (2010). *Military and Security Developments Involving the People's Republic of China*. Department of Defense.

Director of National Intelligence (2015). Intelligence community directive 203, analytical standards.

Dobson, A. (1995). *Anglo-American Relations in the Twentieth Century*. Routledge.

Dollar, D., R. Hass, and J. A. Bader (2019). *Assessing U.S.-China relations 2 years into the Trump presidency*. Brookings Institute. www.brookings.edu/articles/assessing-u-s-china-relations-2-years-into-the-trump-presidency/.

Doshi, R. (2021). *Hu's to Blame for China's Foreign Assertiveness?* Brookings Institution.

Downs, G. W. and D. M. Rocke (1994, May). Conflict, agency, and gambling for resurrection: The principal-agent problem goes to war. *American Journal of Political Science 38*, 362.

Doyle, M. W. (2005). Three pillars of the liberal peace. *The American Political Science Review 99*, 463–466.

Dutton, D. (1997). *Anthony Eden: A Life and Reputation*. Arnold.

Economy, E. (2010, November). The end of the 'peaceful rise'? *Foreign Policy.* https://foreignpolicy.com/2010/11/28/the-end-of-the-peaceful-rise/.

Edelstein, D. M. (2002, October). Managing uncertainty: Beliefs about intentions and the rise of great powers. *Security Studies 12*, 1–40. https://www.doi.org/10.1080/09636410212120002.

Edelstein, D. M. (2019). *Over the Horizon: Time, Uncertainty, and the Rise of Great Powers*. Cornell University Press.

Elizalde, M.-D. (2016, April). Observing the imperial transition: British naval reports on the Philippines, 1898–1901. *Diplomatic History 40*, 219–243.

Ells, M. D. V. (1995, November). Assuming the white man's burden: The seizure of the Philippines, 1898–1902. *Philippine Studies 43*, 607–622.

Engel, J. (2010). A better world... but don't get carried away: The foreign policy of George H. W. Bush twenty years on. *Diplomatic History 34*(1), 25–46.

Eysenbach, G. (2004). Improving the quality of web surveys: The checklist for reporting results of internet e-surveys. *Journal of medical Internet research 6*, e34.

Fawcett, L. (2014, May). Revisiting the Iranian crisis of 1946: How much more do we know? *Iranian Studies 47*, 379–399.

Fawcett, L. L. E. (2009). *Iran and the Cold War: The Azerbaijan Crisis of 1946*, Volume 26. Cambridge University Press.

Fearon, J. D. (1994, September). Domestic political audiences and the escalation of international disputes. *American Political Science Review 88*, 577–592.

Fearon, J. D. (1995, June). Rationalist explanations for war. *International Organization 49*, 379.

Fearon, J. D. (1997). The offense-defense balance and war since 1648. https://web.stanford.edu/group/fearon-research/cgi-bin/wordpress/wp-content/uploads/2013/10/The-Offense-Defense-Balance-and-War-Since-1648.pdf.

Fearon, J. D. and A. Wendt (2002). *Rationalism v. Constructivism: A Skeptical View*. SAGE Publications Ltd., pp. 52–72.

Feldman, H. A., J. B. McKinlay, D. A. Potter, K. M. Freund, R. B. Burns, M. A. Moskowitz, and L. E. Kasten (1997, August). Nonmedical influences on medical decision making: An experimental technique using videotapes, factorial design, and survey sampling. *Health Services Research 32*, 343–366.

Finnemore, M. (1996a). *National Interests in International Society*. Cornell University Press.

Finnemore, M. (1996b, May). Norms, culture, and world politics: Insights from sociology's institutionalism. *International Organization 50*, 325.

Finnemore, M. (2003, November). *Changing Norms of Humanitarian Intervention*. Cornell University Press, pp. 52–84.

Finnemore, M. and K. Sikkink (1998, October). International norm dynamics and political change. *International Organization 52*, 887–917.

Ford, J. (2017, January). The pivot to Asia was Obama's biggest mistake. *Foreign Policy*.

Fordham, B. O. (2011). Who wants to be a major power? explaining the expansion of foreign policy ambition. *Journal of Peace Research 48*, 587–603.

Fordham, B. O. (2020, January). History and quantitative conflict research: A case for limiting the historical scope of our theoretical arguments. *Conflict Management and Peace Science 37*, 3–15.

Foster, P. U. (1941). The beast from the abyss. *Blackfriars 22*, 366–372.

Foyle, D. C. (1997, March). Public opinion and foreign policy: Elite beliefs as a mediating variable. *International Studies Quarterly 41*, 141–169.

Frendem, M., M. Joseph, and W. Spaniel (2025). Explaining peace during long and rapid power shifts: A theory of grand bargains. *British Journal of Political Science.* doi:10.1017/S0007123424000577.

Friedberg, A. L. (2010). *The Weary Titan: Britain and the Experience of Relative Decline, 1895–1905*. Princeton University Press.

Gaddis, J. L. (2006). *The Cold War: A New History*. Penguin Publishing Group.

Garfinkel, B. and A. Dafoe (2019, September). How does the offense-defense balance scale? *Journal of Strategic Studies 42*, 736–763.

Gentile, G., M. Shurkin, A. Evans, M. Grisé, M. Hvizda, and R. Jensen (2021). The history of the third offset strategy. Rand Corporation. www.rand.org/pubs/research_reports/RRA454-1.html.

George H. W. Bush Foundation for U.S.-China Relations (2025). The U.S.-China relations legacy of President George H. W. Bush. https://bushchinafoundation.org/u-s-china-legacy/.

Gibler, D. M. (2008, June). The costs of reneging. *Journal of Conflict Resolution 52*, 426–454.

Gilbert, M. (1966). *The Roots of Appeasement*. Weidenfeld & Nicolson.

Gilbert, M. (1972). *The Roots of Appeasement*. Weidenfeld & Nicolson.

Gilbert, M. (1983). *Finest Hour. Winston S. Churchill, 1939–1941*. Houghton Mifflin Company.

Gilder, G. (2010, February). Why antagonize China? *The Wall Street Journal*.

Gilderhus, M. T. (2006, March). The monroe doctrine: Meanings and implications. *Presidential Studies Quarterly 36*, 5–16.

Gilpin, R. (1983). *War and Change in World Politics*, Volume 1983. Cambridge University Press.

Gilpin, R. (1988, 21). The theory of hegemonic war. *Journal of Interdisciplinary History 18*, 591.

Glaser, B. (2012). Armed clash in the South China Sea. The Council on Foreign Relations. https://cdn.cfr.org/sites/default/files/pdf/2012/04/CPA_contingency memo_14.pdf.

Glaser, C. L. (2010). *Rational Theory of International Politics*. Princeton University Press.

Glaser, C. L. (2015, April). A U.S.-China grand bargain? The hard choice between military competition and accommodation. *International Security 39*, 49–90.

Glaser, C. L. and C. Kaufmann (1998). Offense defence balance and can we measure it? *International Security 22*, 44–82.

Goddard, S. E. (2018). *When Right Makes Might: Rising Powers and World Order*. Cornell University Press.

Goemans, H., K. Gleditsch, and G. Chiozza (2009). Introducing archigos: A dataset of political leaders. *Journal of Peace Research 46*, 269–283.

Goemans, H. and W. Spaniel (2016, January). Multimethod research: A Case for Formal Theory. *Security Studies 25*, 25–33.

Goemans, H. E. and K. A. Schultz (2017, October). The politics of territorial claims: A geospatial approach applied to Africa. *International Organization 71*, 31–64.

Goertz, G. and P. F. Diehl (1995, February). The initiation and termination of enduring rivalries: The impact of political shocks. *American Journal of Political Science 39*, 30–52.

Goldfien, M., M. Joseph, and D. Krcmaric (2023, August). When do leader backgrounds matter? evidence from the president's daily brief. *Conflict Management and Peace Science 41*, 4, 414–437.

Goldfien, M., M. Joseph, and R. McManus (2026). The domestic sources of international trust. *The American Political Science Review* forthcoming.

Goldfien, M. A. and M. F. Joseph (2023, March). Perceptions of leadership importance: Evidence from the CIA's president's daily brief. *Security Studies 32*, 205–238.

Goldfien, M. A., M. F. Joseph, and R. W. McManus (2022, September). The domestic sources of international reputation. *American Political Science Review*, 1–20.

Goldstein, E. (2010). *Origins of the Anglo-American Special Relationship, 1880–1914*. Cambridge University Press.

Goodman, M. S. (2015). *The Official History of the Joint Intelligence Committee*. Routledge.

Gorodetsky, G. (1994). *The Formulation of Soviet Foreign Policy: Ideology and Realpolitik*. Frank Cass and Co.

Gortzak, Y. (2005, February). Offense-defense theory: An empirical assessment. *Journal of Conflict Resolution 49*, 67–89.

Grynaviski, E. (2018). *America's Middlemen : Power at the Edge of Empire*. Cambridge University Press.

Gurantz, R. and A. V. Hirsch (2017, July). Fear, appeasement, and the effectiveness of deterrence. *The Journal of Politics 79*, 1041–1056.

Haas, M. L. (2005). *The Ideological Origins of Great Power Politics, 1789–1989*. Cornell University Press.

Hamilton, L. (2017). Trump's impulsiveness challenges are vital to U.S.-China relationship. *Huffpost*.

Harbutt, F. J. (2010). *Yalta 1945: Europe and America at the Crossroads*. Cambridge University Press.

Harding, H. (2015, July). Has U.S. China policy failed? *The Washington Quarterly 38*, 95–122.

Harper, B. F. (2018). *The Iranian Crisis and the Birth of the Cold War: The Bridge to Victory*. Lexington Books.

Harriman, W. A. and E. Abel (1975). *Special Envoy to Churchill and Stalin, 1941–1946*. Random House.

Haslam, J. (2003, June). The Cold War as history. *Annual Review of Political Science 6*, 77–98.

Haslam, J. (2021). *The Spectre of War*. Princeton University Press.

Hass, R. and A. Denmark (2020). More pain than gain: How the US-China trade war hurt America. Brookings Institute. www.brookings.edu/articles/more-pain-than-gain-how-the-us-china-trade-war-hurt-america/.

Hauner, M. (1978, November). Did Hitler want a world dominion? *Journal of Contemporary History 13*, 15–32.

Haynes, K. and B. Yoder (2020, January). Offsetting uncertainty: Reassurance with two-sided incomplete information. *American Journal of Political Science 64*, 38–51.

He, K. (2016, March). Explaining United States–China relations: Neoclassical realism and the nexus of threat–interest perceptions. *The Pacific Review 30*, 133–151.

Henley, L. (2023). Deterrence and dissuasion in the taiwan Strait.

Herkert, A. (2017, December). U.S. intelligence and cross-strait relations. *American Intelligence Journal 34*, 102–110.

Hess, G. R. (1974, March). The Iranian crisis of 1945–46 and the Cold War. *Political Science Quarterly 89*, 117–146.

Hess, G. R. (1992, January). Accommodation amid discord: The United States, India, and the third world. *Diplomatic History 16*, 1–22.

Hillgruber, A. (1974, January). England's place in Hitler's plans for world dominion. *Journal of Contemporary History 9*, 5–22.

Hitler, A. (1941, June). The Hitler proclamation. *New York Times*, 4.

Hoffman, A. M. (2002, September). A conceptualization of trust in international relations. *European Journal of International Relations 8*, 375–401.

Holmes, M. (2013). The force of face-to-face diplomacy: Mirror neurons and the problem of intentions. *International Organization 67*, 829–861.

Holmes, M. (2018, March). *Face-to-Face Diplomacy*. Cambridge University Press.

Hopf, T. (1994). *Peripheral Visions: Deterrence Theory and American Foreign Policy in the Third World, 1965–1990*. University of Michigan Press.

Horowitz, M., B. M. Stewart, D. Tingley, M. Bishop, L. R. Samotin, M. Roberts, W. Chang, B. Mellers, and P. Tetlock (2019, October). What makes foreign policy teams tick: Explaining variation in group performance at geopolitical forecasting. *The Journal of Politics 81*, 1388–1404.

House Permanent Select Committee on Intelligence (2020). The China deep dive: A report on the intelligence community's capabilities and competencies with respect to the People's Republic of China. https://democrats-intelligence.house.gov/uploadedfiles/hpsci_china_deep_dive_redacted_summary_9.29.20.pdf.

Houweling, H. and J. G. Siccama (1988, March). Power transitions as a cause of war. *Journal of Conflict Resolution 32*, 87–102.

Howard, M. (1961). *The Franco-Prussian War: The German Invasion of France 1870–1871*. Macmillan.

Ikenberry, J. G. (1998). Institutions, strategic restraint, and the persistence of American postwar order. *International Security 23*, 43–78.

Jackson, M. O. and M. Morelli (2011). The Reasons for Wars: An Updated Survey. In Christopher J. Coyne and Rachel L. Mathers (Eds.), *The Handbook on the Political Economy of War* (pp. 34–57). Edward Elgar.

James, C. (1937). *World Revolution, 1917–1936: The Rise and Fall of the Communist International*. Duke University Press.

Jervis, R. (1978, January). Cooperation under the security dilemma. *World Politics 30*, 167–214.

Jervis, R. (1989a). *The Logic of Images in International Relations*. Columbia University Press.

Jervis, R. (1989b, June). Rational deterrence: Theory and evidence. *World Politics 41*, 183–207.

Jervis, R., R. N. Lebow, and J. G. Stein (1989). *Psychology and Deterrence*. Johns Hopkins University Press.

Johnson, R. (2019). Trump's tone-deaf appeal to farmers hurting from trade war: "Greatest harvest is yet to come". *The Hill*. https://thehill.com/opinion/energy-environment/425294-trumps-tone-deaf-appeal-to-farmers-hurting-from-trade-war-greatest/.

Johnston, A. I. (2013, April). How new and assertive is China's new assertiveness? *International Security 37*, 7–48.

Johnston, A. I. (2019, April). The failures of the "failure of engagement" with China. *The Washington Quarterly 42*, 99–114.

Joseph, M. F. (2021, January). A little bit of cheap talk is a dangerous thing: States can communicate intentions persuasively and raise the risk of war. *The Journal of Politics 83*, 166–181.

Joseph, M. F. (2023, March). Do different coercive strategies help or hurt deterrence? *International Studies Quarterly 67*. DOI:10.1093/isq/sqad018.

Joseph, M. F. and M. Poznansky (2018, May). Media technology, covert action, and the politics of exposure. *Journal of Peace Research 55*, 320–335.

Joseph, M. F. and M. Poznansky (2024, November). Secret innovation. *International Organization 78*, 766–799.

Joseph, M. F., M. Poznansky, and W. Spaniel (2022, April). Shooting the messenger: The challenge of national security whistleblowing. *The Journal of Politics 84*, 846–860.

Kagan, R. (2005, May 15). The illusion of "managing" China. *The Washington Post*.

Kennedy, P. M. (1976). The tradition of appeasement in British foreign policy 1865–1939. *British Journal of International Studies 2*, 195–215.

Kennedy, P. M. (1988). *The Rise of the Anglo-German antagonism, 1860–1914*. Humanity Books.

Kennedy, P. M. (1989). *The Rise and Fall of the Great Powers: Economic Change and Military Conflict from 1500 to 2000*. Vintage Books.

Keohane, R. (2005). *After Hegemony: Cooperation and Discord in the World Political Economy*. Princeton University Press.

Kertzer, J. D. (2016). *Resolve in International Politics*. Princeton University Press.

Kertzer, J. D. (2020, December). Re-assessing elite-public gaps in political behavior. *American Journal of Political Science. 66*, 3, 539–553

Kertzer, J. D. and R. Brutger (2016, January). Decomposing audience costs: Bringing the audience back into audience cost theory. *American Journal of Political Science 60*, 234–249.

Khong, Y. (1992). *Analogies at War*. Princeton. University Press.

Kim, W. and J. D. Morrow (1992, November). When do power shifts lead to war? *American Journal of Political Science 36*, 896.

King, G., R. Keohane, and S. Verba (1994). *Designing Social Inquiry: Scientific Inference in Qualitative Research*. Princeton University Press.

Kissinger, H. (1979). *White House Years*. Christopher Van Hollen.

Kitchen, M. (1986). *British Policy towards the Soviet Union during the Second World War*. St. Martin's Press.

Kitfield, J. (2012, June). Is Obama's "pivot to Asia" really a hedge against China? *The Atlantic*. www.theatlantic.com/international/archive/2012/06/is-obamas-pivot-to-asia-really-a-hedge-against-china/258279/.

Klau, T., G. Verhofstadt, A. Palacio, E. Letta, D. Trenin, D. Kramer, and D. Mac-Shane (2016). What's Obama's European legacy? *Politico*. www.politico.eu/article/what-will-define-barack-obamas-european-legacy-eu-us/.

Klein, J. P. (2006, May). The new rivalry dataset: Procedures and patterns. *Journal of Peace Research 43*, 331–348.

Knecht, T. and M. S. Weatherford (2006, 9). Public opinion and foreign policy: The stages of presidential decision making. *International Studies Quarterly 50*, 705–727.

Krainin, C. (2017, January). Preventive war as a result of long-term shifts in power. *Political Science Research and Methods 5*, 103–121.

Krebs, R. R. and P. T. Jackson (2007, March). Twisting tongues and twisting arms: The power of political rhetoric. *European Journal of International Relations 13*, 35–66.

Kugler, J. and D. Lemke (1996). *Parity and War: Evaluations and Extensions of the War Ledger*. University of Michigan Press.

Kuniholm, B. R. (2014). *The Origins of the Cold War in the Near East: Great Power Conflict and Diplomacy in Iran, Turkey, and Greece*. Princeton University Press.

Kurizaki, S. (2007, August). Efficient secrecy: Public versus private threats in crisis diplomacy. *American Political Science Review 101*, 543–558.

Kushner, T. (1989, March). Beyond the pale? British reactions to Nazi anti-semitism, 1933–39. *Immigrants & Minorities 8*, 143–160.

Kydd, A. H. (2005). *Trust and Mistrust in International Relations*. Princeton University Press.

Lake, D. A. and R. Powell (1999). *Strategic choice and International Relations*. Princeton University Press.

Larson, D. (1985). *Origins of Containment: A Psychological Explanation*. Princeton University Press.

Larson, D. W. (2000). *Anatomy of Mistrust: U.S.-Soviet Relations During the Cold War*. Cornell University Press.

Lawson, L. (1922, December). *VI. The Monroe Doctrine*. Columbia University Press, pp. 125–146.

Layne, C. (1997). From preponderance to offshore balancing: America's future grand strategy. *International Security 22*, 86–124.

Leffler, M. P. (1999, April). The Cold War: What do "we now know"? *The American Historical Review 104*, 501.

Lemke, D. (2003, October). Investigating the preventive motive for war. *International Interactions 29*, 273–292.

Levendusky, M. S. and M. C. Horowitz (2012, March). When backing down is the right decision: Partisanship, new information, and audience costs. *The Journal of Politics 74*, 323–338.

Levy, J. S. (1984, June). The offensive/defensive balance of military technology: A theoretical and historical analysis. *International Studies Quarterly 28*, 219.

Levy, J. S. (1998, June). The causes of war and the conditions of peace. *Annual Review of Political Science 1*, 139–165.

Lieb, R. and B. Schwarz (2001, January). The year 2001 survey: CEO perspectives on the current status and future prospects of the third party logistics industry in the United States. *Supply Chain Forum: An International Journal 2*, 36–44.

Lieberthal, K. (2011, December). The American pivot to Asia. *Foreign Policy*. https://foreignpolicy.com/2011/12/21/the-american-pivot-to-asia/.

Lomas, D. W. B. (2016). *Intelligence, Security and the Attlee Governments, 1945–51: An Uneasy Relationship?* Manchester University Press.

Lowenthal, M. M. (2019). *Intelligence: From Secrets to Policy.* CQ Press.

Ludbrook, J. and H. Dudley (1998, May). Why permutation tests are superior to t and f tests in biomedical research. *The American Statistician 52*, 127.

Luthin, R. H. (1937, November). The sale of Alaska. *The Slavonic and East European Review 16*, 168–182.

Lynn, K. K. (2013). *The Inauguration of Organized Political Warfare: Cold War Organizations Sponsored by the National Committee for a Free Europe/Free Europe Committee.* Helena History Press.

Maisky, I. M., G. Gorodetsky, O. Ready, and T. Sorokina (2016). *The Maisky Diaries: The Wartime Revelations of Stalin's Ambassador in London.* Yale University Press.

Mathews, J. J. (1963, September). Informal diplomacy in the venezuelan crisis of 1896. *The Mississippi Valley Historical Review 50*, 195.

Maurer, J. H. (1997, June). Arms control and the Anglo-German naval race before World War I: Lessons for today? *Political Science Quarterly 112*, 285–306.

May, E. R. (1975, December). *The Making of the Monroe Doctrine.* Harvard University Press.

McHale, T. R. (1961). The development of American policy toward the Philippines. *Philippine Studies 9*, 47–71.

McManus, R. W. (2017, August). *Statements of Resolve.* Cambridge University Press.

Mearsheimer, J. J. (2001). *The Tragedy of Great Power Politics.* Norton.

Medeiros, E. S. (2005). Strategic hedging and the future of Asia-Pacific stability. *The Washington Quarterly 29*, 145–167.

Medeiros, E. S. and J. Blanchette (2021). Beyond colossus or collapse: Five myths driving American debates about China. War on the Rocks. https://warontherocks.com/2021/03/beyond-colossus-or-collapse-five-myths-driving-american-debates-about-china/.

Mercer, J. (1996). *Reputation and International Politics.* Cornell University Press.

Messer, R. L. (1982). *The End of an Alliance: James F. Byrnes, Roosevelt, Truman, and the Origins of the Cold War.* University of North Carolina Press.

Miller, M. K., M. Joseph, and D. Ohl (2016, May). Are coups really contagious? An extreme bounds analysis of political diffusion. *Journal of Conflict Resolution, 62, 2*, 410–444.

Ministry of Foreign Affairs (1957a). *Correspondence between the Chairman of the Council of Ministers of the USSR and the Presidents of the USA and the Prime Ministers of Great Britain during the Great Patriotic War of 1941–1945, Vol. 1.* Foreign Languages Publishing House; distrib. by Chicago Council of American Soviet Friendship, Inc.

Ministry of Foreign Affairs (1957b). *Correspondence between the Chairman of the Council of Ministers of the USSR and the Presidents of the USA and the Prime Ministers of Great Britain during the Great Patriotic War of 1941–1945, Vol. 2.* Foreign Languages Publishing House; distrib. by Chicago Council of American Soviet Friendship, Inc.

Mitchell, S. M. and B. C. Prins (1999, March). Beyond territorial contiguity: Issues at stake in democratic militarized interstate disputes. *International Studies Quarterly 43*, 169–183.

Mitzen, J. (2006, September). Ontological security in world politics: State identity and the security dilemma. *European Journal of International Relations 12*, 341–370.

Monteiro, N. P. (2014). *Theory of Unipolar Politics.* Cambridge University Press.

Moran, C. M. W. (2002). *Churchill at War, 1940–1945.* Carroll & Graf.

Moravcsik, A. (1997, August). Taking preferences seriously: A liberal theory of international politics. *International Organization 51*, 513–553.

Morgenthau, H. J. H. J. and K. W. Thompson (1948). *Politics among Nations: The Struggle for Power and Peace.* McGraw-Hill.

Mosse, W. (1958). *The European Powers and the German Question, 1848–71.* Cambridge. University Press.

Mosse, W. E. (1951). The crown and foreign policy. Queen Victoria and the Austro-Prussian conflict, March–May, 1866. *The Cambridge Historical Journal 10*, 205–223.

Mowat, R. (1925). *The Diplomatic Relations of Great Britain and the United States.* Longmans.

Murray, M. (2018, December). *Weltpolitik.* Oxford University Press, pp. 87–112

Mylonas, H. (2013). *The Politics of Nation Building.* Cambridge University Press.

Nakatsuji, K. (1999). Nancy Pelosi and human rights in China. *Ritsumeikan International Studies 12.* www.ritsumei.ac.jp/ir/isaru/assets/file/journal/12-2_nakatsuji .pdf.

Nathan, A. J. (2019). The new Tiananmen papers inside the secret meeting that changed China. *Foreign Affairs.* www.foreignaffairs.com/articles/china/2019-05-30/ new-tiananmen-papers.

Naughton, B., A. R. Kroeber, G. de Jonquières, and G. Webster (2015). What will the TRP mean for China? *Foreign Policy.* https://foreignpolicy.com/2015/10/07/china-tpp-trans-pacific-partnership-obama-us-trade-xi/.

Neilson, K. (1993, August). "Pursued by a bear": British estimates of Soviet military strength and Anglo-Soviet relations, 1922–1939. *Canadian Journal of History 28*, 189–222.

Nicolson, H. and N. Nicolson (2004). *Harold Nicolson Diaries and Letters 1907–1964.* Weidenfeld & Nicolson.

Obama, B. (2011, November 17). Remarks by President Obama to the Australian parliament. The White House, Office of the Press Secretary.

Obama, B. (2014, November 15). Remarks by President Obama at the University of Queensland. The White House, Office of the Press Secretary.

O'Callaghan, J. and M. Mogato (2012). The U.S. military pivot to Asia: When bases are not bases. *Reuters.*

Office of the Historian (2024). Blaine and pan Americanism, 1880s/1890s. https:// history.state.gov/milestones/1866-1898/blaine.

Oneal, J. R., F. H. Oneal, Z. Maoz, and B. Russett (1996, February). The liberal peace: Interdependence, democracy, and international conflict, 1950–85. *Journal of Peace Research 33*, 11–28.

O'Neill, B. (1999). *Honor, Symbols, and War.* University of Michigan Press.

Orde, A. (1996). *The Eclipse of Great Britain: The United States and British Imperial Decline, 1895–1956.* Bloomsbury Publishing.

Organski, A. F. K. and J. Kugler (1980). *The War Ledger.* University of Chicago Press.

Overy, R. and A. Wheatcroft (2009). *The Road to War.* Random House.

Pagunsan, R. (2010). British consular reports on Filipino anti-colonial struggles and Philippine-British relations, 1896–1902. *Philippine Social Sciences Review 62.*

Paine, J. and S. A. Tyson (2020). *Uses and Abuses of Formal Models in Political Science.* SAGE Publications Ltd., pp. 188–202.

Palmer, G., V. D'Orazio, M. Kenwick, and M. Lane (2015, April). The mid4 dataset, 2002–2010: Procedures, coding rules and description. *Conflict Management and Peace Science 32*, 222–242.

Panda, A. (2018, October 6). How the partisan policies of Donald Trump's administration rubbed salt in wounded China-US ties. *South China Morning Post.*

Papp, N. G. (1979). The democratic struggle for power in hungary: Party strategies 1945–46. *East Central Europe 6*, 1–19.

Parks, B. C., A. A. Malik, B. Escobar, S. Zhang, R. Fedorochko, K. Solomon, F. Wang, L. Vlasto, K. Walsh, and S. Goodman (2023). Belt and road reboot: Beijing's bid to de-risk its global infrastructure initiative. https://docs.aiddata.org/reports/belt-and-road-reboot/Belt_and_Road_Reboot_Full_Report.pdf.

Parks, C. D., R. F. Henager, and S. D. Scamahorn (1996, March). Trust and reactions to messages of intent in social dilemmas. *Journal of Conflict Resolution 40*, 134–151.

Penn, E. M., J. W. Patty, and S. Gailmard (2011, April). Manipulation and single-peakedness: A general result. *American Journal of Political Science 55*, 436–449.

Pesek, W. (2021, May 28). China missing Trump terribly as biden hits 'hard power'. *Forbes.* www.forbes.com/sites/williampesek/2021/05/28/china-missing-trump-terribly-as-biden-hits-hard-power/.

Pflanze, O. (1990a). *Bismarck and the Development of Germany, vol. 2, The Period of Consolidation, 1871–1880.* Princeton University Press.

Pflanze, O. (1990b). *Consolidation and Cleavage.* Princeton University Press, pp. 3–31.

Pollard, R. (1985). *Economic Security and the Origins of the Cold War, 1945–150.* Columbia University Press.

Pons, S. (2012). *The Global Revolution.* Oxford University Press.

Popper, K. (1959). *The Logic of Scientific Discovery.* Hutchinson & Co.

Posen, B. (2014). *Restraint: A New Foundation for U.S. Grand Strategy.* Cornell University Press.

Powaski, R. (2018, September). *Ideals, Interests, and U.S. Foreign Policy from George H.W. Bush to Donald Trump.* Springer International Publishing.

Powell, R. (1993, March). Guns, butter, and anarchy. *American Political Science Review 87*, 115–132.

Powell, R. (1996, December). Uncertainty, shifting power, and appeasement. *The American Political Science Review 90*, 749–764.

Powell, R. (1999). *In the Shadow of Power: States and Strategies in International Politics.* Princeton University Press.

Powell, R. (2006, January). War as a commitment problem. *International Organization 60*, 169–203.

Powell, R. (2017, April). Research bets and behavioral IR. *International Organization 71*, S265–S277.

Powers, K. E. (2022). *Nationalisms in International Politics*. Princeton University Press.

Press, S. (2022, March). Buying sovereignty: German "weltpolitik" and private enterprise, 1884–1914. *Central European History 55*, 15–33.

Qimao, C. (1996, November). The Taiwan Strait Crisis: Its crux and solutions. *Asian Survey 36*, 1055–1066.

Raine F. S. (1994). The Iranian Crisis of 1946 and the Origins of the Cold War. In M. P. Leffler and D. S. Painter (Eds.), *Origins of the Cold War An International History* (pp. 93–117). Routledge.

Ramsay, K. W. (2017, May). Information, uncertainty, and war. *Annual Review of Political Science 20*, 505–527.

Raymond, D. N. (1921, December). *British Relations with France and Germany, 1860–1870*. Columbia University Press, pp. 17–36.

Redding, R. E., M. Y. Floyd, and G. L. Hawk (2001, July). What judges and lawyers think about the testimony of mental health experts: A survey of the courts and bar. *Behavioral Sciences & the Law 19*, 583–594.

Renshon, J. (2015, May). Losing face and sinking costs: Experimental evidence on the judgment of political and military leaders. *International Organization 69*, 659–695.

Renshon, J. (2016, August). Status deficits and war. *International Organization 70*, 513–550.

Reynolds, D. (1994). The European Dimension of the Cold War. In M. P. Leffler and D. S. Painter (Eds.), *Origins of the Cold War An International History* (pp. 167–177). Routledge.

Ripsman, N. M. and J. S. Levy (2008, October). Wishful thinking or buying time? The logic of British appeasement in the 1930s. *International Security 33*, 148–181.

Roberts, G. (2011). *Molotov: Stalin's Cold Warrior*. Potomac Books.

Rock, S. (1989). *Why Peace Breaks Out*. University of North Carolina Press.

Rock, S. R. (2000). *Appeasement in International Politics*. University Press of Kentucky.

Rosato, S. (2007, December). The flawed logic of democratic peace theory. *The American Political Science Review 97*, 585–602.

Rosato, S. (2015, January). The inscrutable intentions of great powers. *International Security 39*, 48–88.

Ross, R. S. (2013). Us grand strategy, the rise of China, and US national security strategy for East Asia. *Strategic Studies Quarterly 7*, 20–40.

Rothwell, V. (1992). *Anthony Eden: A Political Biography 1931–57*. Manchester University Press.

Sartori, A. E. (2005). *Deterrence by Diplomacy*. Princeton University Press.

Saunders, E. (2011). *Leaders at War: How Presidents Shape Military Interventions*. Cornell University Press.

Saunders, E. N. (2017, April). No substitute for experience: Presidents, advisers, and information in group decision making. *International Organization 71*, S219–S247.

Schake, K. N. (2017). *Safe Passage: The Transition from British to American Hegemony*. Harvard University Press.

Schelling, T. C. (1957, March). Bargaining, communication, and limited war. *Journal of Conflict Resolution 1*, 19–36.

Schelling, T. C. (1960). *The Strategy of Conflict*. Harvard University Press.

Schelling, T. C. (1966, September). *Arms and Influence*. Yale University Press.

Schiff, A. (2020). The U.S. intelligence community is not prepared for the China threat. *Foreign Affairs*. www.foreignaffairs.com/articles/united-states/2020-09-30/us-intelligence-community-not-prepared-china-threat.

Schimmelfennig, F. (2001, March). The community trap: Liberal norms, rhetorical action, and the eastern enlargement of the European union. *International Organization 55*, 47–80.

Schub, R. (2023). Informing the leader: Bureaucracies and international crises. *American Political Science Review 116*, 4, 1460–1476.

Schultz, K. (1999, April). Do democratic institutions constrain or inform? Contrasting two institutional perspectives on democracy and war. *International Organization 53*, 233–266.

Schultz, K. A. and H. E. Goemans (2019, July). Aims, claims, and the bargaining model of war. *International Theory, 11, 3*, 344–374.

Schweller, R. L. (1992, June). Domestic structure and preventive war: Are democracies more pacific? *World Politics 44*, 235–269.

Schweller, R. L. (2004). Unanswered threats: A neoclassical realist theory of underbalancing. *International Security 29*, 159–201.

Scobell, A. (2003, September). *Show of Force: The 1995–1996 Taiwan Strait Crisis*. Cambridge University Press, pp. 171–191.

Sechser, T. S. (2010, October). Goliath's curse: Coercive threats and asymmetric power. *International Organization 64*, 627–660.

Sechser, T. S. (2011, September). Militarized compellent threats, 1918–2001. *Conflict Management and Peace Science 28*, 377–401.

Seed, G. (1958, June). British reactions to American imperialism reflected in journals of opinion 1898–1900. *Political Science Quarterly 73*, 254–272.

Seed, G. (1968, November). British views of American policy in the Philippines reflected in journals of opinion, 1898–1907. *Journal of American Studies 2*, 49–64.

Seligmann, M. and F. Nägler (2015). *The Naval Route to the Abyss*. Routledge.

Seydi, S. (2006, April). Making a cold war in the Near East: Turkey and the origins of the Cold War, 1945–1947. *Diplomacy & Statecraft 17*, 113–141.

Shambaugh, D. (1996, October). Containment or engagement of China? Calculating Beijing's responses. *International Security 21*, 180–209.

Shambaugh, D. (2013, May). Assessing the US "pivot" to Asia. *Strategic Studies Quarterly 7*, 10–19.

Shirer, W. L. (1990). *Rise and Fall of the Third Reich: A History of Nazi Germany*. Simon & Schuster.

Shuman, M. (2021). Xi Jinping turned me into a China hawk. *Politico*. www.politico.eu/article/xi-jinping-turned-me-into-a-china-hawk/.

Singer, J., S. Bremer, and J. Stuckey (1972). *Capability Distribution, Uncertainty, and Major Power War, 1820–1965*. SAGE Publications, pp. 19–48.

Siverson R. M. and R. A. Miller (1995). The Power Transition: Problems and Prospects. In Jacek Kugler and Douglas Lemke (Eds.), *Parity and War* (pp. 57–73). University of Michigan Press.

Skidmore, D. and W. Gates (1997, May). After Tiananmen: The struggle over U.S. policy toward China in the Bush administration. *Presidential Studies Quarterly 27*, 514–539.

Smith, G. (1941). *The Treaty of Washington, 1871: A Study in Imperial History*. Cornell University Press.

Smith, R. (1988). A climate of opinion: British officials and the development of British Soviet policy, 1945–7. *International Affairs 64*, 631–647.

Snyder, J. (1993). *Myths of Empire: Domesitc Politics and International Ambition.* Cornell University Press.

Snyder, J. and E. Borghard (2011, August). The cost of empty threats: A penny, not a pound. *American Political Science Review 105*, 437–456.

Snyder, R. C., R. Jervis, R. N. Lebow, J. G. Stein, P. M. Morgan, and J. L. Snyder (1987). *Psychology and Deterrence*, Volume 8. Johns Hopkins University Press.

Spaniel, W. (2019). *Bargaining Over the Bomb: The Successes and Failures of Nuclear Negotiations.* Cambridge University Press.

Stafford, D. (1982, May). A moral tale: Anglo-German relations, 1860–1914. *The International History Review 4*, 249–263.

Stein, R. M. (2015, August). War and revenge: Explaining conflict initiation by democracies. *American Political Science Review 109*, 556–573.

Steinberg, J. (1966). *Yesterday's deterrent: Tirpitz and the birth of the German battle fleet.* Macmillan.

Steinberg, J. (2011). *Bismarck: A Life.* Oxford University Press.

Steinberg, J. (2020). What went wrong? U.S.-China relations from Tiananmen to Trump. *Texas National Security Review 3*(1), 119–133.

Steiner, P. M., C. Atzmüller, and D. Su (2017, June). Designing valid and reliable vignette experiments for survey research: A case study on the fair gender income gap. *Journal of Methods and Measurement in the Social Sciences 7*. https://doi.org/10.2458/v7i2.20321.

Stettinius, E. (1949). *Roosevelt and the Russians: The Yalta Conference.* Doubleday.

Stone, D. (2008, October). The "Mein Kampf ramp": Emily Overend Lorimer and Hitler translations in Britain. *German History 26*, 504–519.

Strang, G. B. (2008, September). The spirit of Ulysses? Ideology and British appeasement in the 1930s. *Diplomacy & Statecraft 19*, 481–526.

Strasser, H. and C. Weber (1999). On the asymptotic theory of permutation statistics. WU Vienna. https://doi.org/10.57938/ff565ba0-aa64-4fe0-a158-86fd331bee78.

Stuart, R. C. (1988). *United States Expansionism and British North America, 1775–1871.* University of North Carolina Press.

Swaine, M. (2018). Chinese views on the U.S. national security and national defense strategies. *China Leadership Monitor 56.* https://carnegieendowment.org/posts/2018/05/chinese-views-on-the-us-national-security-and-national-defense-strategies?lang=en.

Talmadge, C. (2015). *The Dictator's Army: Battlefield Effectiveness in Authoritarian Regimes.* Cornell University Press.

Tan, A. (2016). *Handbook of US-China Relations.* Edward Elgar.

Tarar, A. (2016, December). A strategic logic of the military fait accompli. *International Studies Quarterly 60*, 742–752.

Taylor, A. J. P. (1954). *The Struggle for Mastery in Europe: 1848–1918*. Oxford University Press.

Taylor, A. J. P. (1961). *Origins of the Second World War*. Simon & Schuster.

The White House (2020, May). The United States strategic approach to the People's Republic of China. https://trumpwhitehouse.archives.gov/articles/united-states-strategic-approach-to-the-peoples-republic-of-china/.

Thompson, W. R. (2001, December). Identifying rivals and rivalries in world politics. *International Studies Quarterly 45*, 557–586.

Trachtenberg, M. (2019). *A Constructed Peace*. Princeton University Press.

Trager, R. F. (2010, May). Diplomatic calculus in anarchy: How communication matters. *American Political Science Review 104*, 347–368.

Trager, R. F. (2011, July). Multidimensional diplomacy. *International Organization 65*, 469–506.

Trager, R. F. (2016, May). The diplomacy of war and peace. *Annual Review of Political Science 19*, 205–228.

Tyerman, C. (1996). *England and the Crusades, 1095–1588*. University of Chicago Press.

Valentin, V. (1937, December). Bismarck and England in the earlier period of his career. *Transactions of the Royal Historical Society 20*, 13–30.

van Evera, S. (1998). Offense, defense and the causes of war. *International Security 22*, 5–43.

Vasquez, J. A. (1993). *The War Puzzle*. Cambridge University Press.

Veeser, C. (2003, June). Inventing dollar diplomacy: The gilded-age origins of the Roosevelt corollary to the Monroe doctrine. *Diplomatic History 27*, 301–326.

Volgy, T. J. (2011). *Major Powers and the Quest for Status in International Politics: Global and Regional Perspectives*. Palgrave Macmillan.

VonPoschinger, H. and S. Whitman (2007). *Conversations with Prince Bismarck*. Kessinger Publishing.

Walker, J. S. (1986, October). The origins of the Cold War: Reviving and revising an old debate. *The Public Historian 8*, 81–86.

Walt, S. (2018). *The Hell of Good Intentions: America's Foreign Policy Elite and the Decline of U.S. Primacy*. Farrar, Straus and Giroux.

Walt, S. M. (1992, March). Alliances, threats, and the US grand strategy, a reply to Kaufmann and Labs. *Security Studies 1*, 448–482.

Waltz, K. N. (1979). *Theory of International Politics*. McGraw-Hill.

Waltz, K. N. (1990, September). Nuclear myths and political realities. *American Political Science Review 84*, 731–745.

Wark, W. K. (1985). *The Ultimate Enemy: British Intelligence and Nazi Germany, 1933–1939*. Cornell University Press.

Watt, D. (1989). *How War Came: The Immediate Origins of the Second World War 1938–1939*. Heinemann.

Wawro, G. (2023, August). *The Franco-Prussian War*. Cambridge University Press.

Weeks, J. L. (2008). Autocratic audience costs: Regime type and signaling resolve. *International Organization 62*, 35–64.

Weinberg, G. L. (1980). *The Foreign Policy of Hitler's Germany: Starting World War II, 1937–1939*. University of Chicago Press.

Weisiger, A. (2013). *Logics of War: Explanations for Limited and Unlimited Conflicts.* Cornell University Press.

Weisiger, A. and K. Yarhi-Milo (2015, May). Revisiting reputation: How past actions matter in international politics. *International Organization 69,* 473–495.

Wendt, A. (1992, April). Anarchy is what states make of it. *International Organization 46,* 391–425.

Wike, R. (2014). How America's opinion of China has changed since Tiananmen. Pew Research Center. www.pewresearch.org/short-reads/2014/06/03/how-americas-opinion-of-china-has-changed-since-tiananmen/.

Wolford, S. (2007, October). The turnover trap: New leaders, reputation, and international conflict. *American Journal of Political Science 51,* 772–788.

Woodward, E. (1935). *Great Britain and the German Navy.* Taylor & Francis.

Woodward, E. L. (1970a). *British Foreign Policy in the Second World War, Vol 3.* H.M.S.O.

Woodward, E. L. (1970b). *British Foreign Policy in the Second World War, Vol 4.* H.M.S.O.

Woodward, E. L. (1970c). *British Foreign Policy in the Second World War, Vol 5.* H.M.S.O.

Yarhi-Milo, K. (2014). *Knowing the Adversary: Leaders, Intelligence, and Assessment of Intentions in International Relations.* Princeton University Press.

Yegorova, N. I. (1996). *The "Iran Crisis" of 1945–1946: A View from the Russian Archives.* Cold War International History Project, Woodrow Wilson International Center for Scholars.

Yoder, B. K. (2019, January). Retrenchment as a screening mechanism: Power shifts, strategic withdrawal, and credible signals. *American Journal of Political Science 63,* 130–145.

Zhang, B. (2011, March). The security dilemma in the U.S.-China military space relationship. *Asian Survey 51,* 311–332.

Zhang, K. (2023, December). *China's Gambit.* Cambridge University Press.

Zoellick, R. (2005). Whither China: From membership to responsibility? Remarks to National Committee on U.S.-China Relations. http://2001-2009.state.gov/s/d/former/zoellick/rem/53682.htm.

Index

Page numbers in *italics* refer to figures, page numbers in **bold** refer to tables and page numbers followed by 'n' refer to footnotes.

For EU product safety concerns, contact us at Calle de José Abascal, 56–1°,
28003 Madrid, Spain or eugpsr@cambridge.org.

www.ingramcontent.com/pod-product-compliance
Ingram Content Group UK Ltd.
Pitfield, Milton Keynes, MK11 3LW, UK
UKHW012143210626
472488UK00008B/89